ANTICHRIST

Also by Bernard McGinn

Visions of the End: Apocalyptic
Traditions in the Middle Ages

The Calabrian Abbot: Joachim of Fiore
in the History of Western Thought

The Foundations of Mysticism:
Origins to the Fifth Century

The Growth of Mysticism: Gregory the
Great through the Twelfth Century

Apocalypticism in the
Western Tradition

ANTICHRIST

Two Thousand Years of the Human Fascination with Evil

Bernard McGinn

HarperSanFrancisco
A Division of HarperCollinsPublishers

FIRST EDITION
Book design by Ralph Fowler
Set in Granjon by TBH/Typecast

Library of Congress Cataloging-in-Publication Data

McGinn, Bernard.
    Antichrist : two thousand years of the human fascination with evil / Bernard
McGinn. —1st ed.
        p.   cm.
    Includes bibliographical references and index.
    ISBN 0–06–065543–7 (cloth : alk. paper)
    ISBN 0–06–065282–9 (pbk. : alk. paper)
    1. Antichrist—History of doctrines.   I. Title.
BT985.M29   1994
236—dc20

94-14396
CIP

95 96 97 98 ❖ RRD(H)   10 9 8 7 6 5 4 3

This edition is printed on acid-free paper that meets the
American National Standards Institute Z39.48 Standard.

It is therefore necessary for us to marke diligently, and to espie out this felowe: and it is convenient for us also, to geve the eies of our heartes attentively unto this purpose (especially the worlde that is now) to th'intent we maye be hable to knowe (out of the scriptures) both him and all his wyles, and to beware of him, that he begyle us not.

> [Rudolph Walther]
> *Antichrist, that is to saye: A true report, that*
> *Antichriste is come . . . : translated out of*
> *Latine into Englishe, By J. D.* (Southwarke:
> Christopher Trutheall, 1556), fol. 70r.

Die zyt die kumt, es kumt die zyt:
Ich vorcht der endkrist sy nit wyt.

[The time comes, it is quite clear,
The Antichrist is very near.]

> Sebastian Brant
> *The Ship of Fools,* CIII.92–93.

CONTENTS

One generation in three has the chance to witness the end of a century, but only one generation in more than thirty gets to confront the close of a millennium. However skeptical the contemporary "postmodern" world may think itself to be about the possibility of knowing the future, it is likely that this final decade of the last century of the second millennium of the Christian era will produce an abundant crop of predictions regarding the coming third millennium, as well as fears that the end of history itself may be near.

According to a view popular in the nineteenth century, the turn from the first to the second millennium c.e. was greeted by terrors throughout western Europe as the populace awaited the onslaught of Antichrist and the coming of the Last Judgment. Upon waking up on New Year's Day in 1000 c.e. (it should really have been 1001, a thousand years from the traditional date for Christ's birth), the supposed universal relief that the world had not ended gave rise to concerted efforts to begin building a new and better world.

Historical fables like the "Terrors of the Year 1000" have a way of reproducing themselves as real events. In all likelihood some will view the approaching year 2000 in terms of such foreboding, perhaps even fearing the imminence of Antichrist.[1] If they were to search hard enough, these contemporary speculators could even find ancient prophecies predicting the end of the world for the year 2000. For example, a treatise of one Scheltco à Geveren, translated into English in 1578, adapted Talmudic passages on the six-thousand-year duration of the world as follows: "Two thousand Vayne, two thousande Lawe, two thousand Christe. And for our sinnes whiche are many and marveylous, some yeares which are wantyng, shal not be expired."[2] The "many and marvelyous" sins of the sixteenth century were apparently insufficient to shorten the end, but the Protestant divine doubtless would have found the sins of the late twentieth century even more prevalent and peculiar, so Scheltco's prophecy may be due for a revival in the next few years. But this is scarcely necessary; no age in Christian history has lacked its own ingenious proofs of the imminence of the end of time.

This book is not written for those who are convinced that Antichrist is imminent and that the world will end in the year 2000 (though I shall not resist them if they choose to read it). Rather, I write in the conviction that Antichrist has *already* come—that is, that the most important message of the Antichrist legend in Western history is what it has to tell us about our past, and perhaps even about our present attitudes toward evil.

For over twenty years I have studied Christian ideas about the end of the world. Antichrist's role in the development of Christian eschatology— meaning doctrine about the end—is an extensive one; so large, in fact, that no modern survey of his story exists.[3] Hence, the question I will address in this book is not "Why another book on Antichrist?" but "Why a book about Antichrist at all?" The introduction will set out my brief for why the study of Antichrist traditions still has more than antiquarian interest. The chapters that follow will fill out the picture by providing a chronological account of the development of the Antichrist legend.

For many reasons, this book has been in gestation longer than I originally intended. Although I had often pondered the possibility of such a work, I might never have actually undertaken it if not for the initiative of Thomas Grady of Harper Collins. Perhaps I should have been more cautious—especially given Antichrist's notable ability to deceive—but the invitation was an offer that I felt I could not refuse. I wish to thank Grady not only for the opportunity he extended but also for the patience he showed during the stages of the book's preparation. I would also like to express my gratitude to a number of friends whose suggestions regarding sections of the manuscript have been of great value. Michael Fishbane read the first chapter and helped me achieve greater clarity in my understanding of the interaction of myth and legend in the Jewish materials. Robert M. Grant's expert knowledge of early Christianity enriched parts of chapter 3. Richard K. Emmerson made helpful suggestions concerning chapter 4, while Martin Marty and Roberto Rusconi gave me assistance in chapters 8 and 9 where I ventured into postmedieval periods with considerable trepidation. Holly B. Elliott made many helpful suggestions about the style and presentation of the book, as did Caroline Pincus. Lindsay Kefauver assisted with the illustrations. I would like to give special thanks to the various libraries, museums, and publications that granted permission to use these illustrations. My research assistant, Shawn Madison Krahmer, contributed her fine editorial gifts. Finally, my wife, Patricia, provided invaluable assistance and encouragement, especially in the final editing.

Chicago, March 1994

ANTICHRIST
AS EPITOME OF
HUMAN EVIL

Why a book about Antichrist? Certainly not because Antichrist dominates popular imagination today as he once did in the later Middle Ages or in the sixteenth century. Nor just because Antichrist is an interesting historical relic, an antiquarian's delight. Too many people still believe in a literal and imminent Antichrist for skeptics to pronounce his epitaph with easy security. The Antichrist legend remains elusive, not only because of its long and complex history but also because of the diversity of attitudes it evokes in the modern world.

This diversity was not created overnight. It was present even three centuries ago, when literal belief in Antichrist was far more widespread than today. Sir Isaac Newton, one of the originators of modern science, belonged to a long line of great thinkers who were obsessed with calculating the time of Antichrist and the approach of the end. In an unpublished tract on the Apocalypse, he rather testily warned, "if God was so angry with the Jews for not searching more diligently into the Prophecies which he had given them to know Christ by, why should we think he will excuse us for not searching the Prophecies which he hath given us to know Antichrist by?"[1] But Newton's efforts to work out the time of the coming of Antichrist from the book of Daniel and the Apocalypse were not appreciated by all. Bishop Thomas Newton in his *Dissertations on the Prophecies* (1758) quoted the Enlightenment philosopher Voltaire's ironic statement: "Sir Isaac Newton wrote his comment upon the Revelation to console mankind for the great superiority that he had over them in other respects."[2] In the eighteenth century, then, we can already find two different approaches to Antichrist's role in apocalyptic eschatology. (*Eschatology* literally means "teaching about the end." It is here understood as any theology of history based upon a divinely revealed message about the last events. *Apocalyptic eschatology,* or apocalypticism, is the form of eschatology believing that these events are in some sense imminent.) Many, like Newton, believed that the Bible, properly understood, provided a blueprint for the close of history and Antichrist's coming. Others, like Voltaire, thought that such beliefs were pure folly.

In this book, I try to find a third way, an approach to Christian eschatology that takes it seriously but not literally. It is a mistake to think that Christian beliefs about the end, whether understood as imminent or not, are mere relics of the past or unfortunate aberrations of superstitious minds, past and present. Views of the end of time—and even the absence of such views—have much to tell us both about society's perceptions of the meaning of history and about its understanding of evil. They may also help reveal something about society's self-understanding.

From this perspective, the Antichrist legend can be seen as a projection, or perhaps better as a mirror, for conceptions and fears about ultimate human evil. Even for those who no longer see Antichrist as a living reality, the study of Antichrist, both in his historical manifestations and in his current transformations, can be revealing. Perhaps Antichrist today is not so much dead as disguised, having changed roles in new scenarios of the end that allow human evil a key, though not the only, role in impending destruction.

Belief in a final human opponent of all goodness, the Antichrist, provides a special focus for understanding Western conceptions of evil, one that is somewhat different in scope even from those available through investigating the extensive traditions concerning the devil.[3] However much Antichrist's history is entwined with that of God's superhuman spiritual adversary, he differs from the devil in being conceived of primarily as a human agent.[4] The issue raised by belief in Antichrist, then, is that of the relation between human agency and evil, especially the possibility of a completely evil human being.

For many people today the possibility of a totally evil human being is as inconceivable as the idea of someone perfectly good. In our own century, when psychological and sociological accounts of human motivation have done so much to explain why some people do good acts while others seem driven to commit evil, we are loath to think that any human being could be either completely good or completely evil. The Antichrist legend challenges these modern assumptions, because it is based on the conviction that total evil *can* be realized in an individual human and even in a human collectivity. Many societies have believed in the existence of an absolutely evil spiritual agent of a superhuman nature—the devil, Satan, or some similar being—whose very freedom from the human condition makes possible a singleness of purpose no human could hope to enjoy. But only in Christianity (and to a lesser extent in the related monotheistic religions of Judaism and Islam) has the figure of a completely corrupt human agent played so large a role.

The reasons for this peculiarity appear to be twofold. First, all three Western forms of monotheism include a certain form of apocalypticism, one that bestows value on current events, viewing present conflicts as images or prototypes of the final decisive battle between the forces of good and evil. Thus, if humans oppose God's present saving work, it means such opposition will also take place at the end, though in the most extreme and final way. At the same time, these present conflicts can help shape the view of the ultimate struggle to come. The second factor, the one that gave the Antichrist legend its unique power in the history of Christianity, is revealed by simple reflection on the name Antichrist. The roots of the Antichrist legend are found in the apocalyptic and messianic beliefs of late Second Temple Judaism (from the third century B.C.E. to 70 C.E.). These beliefs often involve individuals or groups opposed to the hoped-for messiah who is to rescue Israel from the forces of evil. But such "antimessiahs" are not yet Antichrist. The full-blown legend of Antichrist was born only when some Jews of the first century C.E. came to believe that the messiah had actually arrived in the person of Jesus of Nazareth.[5] Early Christianity was founded on the conviction that Jesus of Nazareth, now established as Savior and messiah by his resurrection from the dead, would soon return to earth to manifest openly the new age begun with his rising. But just as Jesus had faced opposition during his lifetime, and just as his followers were now experiencing hatred and persecution, they soon came to believe that the returning God-man would have to encounter the epitome of human opposition to goodness in order to realize the fullness of his reign on earth. The roots of the Antichrist legend are thus firmly planted in the early church's developing views of Christ.

The history of Antichrist can be conceived as one way of writing the history of Christianity or at least the history of the hatreds and fears of Christians. The image of the totally evil human being has been molded by the personalities and deeds of many individual rulers and leaders—Simon Magus, Nero, Justinian, Muhammad, Frederick II, John XXII, Luther, Peter the Great, Napoleon, Mussolini, and so on—all of whom have come to be viewed as enemies of the good. The Antichrist image has also been affected by collective views that would identify either the final enemy himself, or at least his immediate predecessors and followers, with groups of opponents and outsiders viewed as embodiments of evil, especially Jews, heretics, and Muslims.

The development of the legend of Antichrist over the centuries is complex and still obscure in many particulars. The ancient questions concerning Antichrist are legion. Will he be one or many? Jew or Gentile? Fully human or part demon? False teacher or imperial persecutor? What are the signs of his coming? How long will he remain? How will he be destroyed? Will his death mark the end of the world? To these centuries-old queries we can add the critical questions of modern history and theology: What are we to make of the Antichrist legend? What can it possibly mean for us?

The history of Antichrist, as I present it here, suggests that Christian ideas about the nature of final human evil have developed through the interaction between two polarities, what we can call the external-internal polarity and the dread-deception polarity. The first polarity involves the believer's perception of his or her own relation to ultimate evil: Is this evil primarily conceived of as an external force that will threaten or attack the righteous among whom the believer is numbered, or will it come from within the righteous themselves, even from within the believer's own heart? Both external and internal poles of Antichrist beliefs have been present from the beginning. The history of the legend certainly gives more attention to dramatically portrayed accounts of Antichrist conceived of as an identifiable external foe, either individual or collective. Yet biblical texts, such as the First Epistle of John (which contains the earliest appearance of the word *Antichrist*), and major Christian thinkers—from Origen, Augustine, and Gregory the Great among the ancients, through medieval poets like William Langland and Reformation radicals, down to modern novelists and psychologists who have used Antichrist motifs—all have insisted that the true meaning of Antichrist is to be found within, that is, in the spirit that resists Christ present in the hearts of believers.

The fundamental nature of the evil represented by Antichrist has been expressed primarily through the polarity of dread and deception. The Final Enemy, especially when thought of in external and individual terms, has often been pictured as a tyrannical persecutor, a monster of cruelty whose fundamental purpose is to wreak death and destruction on true religion. Although the motif of overwhelming pride by which a human being lifts himself up to be worshiped as God has certainly not been lacking (being forcefully expressed in the Second Epistle to the Thessalonians, the earliest Christian account of the final foe), it is more often the note of fear and dread of the cruelty of the coming proud tyrant that we find in descriptions of Antichrist's career. This helps explain why the great persecutors of the past have been used so extensively in shaping details of the developing legend.

Not by dread alone, however. Antichrist as the false messiah, the "pseudo-Christ," is first and foremost the great deceiver, the arch-hypocrite. The history of the Antichrist legend reveals, above all, how Christians have viewed the perversion of true religion, the masquerades that can be used to hide evil intent under the guise of religious probity. Here the relation between external and internal views of Antichrist re-enters the picture. Most portrayals of Antichrist's deceit have cast it in external terms; that is, they have tried to identify certain forms of religious leadership, such as the papacy, or certain kinds of religious activity as the likely offices and modes in which Antichrist would make his appearance. But the notion of deceit, of pretending to be Christian when intending the reverse, can also be internalized. Augustine of Hippo, preaching on the First Epistle of John, identified Antichrist with heretics and schismatics who departed from the true church, but he went on to speak also of Antichrists who remain within—those who confess Christ with their mouths but deny him by their deeds. He concluded, "everyone must question his conscience whether he be such."[6] Augustine's question, I would argue, constitutes the real meaning of the Antichrist. It explains why the Antichrist legend is not merely a fascinating historical artifact but also a legend that continues to provoke modern reflection.

The philosopher Paul Ricoeur's seminal work, *The Symbolism of Evil,* showed how contemporary reflection on the symbols found in the ancient myths of the origin of evil could still "give rise to thought"; that is, they provide an "occasion for thought, something to think about."[7] This book is written in the hope that a historical reflection on the development of the legend of Antichrist can serve an analogous function by revealing that ultimate human evil, even if we no longer view it as enshrined in a single personality, can include our seemingly ineradicable capability for religious self-deception.

One book cannot hope to do justice to all the intricacies of Antichrist's story. Specialists in various aspects of this history will doubtless point to areas that I have neglected or treated in too summary a fashion. My aim has been to provide the general reader with a synoptic sketch of the story of the final enemy from his foreshadowings in Second Temple Judaism down to his present ambiguous existence, poised between still-fervent belief in a literal Antichrist on the part of Christian Fundamentalists on the one hand, and neglect and dismissal or perhaps an often-unrecognized internal existence on the other. The evidence for this story is varied. Much of it will come from theological works and biblical interpretations, but Antichrist has also played a part in art, in popular literature, and in some of the greatest literary masterpieces of the Western tradition, from Dante to Dostoevsky and beyond.

My account will proceed along chronological lines, guided by the central theme of what changing images of Antichrist as the totally wicked human can tell us about the understanding of evil in the history of Christianity. The first chapter outlines the prehistory of Antichrist, that is, the development of human opponents to God and his messiah in the apocalyptic traditions of Second Temple Judaism. The story proper begins in chapter 2, which discusses the coalescence of these Jewish traditions into a full-fledged Antichrist in the circles of the Jesus movement of the second half of the first century C.E. Chapter 3 addresses the luxuriant growth of the legend down to 500, a concluding date that not only marks (roughly speaking) the end of ancient culture but also was the date set by the most popular early Christian form of apocalyptic speculation for Antichrist's coming and the end of the world.

Chapter 4 deals with early medieval views of the Antichrist, both in the Eastern Orthodox realm of the Byzantine Empire—the real center of Christian civilization during these centuries—and in the fragmented barbarian world of Western Christianity. During this period, an important series of Byzantine apocalypses established a new and more complete scenario of the final events that included important innovations in the Antichrist legend. These materials migrated to the West where, mingled with many traditional motifs, they were given form in a famous tenth-century document, the monk Adso's *Letter on the Antichrist*, which set the standard Western view for centuries to come. An appendix to chapter 4 briefly treats the Antichrist-like figures of Armillus and the Dajjāl, the Jewish and Islamic parallels to the Christian final enemy.

The later medieval period in the West is covered in chapters 5, 6, and 7. While Adso's version remained the baseline for most Antichrist speculation during these four centuries (and deeply influenced art and literature), important changes in Western eschatological ideas, especially those pioneered by the twelfth-century prophet Joachim of Fiore, allowed many new roles to be ascribed to the Antichrist, not least of which was the Antichrist as an evil pope of the last days.

The possibility of a papal Antichrist is one bond of continuity between the late Middle Ages and the period of the Reformation that begins chapter 8, although Reformation notions of a papal Antichrist differed from most medieval ones in identifying the papacy itself, and not merely some coming evil tenant of the throne of Peter, as the Antichrist. Two significant developments characterize the history of the legend in the four centuries between 1500 and roughly 1900. The first mirrors the split in Western Christianity itself: Antichrist belief among Catholics remained largely a series of variations on inherited medieval materials, while Protestant belief in Antichrist, which increased in the seventeenth century, tended to deteriorate either into a monotonous insistence on the pope-Antichrist motif or into such broad Antichrist rhetoric directed against so many foes, both real and imagined, that it lost much of its invective power. This repetition and lack of creativity, coupled with the Enlightenment critique of certain elements of Christianity, especially those like Antichrist that contained so much legendary and bizarre material, led to considerable decline in the status of Antichrist, even among believers, in the eighteenth and nineteenth centuries, though Antichrist belief remained powerful in Russia. This is all treated in chapter 9.

Finally, the last chapter deals with Antichrist over the past hundred years. Catholic theological use of Antichrist has been minimal in this century; in Protestantism, Antichrist beliefs remain strong primarily in Fundamentalist circles, though in repetitious forms. This accounts for my relatively brief treatment of these rather simplified forms of contemporary Antichrist belief. The most fascinating appeals to the Antichrist legend in our era, the ones suggesting that the legend can continue to inspire thought about the meaning of evil, have come from novelists and from the psychologists, such as Carl Gustav Jung. I am not convinced by Jung's interpretation of the significance of Antichrist, but I think that those who ponder the mystery of evil could learn much by considering the question that obviously fascinated the Swiss psychologist: "Why Antichrist?"

CHAPTER ONE

PERVERSION, BLASPHEMY, AND ABOMINATION

JEWISH VISIONS OF GOD'S ENEMIES AND THE LAST DAYS (C. 200 B.C.E.–50 C.E.)

The origins of the Antichrist legend are inseparable from the history of Jewish speculations about the endtime and its proximity. Jewish scribes and seers created a powerful new religious vision of the meaning of history in the last three centuries before Jesus, one that was in full bloom during his lifetime. While it would be anachronistic to speak of an Antichrist before some Jews in the middle of the first century C.E. came to identify Jesus of Nazareth as the messiah or Christ (the anointed one), earlier Jewish views of apocalyptic adversaries form a necessary part of the background to the Antichrist legend.

The Jews of the last centuries B.C.E. did not share belief in a single human opponent of the coming messiah or messiahs. What they did share, and what proved to be so potent both in its originality and ambiguity, was the growing conviction that just as there was one malevolent angelic power who led the forces of evil throughout history, so too would human evil reach a culmination in the last days. The persecution and blasphemies of Antiochus IV, the Seleucid emperor from 175 to 164 B.C.E., were the most obvious historical catalysts of this view, but later trials and troubles also played their parts.

This form of apocalyptic contrast between good and evil incorporated many layers of oppositional thinking reaching as far back as the mythic struggle between Baal and the Dragon. These historical patterns, founded positively on the memory of Israel's great kings of the past and renewed Jewish hopes for a coming messianic ruler, and negatively on the memory of persecutors past and fear of worse ones in the future, took on new meanings in the era that gave birth to apocalyptic eschatology. This apocalyptic eschatology formed the matrix of early Christianity, so that as the messiah of Jewish apocalyptic hopes became the Christ of Christian belief, the traditions about apocalyptic messianic adversaries formed the foundation for the legend of Antichrist. Few phenomena in the history of Western religious traditions have been so important, or so controversial, as apocalyptic eschatology. Although the past generation of scholars has worked extensively on almost all aspects of the origins of apocalypticism, many disputes still remain.[1] The brief account of apocalypticism given here forms a necessary context for investigating how the figure of a final human epitome of evil came into being.[2]

Political Disruptions and the Rise of Jewish Apocalyptic

The conquest of Jerusalem and destruction of Solomon's temple by the Babylonians in 587 B.C.E. might well have marked the end of the Jewish people, especially in light of the mass deportations of the survivors to Babylon. But the devotion of the Jews to their God and to their holy city, Jerusalem, led to the return of the exiles under the more lenient Persians and the building of a second temple (c. 536–515 B.C.E.). The period of Second Temple Judaism was to last until the Roman conquest and destruction of Jerusalem in 70 C.E.[3] Despite the straitened circumstances of the Jews in this era of empires in conflict, it was a period of religious creativity, especially after Alexander the Great (356–323 B.C.E.) conquered the Persian empire and most of the ancient Near East. Alexander's career ushered in a new political order as well as a new cultural and religious situation. The world of Hellenism and the mingling of traditions it entailed brought a challenge to the Jews of the last three centuries B.C.E. that resulted in major changes in their religious views, not least in the birth of apocalyptic eschatology.

The disruptions of the old political and religious order sparked the creation of new forms of religious literature produced by new kinds of religious leaders with new messages about God, the world, and history. The stimulus, though scarcely the whole explanation, for this creativity lay in the Jewish reaction to Hellenization, the process by which Alexander and his successors, the warring Greek generals who ruled the Near East after his death, sought to spread Greek language and culture to the subject peoples. Among the most important new forms of religious literature produced by the Jews after 250 B.C.E. were the apocalypses (literally, "revelations" or "unveilings"). A key, though not the only, part of their message was the new understanding of history we call apocalyptic eschatology.

Apocalypses are a genre of revelatory literature—that is, texts in which a message from the divine world is given to a believing community. Various kinds of revelations flourished throughout the Hellenistic world. The Jewish apocalypses were part of a broad religious phenomenon, though with their own distinctive marks. One scholar holds that the apocalypse is "a genre of revelatory literature with a narrative framework, in which a revelation is mediated by an otherworldly being to a human recipient, disclosing a transcendental reality which is both temporal, insofar as it envisages eschatological salvation, and spatial insofar as it involves another, supernatural world."[4]

As a group, the apocalypses introduced new constellations of religious meaning into ancient Judaism. We can begin our investigation by highlighting some of the distinctive ways in which the genre sought to convey its message. Two crucial characteristics of apocalypses are their narrative nature and the mediated character of the content. Apocalypses are stories; they tell a story about how the message was received, and they include a story as part of their content. And apocalypses are mediated; they come to particuar historical sages through certain divine or heavenly messengers. The account of the reception of the message usually says something about the sage who is purported to have received the message and the situation in which the heavenly revealer appeared.

The stories told in the apocalypses are varied but tend to fall into two broad categories, as the above definition suggests. One group of apocalypses concentrates on the revelation of secrets about the mysteries of the universe, especially of the heavenly realm. These apocalypses often involve an otherworldly journey in which the human recipient is taken on a tour of the heavenly realms (and later also of hell).[5] Another group of apocalypses, which usually do not contain a heavenly journey, concentrate on the revealing of a temporal secret, a message about the course of history. These often contain a sketch of world ages leading up to the revelation of the imminent events of the end of history and the beginning of the new divine age or aeon. The narrative always implies and often explicitly provides a sketch or scenario of the last events and the roles assigned to the various actors. Antichrist will eventually assume one of the largest and most interesting parts in this grand scenario.

The fifteen or so surviving Jewish apocalypses from the period dating roughly from 250 B.C.E. to 150 C.E. are all mediated revelations in which the message is communicated to the human seer by a heavenly figure, usually an angel. Jewish apocalypses also share another form of mediation in that they are all pseudonymous; that is, they are ascribed to ancient wise men, the biblical heroes of old, such as Enoch, Ezra, Abraham, and Daniel. This double mediation exposes two of the most important dimensions of the apocalyptic mentality. The first is the stress on divine transcendence. The God of the apocalypses is paradoxically both farther away and yet nearer than the God of the prophets. He is more distant both because he cannot be attained directly but only through intermediary spirits, his angelic messengers, and because divine control over the world is not evident in the midst of the confusions and trials of the present time when the powers of evil seem triumphant. And yet he is nearer, at least to the seers, for they achieve what no previous Jewish religious leaders had accomplished—they ascend into heaven itself.[6]

The seer receives the message through an angel; the believer receives it through the book written in the seer's name by a scribe who has adopted his persona. The apocalypses are thus part of an important move in Second Temple Judaism toward the fixing of revelation in the written word. Although the precise sociological contexts within which the surviving apocalypses were written remain hidden to us, these texts were clearly the products of learned scribal circles in which visionary experiences were cultivated. Given the growing emphasis on the sacred book, however, such visionary experiences were achieved through identifying with the ancient biblical seers, and the visions were communicated in written form using the names of these heroes as signs of the books' validity. Scribal circles of this sort, combining visionary experiences and learned skills, imply a very different form of religious leadership from that of the priests and sacred kings, the traditional leaders in ancient Judaism.

Apocalyptic eschatology is the term generally used to denote the horizontal or time dimension of the revelations found in the apocalypses. The revelations that concentrate on the course of time from the present to the end, such as the Book of Daniel, the Animal Apocalypse (1 Enoch 85–90), and the Apocalypse of Weeks (1 Enoch 93 and 91)—all from the mid–second century B.C.E.—can be termed historical apocalypses. While this mode of understanding history and its end first came to expression in the apocalypses, it soon made its way into other types of literature of Second Temple Judaism. The Qumran community of Jewish ascetics living near the Dead Sea from about 150 B.C.E. to 70 C.E. collected apocalypses and held strong apocalyptic beliefs that are reflected in its writings but apparently did not compose apocalypses of its own.

In order to understand the horizontal or time component of the apocalypses, some definitions are necessary. Eschatology and apocalypticism have often been used interchangeably, but I view apocalypticism as one type of eschatology, and hence I speak of apocalyptic eschatology as a subtype. Eschatology is any form of belief about the nature of history that interprets historical process in the light of the final events (Greek *ta eschata*). All Christian views of history are eschatological in this sense, whether or not they stress the approaching end and the sequence of events leading to it. Apocalyptic eschatology, however, goes a step further in emphasizing a deterministic view of history. In apocalyptic eschatology the last things are viewed in a triple pattern of crisis-judgment-reward, and their imminence can be discerned in the events of the present through the revealed message found in the sacred book.

The revelation given to the apocalyptic seer involves a sense of the totality of world history, often expressed in an enumeration of ages of world history. The oldest of these revelations is the Apocalypse of Weeks, now part of a compilation of apocalyptic texts known as 1 Enoch. It gives a plan of the whole of history according to a model of ten weeks of years.[7] Such enumerations function as ways of demonstrating God's total control of history and especially of the final events that give meaning to the whole.

In the Apocalypse of Weeks, the present time is seen as the seventh week, a time when an "apostate generation" will rise up whose "deeds shall be many and all of them criminal" (1 Enoch 93:9). This sense of present-day evil as a sign of the crisis of history appears in greater detail in other apocalypses. The best known of these is the apocalypse of Daniel 7–12 (the only apocalypse to be included in the subsequent canon of the Hebrew Bible). Here the triple paradigm of crisis-judgment-reward appears clearly, though there is no account of universal history; in its place we have a prophecy of four recent world empires presented in Daniel 7 under the image of four beasts. This prophecy illustrates one of the most common features of the apocalyptic view of history and its end—the function of *vaticinia ex eventu,* or history disguised as prophecy. Daniel, supposedly writing in the sixth century B.C.E., describes the "future" empires of Babylonia, Media, Persia, and that of Alexander and his successors. Each of these is bad, but the last is the worst: "It will devour the whole earth, trample it underfoot and crush it" (7:23).[8] The eleventh horn of this beast (whom we will meet often in this book) is portrayed in such detail (for example, 7:24–27, 8:9–14 and 23–26, 9:27–28, 11:21–12:45) that there can be no doubt that the writer is describing Antiochus IV Epiphanes, the Hellenistic ruler of Syria who began a violent persecution of the Jews in 167 B.C.E. to compel them to adopt Greek customs. The reader is expected to believe that the apocalyptic seer had long ago revealed the heavenly secret that an evil ruler would initiate a final crisis of persecution that is now present, but that would soon be followed by the tyrant's defeat and destruction.

In the apocalypses, history disguised as prophecy often passes over at some point into true prophecy, and this point helps scholars date pseudonymous works. For example, the scribe who composed Daniel between 167 and 164 B.C.E. moved into true apocalyptic prediction by promising an imminent divine judgment on the forces of evil that historically never happened—Antiochus IV died of natural causes. According to this unfulfilled prophecy, the persecution inflicted by the "little horn" of the fourth beast was to be brief, variously calculated as "three and a half times" (that is, years), or 1260 or 1150 days. Then, "a court will be held and his power will be stripped from him, consumed and utterly destroyed" (7:25; cf. 8:25, 11:40–45, and 12:7). Definitive divine judgment upon the wicked—frequently both wicked humans and the evil spiritual powers that inspire them—is a constant element in the apocalyptic view of history.

The defense of divine control underlying the apocalyptic worldview does not stop with the punishing of God's opponents. It also includes final vindication or reward for the just, especially for those who suffered for righteousness' sake during the time of crisis and persecution. This reward is conceived of in various ways in the apocalypses, but the common element is hope for some way of transcending death.[9] Often there is an earthly as well as a heavenly aspect to the reward, especially in the historical apocalypses. This may involve the expectation of a coming ideal kingdom under a just ruler anointed by God, that is, a messiah.[10] While the expectation of a definitive earthly savior or redeemer is not identical with apocalypticism, the two were closely connected in Jewish history, especially from the late Second Temple period on.[11] Hope for a final reward also led to belief in the resurrection of the dead, a view that made its earliest scriptural appearance in the book of Daniel: "Of those who lie sleeping in the dust of the earth many will awake, some to everlasting life, some to shame and everlasting disgrace" (12:2).

Apocalyptic eschatology can be distinguished from other forms of expectations about the end of history not only through the distinctive triple pattern it employs but also because of its sense of the imminence, often even the actual presence, of the final events. The nearness of the end has long been seen as a hallmark of the apocalyptic mentality; however, it is important to distinguish between chronological and psychological imminence. Some apocalyptic texts provide timetables, usually more or less cryptic, for calculating the endtime. Daniel, with its many variations on the pattern of the three and a half times noted above, as well as the calculations based on the seventy weeks of years originally found in Jeremiah (see Dan. 9), is a good example, one that apocalyptic aficionados down through the centuries have found impossible to resist tying to the events of their own time. But other apocalypses provide only a rather general sense that the end is near, and some even emphasize that no human calculation can ever disclose the time hidden in God's determination. Nevertheless, apocalyptic eschatology always involves a sense of psychological imminence—that is, a belief that the most important thing about the present is that it is witnessing the beginning of the events that must inexorably lead to the end. This end, however far or near in the chronological sense, is psychologically present as the motive for the believer's efforts. Such an outlook is based on the apocalypticist's conviction about the legibility of history. Although God may keep the secret of the exact time of the end to himself, his revelation of at least a part of his plan for history through a seer enables the believer to see current events as signs that have been foretold, signs that call to action.

The apocalypses were texts designed to have clear and powerful effects on their readers. Thus, the function of the historical apocalypses, what we may call apocalyptic piety or spirituality, is also important for understanding the phenomenon.[12] The historical apocalypses have been seen most often as a literature of consolation directed to persecuted believers in times of severe stress. Since the apocalypses arose in Judaism during an age when the Jews were subject to foreign powers and often persecuted for their religion, this dimension has always been important. From this perspective, the apocalypses also imply a strong element of theodicy, that is, a defense of the basic goodness of God and his control over history despite the evil so evident in the world. But the flexibility of apocalyptic eschatology allowed it to be used not only to console the persecuted; it could also strengthen support for the establishment, both political and spiritual, and it was used in this way especially in later Christian history.

The essential features of apocalyptic piety, whether exercised by persecuted minorities or embattled majorities, are much the same. The most obvious is the call to decision. Convinced that the final struggle between the forces of good and evil has already begun, apocalyptic believers experience the necessity for ultimate decision. The apocalyptic worldview has no room for moral ambiguity, for any shades of gray. By viewing opponents as adherents of absolute evil, apocalypticism allows for a total opposition, a thirst for complete defeat of and dire vengeance on the wicked. Its moral absolutism forms the most disturbing (and historically the most destructive) aspect of apocalypticism.

Facing the final struggle demands not only decision but also patience and endurance and sometimes the courage to take action. Later apocalyptic propagandists, following the lead of the scriptural apocalyptic texts of Daniel and John, usually call on their adherents to endure trial and suffering until the intervention of divine justice that will destroy the forces of evil once and for all and grant the just their expected reward. At times, however, apocalypticists have summoned their followers to take up arms to be ready to fight with God and his angelic hosts against the forces of evil, either by overthrowing the power of satanic rulers (we might call this the revolutionary function of apocalypticism) or by defending God's threatened kingdom and ruler against the final onslaught of evil (the confirmatory or supportive function).[13]

Apocalyptic piety is marked both by fervent hope in the coming reward and by absolute conviction regarding the justice of one's cause. Thus, apocalypticism can be seen as a way of dealing with what historian of religions Mircea Eliade called "the terror of history," the human fear of consciously and voluntarily creating history.[14] Apocalypticism provides believers with an already determined structure of meaning within which they can deal with the crises, the evil, and the absence of meaning they encounter in the world around them. Apocalyptic eschatology is profoundly deterministic on the level of universal history—God's plan for the ages and for the end of time cannot be altered—but it usually stresses individual freedom by emphasizing how believers are called to affirm the divine plan by their adherence to the good and their willingness to endure suffering for its sake. The divine vindication upon which apocalyptic hopes are based is no partial reward but a complete and ultimate one—the transcendence of death conceived of both individually and collectively.

The Interaction of Myth, Legend, and History

The apocalypses of Second Temple Judaism and their Christian successors present their message of the meaning of history not through philosophical discourse or staightforward historical account but by means of a symbolic narrative forming a unique combination of myth, legend, and history. The mythological elements in apocalypticism have been the subject of considerable study since the biblical scholar Hermann Gunkel first discussed this dimension in 1895.[15]

The use of myth and mythlike features in apocalypticism can be understood in terms of both the sources used and the presentation of the understanding of history. Regarding sources, scholars agree that the apocalyptic authors used mythological traditions, especially those relating to the ancient Near Eastern "combat myth," the narrative of the struggle between a high god and the monster of chaos at the time of the creation or formation of the world. But the apocalypticists did not merely repeat the myths; they adapted, expanded, and transformed them in a variety of ways. Gunkel studied the connections between the apocalypses and Babylonian materials; more recent work has shown that Canaanite and Ugaritic versions of the combat myth show the closest parallels.[16]

Myths also function as archetypal narratives that exercise a special power over the human imagination, as psychologists such as C. G. Jung, religionists like Mircea Eliade, and philosophers like Paul Ricoeur have shown. Recently, biblical scholar Adela Yarbro Collins has drawn attention to the way in which apocalypses, such as the Apocalypse of John, use subtle interactions between the "old story," the primordial narrative of the cosmic combat, and the "new story" of the historical account of trial and opposition (often presented through history disguised as prophecy) to create their effect.[17] But the new story presented in the apocalypses is never history in the modern sense; it is a form of symbolic narrative better described as legend rather than history. A consideration of the relation of myth, history, and legend in the historical apocalypses is essential for understanding the creation and development of Antichrist.

Myth, from the Greek *mythos* (speech, account, or plot), has been used in a wide variety of ways since the word became popular in academic circles in the mid–nineteenth century. I am using it here in the sense of a sacred story or narrative intended to explain a basic fact or value about the world by relating it to the time of beginning.[18] Myth explains, not in an intellectual way by giving an argument, but rather by presenting an account of origins or essential structures that mediates meaning to the present.

Myths function in a variety of ways. Certainly, myths seek to resolve conflict and alleviate social anxiety.[19] But more essentially, myths, especially creation myths, establish the world of meaning within which ancient societies lived and tried to make sense of reality. One can even argue that the use of myth in the broad sense is a requirement of all human culture, even in modern society, where secular analogues of ancient myths, such as the myth of "the American way of life," continue to be powerful.

The relationship between myth and history is too complex to permit easy generalizations. Myths in the classic sense, as Mircea Eliade demonstrated, take place in a special sacred time before history—*in illo tempore*. But the crucial factor in constituting the myth, according to Paul Ricoeur, is a culture's conception of the bond between its own historical time and the mythic *in illo tempore*.[20] It is popularly thought that "myth" (at least broadly conceived) represents a "primitive" stage of human development succeeded by a higher phase in which "history" reigns supreme. But this view is problematic, for it can explain neither the historical development of ancient cultures nor the prevalence of myths in our contemporary mass culture—myths that are often most powerfully conveyed through the media.

Societies have conceived of the relation between myth and history in many ways. In ancient Israel the relationship is complex and controversial. Ricoeur claims that what is most distinctive in Israel's way of framing the connection is that ". . . in Israel the quasi myths or myth fragments borrowed from neighboring cultures were incorporated into the great narrative ensembles . . . in the form of historicized myths, as is the case in *Genesis* 1–11. This reinterpretation of myth on the basis of history appears quite specific to the literary sphere of ancient Israel."[21]

For Ricoeur, Hebrew thought, like Greek philosophy, not only rejected myth but also reinvented it—in Israel's case in the form of "a broken and historicized myth."[22] Other investigators, such as the Jewish scholar Michael Fishbane, emphasize that the creative use of myth throughout the Jewish tradition, from early strands of the Hebrew Bible through medieval Jewish mysticism, includes a series of trajectories that cannot be captured under a single heading, such as "broken myth."[23] It is within this more complex perspective of the intermingling of myth and history, especially in Second Temple Judaism, that apocalyptic eschatology is best understood. In order to grasp the transformation of myth in apocalyptic discourse, we need to introduce a third type of narrative, legend.

The distinction of myth, legend, and folktale (German *Mythus, Sage, Märchen*) can be traced back to the work of the famous Grimm brothers in the first half of the nineteenth century and has been developed in a variety of ways by students of folklore, ethnographers, and historians of religion.[24] Hermann Gunkel and Hugo Gressmann applied these distinctions to the study of the Hebrew Bible in the first half of the twentieth century, separating a variety of biblical legends from myths of origins.[25] Nevertheless, the term *legend* has often been used almost interchangeably with *myth* by many scholars.[26]

In relation to apocalyptic literature, it is important to maintain a distinction between myth and legend. Legend (from the Latin *legenda,* things to be read) differs from myth in that it claims to have happened *in* history, often (though not necessarily) long ago. These claims are not always fictitious; real historical events do shape the narrative, as we will see in the case of Antichrist. The primary actors in legends are human figures, though often of a heroic and larger-than-life character. Like myth, and unlike the folktale with its imaginary "once upon a time" introduction and "happily ever after" conclusion, the legend has an archetypal function: It reveals something of fundamental importance about the world and especially about human society. It is not just an exemplary tale.[27] It is history aspiring to the level of myth—that is, the retelling of significant historical events in an archetypal way by invoking mythic language and symbols.

The Hebrew Bible abounds with legendary accounts. They are also found in the New Testament (for example, the infancy narratives of the Gospels). Apocalyptic legends, however (of which Antichrist is the foremost), form a special variety. The legends found in the historical apocalypses are distinctive because they are *future* narrative projections combining mythic and historical materials. This unusual mixture is seen not only in the story of Antichrist but also in the development of many other apocalyptic elements. The origin of this form of narrative lies in what we can call current events, that is, with historical memory of what has been experienced recently (or relatively recently) by a community. Thus, the experience of the Jews of the Second Temple period under the sway of Babylonian, Median, Persian, and Hellenistic rule forms the historical core of the vision of the four beasts in Daniel 7, and it is also the basis for the various subsequent symbolic retrievals of the same history.[28] But in the apocalyptic narrative this history is mythologized and its temporal referent altered through the technique of history as prophecy to create a new genre: the future, or apocalyptic, legend.

The mythologizing of the historical basis in Daniel is evident in the way the four kingdoms are presented symbolically as four beasts, with the current Hellenistic kingdom figured as a terrifying monster that cannot but recall the dragon of chaos (Dan. 7:7 and 19–20). Mythic structures are used to heighten the significance of the historical events being described. The opposition between the community of Israel and its persecutors becomes part of the primordial struggle between good and evil when seen in light of mythic symbols and patterns. Such mythic patterns, of course, are found throughout the Hebrew Bible, not least in its other "legendary" strata. What is distinctive about the apocalyptic legends as compared with other forms of legends (think of the "hero legends," like those of David) is their location not in the past, but in the future. Both because of the way in which the *vaticinia ex eventu* (historical events presented as prophecy) interpret the past as future, and because the whole purpose of the historical apocalypses is to prepare for an imminent future in the light of present events, remythologized history becomes a new and potent form of legend—that is, a *coming* (not past) historical event of archetypal significance.

In apocalypticism, historical events form the necessary mediating link between the mythic beginning and the legendary (that is, parahistorical) end. Thus, for example, recent historical events and persons, such as Antiochus IV, when viewed through the prism of mythic structures, take on a formative—not merely auxiliary—role in creating the legend of the ultimate human (that is, historical) opponent of all good, though in the case of Daniel this figure is better called a Final Tyrant or Antimessiah than an Antichrist in the proper sense. But before we examine the stages, both historical and structural, in the opposition between good and evil that led from the Final Tyrant to the Antichrist, we need to reflect on the symbolic character of apocalyptic narrative in general.

The interpenetration of myth and history that created the apocalyptic legend has been spoken of above as a symbolic one, or at least as one that expressed itself in symbolic form. To read the Jewish and Christian apocalypses is to enter a vivid and often confusing world of bright colors, strange animals, bizarre enumerations, and often striking images and characters of heaven and earth. Though some critics have dismissed the apocalypses as replete with puerile allegories (and there are certainly many of these), apocalyptic texts are actually filled with images that call into question any simplified modern distinction between "bad" allegory and "good" symbolism.[29] An emerging consensus evident in recent literature on apocalypticism is the insistence on paying careful attention to this symbolic mentality.[30]

The symbolism of apocalyptic eschatology is replete with moral or ethical dualism.[31] No apocalyptic text considers evil to be a separate principle or cause independent of God's will; hence, any form of ontological or cosmological dualism is ruled out. However, apocalyptic texts continuously highlight the opposition between good and evil leaders and communities—the contrast between the "wicked" human beings and those "wise" in the ways of the Lord (for example, Dan. 12:10), as well as the opposition between good and evil angelic figures. Along with this ethical dualism, we can also point to a broad "locational" dualism, according to which oppositions of temporal and spatial patterns and figures abound in apocalyptic eschatology. A rich variety of symbols replicate over and over the contrast between good and evil, triumph and catastrophe, that ancient myths portrayed through the struggle between the Dragon of chaos and the Divine Warrior.

This conflict is often presented in terms of the contrast between "this age" (Hebrew *ha'olam hazzeh*), or aeon, and the "age to come" (*ha'olam habba'*)—that is, the perception of the present as under the control of evil and the hope for a future shattering of history that will initiate divine rule. The contrast between present and future ages is so prevalent that some investigators have seen it as the distinguishing mark of apocalyptic eschatology.[32] The underlying oppositional mentality is also evident in some of the numerical symbols used to present the crisis-judgment-reward scenario of the end. The most important of these is the contrast between seven and its multiples (traditionally numbers representing fullness and perfection) and half-seven (that is, three and a half and its multiples), an obvious marker for failure and imperfection.

Spatial symbols also display the law of opposition. Earth is set over against heaven, a contrast that does not preclude important correspondences between the two realms, as we will see.[33] This age and the age to come can be envisaged as a kingdom of evil and a divine kingdom, or more concretely as Babylon and Jerusalem, seen both as ideal places and specific locations in which the powers of evil and of good will wage their final war. The idea of locating good and evil, especially ultimate good and evil, in specific places is probably as alien to modern religion as the medieval idea that physical objects, like relics, can contain divine power. But Jerusalem, at least for apocalypticists, was both a symbol of the final victory of God and the concrete place where that victory was to be achieved.

The overarching need to oppose symbols is also evident when we turn to the images of living beings—animal, monstrous, human, and angelic—that pervade the apocalyptic narratives. Good plays need strong characters and characters representing different viewpoints. In the apocalyptic scenario, what the players lack in psychological development is partially compensated for by their symbolic power. Through their symbolism, these gaudy and implausible figures display aspects of the characteristic apocalyptic drive to finalize the struggle between good and evil.

Angelic and Human Opposition to God

THE ORIGINS OF SATAN

Among the many contributions of apocalyptic eschatology to the religious history of the West, few have been as important as the development and dissemination of the myth of Satan, God's angelic opponent in the struggle between good and evil. To be sure, evil spiritual powers of greater or less malignancy appear in almost all religious traditions,[34] and the combat myth of the conflict between the Creator God and his opponent, the Dragon of chaos, was rooted in the religions of the ancient Near East. The historical origins of the myth of Satan conceived of as the leader of the disloyal spiritual opposition in the cosmos predate the rise of apocalyptic eschatology, and it can be argued that the full-blown concept of Satan had already appeared in Jewish traditions in the Second Temple period prior to the rise of apocalypticism. However, the crystallization and spread of the myth of Satan clearly owes much to apocalypticism in both Jewish and Christian traditions. The tendency of the apocalyptic imagination to conceive of reality in terms of eschatological opposition between good and evil gave Satan a stature he had not enjoyed hitherto and one that has continued for almost two millennia.

A fully satisfactory explanation of how the figure of Satan emerged in the Jewish tradition has yet to be developed. In a world of many gods and spiritual powers, the division between benign and malign forces does not create problems of theodicy: Some superhuman beings are good in relation to the world and humanity; others are evil, that is, unfavorable and hostile. The gradual evolution of the conception of a single all-powerful God among the Jews eventually made the question of the origin of evil one of central importance. If God is a good creator, whence comes evil?

In many early strata of the Hebrew Bible, God is responsible for both the good and the bad things that happen to humans. In the hymn of Moses found in Deuteronomy 32, Yahweh proclaims, "See now that I, I am He, and beside me there is no other god. It is I who deal death and life; when I have struck it is I who heal (and none can deliver from my hand)" (Deut. 32:39).[35] The prophet known as Second Isaiah, writing at the time of the Babylonian exile, was even more direct: "I am Yahweh, and there is no other. I form light, and I create darkness; I produce well-being and I create evil; I Yahweh do all these things."[36] Though it was always capable of revival, the idea that all that befalls humans, both for good and for ill, comes from God soon erected stumbling blocks for a Judaism that wished to defend God's goodness. The "satanic" solution to this problem was formed out of the interaction of at least four elements present in Jewish tradition: (1) the invoking of the ancient combat myth of the Creator's struggle against the monster of chaos; (2) the role of an angelic messenger who comes down to the world to do God's "dirty work"; (3) the bizarre story of the angels who descended from heaven to intermarry with human women (Gen. 6:1–6); and (4) the attacks of the prophets on the kings who had rebelled against Yahweh by daring to persecute his people.

In terms of antiquity, the combat myth comes first. Best known in its Akkadian form (the *Enuma elish*), probably dating from the late second millennium B.C.E., the myth tells the story of the struggle between Marduk, the champion of the gods, and Tiamat, the female Dragon of the waters of chaos who heads the older divine powers. (For the people of the ancient Near East, the sea and its storms always symbolized evil.) The Akkadian version explains the origin of the universe: Marduk creates the cosmos and humanity from Tiamat's corpse and the blood of her consort, Kingu.[37] But not all versions of the myth are equally concerned with the construction of the present world. The surviving version of the Canaanite myth of the combat between the god Baal and Yamm, or the sea, coming from the ancient city of Ugarit in the fourteenth century B.C.E., is more about establishing proper kingship, though the possibility of lost cosmogonic aspects cannot be excluded.[38] Cosmogony and the establishing of correct rulership are the two poles between which move the myths loosely called combat myths.

There is no need here to try to survey the different versions of ancient combat myths (usually fragmentary) and the possible channels of transmission to the ancient Hebrews (often quite conjectural). The important thing is to recognize how the Jews, from a very early period after their entry into Palestine, adapted the mythic structures to serve their own religious purposes. Already in the early "Song of the Sea" found in Exodus 15:1–18 (c. 1100 B.C.E. [?]) we find motifs and language from the combat myth used to emphasize the importance of the foundational event in Israel's religious identity: the crossing of the Red Sea and deliverance from Pharaoh.[39] The use of such mythic language is heightened in the Psalms (for example, Ps. 77:16–19), where we find the monster named as Leviathan (Ps. 74:14–15, Ps. 104:26) or as Rahab (Ps. 89:9–10). The book of Job also refers to both Rahab (9:13) and Leviathan (3:8, 7:12, 40:25–41:25) as opponents of God. Perhaps the most powerful use of the mythic paradigm comes in Isaiah 51:9–10, where Yahweh's imminent deliverance of his people from their exile in Babylon is placed in the perspective of the cosmogonic struggle:

> Awake, awake! Clothe yourself in strength, arm of Yahweh. Awake, as in the past, in times of generations long ago. Did you not split Rahab in two, and pierce the Dragon through? Did you not dry up the sea, the waters of the great Abyss, to make the seabed a road for the redeemed to cross?

The distance between this text and the apocalyptic, future-oriented use of the mythic combat pattern is not great.[40]

The origin of the name Satan is rooted in the second element, that of the angelic messenger who does God's "dirty work" on earth. The word comes from the verb *satan,* meaning "to oppose," which in its noun form is used in the Hebrew Bible both for human (2 Sam. 19:22) and angelic opposers. The most noted occurrence of an angelic opposer is found in Job where Satan functions as one of the "sons of God" (*bene ha-elohim*), that is, the members of Yahweh's heavenly court (see, for example, Job 1:6–12, 2:1–7). In these texts and in others, such as Zechariah 3:1–2, it is clear that Satan is a powerful angel deputed to be God's accuser against the human world. An interesting contrast between two biblical accounts of the same incident reveals Satan's growing independence as a malevolent force.

In 2 Samuel 24, written sometime in the seventh century B.C.E., we are told that David's decision to undertake a census of the Israelites, although instigated by God, was eventually repented by the king as a grave sin. In the rewriting of this incident found in 1 Chronicles 21:1–17 (c. 400 B.C.E.), God has been relieved of responsibility by placing the blame on Satan: "Satan rose against Israel and incited David to take a census of the Israelites" (21:1). This is the earliest passage in the Hebrew Bible that can be

read as giving the angelic accuser of the heavenly court an apparently independent realm of operation as a source of evil.[41]

The third inherited body of traditions that played a role in the evolution of the Satan myth appears in the Bible in Genesis 6:1–4. "When
men had begun to be plentiful on the earth, and daughters had been born
to them, the sons of God [*bene ha-elohim*], looking at the daughters of
men, saw they were pleasing, so they married as many as they chose"
(6:1–2). Their offspring were the *nephilim,* or giants of old. This ancient
tradition had a rich mythic development in apocalyptic literature. The
primary witness is found in the Book of Watchers (1 Enoch 1–36), a compilation of texts now generally recognized as the oldest surviving apocalypse.[42] In place of the sparse and neutral account of Genesis, the Book of
Watchers, especially in chapters 6 to 11 (probably mid–third century
B.C.E.), spins a rich tale of evil originating in the world through the descent
of two hundred bad angels who intermarry with human women as an act
of rebellion against God. These angels teach the women magical arts and
father a race of destructive giants (1 Enoch 6–7). Most important for the
development of the Satan myth, these angels have a leader, variously
called Semihazah and Asael (the differing names reflect different traditions that have become intermingled in the text).[43] What is clear is the way
in which the author has projected the world judgment of Noah's time into
a coming condemnation of the evil angels and their Satanlike leader.

The final component in the evolution of Satan involves the intermingling of human and celestial opponents of God in a way that brings it close
to the formative stages of the Antichrist legend. Isaiah 14:12–13, dating in
its present form from the mid–sixth century B.C.E., satirizes an earthly
king of Babylon who dared to try to ascend to heaven:

> How did you come to fall from the heavens, Daystar, son of Dawn [*helel
> ben-shahar*]? How did you come to be thrown to the ground, you who en-
> slaved the nations? You who used to think to yourself, "I will climb up to
> the heavens; and higher than the stars of God I will set my throne."

This account, which obviously involves considerable mythic coloring
in its picture of a rebellion against the powers of heaven, is notable for its
mythologizing of contemporary history—that is, its insertion of the new
story of the attack of a Babylonian king (probably either Nebuchadnezzar
or Nabonidas) on Yahweh's temple into the old story of the conflict between younger and more ancient gods.[44] Lucifer, the name given to the

mythologized rebel king in the Vulgate Latin translation of the Bible, was later to become a synonym for Satan in Christianity. Similar attacks against powerful kings who claimed divine status for themselves are found in the oracle against the king of Tyre in Ezekiel 28 and against Pharaoh in Ezekiel 29. This fusion of human and angelic opposition to God influenced both the developing figure of Satan and the evolution of the idea of a Final Tyrant in Jewish apocalypticism.

A passage from the exiled prophet Ezekiel describing a human opponent of Yahweh was to have a profound effect on the later development of Antichrist, if not directly on the Satan myth. Ezekiel 38–39 contains a long oracle against "Gog, prince of Rosh, Meshech and Tubal" (38:2).[45] This account of the invasion of a northern foe and his defeat and death in the mountains of Israel picks up on themes found in both Jeremiah and Isaiah but differs from the earlier prophets in putting Gog's invasion "at the end of the years." Though the Ezekiel passage was not originally an apocalyptic text in the technical sense of the term, its remarkable imagery and sense of historical progression made it ripe for incorporation into apocalyptic traditions.[46] Gog (the origin of the name is unknown but may reflect the mythic Lydian king, Gyges) appears as an enemy of the chosen people at the endtime, and thus the account of his career and fate could easily be linked to that of Antichrist in Christian tradition.[47]

THE FINAL TYRANT

Mingling angelic and human opposition to God is evident in the earliest explicit appearance of a Final Tyrant figure in apocalyptic literature, an appearance that continues to influence the history of the Antichrist legend down to the present: the "little horn" of the apocalyptic section of the book of Daniel. As we have seen, Daniel 7–12 contains a symbolic presentation of the history of the Near East from the time of the Babylonian Empire of Nebuchadnezzar in the sixth century B.C.E. to the second-century Hellenistic kingdoms. It culminates in an account of the career of Antiochus IV Epiphanes, portrayed as the "little horn."

Antiochus was infamous in Jewish history. Shortly after gaining the throne he was approached by the Jerusalem high priest Jason, who urged him to pursue a policy of forceful Hellenization in the Holy City (1 Macc. 1:11–16; 2 Macc. 4:7–17). Squabbles between Jason and other claimants for power eventually resulted in Antiochus capturing Jerusalem and plundering the temple in the year 169 B.C.E. (1 Macc. 1:20–28; 2 Macc. 5:11–27). In 167, for motives that are still unclear, Antiochus went further and banned Jewish religious practices altogether (1 Macc. 1:41–64; 2 Macc. 6:1–17). Even worse, he profaned the temple by erecting an altar to Zeus in it: "On the fifteenth day of Chislev in the year one hundred and forty-five [December 8, 167 B.C.E.] the king erected the abomination of desolation above the altar" (1 Macc. 1:54).[48] These actions and the savage persecution of Jews who continued to adhere to the Torah led to the outbreak of the revolt of the Maccabees. In December of 164, Judas Maccabeus and his followers purified the temple desecrated by Antiochus (1 Macc. 4:36–60; 2 Macc. 10:1–9). The persecutor himself had died a few weeks earlier.

The author of Daniel struggled to make sense of this traumatic national experience within the framework of apocalyptic eschatology. In presenting the evil of Antiochus's actions, he used ancient mythic patterns of the revolt against God to highlight a presentation of this human persecutor as the tyrant of the endtime, the ultimate human adversary of God's people. Daniel's portrayal of Antiochus IV as an endtime opponent of God surpasses anything found in previous Jewish literature.[49]

From the perspective of the full development of Antichrist, however, much is lacking, most especially opposition between the Final Tyrant and a human messiah. Antiochus's real opponent is God. Even the quasi-human leader of the forces of good, the "one like a son of man" found in Daniel 7:13–14, is not explicitly messianic but seems to represent the angelic patron of the "people of the holy ones" (that is, the Jews).[50] Still, from the perspective of later attempts to find scriptural warrants in the Old Testament for Antichrist, Daniel's portrayal of Antiochus always remained a central text.

Antiochus IV as the "little horn" in Daniel 7–12, although he battles against the angelic powers and even against God himself, remains a human king. No other early Jewish product of apocalyptic eschatology paints such a highly developed portrait of a *human* opponent of God in the last days. Clearly, the apocalyptic worldview of the last centuries B.C.E. increasingly emphasized the opposition between God and his enemies, both human and angelic, and belief in a coming messiah of the new aeon was often accompanied by speculation on various human adversaries conceived of both as final tyrant and sometimes as ultimate false prophet.

THE APPEARANCE OF BELIAL

Jewish monotheism never succumbed to any form of metaphysical dualism in which good and evil were explained by recognizing them as two ultimate principles, but an increasing ethical dualism is evident in the last centuries B.C.E. Evil came to be seen more and more as the effect of certain malevolent personalities, angelic and human. (We must remember that the distinction between powerful human rulers who claimed divine status and superhuman angelic powers who were believed to have bodily forms was not always clear.)[51] The most important of these figures epitomizing apocalyptic opposition is the evil angel Belial (alternatively Beliar), who appears in a number of writings of late Second Temple Judaism.[52]

The Book of Jubilees is a retelling of Genesis and parts of Exodus. It purports to have been given to Moses on Sinai, but it was actually written in the second century B.C.E., most likely around 160. It reflects a view of Judaism not unlike that of the Qumran community to be discussed presently.[53] Jubilees is not an apocalyptic document as such, but it is important to our theme for its richly developed picture of angelic opposition to God under the leadership of "Mastema," a name obviously related to Satan.[54] But Jubilees also uses the name Beliar for this evil Prince, as when Moses prays, "O Lord, let your mercy be lifted up upon your people, and create for them an upright spirit. And do not let the spirit of Beliar rule over them to accuse them before you . . . " (1:20; see also 15:33). This appears to be the earliest personalized use of this name, which is derived from a root meaning "base" or "worthless" (see, for example, Deut. 13:14, 1 Sam. 2:12).

Beliar or Belial was to have a long, if not noble, history. This name for the Prince of Demons occurs most often in the Testaments of the Twelve Patriarchs, the purported final utterances of the sons of Jacob.[55] The Testaments doubtless contain Jewish materials dating back to the second century B.C.E., but since there is still no agreement about the actual date of the work's formation, or even whether it is a Jewish piece with Christian interpolations or a Christian composition using Jewish sources, its use here is both problematic and unnecessary, since it says nothing about Belial that cannot be found in other texts.[56]

The name Beliar is frequently used in the writings of the Qumran community to refer to the leader of opposition to God. The community at Qumran was made up of Essenes who broke with the Jerusalem temple priesthood sometime in the second century B.C.E. (perhaps around 170) and later withdrew to the Judaean desert, where they established a center at Qumran near the Dead Sea.[57] This community continued to exist until about 68 C.E. when it was destroyed by the invading Romans. The discovery between 1947 and 1956 of the scrolls the Qumran sectarians had hid-

den in eleven nearby caves at the time of the Roman conquest is justly regarded as one of the most important archaeological finds of the century.

Without attempting any detailed description of the beliefs of the
Qumran community, it is important to note some essentials of the sect's
ideology in order to understand the importance of its apocalyptic stance
and its contribution to the evolution of Jewish conceptions of final adversaries.[58] Convinced that the priesthood had become corrupt, possibly at
the time of the murder of the High Priest Onias III (c. 170 B.C.E.) and the
beginning of hellenization under Jason, the group had separated itself
from the Jerusalem temple and its worship. It soon came to follow a
priestly leader known as the Teacher of Righteousness who was opposed
first by the Teacher of the Lie and subsequently by a Wicked Priest. (Exactly who these people were is a matter of dispute, but they appear to be
historical characters.) For the Qumran sectarians, the contrast between
good and evil leaders reflected the strict ethical dualism and sense of apocalyptic predestination by which God rules the world down to the end of
the aeon through the opposed Spirit of Truth and Spirit of Perversity.[59]
The Qumran literature highlights with particular intensity the internal
aspects of the basic oppositional structure of apocalyptic thought. History
is a perpetual war between the forces of good—both angels and humans—and the angelic and human representatives of evil under the command of Belial.

According to some texts, the community awaited the imminent arrival of two messiahs, the messiah of Aaron (a priestly figure) and the messiah of Israel (a royal descendant of the house of David). The two would
take leading roles in the final apocalyptic war in which the combined
forces of good people and angels would be thrice victorious and thrice defeated by the angels and people under Belial's command, until God's direct intervention in the seventh battle would usher in the messianic age.[60]
In one text, the Melchizedek Scroll from the mid–first century B.C.E. (11Q
Melch), the mysterious Priest-King of Genesis 14 appears as a heavenly
apocalyptic redeemer who will judge the sons of Belial.[61] The Qumran
documents are notable examples of the tendency of apocalyptic eschatology to merge the heavenly and the earthly on what may be called the ver-
tical or spatial pole of apocalyptic thought; at the same time, on the
horizontal or temporal pole, they mingle the present and the future so that
current trials and conflicts can be interpreted by, and sometimes even be
seen as part of, the ultimate clash between good and evil.[62]

In the major Qumran texts, which seem to date from the second half of the second century B.C.E., Belial appears as the Prince of Evil, the equivalent of Satan. Belial's role is especially pronounced in the noted War Scroll (1QM), which describes the apocalyptic war between the armies of light under Michael's command and those of darkness under Belial's (for example, 1QM 1:1.5.13; 4:2; 11:8; and 13:2). The Thanksgiving Hymns (*Hodayot* found in 1QH) speak of a coming apocalyptic crisis in which the fiery "floods of Belial" will destroy the physical universe.[63] Thus at Qumran Belial became *the* author of evil, but he always remained an angelic figure, as did his counterpart Melchiresha', the commander of the good angelic forces. The Qumran sectarians, however, believed that Belial's army included both angels and humans, and therefore some of the "sons of Belial" begin to take on characteristics of an apocalyptic human adversary, at times even an "antimessiah."

Several early texts from the Qumran collections contain descriptions of such evil human opponents to the coming messiahs.[64] One fragmentary and somewhat late text (4Q psDan Aa, last third of the first century B.C.E.) can be taken to describe a blasphemous human ruler of a destructive and persecuting realm in the era of coming apocalyptic struggle. This ruler goes even further than Daniel's Antiochus IV by demanding worship for himself as son of God.[65] This text could be a missing link between the picture of Antiochus IV found in Daniel and the Jewish traditions that may be reflected in such early Christian documents as 2 Thessalonians and the Little Apocalypse of the synoptic Gospels (see Matt. 24:1–25:46; Mk. 13:1–37; Luke 21:5–38).

Two other late Second Temple Jewish writings (which may or may not have any connection with Qumran) also witness to how Belial could be associated with human figures or even take on human characteristics. The first of these is the Ascension of Isaiah, a work that in its present form is clearly a Christian compilation.[66] Modern scholarship, however, has shown that the Ascension consists of an original Jewish text with some Christian interpolations (the Martyrdom of Isaiah found in chaps. 1–5) and a later independent Christian Ascension of Isaiah (chaps. 6–11) that was joined to it. In the Martyrdom of Isaiah, Beliar is partly fused with *two* human agents—a wicked king and a false prophet—quite possibly to form a precise counterpoint to the dual messiah concept of one messiah as king, the other as prophet. Whether the Martyrdom of Isaiah was a product of the Qumran community or not,[67] the portrayal of Beliar acting in, and at times identified with, human agents in an apocalyptic setting makes it the most important early Jewish witness after Daniel for developing views of human apocalyptic adversaries.

Another text of late Second Temple Judaism, one that may have an Essene origin, deserves mention for its evidence of the Jewish apocalyptic tendency to see current human persecutors as agents of ultimate evil. Early Christian witnesses mention both an Assumption and a Testament of Moses. A fragmentary work surviving in one defective Latin manuscript appears to be a version of this Testament.[68] While cast in the genre of a testament, or last will, of Moses, the content of the text is pure apocalyptic eschatology involving a review of Israel's history through history disguised as prophecy (chaps. 2–8) and an unusual version of the last events in chapters 9 and 10.[69] The connection with the Antichrist tradition is found in chapter 6, where the "wanton king" who rules for thirty-four years must be Herod the Great (37–4 B.C.E.), and the "powerful king from the West" (6:8–9) who destroys part of the temple is the Roman consul Varus. But the description of these apocalyptic agents of the turn of the era is followed by an obscure account of corrupt priests in chapter 7 and the attack against them by "a king of the kings of the earth who, having supreme authority, will crucify those who confess their circumcision" (8:1), which sounds like yet another apocalyptic reflection on Antiochus Epiphanes. In its present form the Testament of Moses probably dates to the early decades of the first century C.E. However we evaluate the layers in this controversial document,[70] for our purposes it is enough to note that the Testament, like other documents,[71] demonstrates that from the time of Antiochus to that of Herod, apocalyptically minded Jews were incorporating their human opponents into the framework of the scenario of the end as special manifestations of the power of evil.

GOD'S ADVERSARIES ARE KNOWN BY THEIR FRUITS

We can ask, in conclusion, what *kind* of human evil these gestating Antichrist-like figures in late Second Temple Judaism convey. What is most evident, especially in the paradigmatic account of the "little horn" in Daniel, are two aspects of external violence: *blasphemy* against God and *persecution* of God's faithful. Also clear is the role of the evil persecutor in profaning the temple and perverting the Torah, God's law. The Qumranic view of human opposition to divine powers in the last days adds the element of *false religious leadership* through the hypocrisy of the pseudo-prophet.[72] This can perhaps be tied to the emphasis found both at Qumran and in other Jewish traditions on internal conflict between good and evil, the psychological dualism of the struggle of the spirits of good and evil within the human heart.[73] All these elements, variously mutated over the centuries, contributed to the image of Antichrist.

The understanding of ultimate human evil found in apocalyptic eschatology, however, is more concerned with action than with motivation. "By their fruits shall you know them" (Matt. 7:16). The evil ruler is evil because he blasphemes against God and attacks the faithful remnant. The wicked priest or prophet is bad because he perverts the Law, especially through deception. What is most striking (from a modern perspective) about the portrayal of final human evil in its Jewish origins is the deterministic nature of the malice of these final adversaries. They are evil because they do evil. Although the Qumran documents speak of the two spirits at war in the human heart, the sectarians' sense of clear opposition between themselves and their foes made it easy for them to be convinced that their opponents had been totally possessed by the Spirit of Perversity. The great temptation of apocalyptic eschatology is always to externalize good and evil in terms of present historical conflicts.

CHAPTER TWO

CHRIST'S
ALTER EGO

THE SECOND ADAM
AND HIS OPPOSITE (50–100)

The true birth of Antichrist is inseparable from belief that Jesus of Nazareth, an itinerant Jewish preacher active around 30 C.E., was the messiah, that is, Christ (the Greek *Christos,* "anointed one," is the equivalent of messiah). But Jesus, as Christians have continued to maintain for almost two millennia, was a different kind of messiah from those anticipated in Second Temple Judaism, not least because he was a messiah who not only had come, but was also still to come. His earliest followers, believing that Jesus had risen from the dead and had ascended to his heavenly Father, focused their hopes on his *parousia,* that is, his triumphant return at the last hour to demonstrate the fullness of his messianic and divine power over history by bringing it to its conclusion.

Identification of Jesus with the returning messiah was the basis for the creation of the Antichrist legend. Antichrist was not an accident or a superfluous addition to Christian faith. It resulted logically from the opposition between good and evil implied in the acceptance of Jesus as divine Son of Man, Christ, and, later, Word of God. Early Christians needed the legend of Antichrist.

The Mystery of Jesus

According to the Gospel ascribed to Matthew, Jesus once asked his closest followers, "But you, who do you say I am?" (Matt. 16:15). The question remains pertinent today. Although probably no figure in the history of world religions has had as much written about him, few remain as mysterious and as subject to controversy. Every age in Christian history has viewed the image of Jesus according to its own ideas of what is central to religion, as historian of Christianity Jaroslav Pelikan has shown in his *Jesus Through the Centuries*.[1] The belief of some Jews that Jesus, the wandering preacher executed in Jerusalem, had risen from the dead and been established as the messiah or Christ was the decisive step both in the path that led to the formation of a new religion and in the creation of the legend of the Antichrist. And one cannot understand the Antichrist without knowing the issues surrounding the life of Jesus and the character of the "Jesus movement" in its earliest stages.

Historically speaking, the paradox about Jesus is that we have more material about him and more sayings attributed to him than almost any other figure of his time, and yet there is little agreement about what he may have "really" said or even about the details of his life and ministry. Much of the problem stems from the fact that Jesus himself wrote nothing; the abundant materials about his life are almost universally from "interested" sources, that is, from his own followers. The earliest external references we possess come from Roman sources near the end of the first decade of the second century (Pliny, Letter 10.96; and Tacitus, *Annals* 15.44). These tell us more about his followers than about Jesus himself. Centuries of Christians have taken the Gospel accounts largely at face value and found little difficulty in explaining away their inconsistencies. Since the Enlightenment critique of Christianity, however, and especially after the triumph of the historical-critical method of biblical interpretation, which strives to understand the text in terms of its original context and intention, the problems concerning the historical Jesus have increased exponentially.

Of course, only a lunatic fringe has ever thought that Jesus did not exist at all. And today few would go as far as the German biblical scholar Rudolf Bultmann did just a few decades ago in reducing the secure historical information about Jesus to a bare minimum. There is no good reason to doubt that Jesus was active at the beginning of the third decade of the first century and that his preaching centered on announcing the "kingdom" or "reign of God." New Testament scholars agree that few, if any, passages in the Gospels give the "very words of Jesus," but almost all are willing to identify some passages that reflect, in more or less accurate fashion, his actual preaching. (Of course, it is difficult to find two biblical scholars who completely agree on what these passages are!) Finally, all admit that Jesus died by crucifixion in Jerusalem.

A crux of contemporary disagreement begins with the issue of how Jesus understood the kingdom of God. Did he think this was a divine event soon to occur in history, or was it a new awareness of God's presence in the hearts of true believers? A powerful tradition of modern biblical scholarship has interpreted Jesus' preaching of the kingdom in an essentially apocalyptic sense, that is, as an imminent and final stage of history. According to this view, Jesus was a preacher convinced of the coming of the new age, which he identified with the kingdom of God.

The scholarly tide arguing for a strictly apocalyptic (*consistent eschatology* was the term often used) view of Jesus, which ran strong for fifty years, began to turn in the middle of the present century and has been largely, though by no means completely, reversed in recent New Testament studies. Some scholars argue that Jesus had nothing at all to do with apocalyptic or even eschatological ideas,[2] but a more prevalent view maintains that he used apocalyptic themes to convey a new message about the present immanence rather than the coming imminence of the kingdom (this view is frequently called *realized eschatology*).[3] However, some investigators have continued to argue in various ways that Jesus is best understood as a kind of apocalyptic preacher.[4]

The precise contours of the doctrinal and ethical message of Jesus will doubtless continue to be evaluated in diverse fashion in the years ahead. The ongoing diversity of viewpoints depends largely on the variety of presuppositions scholars bring to their research. Among these is the question of the originality of Jesus. Traditional Christian explanations of the Gospels, assuming that Jesus was aware of his messianic and even divine nature, saw essential continuity between his preaching and the witness of the early church's written documents. From this perspective, the Gospel passages in which Jesus speaks of himself as Son of Man and messiah *must* have been a part of his original message. Modern critical New Testament scholars have largely adopted a "double-negative" hermeneutical principle based on the idea of Jesus as an original but misunderstood "religious genius." According to this view, the basic principle for determining what Jesus might have said is to see what cannot be reduced either to contemporary Judaism or to the subsequent preaching of the early church and to identify whatever remains with his unique message.[5] Although not as fully developed, other studies stress the "Jewish" Jesus, identifying the possibly authentic surviving parts of his message using the criteria of what an early first-century "sectarian" Jew would have held about Torah, temple, and Messiah.

A good example of the ongoing debate about Jesus' preaching can be found in the disputes about the use of the term *the Son of Man* (*ho huios tou anthrōpou*) in the synoptic Gospels.[6] The expression is not a Greek one, but it reflects a generic term in Hebrew and Aramaic for a human being. However, in Daniel 7:13, and in some Jewish apocalyptic texts contemporary with Jesus (for example, 1 Enoch 48–49; 4 Ezra 13), the term indicates an apocalyptic heavenly being who has the appearance of a man or becomes a man.[7] The *Son of Man* occurs seventy-four times in the synoptics in reference to Jesus, representing some thirty-seven logia, or sayings traditions. At least sixteen of these are in passages dealing with the endtime (for example, the parallel texts in Matt. 24:30, Mark 13:26–27, Luke 17:22–30; and such other passages as Mark 14:62 and Luke 12:8–9). It is obvious that most of these texts reflect the post-Easter faith of the early believers who identified Jesus with the Son of Man conceived of as a messiah coming at the end of days—the earliest form of Christology, that is, the interpretation of who Jesus was and what he did. But did Jesus himself use the term, and did he use it to refer to himself? And if he did, what did he mean by it?

The German New Testament scholar Rudolf Bultmann, in his classic work, *The History of the Synoptic Tradition,* thought that Jesus had used the expression, but only to refer to another figure, an eschatological judge.[8] Other biblical experts, such as Norman Perrin and Philipp Vielhauer, argued that Jesus himself never used the term.[9] More recently, biblical scholars like E. P. Sanders, M. E. Boring, and Adela Yarbro Collins once again advance the case for Jesus' use of the expression, though they are not sure that he used it to refer to himself.[10] The continuing debate, argued with impressive philological skill and textual ingenuity by all parties, is symptomatic of the continuing mystery of Jesus.

Christ and Antichrist in Earliest Christianity

Whatever the debates about Jesus' own views, there is fairly broad agreement that the "Jesus movement," that is, the groups of Jews who accepted him as messiah in the years immediately after his death, understood him in primarily apocalyptic terms. In Ernst Käsemann's famous expression,

"Apocalyptic . . . was the mother of all Christian theology."[11] But we should also recall Gerhard Ebeling's response to Käsemann: "What stands at the beginning of Christian theology is apocalyptic *modified* by faith in Jesus."[12] In other words, recognizing the centrality of the apocalyptic dimension in early Christianity is the beginning of interpretation, not its end, because of both the complexity of Jewish apocalyptic traditions and the radical new possibilities introduced into speculation on history and the endtime by the belief that Jesus had risen from the dead as heavenly Son of Man and messiah. Since the legend of Antichrist developed as the dialectical counterpart to the emerging view of Jesus as Christ in early Christianity, a brief look at nascent Christology is needed before we see what the primitive Christian documents say about the Final Enemy.

The first issue to be considered is the identification of the risen Jesus with the Son of Man. This title is strangely absent in the earliest *written* stratum of Christianity, the letters of Paul (c. 50–57 C.E.). It appears in four relatively independent traditions of early Christianity, however, which come to us in somewhat later written forms. First, there is the lost document generally called Q (from the German *Quelle,* "source"), the existence of which New Testament scholars have postulated in order to explain common sayings of Jesus found in Matthew and Luke but absent in Mark.[13] Q is thought to represent early Palestinian Christianity with a strong apocalyptic flavor. Second, we have the Gospel of Mark, which is usually seen as prior to Matthew and Luke but which in its surviving form is also usually thought to have been written after 70 (after the fall of Jerusalem at least).[14] In the Gospel of John, probably written in the last decade of the first century C.E., Jesus is sometimes still described as the Son of Man (for example, 1:51, 3:13–14; 5:27; 6:27, 54, and 63; 8:28; 12:23 and 34; 13:31) but with accents that take on a different meaning in light of the author's highly developed Christology. Finally, the Apocalypse of John (the product of a different strand of Christianity from the Gospel but probably roughly contemporary) occasionally speaks of the risen Lord as Son of Man (for example, Apoc. 1:13 and 14:14 directly; 1:7 indirectly).[15]

It seems evident that identifying the risen Jesus with the apocalyptic Son of Man was a widespread practice in the earliest strands of Christianity but one that did not last much beyond the first century and that was already being superseded in some circles much earlier, when Paul wrote his letters. Within a Jewish apocalyptic milieu, seeing Jesus as the Son of Man was a potent means of linking a human life (that of the preacher from

Galilee) with a heavenly being whose advent was associated with the imminent final scenario of crisis-judgment-vindication. In other words, it was the beginning of what was to become—and still is—the central affirmation of Christian belief, the affirmation that Jesus was a heavenly/divine figure as well as an earthly/human one. But even from the viewpoint of apocalyptic eschatology, there was a decisive change: Jesus was an apocalyptic messiah who had *already* come and was yet *still* to come! The decisive event of his rising from the dead was taken as the beginning of the new age, though not as its definitive triumph. Implicit in this is the fundamental eschatological perspective that distinguishes Christian views of history, both apocalyptic and nonapocalyptic, the pattern that New Testament scholar Oscar Cullmann described as the "already and not yet" character of the Christian present.[16]

Belief in this pattern meant that the history of the present evil age had not quite ended. Some events were still to come, and other actors might still have roles to play on the great stage of history. The context within which these events and actors were shaped was the Christian expectation of Christ's return to finalize the triumph over the forces of evil begun by his rising from the dead. The most powerful early Christian accounts of this return or *parousia,* not surprisingly, are also central texts in the formation of the Antichrist legend.[17]

How the Synoptic Gospels Envisioned the End

The text often called the Little Apocalypse or Synoptic Apocalypse (Mark 13:1–37; Matt. 24:1–25:46; Luke 21:5–38) has long fascinated Christians. Although the wealth of modern studies on this passage precludes easy summary, a detailed analysis by New Testament scholar Lars Hartman, which shows this text's relation to earlier Jewish apocalypticism as well as its connections with the accounts of the last events found in 1 and 2 Thessalonians, offers an excellent exposition of its meaning.[18] Hartman maintains that the Little Apocalypse, especially in the version in Mark—arguably its most primitive surviving form—was based on a scriptural midrash, or meditation, on the description of the last events found in Daniel. His notations of its direct dependence on texts from the Hebrew Bible are given here in brackets;[19] Matthew's variations and additions are italicized here.

I. *Introduction (Mark 13:1–5).*

II. *First Discussion of Signs (Mark 13:5b–8).*

Take heed that no one leads you astray. Many will come in my name saying "I am" (*the Christ*) and they will lead many astray. And when you hear
of wars and rumors of wars, do not be alarmed; this must take place
[Dan. 2:28–29], but the end is not yet. For nation will rise against nation
[2 Chron. 15:6] and kingdom against kingdom [Isa. 19:2]; there will be
earthquakes in various places, there will be famines; this is but the beginning of the sufferings.

III. *First Section of Moral Advice (Mark 13:9–13).*

IV. *Second Discussion of Signs (Mark 13:14–20).*

When you see the Abomination of Desolation (*spoken of by the prophet
Daniel*) [Dan. 11:31, 12:11] set up where it ought not to be [Dan. 11:31],
(*standing in the holy place*) [Dan. 9:27]—let the reader understand—then
let those who are in Judaea flee to the mountains [Gen. 19:17], let him
who is on the housetop not go down to take what is in his house; and let
him who is in the field not turn back to take his mantle [Gen. 19:17]. And
alas for those who are with child and for those who give suck in those
days! Pray that it may not happen in winter (*or on the Sabbath*). For in
those days there will be such tribulation as has not been from the beginning [Dan. 12:1] of the creation which God created until now, and never
will be. And if the Lord had not shortened the days, no human being
would be saved; but for the sake of the elect whom he chose, he shortened
the days.

V. *Second Section of Moral Advice (Mark 13:21–23).*

And then if anyone says to you, "Look, here is the Christ!" or "Look,
there he is!" do not believe it. For false Christs and false prophets will
arise [Deut. 13:2], and show (*great*) signs and wonders, to lead astray if
possible the elect. But take heed; I have told you all things beforehand.

VI. *Third Discussion of Signs (Mark 13:24–27).*

But in those days, after that tribulation (*Immediately after the tribulation of
those days*) the sun will be darkened [Joel 2:10, 4:15], and the moon will not
give its light [Isa. 13:10], and the stars will fall from heaven [Isa. 34:4], and
the powers in the heavens will be shaken [Isa. 34:4]. (*Then will appear the
sign of the Son of Man in heaven*) And then (*all the tribes of the earth will
mourn*) they will see the Son of Man coming in (*on*) clouds (*of heaven*)
[Dan. 7:13] with great power and glory. And then he will send out the

angels (*with a loud trumpet call*), and (*they will*) gather his elect from the four winds [Deut. 30:3ff.], from the ends of the earth to the ends of heaven [Zech. 2:10].

The Little Apocalypse, like almost all apocalypses, finds in wars, catastrophes, and apostasy sufficient signs of the time of crisis. But is there a recognizable Antichrist, or even Antichrist-like, figure among these signs?[20] This text lacks a clear picture of a Final Tyrant in the manner of Antiochus Epiphanes, but three elements of final human opposition to goodness found in the Little Apocalypse have been important in the history of Antichrist traditions, for they reflect an early, inchoate but still significant stage in Antichrist beliefs. The first of these is the many who will come saying "I am (*the Christ*)" (Mark 13:6, Matt. 24:5, Luke 21:8); the second is the notice of the "Abomination of Desolation" (*to bdelugma tēs erēmōseōs*) drawn from Daniel (Mark 13:14 and Matt. 24:15); and the third is the prediction of "false Christs and false prophets" (Mark 13:22, Matt. 24:24, Luke 21:8).

Although it would appear from the structure of the Little Apocalypse that these three kinds of opposition form distinct moments in the scenario of the last events, it was easy for other Christian speculations about the end either to conflate them in various ways (as Paul may have done) or to see them as indicating the presence of both multiple opposition to Christ and a single Final Enemy. One common subsequent variation on the latter view linked the "many [who] will come in my name saying 'I am'" found in Mark 13:5b (the beginning of the discourse) with the "false Christs and false prophets" of the later part (Mark 13:22). The assertion "I am" (*ego eimi*) is a claim of divinity in the Hebrew Bible, as many commentators have noted, and it also recalls the boastful horn of Daniel who "will utter incredible blasphemies against the God of gods" (Dan. 11:36, cf. 7:8, 11, 20, and 25; 8:10–11 and 25).[21] In a communal or group interpretation that joins the first and third elements, however, the major emphasis is not so much on the tyranny and persecution motif as on the falsity and deception by which the pseudochrists and pseudoprophets will seek to lead the elect astray, once again underlining the importance of the false prophet motif.

The other important element is the appearance of the mysterious Abomination of Desolation. In its original form in Daniel, as we have seen, this was a reference to Antiochus IV's erection of a statue of Zeus in the Jerusalem temple. In the Little Apocalypse in the synoptic Gospels, it is to be understood as a reference to the sacking and destruction of the temple by the Romans in 70 C.E., viewed as an apocalyptic sign by the Christian community.[22] In the original form of the Little Apocalypse (which seems prior to the fall of Jerusalem), the referent is harder to determine.[23] In subsequent Christian exegesis, however, beginning as early as Irenaeus in the late second century,[24] the Abomination of Desolation was taken as a symbolic designation of the "Man of Sin, the Son of Perdition" (*ho anthropos tēs anomias, ho huios tēs apoleias,* 2 Thess. 2:3), who also sets himself up in the temple (compare 2 Thess. 2:4 with Matt. 24:15).[25] This interpretation of the original meaning of the Abomination of Desolation is only conjectural, but it raises the question of the relation of the Little Apocalypse to the teaching on the *parousia* found in 1 and 2 Thessalonians, to which we now turn.

The Scenario According to Thessalonians

A major disagreement exists regarding the Thessalonian letters, though its importance for the development of views of Antichrist may not be all that crucial. Scholars agree that 1 Thessalonians is an authentic letter of Paul, indeed the earliest product of the apostle's pen and therefore the first surviving Christian document, written shortly after 50 C.E. With regard to 2 Thessalonians, however, commentators seem almost evenly split between those who argue that it is also by Paul and was written shortly after 1 Thessalonians to correct misunderstandings of that letter among the believers of Thessalonika and those who claim that a difference in apocalyptic perspective and a more advanced Christology indicate that the work is an imitation of Paul from the first generation of his disciples (70s or 80s C.E.).[26] Where experts continue to disagree, outsiders should be cautious; but I will treat both letters as evidence for Paul's apocalyptic thought in the 50s. In any case, according to Lars Hartman, both show knowledge of the same midrash on Daniel that stands behind the Little Apocalypse of the synoptics.[27]

In 1 Thessalonians Paul gives an instruction (4:13–5:11) concerning the "day of the Lord" (*hemera kyriou,* 5:2). The basic concerns appear to be twofold: the fate of the dead in relation to the living at the imminent return of the Lord (*parousia,* 4:15);[28] and the necessity for watchfulness since that day "is going to come like a thief in the night" (5:2, see Matt. 24:43 and Luke 21:34–35). The latter issue has clear parallels with the Little

Apocalypse; the former appears to be a problem raised in the Thessalonian community by Paul's preaching. There has been considerable discussion of what the apostle means by his appeal to the "Lord's own teaching" (*en logō kyriou,* 4:15), but it seems to indicate not so much a distinct saying of Jesus as a fundamental part of the *kerygma,* the message Paul preached to the Thessalonians. Although the 1 Thessalonians passage is addressed to a particular issue rather than to a general account of the end, it shows a number of similarities with the Little Apocalypse, especially the versions in Matthew and Luke.[29] First Thessalonians displays a clear sense of the proximity of the return of the "Lord"—not the Son of Man—but it does not discuss active opposition to Christ's triumphant return. There is no direct reference to an Antichrist.

Second Thessalonians, on the other hand, provides a detailed account of the Final Enemy, one that remained central in all later Christian speculation, even though it does not use the technical term *Antichrist.* Second Thessalonians insists that a series of preliminary events are necessary before the end, while 1 Thessalonians teaches the imminence of that event. The contrast is stark and will doubtless continue to be debated by investigators because of their differing views both of the nature of apocalyptic eschatology and of the character of Paul's thought. If 1 Thessalonians expresses the whole of Paul's apocalyptic thought, then it is obvious that 2 Thessalonians cannot be authentic. But does anything, either in the nature of apocalyptic eschatology or Paul's own complex thought, rule out the alternative view, namely, that the apostle communicated different aspects of his teaching according to the circumstances?

Given the central importance of 2 Thessalonians 2:1–12 to all later Christian views of Antichrist, it seems helpful to give the complete text, along with the direct parallels to the Hebrew Bible and the synoptic Little Apocalypse in brackets.[30]

> And now, brothers, about the coming [Matt. 24:3, 27] of the Lord Jesus Christ and his gathering of us to himself [Matt. 24:31; Mark 13:27]: I beg you, do not lose your heads or alarm yourselves [Mark 13:7, Matt. 24:6], whether at some oracular utterance, or pronouncement, or some letter purporting to come from us, alleging that the Day of the Lord is already here. Let no one deceive you in any way whatever [Mark 13:5]. That day cannot come before the rebellion [*apostasia*] against God [Isa. 14:13; Ezek. 28:2–9], when the Man of Sin [or lawlessness] will be revealed, the Son of Perdition. He is the Enemy.[31] He rises in his pride against every god [Dan. 11:36], so

called, and every object of men's worship, and even takes his seat in the temple of God [Dan. 9:27; Matt. 24:15] claiming to be God himself. You cannot but remember that I told you this while I was still with you; you must now be aware of the restraining hand [*katechon*] which ensures that he shall be revealed only at the proper time. For already the secret power [*mystērion*] of wickedness is at work, secret only for the present until the Restrainer [*katechōn*] disappears from the scene. And then he will be revealed, that wicked man [*ho anomos*] whom the Lord Jesus will destroy with the breath of his mouth [Isa. 11:4], and annihilate by the manifestation of his coming [*parousia*]. But the coming [*parousia*] of that wicked man is the work of Satan. It will be attended by all the powerful signs and miracles of the lie [*pseudos*] [Mark 13:22], and all the deception that sinfulness can impose on those doomed to destruction. Destroyed they shall be, because they did not open their minds to the love of the truth, so as to find salvation. Therefore God puts them under a delusion, which works upon them to believe the lie, so that they may all be brought to judgment, all who do not believe the truth but make sinfulness their deliberate choice.

The sequence of last events that Paul advances here has significant parallels with those found in the Little Apocalypse, though there are also some differences. One obvious difference is the necessity for removing the "restraining hand or force" (neuter *to katechon* of v. 6), or "Restrainer" (masculine *ho katechōn* of v. 7), before the "Man of Sin" can appear. This mysterious reference has baffled exegetes from the start. As early as Tertullian (c. 200), it was interpreted as a reference to the Roman Empire (and Roman emperor as *ho katechōn*). Another interpretation, found in Theodore of Mopsuestia in the fifth century and revived in our time,[32] sees it as a reference to the necessity of preaching the gospel throughout the world before the end (see Matt. 24:14), in which case Paul himself would be *ho katechōn*.

In the second stage of the last events, the letter seems to combine the three moments or groups of final opposition found in the Little Apocalypse (the ones claiming "I am," the Abomination of Desolation, and the "false Christs") into one.[33] The rebellion, or falling away (*apostasia*), is at the same time the revelation of the Man of Sin. If the synoptics had room for both a group of opposers and the mysterious Abomination of Desolation, in 2 Thessalonians opposition is crystallized in a single figure who combines the motifs of rebellion, blasphemy, and deception and who acts by the power or energy of Satan (*kat'energeian tou Satana*) in the last days.

What is most significant, however, is the way in which this human op-poser has gained specificity and strength by his apocalyptic contrast with Jesus, the risen Lord. Like the returning Jesus, his coming is described as a *parousia* (v. 9) that has its own special moment (*kairos,* v. 6). In an implied one-on-one final combat, he will be slain by the "breath of the mouth of the Lord Jesus" (combining Ps. 2:9 and Isa. 11:4) and by the "manifestation of his coming," an expression for the power of the returning Lord. Jesus has taken over the powers of judgment ascribed to God in the Hebrew Bible, but the Man of Sin, rather than Satan himself, has assumed center stage in the final conflict. The mythic implications of this shift deserve some consideration.

The archetypal story of the Fall in chapters 2 and 3 of Genesis may well help explain this shift. Although the myth of Adam played no large role in the preaching of Jesus, it was important for the apostle Paul, as philosopher Paul Ricoeur has pointed out in his work *The Symbolism of Evil.* "By means of the *contrast* between the 'old man' and the 'new man,'" states Ricoeur, Paul "set up the figure of Adam as the inverse of that of Christ, called the second Adam (1 Cor. 15:21–22, 45–49; Rom. 5:12–21). . . . It was Christology that consolidated Adamology."[34] Christ was seen as a symmetrical but greater Adam. For early Christians, the second Adam gave the myth of the first Adam its full structure, explain-ing evil both as a result of the first man's error or deviation and as an already present and prehuman force, symbolized in the serpent who tempted him.

Ricoeur's reconstruction of the evolution of the Adamic myth is helpful for uncovering important aspects of the early Christian view of evil. But the evidence of the Little Apocalypse, and especially of 2 Thessa-lonians, exposes a limitation in his presentation. The possibility of human fallibility appears not only at the beginning *but also at the end* of time. If the "myth" of the Second Adam was what finally gave the myth of the First Adam its full structure, then we can also say that the emergence of Jesus as apocalyptic Son of Man made the legend of the coming Son of Perdition possible and gave it much of the power it has exerted for two millennia. Just as the archetypal myth of the Fall balances the narration of Adam's loss of innocence with the drama of Christ's temptation and vic-tory over evil on the cross, the Antichrist legend fuses history and myth into an increasingly complex narrative of how resistance to evil by the faithful will finally be overcome in the most difficult of temptations, that presented by Christ's alter ego, the Man of Sin.

This insight helps explain the rather minor role Satan plays in the last days in relation to his human agent, the Antichrist. If the origin of evil is to be explained on the basis of the Fall of the First Adam, and salvation is made available through the New Adam who is Jesus Christ, then final victory (that is, ultimate salvation) will not be achieved until the defeat of the last and most evil Adam, Antichrist. Given the anthropological nature of the central Christian myth of evil, Antichrist is as necessary to it as Adam and Christ.[35]

Finally, we may return to the historical question of the origin of these early portrayals of the *parousia*. The common features of both the Little Apocalypse found in the synoptic Gospels and the Letters to the Thessalonians, especially as analyzed by Lars Hartman, point, as we have said, to an origin in an apocalyptic "meditation" on key texts in the Hebrew Bible, especially from Daniel, treating the events of the last days. The hypothetical stages that the original text went through in its movement toward its surviving witnesses are highly speculative, but if it was known to Paul (either in written or oral form) by the year 50 c.e., it must have been the product of very early Christian scribal circles. If Jesus himself had spoken of the Son of Man (as many scholars now admit), there may be good reason to think that parts of this text go back to his own preaching, though this will scarcely be acceptable to those who wish to distance Jesus from true apocalyptic eschatology.[36]

A New Historical Model: Nero and Antichrist

The role of Antiochus IV as a prism concentrating images of human opposition to God in an apocalyptic perspective has been important both in this chapter and in the last. The Hellenistic king's attack on Jewish religious practices and on the temple as reflected in Daniel and texts influenced by Daniel has remained crucial to Antichrist traditions down to the present. But the growing Christian movement soon began to separate itself from the Jewish temple and its worship, as other groups of Jews, such as the Qumran community, had done in previous centuries. After the destruction of the temple by the Romans in 70 c.e., both Jews and Christians had to confront a new religious situation, one that profoundly affected their respective beliefs and the increasingly divergent roads these religious traditions would take. From the viewpoint of the history of Antichrist, the time was ripe for new historical input into the evolution of the figure of

God's final opponent. Yet the Emperor Vespasian (69–79 C.E.), whose armies under the command of his son Titus destroyed Jerusalem, did not supply the new elements in the Antichrist legend. His predecessor, Nero, emperor from 54 to 68 C.E., did instead.[37]

Nero was a paradigm of megalomania, evil, and cruelty according to Roman historians as well as Christians and Jews.[38] His sin of matricide and his claims to divine status were major elements in his unsavory reputation. Though modern historians have endeavored to show that his reign was not all bad and that certain groups in Rome and other parts of the empire supported him, his name has become a synonym for tyrant (and even in some languages for Antichrist!).[39] From the Christian perspective, Nero's role in the development of the Antichrist legend was linked to his identification as the first imperial persecutor of the new sect,[40] while from the viewpoint of the inner logic of the mythic meaning of Antichrist, another aspect of his life (or, better, afterlife) appears even more important—the belief that Nero was to rise from the dead.

The circumstances surrounding Nero's suicide by sword blow in 68 C.E.—let alone the more bizarre aspects of his reign—were so mysterious they gave rise to a host of stories and legends. The emperor's making peace with the Parthian Empire in the East as well as the favor he enjoyed with some of the lower classes soon contributed to the rumor that he had not died but had fled to Parthia to gather armies so he could return to destroy his opponents and reclaim Rome.[41] Imposters pretending to be the returning Nero appeared in 69 and in 80 C.E. In the year 88, a more serious pretender surfaced in Parthia and, according to the Roman historians, almost succeeded in bringing about a war between these ancient superpowers. The Roman legends of Nero envisaged an emperor who had fled but who would return from the East to conquer Rome—another version of the ancient oracles centering on the conflict between the East and the West.[42] Jewish and Christian texts would later develop both historical and legendary aspects of Nero's career in the language of apocalyptic eschatology.[43]

We know that the conception of a returning Nero affected Jewish eschatological ideas of the first and second centuries primarily through his appearance in the Sibylline Oracles, poetic imitations of pagan oracles created by Jews living outside Palestine to show the superiority of Judaism and to predict coming divine judgment on the sinful Gentiles.[44] In Book 4 of the Sibyllines, which apparently was written late in the first century C.E., Nero appears in the midst of other contemporary signs of growing evil as a king who fled to the East but who will come back to wreak vengeance on Rome: "Then the strife of war being aroused will come to the West, and the fugitive from Rome will also come, brandishing a great spear, having crossed the Euphrates with many myriads."[45]

Book 5, written in Egypt around 100 c.e. and bitterly anti-Roman, moves beyond echoing the pagan legends of the returning emperor toward a full presentation of Nero as the apocalyptic opponent of the messiah. No less than five passages contain an extensive development of the story of the evil emperor.

Nero first appears in verses 28 to 34, where aspects of his life and deeds are prophetically recounted (remember the Sibyl was thought to have been writing in the time of Noah). He is described as having disappeared but also as becoming destructive again when he returns "declaring himself equal to God," like the rebellious kings of the Hebrew Bible. A longer account of Nero's return in verses 93 to 110 describes him as "a savage-minded mighty man, much-bloodied, raving nonsense" (v. 96). Here he comes from Rome (which he has already conquered) to overcome Alexandria and attack Jerusalem. But he will be forestalled by a king sent from God, obviously the messiah.[46] Verses 137 to 154 contain another account of Nero's life and evil deeds disguised as prophecy, explicitly mentioning his flight to the Medes and Persians and using mythological language of his predicted return: "For on his appearance the whole creation was shaken and kings perished" (vv. 152–53). More mythological language is found in the passage in verses 214 to 127, an oracle of doom against Corinth, which will be destroyed when Nero returns:

> For to him God gave strength to perform
> things like no previous one of all the kings.
> For, first of all, cutting off the roots from three heads
> mightily with a blow, he will give them to others to eat,
> so that they will eat of the flesh of the parents of the impious king.[47]

A final passage in Book 5 also approaches the Antichrist legend by contrasting the action of the returning Nero as the agent of final apocalyptic conflict (vv. 361–84) with the coming of "a blessed man from the expanses of heaven" who rebuilds the temple and initiates a messianic period (vv. 414–33).[48]

In these materials there is no reference to Nero's death. He is presumed to be alive in the East, waiting to return.[49] This also appears to be the case in another Nero legend in the Sibylline Oracles, once again in an apocalyptic context of a final Antichrist-like figure. Book 3 is the oldest of the Sibyllines, with parts going back to the mid–second century B.C.E., but verses 63 to 74 are probably an interpolation from not long after 70 C.E. Here, Nero has become Beliar.

> Then Beliar will come from the *Sebastenoi*[50]
> and he will raise up the height of the mountains, he will raise up the sea,
> the great fiery sun and shining moon,
> and he will raise up the dead,[51] and perform many signs
> for men. But they will not be effective in him.
> But he will, indeed, also lead men astray, and he will lead astray
> many faithful, chosen Hebrews, and also other lawless men
> who have not yet listened to the word of God.
> But whenever the threat of the great God draws nigh
> and a burning power comes through the sea to land
> it will also burn Beliar and all overbearing men,
> as many as put faith in him.[52]

The identification of Nero as Beliar in Sibylline Oracle 3 is made more probable because we have an explicit reference to Nero as Beliar incarnate in another text from the late first century C.E. This text, however, is definitely Christian. Earlier (chapter 1) we looked at the role of Beliar in the Martyrdom of Isaiah. In the middle of the Martyrdom (3:13–4:22) is a Christian interpolation that purports to be the content of the vision Isaiah had before his arrest by the evil king Manasseh. This passage, which must date from sometime between 80 and 100 C.E., gives a prophecy of Christ, who is called the "Beloved" (3:13–20), warns of corruption in the church (3:21–31), and ends by describing the reign of Beliar (4:1–13) and the *parousia* of the Beloved (4:14–22).[53] Just as the Beloved comes down from the seventh heaven and is transformed into the appearance of a man (3:13),

> Beliar will descend, the great angel, the king of this world, which he has ruled ever since it existed. He will descend from his firmament in the form of a man, a king of iniquity, a murderer of his mother—this is the king of this world—and will persecute the plant which the twelve apostles of the Beloved will have planted; some of the twelve will be given into his hand (4:1–3).

What follows (vv. 4–14) turns from history disguised as prophecy to bona fide prophecy of the miracles, blasphemy, and world domination of the returning Beliar-Nero: "He will act and speak like the Beloved, and will say, 'I am the Lord, and before me there was no one'" (v. 6). Even the time of his rule is predicted: three years, seven months, and twenty-seven days.[54]

This remarkable text appears to be the earliest Christian adaptation of the Nero legend. It shows that some Christians, developing a trajectory already present in the earlier part of the Jewish Martyrdom of Isaiah, had fused the diabolical last enemy with a human opponent, the persecuting Roman emperor. The underlying logic of this view is plain: Just as the Beloved, conceived of as a heavenly being in the divine sphere (like the Son of Man), had taken on human form to effect redemption, so too Beliar took on human form in Nero. The belief that Antichrist-Nero is the devil incarnate is one of the two major forms of the Christian use of the stories about Nero. Although this form would be rejected by the mainstream tradition, it would have a number of adherents in later centuries.[55]

In a nondualistic religion like Christianity the opposition between good and evil should always remain asymmetrical, not equal. Good must be more powerful than evil. Therefore, theological reasons were soon forthcoming to show that only God, not the devil, can take on a human nature. The devil cannot *become* human precisely because he is *not* God— he does not have the power. So while Satan will inhabit and possess Antichrist as fully as possible, the Final Enemy remains human in the mainline Christian tradition, as the underlying anthropological character of the Adamic myth suggests.

The second Christian use of the Nero legend, one that found its center in contrasting resurrections rather than contrasting incarnations, was to be far more influential in Christian history, though here too subsequent theological reflection denied the Final Enemy a *real* resurrection because such power was seen as belonging to God alone. We find this use in the Johannine Apocalypse, the greatest of all Christian apocalyptic texts. No other apocalypse has been so thoroughly debated; even for those who despise and reject it, the Apocalypse is an unavoidable book.[56] The many disputes over the authorship, date, and structure of the text will probably never be solved; even the picture it presents of Antichrist has been the subject of extensive dispute.

The standard view of the authorship and date of the Apocalypse (as I shall call it hereinafter) is that the work was the product of an early Christian prophet named John and was written in Asia Minor in the last decade of the first century c.e. (The emphasis on the Nero legend in the symbolic lists of emperors in chapter 17 has been a primary argument for a minority who continue to date it shortly after the emperor's demise in 68.)[57] Misplaced zeal for the critical method in the late nineteenth and early twentieth centuries (based on the premise that ancient authors ought to be as consistent as modern professors) led scholars to divide the Apocalypse into varying segments according to diverse principles. Scholars over the past several generations have more and more supported a view of unity of authorship while admitting that John absorbed many earlier traditions, written and unwritten.[58]

If good consensus exists for unity of text and author, there is, unfortunately, still much debate about the structure of the work. Though garish and direct in its language and images, the Apocalypse manages to remain mystifying in its organization and message. As to genre, it is clearly an apocalypse, that is, a revelation mediated to John by the risen Christ (1:12–13) and by various angelic figures (for example, 5:5, 10:9–11, 17:7, and so on). But the Apocalypse has a special character because the author does not adopt the pseudonym of an ancient seer but speaks in his own name, probably reflecting the Christian conviction of the new era begun with the resurrection of Jesus.[59] While it does not contain a review of world history (which would have been meaningless now that the last aeon had actually begun), the Apocalypse is greatly interested in how recent events, especially the history of the Roman Empire, relate to the basic apocalyptic scenario of crisis-judgment-vindication.

It is within this perspective that the Apocalypse's use of the Nero legends appears as a central motif. The interpretive key is the symbolic relation between the historical/legendary Nero, the Roman Empire, and the Antichrist. The key figure is the Beast from the Abyss of Apocalypse 11:7, who is also one of the seven heads of the Beast from the Sea of 13:1–10, the head that received a fatal wound but was restored to life.

It is helpful to look at the structure of the Apocalypse as a series of repeating visions divided into two major "unveilings" of books containing apocalyptic secrets. The first book is the sealed scroll (5:1–5), whose opening by the Lamb of God is found in 6:1 through 11:19. The second book is the small, unrolled scroll held by the mighty angel of chapter 10 (10:2), which the seer is commanded to eat (10:8–11) and whose message is recounted in 12:1 through 21:8. Although the seven seals (6:1–8:1) and seven trumpets of the first revelation (8:2–11:9) contain a full range of apocalyptic signs and wonders, they do not dwell on the figure of Antichrist (with the exception of 11:7–10). Antichrist as the Beast from the Abyss becomes a major figure only in the second part of the Apocalypse.

The mythological framework of heavenly opposition between the forces of good and evil that sets the stage for the coming of the Antichrist is described in chapter 12, the famous vision of the pregnant Queen of Heaven who is attacked by the "huge red Dragon which had seven heads and ten horns" (12:3). This Dragon, identified with the devil in verse 13, does not prevail over the Woman and her "male child," the messiah. He is cast down to earth to "make war on the rest of her children, that is, all who obey God's commandments and bear witness for Jesus" (v. 17). This retrieval of the ancient combat myth is one of the most potent scenes in all apocalyptic literature.[60]

In chapter 13, the way in which Satan wages this final war is taken up. The dependence of Apocalypse 13 on Daniel 7 has long been noted. While Daniel saw four beasts arise from the sea (the watery chaos of opposition to God), John sees one Beast that combines the features of Daniel's four:

> Then I saw a Beast emerge from the sea: it had seven heads and ten horns, and each of its heads was marked with blasphemous titles. I saw that the Beast was like a leopard, with paws like a bear and a mouth like a lion; the Dragon had handed over to it his own power and his throne and his world-wide authority. I saw that one of its heads seemed to have had a fatal wound but that this deadly injury had been healed and, after that, the whole world had marvelled and followed the beast (13:1–3).

Daniel's four beasts were four kingdoms; John's single Beast is also a human rulership, the Roman Empire conceived of as the persecuting emissary of Satan on earth. But if Satan had been the predominant evil figure in chapter 12, from chapter 13 on his human representative, symbolized as the Beast, is the major actor.[61] While chapter 13 gives us many details about the activities of the Beast, such as his forty-two-month reign and his number, "the number of a man, the number 666" (13:18), the head that seemed to have the fatal wound and recovered is the main clue to his identity.

This is borne out by the second lengthy description of the Beast and his activity in chapter 17, where John sees the Prostitute Babylon the Great (meaning Rome) riding on the Beast. The revealing angel tells him:

> The Beast you have seen once was and now is not; he is yet to come up from the Abyss, but only to go to his destruction. And the people of the world . . . will think it miraculous when they see how the Beast once was and now is

not and is still to come. Here there is need for cleverness, for a shrewd mind; the seven heads are the seven hills, and the woman is sitting on them. The seven heads are also seven emperors. Five of them have already gone, one is here now, and one is to come; once here, he must stay for a short while. The Beast, who once was and now is not, is at the same time the eighth and one of the seven, and he is going to his destruction (17:8–11).[62]

Thus the coming Beast is seen as one of the five heads already gone, who will return as the eighth and final head. The passage goes on to describe the ten horns (see Dan. 7:24) as ten kings who will be given power by the Beast to fight along with him against the Lamb (17:12–14). The Lamb will defeat them, but not before they have attacked and destroyed the Prostitute (17:15–17). Although this knotty chapter continues to have its puzzles, comparing this version of the Beast to that in chapter 13 clarifies a number of important issues.

First, it is evident that the Beast is a polyvalent symbol, representing both the Roman Empire (a collective opponent of Christ and his followers) and a final single imperial opponent, the head with the deadly wound (13:3) that "once was and now is not and is still to come" (17:8). Second, it is almost unanimously admitted that this fatally wounded and soon-to-be-revived head is Nero, conceived of for the first time in surviving literature as returning from the dead.[63] Just as the Lamb who opened the sealed scroll was seen "standing [that is, risen] as though it had been slain" (5:6), so his apocalyptic opponent, the Beast from the Abyss, will also arise from death, that is, from the *abyssos*.[64] The contrast between the two animal images for Christ and Antichrist-Nero is realized with marvelous symbolic precision. The dead Nero symbolized as the head of the Beast will *ascend* alive into the world from the Abyss in his own *parousia* to war against the saints and to destroy Rome, as the legends had long predicted. Jesus Christ, the sacrificed Lamb now present in heaven, will *descend* once again to earth in a *parousia* (1:7), coming as the Divine Warrior, the Rider on the White Horse (19:11–16), who will defeat the Beast and his followers and cast them alive "into the fiery lake of burning sulphur" (19:20).[65] Though John does not appear to have known 2 Thessalonians, the theme of the dual *parousia* of Christ and Antichrist is also central to his presentation of the Last Days and bears the same significance from the perspective of the Adamic myth of evil.

The identification of the slain and revived head with Nero also helps explain the mysterious number of the Beast (13:18), that is, 666. Since the second century, various interpretations of 666 have been offered (not helped by the fact that a number of manuscripts read 616 rather than 666).[66] Students of apocalypticism have been uncertain whether to take the number as an example of general number symbolism (according to which we might say that 666 is total imperfection just as 888 would be complete perfection),[67] or of gematria, the special number symbolism popular in antiquity that calculated names according to the numbers signified by the letters. In addition, some have opted for gematria based on Hebrew letters, others on Greek. The simplest and most likely solution is that 666 is a gematria for the Hebrew *nrwn qsr,* that is, "Nero Emperor."[68]

The Beast arising from the Abyss (*to thērion to anabainon ek tēs abyssou*) occurs in only one context in the first part of the Apocalypse, chapter 11, which tells the story of the two witnesses. Christian tradition has read this Beast as another reference to Antichrist, and this position has generally been supported by modern scholarship. It seems likely, however, that this is one of the places where John used an earlier written source (rewritten but still discernible in 11:3–13) that concentrated on the apocalyptic role of Jerusalem.[69] The two witnesses who are sent "to prophesy for those twelve hundred and sixty days" (Jerusalem's time of persecution by the Gentiles) remain mysterious figures but are clearly apocalyptic preachers of the end of time.[70] The miraculous powers of the witnesses are not enough to protect them from "the Beast that comes out of the Abyss [who] is going to make war on them and overcome them and kill them" (11:7). This verse, with language influenced by the account of the "little horn" (Dan. 7:21), appears to be added by John, inserting his Antichrist-Nero figure into the older account and thus also tying together the revelation of the apocalyptic scenario found in the sealed scroll with that in the open scroll.[71] We should note too that it allows, though perhaps in confusing fashion, both Jerusalem and Rome (the focus in chaps. 13–18) significance in the Antichrist's career. Both cities would continue to play important roles in later Christian apocalypticism.

One final aspect of the depiction of Antichrist as the Beast in the Apocalypse needs to be noted. In chapter 13, the Beast is followed by a second Beast that emerges from the ground, having the horns of a lamb and a voice like a dragon (13:11). "This second Beast was servant to the first Beast, and extended its authority everywhere, making the world and all its people worship the first Beast, who had had the fatal wound and had been healed" (13:12). It works miracles on behalf of the first Beast and sees to it that all are branded with the Beast's name or number (13:13–17). It has been pointed out that the Dragon, the first Beast, and the second Beast (described as a "false prophet" in 16:13 and 19:20) form an "unholy trinity" in contrast perhaps to developing Christian belief in the Trinity.[72] But who is the second Beast and what is his relation to Antichrist?

The mythological background of the picture of two Beasts is apparently Jewish speculation about Leviathan and Behemoth. Both of these monsters appear in the Hebrew Bible as forms of the cosmic opposition to God (Isa. 27:1, and especially Job 40:15–41:26). In late Jewish apocalyptic literature they take a larger role, with the added note that Leviathan is a beast from the sea and Behemoth a beast of the land, just like the two creatures in Apocalypse 13.[73] The identification of the second Beast as a false prophet involved in furthering the worship of the Antichrist-Beast may reflect John's criticism of the pagan priests of the imperial cult and may also be related to the pseudoprophets in the Little Apocalypse (Mark 13:22).[74] What is distinctive is that this Beast has become individualized as *the* false prophet of the Antichrist.[75]

The Coalescence of the Antichrist Legend

Our consideration of early Christian evidence for an explicit Antichrist figure has thus far revealed many of the materials upon which later Christians would construct their accounts of the Final Enemy, but it has not provided us with evidence for the title *antichristos* itself. The term first occurs in two of the late documents found in the New Testament. The two Letters ascribed to John, the Beloved Disciple, certainly belong to the "Johannine community," that group of believers who cherished the deeply spiritual interpretation of Jesus and his message that is preserved in the Gospel of John (probably put together in its final form toward the end of the first century C.E.). Despite the antiapocalyptic stance of John's Gospel (traditionally the archetype of immanent or realized eschatology), the evidence of the Johannine Letters indicates that even this group of early Christians knew of the traditions of final opposition between good and evil, though they interpreted these according to their own version of faith in Jesus as Christ.[76]

The letters show that the Johannine community had experienced a severe split over the proper interpretation of their leader's teachings about Jesus. Given the date of the Gospel, this split is likely to have taken place about 100 C.E. One group had left the community, and it was against these secessionists (perhaps proto-Gnostics) that the Letters were written.[77] The author's sense of the danger of the secessionists' teaching led him to see them as the "false Christs and false prophets" tradition taught to be among the signs of the end. What is new, at least in literature that survives, is the use of the term *Antichrist*. The key text is in 1 John 2:

> Children, it is the last hour [*eschatē hōra*].[78] You heard that Antichrist is to come: well, now many Antichrists have made their appearance, and this makes us certain that it really is the last hour. It was from our ranks that they went out—not that they really belonged to us; for if they had belonged to us, they would have remained with us. . . . Who, then, is the Liar? None other than the person who denies that Jesus is the Christ. Such is the Antichrist [*ho antichristos*]: the person who denies the Father and the Son (1 John 2:18a–19d, 22).

The same message is repeated in 4:3 where "everyone who negates the importance of Jesus" is described as reflecting a "Spirit which does not belong to God. It is rather of the Antichrist, something which, as you have heard, is to come—well now, it is already here!" In 2 John 7 those who do not confess that Jesus came in the flesh are hailed with the words, "There is the Deceiver! There is the Antichrist!"

Although there is no mention of Antichrist in John's Gospel, it is clear that traditions about the Final Opponent(s) of Jesus were a part of the preaching of the Johannine community. They appear to have differed little from what we have seen in the Little Apocalypse, for they included both an individual opponent—the Liar (*ho pseustes*, 1 John 2:22) or the Deceiver (*ho planos*, 2 John 7)—and a collective component of false Christs and false teachers. The Letters put such emphasis on the collective component, however, that it is difficult to think that the author has much interest in a final single human opponent. We can also note that this is a resolutely "nonpolitical" rendition of the final opponents. The denial of Christ (which is a denial of both the Father and the Son) is a doctrinal error—a heresy—on the part of false Christians. These Christians are not just precursors of the Antichrist; their existence is a sign that it *is* the last hour: Antichrist is already here. In other words, this is another expression of Johannine immanent, or realized, eschatology. Independent of any relation to external world history, the presence of the false belief and secession of some who pretend to follow Jesus proves that the liar(s) collectively called Antichrist is/are now actually present.

The term *antichristos,* with its ambiguous preposition *anti,* can indicate "in place of Christ," "false Christ," and "opposed to Christ."[79] All three meanings may well have been intended, and all three continued to appear in later use of the word. The author's transformation of Antichrist toward a collective actually within the Christian community itself (or at least among those who claimed to be Christian) remained an important option in the subsequent history of Antichrist, as did his use of the term not only in the plural but also in the singular (probably reflecting earlier teaching). This made it possible for most later Christians to believe in many antichrists as well as in the single final opposer predicted in 2 Thessalonians and the Apocalypse.

The move to an immanent collective view of Antichrist that is evident in the Johannine Letters has been thought by some to reflect a major transition in early Christianity away from apocalypticism as the delay of the *parousia* of the risen Jesus became more and more evident.[80] There can be no doubt that the original apocalyptic fervor of the "Jesus movement" of about 30 to 50 C.E. had diversified, developed, changed, and even cooled, in many segments of the Christian communities by about 100. This was bound to be the case. But only the elusive search for a single-minded explanation of a remarkably diverse religious movement has allowed some investigators to assume that second-century Christians lost their interest in apocalyptic eschatology and proceeded to create a new form of religion on very different bases. Christianity has never lost touch with its apocalyptic foundations.

CHAPTER THREE

PERSECUTION, HERESY, AND SELF-DECEIT

ANTICHRIST IN DEVELOPING CHRISTIANITY (100–500)

The seventy-five years that followed the Apocalypse of John left only partial and scattered evidence concerning Christian belief in Antichrist, though we have no reason to suppose that this indicates loss of faith in Antichrist.[1] Indeed, by about the year 200 C.E. the Antichrist legend had taken provocative new twists.

One important witness to Antichrist beliefs may date from the last generation of the first century, that found in the *Didache,* or *Teaching of the Twelve Apostles.*[2] The apocalypse that forms this work's final chapter shows many similarities with Matthew's version of the Little Apocalypse. This does not necessarily indicate direct literary dependence but perhaps merely access to the same underlying traditions, including a warning that "in the last days the false prophets and corrupters shall be multiplied, . . . and then shall appear the Deceiver of the World as a son of God" (16:3–4). The *Didache* announces three signs of the coming of the Lord: first, "the sign spread out in heaven" (Matt. 24:30); second, "the sign of the sound of the trumpet" (Matt. 24:31a); and third, "the resurrection of the dead" (possibly a reference to the gathering of the elect in Matt. 24:31b).

Polycarp (the bishop of Smyrna born about 70 C.E. and martyred around 156), in his Epistle to the Philippians, probably written about 135 C.E., mentions Antichrist in a brief reference that depends on the Johannine Letters.[3] About the same time, the pseudonymous *Epistle of Barnabas,* a product of Alexandrian Christianity, also mentions Antichrist beliefs. Finally, Justin Martyr, who was executed in Rome about 165 c.e., refers to Antichrist, though unlike Polycarp he does not use the term.[4]

Perhaps the most important Antichrist account of the first half of the second century occurs in another early Christian apocalypse, that ascribed to Peter. Many early Christian apocalypses are difficult to date.[5] The *Apocalypse of Peter,* however, is alluded to by Theophilus, bishop of Antioch toward the end of the second century, and appears to date from 130–140 c.e. This work briefly portrays a false messiah who tries to turn members of the "fig-tree of the House of Israel" away from Christ and to himself and who kills those who do not follow him. It has been suggested that this reflects the history of the Jewish messianic leader Bar-Kochba, who in 133 c.e. killed Christians who refused to acknowledge him and join his war against the Romans.[6] If this is the case, the *Apocalypse of Peter* is an important witness to ongoing Christian adaptation of the Antichrist legend to current events.

Antichrist Teachings of Irenaeus and Hippolytus

In the first centuries of Christianity, various Antichrist traditions coalesced into a full-blown legendary narrative. We see the process clearly in the writings of two important theologians: Irenaeus, the first great theologian of the orthodox or "Great Church" tradition, and Hippolytus, the major early theologian of the Church of Rome. (Irenaeus wrote c. 175–80 c.e., Hippolytus in the early third century.)

Irenaeus was born in Asia Minor (he knew Polycarp), lived for a time in Rome, and died as bishop of Lyons in Gaul in the late second century. A prolific writer, he is best known for his five books *Against Heresies* (*Adversus haereses*), written in Greek but surviving mostly in Latin translation.[7] That Irenaeus, the premier Christian thinker of the second century, included a treatment of Antichrist in his great work witnesses to how important Antichrist traditions were in the common teaching of the second-century "Great Church" of emerging orthodoxy as well as to how a theological genius was able to reveal important new depths in this common belief.

A passage from *Against Heresies* (5.30.1) summarizes Irenaeus's central insight into the meaning of Antichrist. In defending the reading of 666 for the Beast's number in Apocalypse 13:18, the bishop appeals to the evidence of the best manuscripts, to eyewitnesses who had seen John (doubtless Polycarp), and even to reason (*logos*) itself to demonstrate that 666 "shows the recapitulation of that entire apostasy which happened in the beginning, and in the intervening times, and which will happen in the end" (*Against Heresies* 5.30.1). The notion that Antichrist will effect a "recapitulation" (Latin *recapitulatio*; Greek *anakephalaiosis*) of evil is the linchpin of Irenaeus's Antichristology: Antichrist must recapitulate evil, just as Christ recapitulates all good.[8] As the Word truly became flesh in order that the human might become God according to the eternal plan of the beneficent Father, so too Antichrist must come in the flesh as the one who sums up all the evil that separates humanity from God. Over and over, the bishop returns to the necessity of the coming Evil One who "voluntarily recapitulates apostasy in himself" (5.28.2). Irenaeus's reading of the Antichrist tradition moves from the level of the double *parousiai* found in the New Testament texts—the Son of Man versus the Man of Sin—to the new theological level of double recapitulation.

The bishop's recapitulative perspective allowed him to make a number of major contributions to the developing Antichrist legend, from his insightful theological explanation of 666, the number of the Beast,[9] to the overall synthetic presentation by which he brought together the scattered biblical passages of both the Old and the New Testaments on the career of the Final Enemy, the Antichrist.[10] Though the bishop doubtless made his own exegetical innovations, it is difficult to think that he was totally responsible for this synthetic exegesis. We can rather presuppose that he reflects a tradition already well established in the church.

In his account of the career of Antichrist, Irenaeus mingles a variety of scriptural "prophecies," both expected and unexpected.[11] It seems clear that the bishop depended on earlier traditions, both Jewish and Christian, in claiming that Antichrist will be born a Jew, specifically from the tribe of Dan. It is likely that he rejected the idea of a revived Nero as Antichrist because of his adherence to the older tradition that the antimessiah, like the true messiah, must be of Jewish origin. In proving Antichrist's origin from Dan, the bishop cites Jeremiah 8:16 (see 5.30.2) and notes that the tribe of Dan is conspicuously absent from the enumeration of the saved in Apocalypse 7. Here the bishop draws on traditions in Jewish and Christian apocalypticism pointing to the tribe of Dan as the stock from which would come the false messiah.[12]

Irenaeus concentrates his treatment of the Man of Sin on theological significance, not on biographical details, although he mentions some of the now-accepted facts about Antichrist, such as the three-and-a-half-year reign (5.25.3–4). Though he claims that Gnostics and Marcionites are part of the *apostasia* to be recapitulated in Antichrist (see 5.26.2), unlike the author of the Johannine Letters he does not identify current heretics with the actual presence of Antichrist. His sense of the reality of God taking on flesh in Jesus led him to emphasize that Antichrist must be a single human still to come, not a present or future collectivity, however much such might prepare for him. We must also note how powerfully Irenaeus's theology of Antichrist stresses the role of human freedom. Christ's coming was for the resurrection of those who choose the good and the ruin of those who choose evil (5.27.1); the recapitulation of apostasy in the coming of Antichrist will cast final light on the freedom of those who have clearly elected to be punished for eternity (see 5.27.1–2, 5.28.1, and 5.29.1).[13]

The second important theologian who discussed Antichrist traditions was a disciple of Irenaeus. Hippolytus, of Greek origins, served as presbyter in Rome from about 200 to 235, when he died a martyr. Though his theology was not as profound as that of his teacher, Hippolytus left a large body of writings that are significant because they show the church's growing emphasis on exegesis as the preferred form of Christian teaching. Hippolytus's *Commentary on Daniel,* written during the persecution of Christians by Septimius Severus (c. 202–4), is the earliest surviving complete Christian biblical commentary.[14] The work contains important materials on Antichrist in its fourth book. Here the presbyter also refers to an earlier treatise, *On the Antichrist (Peri tou antichristou)*, probably written about 200 C.E.[15] This is the earliest example of a theological treatise devoted to Antichrist.

Hippolytus is notable both for the fullness of the account he supplies of the Final Enemy[16] and because he does so within the context of an explicit redating of the end, which pushes the appearance of Antichrist into the future by several centuries. Hippolytus wrote at a time of renewed belief in the imminent coming of the end, perhaps due to the persecutions.[17] At least in part, his *Commentary on Daniel* and his later *Chronicle* (234 C.E.) were written to show that Christ had come not at the end of the sixth millennium of history—that is, immediately prior to the end of history—but rather in the middle of the final thousand years (5500 *anno mundi*), thus leaving five hundred years between his coming in humility and his glorious return.[18] Hippolytus's redating of the end was to have great importance in the history of Christian apocalypticism.[19]

Though Hippolytus occasionally refers to Irenaeus's teaching on Christ's recapitulation,[20] his account of Antichrist is based not on his master's insight about opposing recapitulations, but rather on a more symbolic view of the necessity for fundamental opposition between Christ and the Final Enemy on every level. As he puts it in chapter 6 of *On the Antichrist*:

> Now, as our Lord Jesus Christ, who is also God, was prophesied of under the figure of a lion, on account of his royalty and glory, in the same way the Scriptures have also aforetime spoken of Antichrist as a lion, on account of his tyranny and violence. For the Deceiver seeks to liken himself in all things to the Son of God. Christ is a lion, so Antichrist is a lion; Christ is a king, so Antichrist is also a king. The Savior was manifested as a lamb, so he too, in like manner, will appear as a lamb, though within he is a wolf.[21]

The passage goes on to note six specific ways in which Antichrist will be a perverted imitation of Christ: (1) Jewish origin; (2) the sending out of apostles; (3) bringing together people scattered abroad; (4) sealing of his followers; (5) appearance in the form of a man; and (6) the building of a temple (in Christ's case, the temple of his body in the resurrection [see John 2:19]; in Antichrist's, the raising of a new stone temple in Jerusalem).[22]

After discussing Antichrist's Jewish origin and the prophetic texts whose mystical meaning reveals the last things, Hippolytus extensively discusses the Final Enemy's career in the last part of his treatise. Antichrist cannot be near until the Roman Empire has been divided into ten kingdoms, or "ten democracies" (*deka demokratia*), as Hippolytus says in one instance.[23] Thus, the Roman Empire is not the kingdom of Antichrist (as it had been in John's Apocalypse), but merely a preparatory stage.[24] The presbyter cites Daniel 9:27 as his authority for claiming that the final week of Jeremiah's seventy years (history's last seven years)[25] will be equally divided between the preaching of the two witnesses, Enoch and Elijah,[26] and the career of Antichrist. Hippolytus's interpretation of the two Beasts of Apocalypse 13 is unusual: He identifies the first Beast with the Roman Empire, so that "he [John] means that the Beast coming up from the earth [Apoc. 13:11] is the kingdom of Antichrist and the two horns are him [Antichrist] and the false prophet after him."[27] Antichrist restores the wounded head of the prior Beast by rebuilding the Roman Empire and persecuting the Christians who will not worship him. Hippolytus, with his Jewish Antichrist, offers no hint of the understanding of the Final Enemy as *Nero redivivus*.

In his *Commentary on Daniel,* while Hippolytus several times refers his readers to his earlier treatise on Antichrist, he advances at least two new details relating to the Final Enemy. First, in trying to harmonize Daniel's use of the Abomination of Desolation (which he recognizes refers to Antiochus IV) with the application of the term to Antichrist, Hippolytus claims,

> Daniel predicted two Abominations, the first of destruction (*aphainismou*), the second of desolation (*erēmōseōs*).[28] What is the one of destruction save that which Antiochus did at that time? What is that of desolation save the universal one when Antichrist comes?[29]

Second, when he investigates the different dates for the duration of Antichrist's reign, Hippolytus introduces an exegetical twist that would have a long history in Christian apocalypticism.[30] Noting that Daniel 12:11–12 speaks of both 1290 days and 1335 days, he says:

> When the Abomination appears and wages war against the saints anyone who is able to survive his days [the 1290] and attain the forty-five days [the 1335], as if waiting for the completion of a pentecost [the traditional 50 days of celebration], will gain the kingdom of heaven. Antichrist enters into only a part of the pentecost in his wish to share in Christ's kingdom (*Comm. on Dan.* 4.55).

Hippolytus is thus the earliest witness to what later became known as the "refreshment of the saints," a brief period between Antichrist's defeat and Christ's return when the surviving faithful were supposed to live in peace awaiting the manifestation of the kingdom of God.[31]

The coalescence of the Antichrist legend found in Irenaeus and Hippolytus is echoed and slightly modified in their contemporary Tertullian (c. 160–220), the first major voice in Latin Christianity. Like the writings of Hippolytus, those of Tertullian reflect a renewal of apocalyptic expectations shortly after 200 c.e. (see his *Against Marcion* 3.24). Like both Irenaeus and Hippolytus, Tertullian thought (at least for most of his career) that the end was not near. He is the first author to identify the "Restraining Force" of 2 Thessalonians 2:6 with the Roman Empire. In his *Apology* 32 he notes that Christians offer prayers for the emperors, since only the continued existence of Rome staves off the end. His treatise on *The Resurrection of the Flesh* is more explicit, stating, "'For that day shall not come unless first comes a falling away' (*discessio*), which he [Paul] means of this present empire."[32] Tertullian's references to Antichrist indicate that he believed both in present "antichrists," especially heretics who rend the church (as in the Johannine Letters, which he is among the first to cite explicitly), and in a coming final Antichrist who will persecute the faithful.[33]

The picture that emerges from these accounts forms, in the words of patristic scholar David Dunbar, "a kind of 'mainline' eschatology which may have been quite widespread during the closing decades of the second century."[34] Antichrist is a Jewish false messiah whose coming is still some time in the future, following the fragmentation of the Roman Empire. Antichrist is seen primarily as a persecuting tyrant who will rebuild Jerusalem and its temple. Exalting himself as God and demanding public worship, he will slaughter those who refuse to worship him. Hippolytus summarizes thus: "After gaining power over all, he, as a savage tyrant [omotyrannos], shall bring tribulation and persecution on the saints, exalting himself over them."[35] His fall after three and a half years will usher in Christ's return to earth.

The Power of "the Lie" in the Later Roman Empire

The full accounts of the Antichrist found at the end of the second and in the early third centuries, however, are only the first level of the complex and at times extravagant edifice of the developing Antichrist legend. The next three centuries of patristic thought show this "mainline" tradition exercising considerable influence, but they also show important variations and new creations.

The three hundred years between 200 and 500 C.E. form a coherent period, both because of the Hippolytan redating of the end that put Antichrist's arrival at about 500 and also because those years witnessed the kind of events that always give new life to apocalyptic traditions. The Irenaean-Hippolytan predictions of Rome's dissolution into a series of independent realms actually took place by 500 C.E., at least in the West, where the barbarian invasions destroyed Roman hegemony in all but name. Such was the power of belief in the empire's necessity as the last barrier before the end, however, that many seem to have been unwilling or unable to recognize its demise. During the three centuries leading to Rome's collapse in the West, no one seems to have written a separate treatise on Antichrist in the manner of Hippolytus, and few devoted as much attention to him as Irenaeus had in his *Against Heresies*. Still, most of the major patristic authors reflect the church's ongoing belief in the key role given to Christ's Final Adversary, and some texts witness to major new developments in the legend.

COMPETING VIEWS OF ANTICHRIST:
SPIRITUAL ANTICHRIST AND DOUBLE ANTICHRIST

Origen of Alexandria (c. 185–254) is generally recognized as the greatest theological mind of early Christianity. His highly spiritual reading of the Bible, as evidenced in his opposition to any literalist reading of the coming reign of Christ and the saints,[36] might seem to indicate that he had little interest in Antichrist. But Origen was also the catechist of the Alexandrian Church and a representative of church tradition. His views on Antichrist, at least as reflected in his surviving works, are ambiguous but are among the most provocative of the patristic era.

Origen argued that Antichrist is necessary because "among men there should be two extremities . . . , the one of goodness, the other of the opposite, so that the extremity of goodness exists in the human nature of Jesus, . . . whereas the opposite extremity exists in him who is called Antichrist." Origen called Antichrist the "son of the evil daemon, who is Satan and the devil,"[37] a designation many later authorities came to think of as a rather suspect term.

Yet Origen thought that for "spirituals," believers capable of deeper insight, another level of meaning could be found in Antichrist. A revealing passage occurs in the second book of what survives of Origen's massive *Commentary on John.* There he applies a spiritual reading to 2 Thessalonians. What Christ, the Word and the Truth and Wisdom, destroys by the breath of his mouth (2 Thess. 2:8) is "the Lie" (*to pseudos*). As Wisdom and Word, he annihilates, by the manifestation of his presence, "everything that is proclaimed as wisdom and is really among the things God seizes 'in their craftiness'" (1 Cor. 3:19, citing Job 5:13).[38] A similar spiritual reading is the leitmotif for his lengthy comment on Matthew's version of the Little Apocalypse, especially the first part dealing with Matthew 24:1–28.[39] There he identifies the Abomination of Desolation as "the word of the lie that is seen to stand in the holy place of Scripture," that is, every form of heresy that misreads or replaces the Scripture. He interprets Antichrist even more universally as "every word that pretends to be the truth when it is not."

In the Johannine Epistles, as we have seen, the presence of Antichrist was understood as the existence of heretics or schismatics. Origen's reading builds on this but goes further by interpreting the now classic texts referring to the coming Final Opponent in terms of the false wisdom, or the lie, present in every soul before it is illuminated by the Word. To the best of my knowledge, this is the earliest fully interiorized reading of Antichrist in Christian history.

The third century c.e. also witnessed two important new developments in the literalist understanding of the figure of Antichrist: the rise of a double Antichrist tradition, and the beginnings of attempts to describe the appearance of the Final Enemy. Both of these innovations are first found in texts that can be plausibly, though not certainly, assigned to the mid–third century.

The traditional Jewish view of the false messiah had obviously conceived of him as a Jew and had centered his activity in Jerusalem. This formed the background to the picture of Antichrist we find in the Little Apocalypse, in 2 Thessalonians, and in more complete fashion in Irenaeus and Hippolytus. But beginning with the Christian parts of the Martyrdom of Isaiah, and especially in John's Apocalypse, the idea of Antichrist as *Nero redivivus* presented an alternative picture of a pagan Final Enemy whose major arena of activity would be Rome, though some role for Jerusalem was not ruled out (see Apoc. 11). Also, as we have seen, the appearance of not one but two Beasts in Apocalypse 13, especially since at least one Christian authority (Hippolytus) identified the second, not the first, with Antichrist, testifies to considerable fluidity in early Christian traditions. One way to deal with this divergence was to admit a duality of Antichrists.[40]

The rather crude verses attributed to the Latin Christian writer Commodian provide what seems to be the earliest evidence for this position. All we know about Commodian comes from his two poems, the "Instructions" and "Song of Two Peoples," or "Apologetic Song" (*Carmen apologeticum*). He has been variously dated from the mid–third to the mid–fifth centuries, with the majority view favoring the earlier date and thus winning for him the title of the earliest Latin Christian poet.[41] Like Irenaeus and many early Christians, Commodian was a convinced millenarian, that is, a believer in a literal thousand-year reign of Christ and the saints on earth (see "Instructions" 1.44). He distanced himself from many second- and third-century Christians by the intransigent tone of his opposition to the Roman Empire, conceiving of it, as John had, as the devil's representative. (This may indicate that he wrote in a time of persecution, perhaps that of the emperor Decius or Valerian.) A brief mention of Antichrist occurs in "Instructions" 1.41, which identifies him as "Nero raised from hell."[42] But in the "Song of Two Peoples," designed to convince both Jews and pagans of the truth of Christianity, Commodian provides a more complex understanding of Antichrist as part of a lengthy apocalyptic section (vv. 791–1060). After a discussion of the *Nero redivivus* and the three and a half years of his persecution, Commodian predicts the Roman Empire will fall and "a king from the East with four peoples" (Persians, Medes, Chaldaeans, and Babylonians) will cross the Euphrates, advance on Rome, and kill Nero and the two Caesars he has adopted (that is, the three kings that the "little horn" of Dan. 7:8 will uproot). His destruction of Rome will usher in the last events (vv. 927ff.). This final Antichrist will then proceed to the land of Judaea, where he will be welcomed by the Jews and perform many prodigies before he is rebuked by God's voice sounding from heaven. Commodian concludes:

> A man from Persia claims to be immortal.
> For us Nero is the Antichrist, for the Jews he is.
> These two are ever prophets in the very end.
> Nero is the destruction of Rome; he of the whole world;
> I tell only a few of the secrets I have read about him.
> (vv. 932–36)[43]

It is clear that this is a new rendition of the old theme of conflict between East and West, which looked forward to the destruction of Western conquerors (first the Greeks, then the Romans) by a revived Eastern ruler (as in the third book of the Sibylline Oracles). Whether or not these two Antichrists reflect any events of the third (or any other) century is still uncertain.[44]

Belief in two Antichrists seems to have been found only in Latin Christianity, but it was widespread for several centuries. The most important Latin apocalyptic author of the early fourth century, Lactantius, taught a modified form of it. In his major summary of the coming end of history contained in the *Divine Institutes* 7.14–26 (composed c. 312 C.E.) Lactantius discussed two final persecutors, though, unlike Commodian, he referred to only the second of these explicitly as Antichrist.[45]

One of the most remarkable aspects of Lactantius's picture of the end is the ecumenical character of his argument. The *Divine Institutes* was an apologetic work written to convince the still largely pagan Latin intelligentsia of the superiority of Christianity. The Romans had always been interested in oracles, and an official collection of Sibylline books was part of Roman state religion. In the short summary of the *Divine Institutes* known as the *Epitome,* Lactantius summarizes his case, claiming "since all these things are certain and true, being foretold by the unanimous annunciation of the prophets, since Trismegistus, Hystaspes and the Sibyls have all foretold the same things, it cannot be doubted that all hope and salvation rests solely in the worship of God."[46] Given this perspective, Lactantius concentrates on nonscriptural sources, especially Vergil and the Sibyl, though he also uses the texts ascribed to the Egyptian sage Hermes (Hermes Trismegistus)[47] and the mysterious *Oracle of Hystaspes,* a text of Persian origin cited by a number of early Christian writers.[48] Although John's Apocalypse and other biblical texts are not directly quoted, Lactantius uses them extensively in implicit fashion.

The North African author accepted the world week understanding of the history's six-thousand-year duration (7.14)—meaning history will last six days, each day a thousand years long—and he adhered to the Hippolytan dating that put Christ's appearance in the middle of the sixth millennium (7.25). Even though he thought that there could be as many as two hundred years before the end, he felt that the apocalyptic clock was already ticking and his readers should accept Christianity to prepare for the horrors to come. The first of these would be the collapse of Rome, an event that the Sibyl had foretold (7.15 and 25). The appearance of ten kings who would divide the Roman Empire would be followed by the coming of "a mighty enemy from the far North," who would destroy three kings in the East, establish dominion over the others, and "afflict the world with unbearable tyranny" (7.16). Lactantius does not call this king Antichrist, but he applies to him so wide a range of the traditions associated with Antichrist it is difficult to think of him as other than a first Antichrist in the manner of Commodian, though not a *Nero redivivus.* His career (see *Divine Institutes* 7.16) is an important prototype for later Christian accounts of one or more evil, Antichrist-like rulers who will precede the Final Opponent.

The standard Christian tradition, based on Apocalypse 11, had predicted two witnesses to preach before the coming of the Final Antichrist. Lactantius, though he uses John's language, speaks of only one "great prophet who will convert humans to him and who will receive power to perform miracles" (7.17).[49] He continues: "When his works are done, another king, born of an evil spirit, will arise from Syria. He will be the subverter and destroyer of the human race." This king is the Final Antichrist who conducts a campaign of four battles against the saints until his final destruction by the returning Lord (7.17–19).[50]

That the double Antichrist was known in other parts of the Latin West is evident from the witness of Martin of Tours (c. 316–397), the famous monastic bishop of Gaul. According to his biographer, Sulpicius Severus, shortly before his death Martin was asked about the end of the world. His reply constitutes a summary of the double Antichrist tradition and belief in Antichrist's conception by the devil himself,[51] perhaps the earliest appearance of the claim, endlessly repeated in succeeding centuries, that Antichrist had already been born.[52] The theme of Antichrist already born but not yet revealed seems to have two roots: first, as a perverted imitation of Christ, who was thought to have spent thirty years of hidden life before his three years of public preaching; and second (at least in some authors), as an explanation of Paul's claim (2 Thess. 2:7) that the mystery of iniquity is already at work.

ANTICHRIST'S PHYSICAL APPEARANCE

The second important theme whose earliest written evidence comes from the third century is that of the Antichrist physiognomies, the physical descriptions of his unusual appearance. These are Eastern rather than Western; indeed, it is curious that they had so little effect on Latin Antichrist beliefs. They form one of the major contributions of the later Christian apocalypses to the development of the Antichrist legend.[53] It is possible that those texts have Jewish roots, but it is also clear that fascination with how physical features reveal character was widespread in the ancient world.[54]

The Syriac *Testament of the Lord* in its present form dates to the fifth century, but its apocalyptic section (chaps. 1–14) appears to be based on a Greek original of the mid–third century. Following an extended description of the signs of the end (chaps. 3–8),[55] chapters 9 to 11 deal with Antichrist. He comes from the East (chap. 10), and he will be difficult to overlook, given the description found in chapter 11:

> And these are the signs of him: his head is as a fiery flame; his right eye shot with blood, his left eye blue-black and he has two pupils. His eyelashes are white; and his lower lip is large; but his right thigh slender; his feet broad; his great toe [or perhaps finger] is bruised and flat. This is the sickle of desolation.[56]

Other Christian apocalypses contain related descriptions. The *Apocalypse of Elijah,* which is really more a series of oracles than an apocalypse, was composed in Greek but survives only in Coptic. It is a Christian work, using Jewish sources, that appears to have been edited in the second half of the third century.[57] A description of the signs preceding Antichrist in chapter 2 is followed in chapter 3 by an account of "Lawless One," detailing the miraculous signs he will perform. The Christ-Antichrist opposition that underlies all belief in Antichrist is well expressed: "He will do the things which the Christ did, except only for raising a corpse—by this you will know that he is the Lawless One: He has no power to give life!" (3:12–13). The description of this hideous human monster follows:

> He is a small *pelec* [word of uncertain meaning], thin-legged, tall, with a tuft of grey hair on his forehead, which is bald, while his eyebrows reach to his ears, and there is a leprous spot on the front of his hands. He will transform himself in the presence of those who see him: at one time he will be a young boy but at another time he will be an old man. He will transform himself in every sign, but the sign of his head he will not be able to change. (3:15–17)

Chapter 4 contains an unusual account of the virgin Tabitha (see Acts 9:36) who is martyred by Antichrist, as well as his struggle with and killing of the two witnesses. The final battles of history are described in the last chapter. Christ sends 64,000 angels to rescue the righteous (5:2–6), but Antichrist pursues them into the desert where he does battle with the angels. After universal conflagration (5:22–24), the Lord judges heaven and earth, and Enoch and Elijah return in "flesh of the spirit" to kill the Lawless One (5:32–35). The *Apocalypse of Elijah* is one of the most complete, but also obscure, accounts of Antichrist in patristic literature.

A third early Christian apocalypse containing a physical description of the Antichrist is the *Apocalypse of the Holy Theologian John*, which pretends to be written by the beloved disciple and author of the Gospel but is a Greek work often dated to the fifth century, although it may well be several centuries earlier.[58] Chapters 6 to 8 give a brief account of Antichrist, emphasizing his bizarre appearance:

> The appearance of his face is gloomy; his hair like the points of arrows; his brows rough; his right eye as the morning star and the left like a lion's. His mouth is a cubit wide, his teeth a span in length, his fingers are like sickles. His footprints are two cubits long, and on his forehead is the writing "The Antichrist."[59]

These accounts indicate widespread interest in Antichrist appearance, if we can judge by other surviving examples.[60] The Antichrist physiognomies currently known to us are found in texts that are often not critically edited and that are difficult to date. Almost every important apocalyptic revealer (Elijah, Ezra, Daniel, John, and even the Sibyl) was eventually credited with providing a physical description of Antichrist, as the chart on pages 72–73 detailing fourteen examples shows.

It is likely that the undercurrent of the Christ-Antichrist opposition was at work in the development of these physiognomies, though the evidence suggests that interest in Antichrist's appearance antedated fascination about that of Christ. Still, it seems that from the third century on curiosity about the physical appearance of both Christ and his nemesis was growing. A legend about a picture of Jesus supposedly sent to King Abgar of Edessa is first found in the Syriac text known as the *Doctrine of Addai* (c. 400), but the traditions on which it is based may be earlier. Actual physical descriptions of Jesus are not found before the sixth century.[61]

Antichrist in the Fourth and Fifth Centuries

Major patristic authors and texts of the fourth and early fifth centuries testify to the continuing development of the Antichrist legend. Only a selection can be discussed here.[62]

EASTERN VIEWS

Cyril (c. 315–386) was the bishop of Jerusalem when it had become a major Christian see because of imperial patronage and its status as a pilgrimage center. His twenty-four *Catechetical Lectures* delivered in the Church of the Holy Sepulchre (c. 350) are among the best witnesses to the instruction given to converts during the period when the Roman world was rapidly becoming Christian. In the last of the lectures devoted to Christology (nn. 10–15) there is a section on Antichrist based on an exegesis of Daniel 7:13–27 (the lection for the day) and the other standard scriptural passages on Antichrist.[63] As in many of the texts already studied, Cyril discusses the signs of the end so that his hearers will "look for Christ" and not "be led astray by that false Antichrist" (15.4). Disunity in the political world and in the church are remote signs of Antichrist; more proximate is the preaching of the gospel to the whole world (see Matt.

24:14), which the bishop sees as almost fulfilled in his day (15.8). The "falling away" of 2 Thessalonians 2:3 is interpreted as heretical departure from the truth, not as the end of the Roman Empire (15.9). Cyril expects a single Antichrist, "a magician highly skilled in guileful and evil art that deals in philtres and enchantments" (15.11). This emphasis on Antichrist as magician may reflect the influence of the legend of Simon Magus on Antichrist traditions, something that will be evident in other accounts from the fourth century on.[64]

As the eleventh king of the fragmented Roman Empire (a position he gains by means of sorcery), Antichrist will attain power over the other kings by both force and fraud and will be accepted as messiah by the Jews (15.12). Satan uses Antichrist as his tool to perform miracles that Cyril insists will all be false (15.14). Perhaps the most interesting aspect of Cyril's summary is found in his analysis of Antichrist and the temple in Lecture 15.15. Because Cyril interprets 2 Thessalonians 2:4 as meaning that Antichrist will rebuild the totally destroyed Jewish temple and enthrone himself there as God,[65] the extant remains of the second temple are a reassuring sign that the Final Enemy is still in the future. The bishop closes with an empassioned plea to his audience:

> So be warned, my friend. I have given you the signs of the Antichrist. Do not merely store them in your memory. Pass them on to everyone without stint. If you have a child after the flesh, teach them to him forthwith. And if you have become a godparent forewarn your godchild, lest he should take the false Christ for the true. For "the mystery of iniquity doth already work." (15.18)

Cyril's account is fairly sober compared to the rich legendary material found in the Pseudo-Hippolytan homily.[66] This text is noteworthy for its insistence that Antichrist is really the devil. Though we have seen this view defended in a number of texts, the Pseudo-Hippolytus underlines it so often, even to the extent of creating a theology of Antichrist as merely appearing to be human,[67] that it is likely the author was consciously reacting against the now preponderant view that Antichrist was not the devil but a human possessed by Satan.[68] The Pseudo-Hippolytus also takes a rather radical view of the miracles the Final Enemy will perform, finding them equal to those performed by Jesus—both in terms of cures and (seeming) good works: "Afterwards he will perform many wonders, by cleansing lepers, raising paralytics, driving out demons, announcing distant events as if they were present, raising the dead, helping widows,

Early Descriptions of Antichrist Physiognomies

TEXT	Height	Hair	Head	Face	Eyes	Pupils	Eye Brows	Eye Lashes	Nose	Mouth
1 Testament of the Lord (Syriac)		fiery flame			R-bloody L-blueblack	2 in left eye		white		
2 Testament of the Lord (Ethiopian)		fiery flame			R-bloody L-dead	2 in left eye		white		
3 Testament of the Lord (Latin)		fiery flame			ANGRY R-bloody L-blueblack	2 in left eye		white		
4 Elijah Apocalypse (Greek)		fiery flame			R-bloody L-radiant	2 in left eye		white		
5 Sibyl (Ethiopian)		little	large		R-bloody L-happy					
6 Sibyl (Arabic)			large		BRILLIANT L-happy					
7 Elijah Apocalypse (Coptic)		tuft of gray	bald				reach to ears			
8 Elijah Apocalypse (Latin)	tall		bald	long						
9 Matthew Apocalypse (Hebrew)	tall and thin	spiky and tuft of white		long	ANGRY				long	
10 Ps.-John Apocalypse (Greek)		points of arrows		gloomy	R-morning star L-like a lion		rough			cubit wide
11 Ezra Apocalypse (Greek)				wild man	R-morning star L-unmoving					cubit wide
12 Ps.-Daniel Apocalypse (Greek)	15 feet	reaches to feet	three crests	long	R-morning star L-like a lion				long	
13 Irish I (Leabher Breac)					1 eye on a gray protuberance		1 under the eye			
14 Irish II (Book of Lismore)	600 x 40 fathoms	black		flat	1 eye on a gray protuberance				3 fiery fumes from nose	reaches to chest

Lips	Teeth	Neck	Arms	Hands	Fingers	Thigh	Legs (Shins)	Feet	Toes	Distinguishing Mark	Group
large					? (see toes)	R-slender		broad	bruised and flat	"Sickle of Desolation"	GROUP I. CHRIST
large				R-torture L-darkness	twisted			broad and twisted		"Sickle of Desolation"	
					large finger broken	R-slender	thin	broad	bruised	"Sickle of Desolation"	
large											
		long			short						GROUP II. SIBYL
	thick	long			short		thin				
				leprous bare spot			thin			Changing of signs	GROUP III. ELIJAH
							thin	broad			
	one missing	leprosy								Changing of signs	
	span long				like sickles			two cubits long		"Antichrist on forehead"	GROUP IV. VARIOUS REVEALERS
	span long				like scythes			two span long		Changing of signs + "Antichrist"	
	iron + diamond jaw	R-iron L-copper	R-4 1/2' long					leave a large track		α τ χ = "Antichrist"	
								flat		Body is one flat surface	GROUP V. IRISH
	no upper teeth						no knees	soles like wheels			

from McGinn, *Portraying the Antichrist*, pp. 26–27

protecting orphans, loving everyone, bringing the contentious to chari-
table accord."[69]

In both cases we can say that the original Hippolytan insistence on a
correspondence in deeds between the messiah and the antimessiah has
been taken to an extreme.

Much of the rest of the Pseudo-Hippolytus reflects common themes,
but several points are worth noting. Although the emphasis is on the single Final Enemy, *pseudochristi* are many, both in the past (Simon Magus is
explicitly mentioned) and in the time to come before the end. In contrast
to Cyril, the Antichrist is presented much more as "tyrant king" (*tyrannos
basileus*) than as a false prophet and magician.[70] The Pseudo-Hippolytus
seems to be the earliest witness (if my dating is correct) to an important element in the developing legend—Antichrist's ability, with demonic aid, to
ascend into the air.[71]

WESTERN VOICES

If Cyril and the Pseudo-Hippolytus may be taken as representative
of a range of Eastern Christian views of Antichrist in the fourth and fifth
centuries, Tyconius, Jerome, and Augustine are both traditionalists and
innovators with respect to Western attitudes. All three authors believed in
the historicity of the final Antichrist, and they represent, in varying de-
grees, a reaction against legendary accretions to his story as well as against
some aspects of traditional apocalyptic eschatology. The writings of Tyconius and Augustine are also important for ways in which they internalize
the meaning of Antichrist.

Jerome (c. 331–420) was arguably the most learned of the major
Latin Fathers, if not the most original.[72] Jerome's views about the final
things are moderate. He identifies the restraining force of 2 Thessalonians
2:6 with the Roman Empire, and he accepts "the traditional interpretation
of all the commentators of the Christian Church" that Rome will be par-
titioned by ten kings who will be overcome by the eleventh king, "the little horn" that signifies Antichrist. He rejects the view that Antichrist is
a demon or the devil himself, "but he is the one man in whom Satan will
totally dwell in a corporeal way."[73] He also prefers the view that the
2 Thessalonians reference to Antichrist enthroned in the temple is to be
understood as the church and not as a rebuilt temple in Jerusalem.[74]

Jerome's understanding of Antichrist is explicitly anti-Jewish. Asked
why God will permit such power and miracles to Antichrist, he responds
that God has allowed this so that the Jews who refused to accept Christ,

the Truth, will now be convicted by their acceptance of the Lie. Antichrist will be born from Jewish stock and of a virgin, in parody of Christ.[75] In recounting the details of his career, Jerome emphasizes a theme that was to have a large future: Antichrist's path to universal power is paved by gold as much as by terror.[76]

Jerome is also the source, for later Western accounts at least, of two important themes concerning the end of the Final Enemy. Commenting on Daniel 11:45 ("He will fix his tent Apedno between the seas, upon a glorious and holy mountain," in the Latin Vulgate translation), he proposes another important parallel between the Truth and the Lie. Since Christ ascended to heaven from the Mount of Olives, the mountain on which Antichrist will fix his tent and throne (Apedno) will also be the Mount of Olives. Jerome claims that this is inherited teaching—"They [Christian teachers] assert that Antichrist will perish in the same place where Christ ascended to heaven"—but his is the earliest written witness to this theme.[77] (As a resident in Bethlehem, the famous exegete may be using a tradition of the local Christian community.) Finally, following Hippolytus, Jerome also notes the discrepancy in Daniel 12 between the 1290 and 1335 days assigned to the Antichrist. He concludes that there must be a surplus of forty-five days after the death of Antichrist, which in his *Commentary on Matthew* he described as "a brief following peace which guarantees total repose to test the faith of believers."[78]

Jerome was a resolute opponent of any form of millenarianism throughout his life. He edited Victorinus's *Commentary on the Apocalypse* (c. 300 C.E.) to remove all hints of the earthly thousand-year kingdom, and he also popularized the new dating of the ages of the world worked out by the church historian Eusebius (c. 260–c. 340), which put Christ's first coming in 5228 *anno mundi* and therefore left room for almost four more centuries of history. Still, the dire events of the early years of the fifth century left Jerome wondering if the Antichrist was not just around the corner (see Letter 123.15–17).

Two of Jerome's contemporaries from North Africa not only rejected millenarianism but also threw cold water on any speculation about the imminence of the end. Tyconius and Augustine are among the most important figures in the history of Western apocalypticism, and it is necessary to interpret their work on Antichrist within the context of their total eschatology. The reaction of these two thinkers against apocalyptic eschatology in favor of a more immanent and agnostic view of the end is striking because they came from what has been called the Bible belt of Western

Christianity, in which apocalyptic views of the more extreme kind had always played a large role.[79]

Tyconius (died at about 390) was a member of the heretical Donatist sect, but he took an independent position and was condemned by his own group for his suspect views. His exegetical manual, *The Book of Rules,* which influenced Augustine, is the best source for reconstructing his thought.[80] Tyconius's most important work, however, was his lost *Commentary on the Apocalypse,* which Augustine knew and used and which was so much mined by Christian exegetes for the next few centuries that it is possible to recover many elements of his interpretation.[81] Although a suspect figure, Tyconius was of great importance in establishing an alternative nonapocalyptic eschatology in Western Christianity. The African did not deny the reality of the last events, but he eschewed any attempts to determine their imminence, and he reinterpreted apocalyptic symbols in terms of the present life of the church and the inner moral experience of souls. In his thought, present antichrists became more important than the coming Antichrist. Tyconius emphasized 1 John's message that Antichrist is anyone whose actions, especially hatred of another, show that he or she does not believe that Christ has come in the flesh.[82] This is the most complete immanent reading of Antichrist since Origen.

Tyconius maintained that there were two parts of the church, a northern part containing the devil and his body, and a southern one containing the whole Christ, the eternal sun. Both parts are found throughout the entire world, though it is the good southern part that is the "Restraining Force" of 2 Thessalonians, keeping the mystery of lawlessness in check until the end.[83] Hence, the "essential Antichrist" is the accumulating body of those within the church itself who deny Christ, although he also believed in a coming final Antichrist who would bring this mass of evil to its completion.[84]

Augustine of Hippo, the dominant figure in Western theology for the next millennium or more, was also hostile to apocalyptic eschatology. But Augustine, like Origen, was a man of the church and its tradition. While he opposed all attempts at reading history's course and determining the endtime,[85] and was cool to legendary accretions to the story of Antichrist, the bishop was still a major channel for the transmission of sober traditions concerning the Final Enemy to the Latin West. Augustine discussed Antichrist both in direct exegetical contexts and in theological summaries (especially in Letter 199 and the *City of God* 18 and 20). His teaching contains nothing that is new, but his emphasis on the significance of present and immanent rather than final opposition is of importance in later Antichrist views.

The heart of Augustine's teaching on Antichrist is to be found in his *Homilies on 1 John.*[86] Here the bishop affirms that the Antichrists spoken of in 1 John 2:18–27 can be understood as heretics and schismatics who have departed from the church, but he also insists that "everyone must question his own conscience whether he be such." Since Antichrist means "contrary to Christ," it is clear that many Antichrists leave the church, but also many remain within it. The denial of Christ implied in the term is not a verbal denial (all Catholics and Donatists admit Christ is God), but a denial by deeds. "There you have the Antichrist—everyone that denies Christ by his works" (Hom. 3.8). As in Origen and in Tyconius, the real Antichrist is any one of us!

By the time of Augustine's death in 430, only a lifetime remained before the last possible date for the coming of Antichrist, if one accepted the Hippolytan calculation. But to many, like Jerome a few years earlier, it may not have seemed that the world was going to last even that long. The rapid decline of the Western Empire and the barbarian pressure felt in both East and West made the end seem nearer than ever. Perhaps Antichrist was already born, maybe even active in the person of a heretic or babarian invader. These last decades before 500 saw no new contributions to the developing legend (at least in written sources that survive to us), but there is evidence, especially from the West,[87] of some who saw the troubles of the time as the coming of the Final Enemy.

Quodvultdeus, a pupil of Augustine, in his *Book of the Promises and Predictions* (c. 450) returns to real apocalyptic eschatology by seeing in his own difficult times, filled with heresy and invasion, the foreshadowing, perhaps even the beginning, of the dread halftime (three and a half years) of the end.[88] In the mid–fifth century, one editor of Victorinus's *Commentary on the Apocalypse* introduced a lengthy passage into the commentary on Apocalypse 13 and 17 regarding the number of the Beast, interpreting it as "Gensericos," that is, Gaiseric, the Arian Vandal king who wasted the Mediterranean world and sacked Rome in 455.[89] Finally, a late sixth-century chronological work, the *Paschal List of Campania* (*Paschale Campanum*), which adheres to Hippolytus's dating of the end, records that both in 493 and 496 c.e. some "arrogant fools" (*ignari praesumptores*) and "crazies" (*deliri*) announced the coming of Antichrist.[90] Obviously, not all had been convinced by Tyconius, Augustine, and others who had tried to defuse expectation of the imminent arrival of the final terror.

The Meaning of Patristic Antichrist Beliefs

Throughout the centuries of the development of Christianity down to 500 C.E., the inverse image of Christ's life and deeds, both past and future, was the driving force behind the organization of disparate texts and ancient mythic traditions about apocalyptic opponents of goodness into an organic whole.[91] Whatever Christ had done during his earthly life or whatever he was expected to do upon his return must also be performed, or at least pretended to, by his opponent, the Antichrist.

Early Christology insisted that the whole Christ was not just the God-man Jesus but also his corporate body—all who had come to participate in him through baptism. Antichrist too came to be thought of as possessing a corporate body—all those wicked people whose presence and power indicate that ultimate human evil is already at work and soon will be fully manifest in that human who will recapitulate every form of sin. The Antichrist legend reveals the Christian understanding of evil as both individual and collective—as realized both in individual sinful decisions and in the power of groups and tendencies to blind individuals to the good.

Both the individual and the collective aspects of Antichrist were mostly seen as external, that is, Antichrist was identified with a final non-Christian World Conquerer who would be a mixture of persecuting tyrant and deceiver (false prophet and magician), while antichrists were conceived of as his predecessors and assistants—Roman officials, and later Jews as well. These external collective identifications were harmful enough when Christianity was a minority, and often a persecuted, religion. They were to prove far more dangerous when it became the religion of the state.

But Antichrist rhetoric was also used internally, to identify certain Christians as apocalyptic enemies because of their heretical beliefs. These uses too were to have an important, and often a destructive, future. But we must not forget that some early Christians, as we have seen with Origen, Tyconius, and Augustine, emphasized a partly interiorized conception of the individual and collective dimensions of the Antichrist legend. To these authors, Antichrist was primarily the power of "the Lie," the deception practiced by all those (and in each of us, as Augustine insisted) who assert that Christ is Lord but who demonstrate the *opposite* by action. These Christian fathers still offer food for thought to those at the end of the twentieth century who have lost belief in any literal Final Opponent.

CHAPTER FOUR

ANTICHRIST
ESTABLISHED

THE FINAL ENEMY IN
THE EARLY MIDDLE AGES
(500–1100)

B y the year 500 c.e. Christianity had become the faith of the ancient Roman world. Despite the new religion's rise to power, it had not given up its apocalyptic hopes. The importance of the Antichrist legend in the centuries that saw the formation of medieval European civilization is undeniable, though not always easy to evaluate.[1] This is due to problems of documentation and also to the variety of ways in which the Last Enemy was understood. The scriptural basis for the Antichrist legend, as we have seen, allowed for both collective interpretations, which saw "false prophets" and "antichrists" as present dangers, often associated with heretics or Jews, as well as belief in a future single opponent of Christ who would combine the most savage persecution with the most insidious deceit.[2] Furthermore, in the West at least, the antiapocalyptic theology of history advanced by Augustine and Tyconius emphasized a moral and internal reading of Antichrist symbolism at the same time that it eschewed any attempt to investigate present events in order to determine the signs of the end.

There can be no question that this internal and moralizing interpretation of Antichrist exercised a powerful role in the West through the twelfth century and beyond.[3] Still, this view never canceled out belief that the last times would see the appearance of a real individual who would be the summation of all evil, nor did the immense influence of Augustine result in the eclipse of truly apocalyptic attitudes toward history on the part of those who continued to live in expectation of the Second Coming.[4] In the Christian East, Augustinian antiapocalypticism had little if any effect, and important new apocalyptic traditions originated there and rapidly spread to the West.[5] The continued development by which the figure of Antichrist gathered to himself new constellations of legendary materials shows how powerful the apocalyptic mentality remained in the centuries between 500 and 1100 C.E. The presence of Antichrist-like figures in both Judaism and Islam in these same centuries further testifies to the power of the image of ultimate human evil as a recapitulating necessity in apocalyptically oriented religions.

In this chapter I will investigate how the patristic traditions surveyed in the previous chapter were conveyed to medieval Christians of both the East and West, as well as how these traditions were enriched by legendary accretions, especially those concerning the Last World Emperor, to form a new and richer scenario of Antichrist's career. Finally, an appendix will look at Jewish and Islamic "antichrists"—the false messiah often called Armillus and the Dajjāl of Islamic lore.

Gregory the Great and the Antichrist Within

Two Christian biblical commentators, Primasius of Hadrumetum in North Africa and Cassiodorus in Italy, show that interest in the traditional teaching on Antichrist remained indeed alive in the sixth century C.E.[6] However, Gregory the Great, bishop of Rome from 590 to 604, was the most significant contributor to the Antichrist legend in this time of the twilight of the ancient world.[7]

Gregory lived through some of the most difficult years of the collapse of the Western Empire, especially after 568 when Italy was invaded and systematically pillaged by the Lombards, whom the Roman historian Velleius Paterculus had described as "a people fiercer than even German ferocity." These dire events led Gregory to the conviction that the end of the world was near. In his *Dialogues* (c. 590) he said, "I don't know what is happening in other parts of the world, but in this country where we live the world no longer announces its end but demonstrates it."[8] But Gregory never proclaimed a date for the end, and despite his conviction about imminent ruin, he expended great efforts through his writing, administration, diplomacy, and missionary activity to form the new Christian society of the West. The pope's combination of a pessimistic sense of impending doom with efforts to ensure a more complete triumph of the gospel was typical of an important strand in medieval apocalypticism.[9]

Gregory used Antichrist primarily as a tool for reform. Though he believed in a real Final Enemy to come, he provided only sparse information about the details of his career, being far more interested in the moral meaning of Antichrist, which is disclosed through a biblical exegesis that seeks moral messages in the many images and types found in holy writ. Following Augustine's line but developing it in greater detail, Gregory wished each Christian to become attentive to the Antichrist within, that is, the elements in his or her own life, especially pride and hypocrisy[10] that constitute us as precursors or members of Antichrist's body. It is not surprising, then, that Gregory's most complete teaching on Antichrist is found in his massive *summa* of Christian morality and spirituality, the *Moral Interpretations on Job* (*Moralia in Job*) composed between 580 and 595. Job in his suffering is a type of both Christ and the church, especially in the last days.

Antichrist is "the head of all hypocrites . . . who feign holiness to lead to sinfulness,"[11] while Job, the type of Christ, signifies the patient and humble suffering that leads us within to God.[12] In a complex figural interpretation, the twin monsters of Behemoth and Leviathan described in Job 40 to 41 stand for both the Devil and his chosen human vessel or "lair" of the endtime, Antichrist. Behemoth, for instance, is used primarily as a type of the devil, but the mention of his tail (Job 40:11) is taken as indicating Antichrist (*Moralia* 32.15.22–18.32). Subsequent exegesis of the Behemoth figure interprets it as both the devil and Antichrist, and a similar reading is applied to Leviathan in *Moralia* Books 33 and 34, where Leviathan's "sneeze" (Job 41:9) signifies Antichrist as the devil's final "explosion."[13] Gregory was able to make these easy transitions in part because he adhered to the outmoded tradition that identified Antichrist as the devil incarnate: "The [devil] himself in the last times will be called Antichrist when he has entered into that vessel of destruction."[14]

Gregory's exegetical ingenuity may amaze—and perhaps also amuse—the modern reader. But the triumph of the moral reading of the Bible in the pope paved the way for much later discussion of the types of Antichrist from the Old Testament, that is, either persons (for example, Doeg the Idumaean of Ps. 51, Abimelech of Judg. 8–9) or animal figures (like Behemoth and Leviathan) that contributed to the medieval view of the Final Enemy. Most of these treatments were more concerned with drawing out the moral evil of the Antichrist than in giving detailed accounts of his career.[15]

In his discussion of Antichrist's deeds, Gregory does include some traditional materials, laying special emphasis on the trials the faithful will undergo when confronted with a figure who is both a violent persecutor and an astounding miracle worker.[16] He also notes that Antichrist's imminence can be known from the decline in the church of charisms, such as prophecy, cures, and miracles—something that will make his prodigies appear all the more convincing.[17] (The pope's *Dialogues,* however, stress the miracles performed by holy men of his own time and thus may strengthen the argument that Gregory did not see the final Antichrist as already alive.)

Gregory appears to have been responsible for some of the subsequent confusion regarding who will destroy Antichrist. Although 2 Thessalonians 2:8 clearly says that Christ himself will slay Antichrist by the breath of his mouth, and Gregory repeats this teaching,[18] he also mentions the tradition that Antichrist will be killed by Michael, the angelic opponent of Satan, a teaching based on Apocalypse 12 and 20:12.[19] Nevertheless, the pope's real emphasis, as noted above, is not on this final Antichrist and his demise but on the Tyconian understanding of the accumulating body of evildoers through the whole course of history. Members of Antichrist have always existed and are always interconnected, whether they know it or not. They are, as he put it in interpreting Job 40:12, Antichrist's testicles: "How many have not seen Antichrist and yet are his testicles because they corrupt the hearts of the innocent by the example of their action?"[20]

The purpose of this emphasis on the presence of Antichrist throughout history, however, is not so much to scapegoat (though Gregory notes the role of the Jews both in rejecting Christ and in the future acceptance of his opponent) as it is to call believers to self-examination. "It is necessary that each of us return to his heart's secret and become very fearful of the harm from his action, lest when merits are demanded, he falls among the number of such people [the members of Antichrist] through the strict justice of God's judgments."[21] The central point of Gregory's extended and influential consideration of Antichrist is perhaps best expressed in the phrase *apud iniquos namque quotidie res Antichristi agitur,* "Antichrist's work is done daily among the wicked." So any rebuking of evil, such as Gregory's own preaching and writing, is nothing less than an attack on the Final Enemy.[22]

Eastern and Western Variations on the Inherited Legend

The internal moral view of Antichrist advanced by Augustine and expanded by Gregory was well represented among the exegetes of the early medieval West, especially the commentators on the Apocalypse and 2 Thessalonians.[23] Most of these interpreters did not express any strong sense of the imminence of the end, but they did provide their readers with basic information about the deeds of the Final Enemy. Their use of Antichrist language tended primarily to emphasize the importance of the moral effort that Christians should make to avoid becoming a part of Antichrist's body.[24] Some authors, however, were closer to real apocalypticism in expressing a sense that Antichrist is near, often including the more usual moralizing concerns.[25] Only a few writers used Antichrist in an overtly historicizing way as a means of identifying a specific group as a part of his entourage or a particular person as a type or predecessor of Antichrist.

One of the most interesting attempts to portray an individual as Antichrist occured in the Byzantine realm. Procopius, the court historian of the emperor Justinian (527–565 C.E.), wrote official accounts of the emperor's wars and triumphs as well as an infamous *Secret History* composed about 550. Besides its well-known racy stories of the sexual escapades of the empress Theodora, the *Secret History* vilifies Justinian in every way possible. After comparing him with the persecutor Domitian (known as a type of Antichrist) in chapter 8, an extended passage in chapter 12 paints the emperor as a "chief of the devils," born of the union of a human mother and a demon.[26] Although Procopius does not use the term *Antichrist,* he is certainly applying elements from the Antichrist legend to Justinian. Did he actually think that the wily emperor was Antichrist, or was he merely using every possible rhetorical device to denigrate someone whom he had come to loathe? It is not easy to say, but since Procopius's writings elsewhere do not display any significant attention to apocalyptic themes, we can conclude that his use was primarily rhetorical. It is important to note, however, that this appears to be the earliest identification of a *Christian* ruler with the Final Enemy.[27] We should not be too surprised at this development. Christian rulers could act—or be seen—as tyrants, and the internalizing aspects of the Antichrist legend allowed for the possibility that the Final Tyrant might well not be a non-Christian persecutor but an evil and deceiving member of the Christian communion. Justinian was to have many successors in this role.

Other identifications of historical individuals or events with Antichrist or his proximate predecessors occur in some early medieval texts. Gregory of Tours in his *History of the Franks,* written late in the sixth century, tells the tale of a heretic of Bourges who could prophesy the future and claimed he was Christ, but whose destruction Gregory hailed as the fall of "an Antichrist."[28] A notice found in the text known as the *Passion of Leodegar* records that after the death of the Merovingian king Childeric in 675, turmoil was so great "that it was openly believed that Antichrist's coming was near."[29] Seventh-century Gaul, to be sure, was a place of great political chaos, and we should scarcely be surprised that these conditions nurtured apocalyptic fears. But there is no simple and constant relation between societal chaos and terror concerning the approaching end. Thus, although a few other texts from the seventh through the ninth centuries use similar language for the end, it is often difficult to judge whether these expressions are mere rhetorical flourishes or whether they reflect popular expectation of Antichrist and the end of time.[30]

The Old High German poem called "Muspilli" (c. 850 c.e.) also reveals a strong sense of the imminence of the end. Written in a Bavarian dialect, the poem tells of the epic conflict between Antichrist and Elijah, the champions of Satan and God. The tradition of Elijah alone as the opponent of Antichrist is an archaic one,[31] and portraying the opposition between the witnesses and Antichrist as an armed struggle is not unknown.[32] The "Muspilli" may demonstrate contact with some ancient Christian sources, but its picture of how Elijah's blood will ignite world conflagration strikes a decidedly Germanic note:

> But many men of God believe that Elijah will be wounded in the battle,
> so that his blood will drip down to earth;
> then the mountains will catch fire, no tree at all will be left standing
> on earth, the waters will dry up,
> the marshland will swallow itself up, the sky will be aflame with fire,
> the moon will fall, and the earth will burn . . .
> Then can no relative help another in the face of the "Muspilli."[33]

The best evidence for expectations of the imminence of the end in the eighth and ninth centuries comes from Spain. A classic case concerns Beatus of Liébana, a Spanish monk of the late eighth century, known for his lengthy *Commentary on the Apocalypse.*[34] Although Beatus's commentary generally reflects the Tyconian-Augustinian moralized reading of the last book of the Bible, in commenting on Apocalypse 7:4 he makes the remarkable statement that there are only fourteen years left to complete the sixth millennium, and therefore presumably only fourteen years also until Antichrist's coming.[35] Incidents in Beatus's own life seem to indicate that he did believe that the Final Enemy would appear in his own lifetime.[36] For instance, he attacked Elipandus, bishop of Toledo, as an Antichrist for teaching Adoptianism, that is, that Christ was only a man who had been adopted to the divine sphere.[37] The same Elipandus wrote to the bishops of the Frankish realms vilifying Beatus for disturbing the faithful by preaching the imminence of the end. Though this may be the canard of an enemy, the text deserves quotation:

> Beatus prophesied the end of the world to Hordonius of Liébana in the presence of the people during the Easter vigil so that they became terrified and crazed. They took no food that night, and are said to have fasted until the ninth hour on Sunday. Then Hordonius, when he felt afflicted with hunger, is said to have addressed the people, "Let's eat and drink, so that if we die at least we'll be fed."[38]

Beatus's *Commentary* is famous in the history of Western apocalypticism for the splendid illuminations that grace some twenty-six of the surviving copies.[39] These include not only portrayals of the monstrous images of Antichrist, such as the first Beast of Apocalypse 13, but also pictures of a human Antichrist.

Spain also provides other evidence of the application of Antichrist language to current events in the early ninth century, especially as directed against the Muslim opponents of Christianity. Christians of the early Middle Ages had great difficulty understanding Islam, the new religious force that burst upon the ancient Mediterranean world in the seventh century. When first confronted by this militant faith, which by 638 C.E. had already captured the holy (and apocalyptic) city of Jerusalem, Christians appear to have thought of the Arab invaders as just another barbarian force, like the Germans or Huns.[40] As the distinctive religious message of the invaders became clear, Christians began to see it not as a new religion (which was unthinkable from the Christian point of view), but as the last and worst of all heresies. Because heretics had long been associated with antichrists and Antichrist, it was an easy move to interpret the rise of Islam as a sign of Antichrist's coming and to see its founder, Muhammad, as a type of the Final Enemy. Abstracting for the moment from Eastern witnesses (to be taken up below), it was in Spain, which since 712 had been largely under Muslim domination, that this theme not surprisingly had its greatest development.[41]

The opposition between Beatus and Elipandus may have had something to do with Islamic-Christian tensions, since Beatus lived in Asturias in the northwest, the only unconquered part of the peninsula, while Elipandus was the primate in the Muslim-dominated southern area. In the mid–ninth century religious polemic in Spain became stronger and took on a decidedly apocalyptic flavor. In Córdoba in the 850s some fifty or more Christians were put to death after deliberately provoking the Muslim authorities by insulting their religion. A controversy erupted over the legitimacy of this form of provocation, with the monks Eulogius and Paulus Alvarus coming forth as defenders of the martyrs. According to Eulogius, the martyr movement began when a Christian named Perfectus denounced Muhammad as one of the "false Christs" prophesied in Matthew 24:16.[42] Eulogius, who was himself imprisoned and eventually martyred, praised those who marched out "against the angel of Satan and forerunner of Antichrist," that is, "Muhammed, the heresiarch."[43] There is no evidence, however, that Eulogius was an apocalyptic propagandist who believed that the end was near.

Paulus Alvarus went further. In his most important work, the *Illuminated Instructions,* Alvarus provided a detailed account of the martyrs and presented the connection between Islam and Antichrist within the framework of a scenario of the last events.[44] His sense of the opposition between the forces of Christ and his martyrs on the one hand and Antichrist and his Muslim members on the other has a vibrantly apocalyptic ring to it. Following Jerome on Daniel and Gregory the Great on Job, he identifies Muhammad with both the eleventh horn of the fourth beast (Dan. 7:8) and the monsters Behemoth and Leviathan—all types of Antichrist.[45] Muhammad is thus the last and worst in a long line of forerunners of Antichrist, beginning with Antiochus IV, and continuing through Nero, Domitian, and others.[46] How much time remains until the end? Alvarus does not say explicitly, but he expects Muslim domination to last only sixteen more years.[47] Alvarus also highlights another apocalyptic theme by identifying the Muslim conquest of Greeks, Franks, and Goths with the uprooting of the three horns (representing kings) by the eleventh horn of the beast (see Dan. 7:24).[48] Thus, this ninth-century Spaniard believed that the Christian martyrs of his time were experiencing the persecution of Antichrist, the Final Enemy conceived of both individually (as Muhammad) and collectively (as the Muslim rulers of his day).

One final representative of a vivid sense of the imminence of Antichrist in the time before 1000 c.e. should be noted: Odo of Cluny (879–942). He was a monastic reformer who, like Gregory the Great, combined apocalyptic pessimism with far-flung ecclesiastical activity (Odo also edited a precis of Gregory's *Moralia*).[49] In the *Life of St. Gerald of Aurillac,* which portrays a feudal lord as a monk in knight's armor, Odo twice mentions the evils of his age as signifying that the time of Antichrist is at hand.[50] This might be seen as mere rhetoric, but Odo's sense of the imminence of the end is found also in his major works, the pessimistic *Occupation,* a poem in seven books on the history of sin and grace, as well as in the three books of his *Collations,* a jeremiad on the evils of the day.[51] The influential Odo indicates that there were probably others who saw the turmoil of the tenth century—"the century of iron," as it has been called—as proof of the imminence of Antichrist, whom Odo, following Gregory, calls *"Vehemoth, rex malorum* [Behemoth, King of the Wicked]."

Antichrist and the Last World Emperor

Important as these aspects of the inherited legend of Antichrist are, what is most revealing about the power of Antichrist in the early Middle Ages is the way in which new materials, both historical and mythical, were adopted and transformed in the legends. This process of creation and development was centered in the Christian East but quite soon also entered the West through translation. From the Western perspective, the fruits of the mingling are most evident in the mid–tenth century, especially in the widely read *Letter on the Origin and Time of the Antichrist* by the monk Adso.

It is often easy to forget that it was the Eastern Roman Empire, the world of Byzantium, that was the real center of power, literacy, and culture in this period. Other parts of the Christian East, especially Syria, played an important role in apocalyptic speculation, though these materials reached the West through Byzantine mediation. Eastern Christianity was the creative source of new apocalyptic speculation for at least three reasons. First, as has already been pointed out, Eastern theologians did not experience the reaction against apocalyptic eschatology present in the

Latin West through the influence of Augustine. Second, Eastern Christians had a more powerful sense of the identity of their still-surviving Rome as the "Restraining Force" of 2 Thessalonians 2:6, an interpretation that, as we have seen, was standard from the early third century at least. Rome—that is, Byzantium—was the only power holding back the onslaught of Antichrist, and hence during this period "imperial eschatology" was a more potent source in the East than in the West for speculation about history's coming end.[52] A third element was the irruption of Islam, a new element first confronted in the East, and one that cried out for an apocalyptic interpretation.

The conversion of the Roman Empire to Christianity in the fourth century C.E. opened up new possibilities for Christian apocalypticism and therefore also for the Antichrist legend. Instead of being the seven-headed Beast of Apocalypse 13 and 17, or even the neutral and ambiguous "Restraining Force" of 2 Thessalonians, the empire could now be seen as a positive element in God's providential plan. Such was the case in the imperializing theology of history created by Eusebius, Constantine's court theologian. One of the characteristics of apocalyptic eschatology is its drive to find meaning in current events by seeing them in light of the scenario of the end.[53] Such *a posteriori,* or after-the-fact, uses of apocalypticism are often reactions to major historical changes (like the conversion of the Empire or the rise of Islam) that do not fit into the received view of providential history. By making a place for such events in the story of the end, the final point that gives all history meaning, apocalyptic eschatology incorporates the unexpected into the divinely foreordained and gives it permanent significance.

The legend of the Last World Emperor is the most important of such *a posteriori* developments in apocalyptic eschatology attendant upon the conversion of Rome to Christianity.[54] The Last Emperor is the symbolic summation of the new positive role for Rome in the endtime. The mythic imagination at work in apocalypticism has always tended strongly toward personification, that is, toward portraying crucial themes and values through archetypal figures rather than abstractions. Indeed, we can find in the rise of the Last Emperor another manifestation of the power of the Adamic myth studied earlier, for the Last Emperor is a symbolic replication of Christ, though his power extends only to overcoming Antichrist's most potent predecessors, not the Final Enemy himself. He usually appears as a warlike ruler who will defeat all Rome's (and now God's) enemies, vindicate the goodness of the just in a messianic time of plenty, and achieve supreme imitation of Christ by handing over world dominion to God, as Christ will do at the end of time, according to Paul in 1 Corinthians 15:24. This act is conceived of as opening the way for the manifestation of Antichrist, and hence there is an important connection between the two apocalyptic figures.

The legend of the Last World Emperor, like that of Antichrist, was not created overnight. The earliest signs of the new apocalyptic focus on the positive role played by the Roman Empire and its coming emperors in the endtime appear in the text known as the *Tiburtine Sibyl*. The history of this Sibylline work is complex and disputed. It is best known in its eleventh-century Latin versions,[55] but the origins go as far back as the fourth century.[56] Paul J. Alexander edited a Greek version of the text, which he called the "Oracle of Baalbek," and dated it shortly after 500 c.e.[57] Alexander's reconstruction of the history of this text is plausible, if still hypothetical.[58]

There does not appear to have been a Last World Emperor in the original Greek version of around 380 c.e., although the surviving Baalbek version displays an interest in contemporary rulers and their relation to the endtime, as well as in Antichrist's career. This combination of concerns provides evidence for a new stage in the history of Christian apocalypticism, one in which imperial apocalyptic eschatology takes on an increasingly powerful role.

The later Western versions (which seem to depend on a lost Latin translation of c. 400) contain a full-blown, and rather distinctive, version of the Last Emperor legend. Did the lost Latin original have a recognizable Last Emperor, that is, a messianic final ruler who prepares the way for Antichrist? There is no way to be sure of this. The earliest securely dated version of the Last Emperor legend occurs in the late seventh-century Pseudo-Methodius (which will be discussed shortly), but this need not preclude earlier manifestations. Those who claim that the Last Emperor first appeared in the Pseudo-Methodius have both textual and contextual arguments on their side.[59] However, others who think that the earliest Latin version of the *Tiburtine Sibyl* may have already contained such a figure can point to some significant differences between the Last Emperor as found in the Sibyl and that in the Pseudo-Methodius, and such differences argue for a separate, if not an anterior, tradition.[60]

An increasingly positive role for the Christian Roman Empire is also evident in two other Eastern texts that contributed much to Antichrist traditions both East and West. These are the *Sermon on the End of the World,* ascribed to Ephrem the Syrian (306–373) but actually a work dating to the late sixth or early seventh century,[61] and the *Revelations,* attributed to the early fourth-century martyr bishop Methodius but really another work of Syriac origin. The Pseudo-Methodius, as it is customarily known, is arguably the most important Christian apocalyptic text after the Apocalypse of John in terms of its wide diffusion and subsequent influence.[62]

The Pseudo-Ephrem *Sermon* insists that present troubles, especially the wars between Greeks and Persians, announce that the end is near. Only one sign of those predicted in the Gospel remains to be fulfilled—the end of the Roman Empire. Although there is no mention of a Last Emperor, in referring to the coming end of Rome the sermon cites 1 Corinthians 15:24,[63] the same text that was later to be used for the Last Emperor's handing over of his realm:

> And when the days of the times of those races have been completed, after they shall have corrupted the earth, the kingdom of the Romans will also rest and the empire of the Christians "will be taken from the midst and handed to God and the Father." Then will come the consummation, when the kingdom of the Romans will begin to be consumed and "every principality and power" will have ended.[64]

The major concern of the Pseudo-Ephrem, however, is with Antichrist, as we shall see presently.

The Pseudo-Methodius, which was probably written about 691 C.E.,[65] is of central importance both because it is the first text to place the rise of Islam within an apocalyptic perspective and also for its full-blown account of both the Last Emperor and Antichrist.[66] According to the Syriac preface (not contained in the Greek and Latin versions), the revelation was made to Methodius by an angel on the "mountain of Senagar," that is, Mount Singara, in present-day northwest Iraq. The work begins with Adam and Eve's expulsion from Paradise and is structured along the lines of the seven-thousand-year duration of world history.[67] In this account special attention is given to the figure of Alexander the Great and his descendants.

The legend of Alexander the Great stretches back centuries in the historical memory of the Mediterranean world and Asia. Our interest in it here is concerned only with its apocalyptic dimensions, which center around the legend that the great conqueror constructed a wall or gate (originally somewhere in the Caucasus) to exclude the wild tribes he encountered there from the civilized world until their release at the end of time. The story is first found in the Jewish historian Josephus in the first century C.E. Josephus identifies these tribes with the Scythians who are also Magog (Ezek. 38:1), the traditional invaders of the last days.[68] This tale was present in at least some of the versions of the Greek Alexander Romance known as the Pseudo-Callisthenes (third century), which was the primary source for the multitude of later accounts. The legend of Alexander's Gate and the enclosed nations, which medievalist Andrew R. Anderson has aptly described as "the story of the frontier in sublimated mythologized form,"[69] took on a more apocalyptic flavor in the fifth and sixth centuries as the enclosed nations of Gog and Magog came to be identified with the invading Huns seen as a sign of the end.[70] Alexander himself was transformed from a pagan king into a worshiper and agent of the true God, and, in the Pseudo-Methodius, to the ancestor of the Roman (that is, Byzantine) emperor and prototype of the Last World Emperor.[71] This cross-fertilization of legends took place in the Syriac world, where the story of Alexander seems to have been particularly popular.[72]

In turning to the events of the last or seventh millennium, the Pseudo-Methodius describes the destruction of the kingdom of the Persians and the irruption of the sons of Ismael (that is, the Arabs) from the desert of Jethrib. The destruction wrought by the latter, recounted in bloody detail, is blamed on the sins of the Christians, especially on their homosexual practices.[73] Methodius is especially concerned about the possibility of Christian apostasy in a time of persecution, doubtless a reflection of the writer's own historical situation.[74] The transition from history disguised as prophecy to true prophecy occurs with the introduction of the Last Emperor: "Then suddenly there will be awakened perdition and calamity as those of a woman in travail, and a king of the Greeks will go forth against them [that is, the Ismaelites] in great wrath, and he will be roused against them like a man who shakes off his wine (Ps. 77:65), and who plots against them as if they were dead men."[75]

He and his sons will make war on the Ismaelites and utterly defeat them, inflicting on them a yoke a hundred times harder than what they had put upon the Christians.

During the ensuing peace, "the Gates of the North [Alexander's Gate] will be opened and those hosts of nations will come forth who were imprisoned there, and the earth will shake before them."[76] Methodius's description of these unclean nations of Gog and Magog is not unlike that found in Pseudo-Ephrem. According to Methodius, they will be destroyed on the plain of Joppa by "one of the captains of the hosts of the angels."[77]

After that, the king of the Greeks will settle in Jerusalem for ten and a half years until he hands over his kingship to God on Golgotha and gives up "his soul to his Creator" as the true Cross is raised to heaven.[78] The Son of Perdition will then be revealed.

Although the Last Emperor is not found in the Bible, the Pseudo-Methodius is most anxious to provide him with a biblical basis, which it fuses with the Christianized Alexander legend. The key texts are the familiar 2 Thessalonians 2:7 concerning the "Restrainer" who must be "removed from the middle" (that is, from Golgotha, the *axis mundi,* or center of the universe), and 1 Corinthians 15:24, which speaks of Christ handing over his kingdom to the Father, an act typologically prefigured by the emperor's surrender. Other passages are joined with these, such as Psalm 78:65, which is taken as a prophecy of the unexpected character of the emperor's action, and Matthew 24:37, which is used as a prediction of his messianic rule. Especially important is Psalm 68:31 ("Cush will hand over the hand to God"), which apparently some had taken as a prophecy that it would be an Ethiopian Last Ruler who would surrender the empire to God, but which Methodius argues refers to the Ethiopian ancestry of the Byzantine Last Emperor who will recapitulate all earthly rulership in himself as Christ's immediate apocalyptic predecessor.[79] It is not necessary, then, to appeal to Jewish messianic traditions, as Paul Alexander did,[80] to understand the origins of the Last Emperor legend. The Last Emperor is solidly rooted in Christian, specifically Syrian Christian, attempts to understand the role of the Roman Empire in the endtime.[81]

Antichrist's Career in Byzantium and the West

We can now turn to the way in which these Eastern Christian texts present Antichrist, the one enemy that the Last Emperor cannot overcome. The accounts are detailed and show interesting additions to the inherited traditions.

THE HERALD OF "WARLIKE RACES"

Paul Alexander's careful survey of the Byzantine sources suggests that the basic scenario of the end in the Christian East after 500 C.E. is that found in the Pseudo-Ephrem *Sermon on the End of the World,* whether or not this text was actually the direct source for all later uses.[82] Its references to Persians and to Huns, but lack of any attention to Islam or to a Last

Emperor, appear to reflect a standard sixth-century view into which legendary accretions were later inserted. The original list of apocalyptic stages are as follows:

1. The appearance of the "warlike races"
2. The surrender of the Roman Empire, without a Last Emperor, but citing 1 Corinthians 15:24
3. The "first" mention or manifestation of Antichrist
4. The "second" mention or manifestation of Antichrist, this time when he comes of age and seizes power
5. The description of the three and a half years (forty-two months) of Antichrist's reign
6. The sending of Enoch and Elijah to succor the human race against Antichrist's onslaught
7. The Second Coming of Christ and death of Antichrist

This text has some anomalies in relation to both previous and subsequent presentations of Antichrist, especially the absence of Antichrist's miracles, but it provides a coherent picture of the final events. In several particulars Pseudo-Ephrem seems to represent a departure that would be important for future developments. First, Pseudo-Ephrem sees two stages in Antichrist's career, as reflected in the difference between numbers 3 and 4 above. This is obviously a development from the theme of "Antichrist already born but not revealed," which we have seen as early as 400 C.E., but here it has achieved a new specificity that will have significant influence.[83] The second development may be more implied than explicit in the Pseudo-Ephrem, because of its lack of a specific Last Emperor figure— that is, the question of the relation of the Last Emperor (or end of Rome) to the two stages of Antichrist's career. How do the two moments or figures relate? Pseudo-Methodius, the *Tiburtine Sibyl,* and other apocalyptic texts of the early Middle Ages will have rather different views on this.

In surveying the Byzantine Antichrist accounts, we note that the *Oracle of Baalbek,* the early sixth-century version of the *Tiburtine Sibyl* (to be investigated presently), shows no acquaintance with Pseudo-Ephrem's picture of Antichrist's place in the final events but represents an idiosyncratic view, possibly of a double Antichrist, that had little if any later influence.[84] Paul Alexander has shown how both the Pseudo-Methodius and the Latin *Tiburtine Sibyl,* as well as a number of later Greek apocalypses, follow the format outlined above, though they also introduce new elements.

Using the seven apocalyptic stages of Pseudo-Ephrem as its core, the Pseudo-Methodius text made some additions as well as some inversions, the most important being the placing of the end of the Empire (number 2) between the first (number 3) and the second (number 4) manifestations of the Antichrist.[85] The same format will also appear in the *Tiburtine Sibyl*. One important contribution of the Syriac form of the Pseudo-Methodius to Antichrist traditions was the speculation that Antichrist, like Christ, would come from Galilee and end in Jerusalem—another powerful symbolic contrast.[86]

Antichrist also appears in the surviving Latin versions of the *Tiburtine Sibyl*, all based on the lost Greek original of the fourth century, but much edited and developed over the centuries to keep pace with changing historical events. The primary texts, representing a mixture of Eastern and Western forms of the legend, are the four eleventh-century Latin versions.[87] Sibylline texts had long been used to give eschatological weight to contemporary dynastic politics. The struggles between claimants to the imperial office, in both the East and the West, appear to provide the background for the explosion of Sibylline prophecies at this time.

In Ernst Sackur's version of the *Tiburtine Sibyl*, the coming of the Antichrist follows immediately on the account of the Last Emperor:

> Then will arise a king of the Greeks whose name is Constans. He will be king of the Romans and Greeks. He will be tall of stature, of handsome appearance with shining face, and well put together in all parts of his body. His reign will be ended after one hundred and twelve years. In those days there will be great riches and the earth will give fruit abundantly. . . .[88]

Antichrist, "the Prince of Iniquity," arises from the tribe of Dan during the time of this final messianic ruler. The Sibylline text emphasizes his signs and wonders, especially "the magic art" by which he seems to bring down fire from heaven. The account, a fairly brief and traditional one, closes with Antichrist slain "by the power of God through Michael the Archangel on the Mount of Olives," an obvious Western motif.[89]

THE DEVIL INCARNATE

A number of somewhat later Byzantine apocalypses, which were not translated into Latin, reflect similar concerns with the rise of Islam and the intermingled careers of the Last Emperor and Antichrist. Perhaps the most complex group of the later pseudonymous apocalypses are those that have been ascribed to the prophet Daniel.[90] The most important of these are the Greek texts and the Slavonic Daniel, which was translated from a lost Greek original.[91] These works are mostly concerned with the succession of emperors of the last times, but they often also include accounts of the Antichrist.

The early ninth-century *Apocalypse of Daniel* has been the subject of considerable research in recent years.[92] Written about 801 C.E. by a sympathizer of the Iconoclast heresy (a movement that denied the legitimacy of sacred images in Christian worship), the first seven chapters concentrate on the conflict between Greeks and Muslims in the eighth century, using elements from the Pseudo-Methodius. An emperor who may be Constantine V is depicted in the language of the Last Emperor in chapter 3,[93] and the mention of the empire being removed from Constantinople and given to Rome in 7:14 appears to refer to Charlemagne's crowning in Rome in 800 C.E.

The story of Antichrist and the last events in the latter part of the text (chaps. 8–14) is rather different from the scenario found in Pseudo-Ephrem and Pseudo-Methodius. It begins with the ingathering of the Jews to Jerusalem under Dan, their king (chap. 8). During his reign, Antichrist viewed as the devil incarnate is conceived in the following bizarre but significant way:

> The Antichrist will go forth from the lower regions and the chasms of Hades. And he will come into a small garidion fish. And he is coming in the broad sea. And he will be caught by twelve fishermen. And the fishermen will become maddened toward each other. One will prevail over them, whose name is Judas. And he takes that fish for his inheritance and comes into a place named Gouzeth and there sells the fish for thirty silver pieces. And a virgin girl will buy the fish. Her name is Injustice [*adikia*] because the son of injustice will be born from her. And her surname will be Perdition [*apoleia*]. For by touching the head of the fish she will become pregnant and will conceive the Antichrist himself. And he will be born from her after three months. And he will suckle from her for four months. He comes into Jerusalem and becomes a false teacher. (9:1–14)

Klaus Berger, a scholar of apocalyptic literature, has suggested that this account should be seen as a "negative imitation of christological traditions."[94] In his tomb inscription of about 200 C.E., Bishop Abercius had praised faith that "set before me for food the fish from the fountain, mighty and stainless, whom a pure virgin grasped, and gave this to friends to eat always, having good wine and giving the mixed cup with bread."[95]

The fish from the fountain (symbolizing baptism) is Christ, who is received by the "pure virgin," that is, the church, or by every believing soul through the Eucharist. The structural symbolic oppositions of these fish stories are evident.[96] Just as Christ the God-man becomes a "fish" to nourish Christians in the Eucharist, Antichrist is a "fish" who becomes a false God-man. Judas is present in each case as a significant intermediary figure. The virgin Church who bears Christ in believers through baptism contrasts with the evil virgin called Injustice who brings forth Antichrist for the Jews.[97]

The chapters that follow (10–14) in the *Apocalypse of Daniel* also display unusual features. After a description of messianic plenty, the Jews make Antichrist their king, and famine and plague immediately follow. A description of demonic affliction of Christians and terrible drought leads into a strange story (a parodic inversion of the temptation of Christ in Matt. 4:2–4 and parallels) of how Antichrist tries to turn stones into bread before the Jews to prove his divinity, only to have one rock become a dragon who upbraids him saying, "O you who are full of every iniquity and injustice, why do you do things of which you are not able?" (13:12). Finally, three witnesses, that is, Enoch, Elijah, and John, preach against Antichrist and are slain by him.[98] There is no account of the Final Enemy's death; the text ends with the promise that the day of the Lord draws near and "the deception of the devil will fall" (14:15).

The folkloric aspects of the *Apocalypse of Daniel* provide good evidence for the continuing creativity of the Antichrist legend. The early medieval period, once dismissed as the Dark Ages, demonstrates new religious and cultural forms built upon elements inherited from early Christianity but using the values of the new peoples—Syriac and Slavic in the East, Celtic and Germanic in the West—who helped create the new Christian societies of these centuries.

I hope it will be obvious, even from this rapid survey, that major developments in Christian understanding of the last events in the period 500 to 1000 C.E. took place largely in the East. Attendant upon the conversion of the empire and the development of a Christian imperial ideology, the figure of the Last World Emperor developed as counterpart to Christ. The Last Emperor would be able to defeat every human force of evil *except* the Antichrist himself. The rise of Islam seems to have been the primary factor in this new scenario of the end, but the ancient tale of the Gates of Alexander and the coming of Gog and Magog also enriched the understanding of the fearful signs of the end. The legend of Antichrist took on new dimensions in this outpouring of apocalyptic texts as old elements combined with new in a complex series of variations.

God's Enemies in Sight at the Turn of the Millennium: Western Views of Antichrist (950–1100)

The latter part of the tenth century, as the year 1000 c.e. approached, has often been seen as a time of intense apocalyptic expectation. Using a handful of texts, a number of historians, especially in the nineteenth century, painted a vivid picture of the "terrors of the year 1000," when all of Europe lived in fear of the end of the sixth millennium and the onslaught of Antichrist.[99] Abbo of Fleury, writing about 995, is one of the most direct witnesses to these fears.[100] Other historians, noting that almost none of the accounts mention the year 1000 itself (or more correctly 1001, since only then would a thousand years from Christ's birth be complete!), have seen the "terrors of the year 1000" as a historical myth designed to emphasize the religious backwardness of the "Dark Ages."[101] Still others have sought a middle path, emphasizing increased apocalyptic expectations both before and after the year 1000 but denying that they were tied to that date in any narrow way.[102]

Perhaps statistically a somewhat larger number of texts from the period 950 to 1050 witnesses to a sense of the imminence of Antichrist and the end than in the previous century, but one could certainly find an even larger number in the years 1150 to 1250. We must also refrain from thinking that every apocalyptic text of the period (for example, Adso's famous *Letter* or the early eleventh-century versions of the *Tiburtine Sibyl*) manifests such "terrors," especially when they contain no speculations on the date of the end. Still, this century was not without importance in the history of Western apocalypticism, especially regarding the Antichrist legend. I will investigate three contributions: the Irish Antichrist tradition; the role of Antichrist in the "terror" texts; and the important treatise of the monk Adso, which set the standard Western view of Antichrist for centuries to come.

ANTICHRIST IN MEDIEVAL IRELAND

Antichrist physiognomies accompanied by unusual legendary accretions belonged to the Eastern imagination at this time. Yet they became prevalent in one place in western Europe—Ireland, at least from the tenth century on.[103] The native imagination, coupled with Irish predilection for apocryphal literature suspect in other parts of Latin Christendom,[104] seems to have had much to do with this unexpected turn of events.

The earliest version of the Irish Antichrist tradition seems to be a tenth-century Latin fragment found in a manuscript from the famous monastery of Mont St. Michel.[105] The early sections of this text apparently deal with a succession of rulers; the latter portion provides a peculiar description of Antichrist's birth and physical appearance. Since this text is little known, I will present a tentative translation of two large portions of the Antichrist section, despite its often obscure Latin:

> The phoenix is a bird which builds its nest for seventy-two years. No one can understand such mysteries and the adornment he makes from his feathers, as well as the sound from his singing. A fire comes from heaven and burns that nest and tree and makes ashes on the earth. Rain comes [from] Africa and puts out the fire. From the ash and the rain will be born the girl from whom Antichrist will come. Two young virgin girls will stand there, called Abilia and Lapidia, from whose breasts will pour the milk by which they will nourish him for five years. When five years are completed, he will begin to reign.

The text proceeds, like the *Apocalypse of Daniel* 9, with a physical description of Antichrist, this time placed in Jesus' mouth, as in the third-century *Testament of the Lord*. It concludes with a brief account of his miracles, a favorite topic in the Irish traditions about the Final Enemy:

> His disciples said to Jesus: "Lord, tell us what he will be like." And Jesus said to them: "His stature will be nine cubits. He will have black hair pulled up [?] like an iron chain. In his forehead he will have one eye shining like the dawn. His lower lips will be large, he will have no upper lips. On his hand the little finger will be the longer; his left foot will be wider. His stance will be similar [?]. He will come to the sea, say 'Dry up,' and it will be dried. He says to the sun, 'Stand,' and it will stop; and he says to the moon, 'Become dark,' and it will be darkened. And the stars will fall from heaven."[106]

Perhaps the most interesting thing about this unusual account is the incorporation of the phoenix legend into the story of Antichrist's birth, something unknown in other sources.[107] Since the resurrecting phoenix had been a Christ symbol from at least the second century, the author of this work is apparently employing new symbolic reversals to present the Final Enemy.

Native vernacular texts that reflect this Irish tradition continued to be produced until the nineteenth century. The most baroque of these is the *Story of Antichrist* found in the late fifteenth-century *Book of Lismore,* though the text may well be earlier. Here Antichrist is born of a harlot from the tribe of Dan and described as a huge monster with no knees (so as not to be able to genuflect!), but with wheels on the soles of his feet and telltale black hair, as in the Latin text just quoted.[108] His strange miracles, such as making trees grow upside down and streams run backward, influenced another important apocalyptic text originating in Ireland and widely diffused throughout the later Middle Ages, the *Fifteen Signs Before Doomsday.*[109] The Irish Antichrist, probably fueled by bizarre descriptions of superhuman figures found in the early Irish sagas, is among the most unusual of the early Middle Ages.

THE SUPPOSED MILLENNIAL TERRORS

As far as the evidence for the so-called terrors of the year 1000 are concerned, we can speak of two classes of texts: (1) those that mention a specific date or time frame indicating expectation of the end for the thousandth year after Christ's birth or Passion; and (2) general expressions of fears of the end from 950 to 1050 without any date being given. Like many other scholars, I find it problematic to lean too heavily on the latter to prove some "special" terrors experienced toward the end of the first millennium c.e. Medieval people lived with enough daily misery and terror to think often of Antichrist without needing a rigidly chronological thousand-year theory. The thousand-year motif was often used as a mere literary device without any real attention to chronology.

The texts that explicitly advert to some kind of millennium in their fears of the end are fairly sparse. Abbo of Fleury was mentioned above. Another witness is the historian Raoul Glaber, whose *History of His Times* 4.6 interpreted a great French pilgrimage to the Holy Land in 1028 as announcing "nothing else but the coming of the Lost One, the Antichrist."[110] When we widen the perspective, however, a fair number of witnesses (given the paucity of texts from this era) link various current events in some way with the imminence of Antichrist.

For instance, a letter written to the bishop of Verdun probably in the 980s attacks the belief of "a multitude" (*innumeros*) that the Hungarian raiders of recent memory were to be identified with Gog and Magog. The letter indicates that some were seeing an apocalyptic dimension in current hardships, but it gives no definite timetable of the end.[111] More interesting, insofar as it represents the first glimmerings of a coming flood, is the use of Antichrist rhetoric at the Synod of Reims in 991 C.E. as recounted by Gerbert of Aurillac. Here Bishop Arnulf, in disgust over the policies and morals of Pope John XV, accused him of being Antichrist, or at least an Antichrist: "Surely, if he is empty of charity and filled with vain knowledge and lifted up, he is Antichrist sitting in God's temple and showing himself as God."[112] This rather daring identification of an *unworthy* pope with Antichrist was such a logical conclusion of the 2 Thessalonians picture of the false teacher enshrined in the temple (which many identified with the Church) that one wonders why it had not been drawn earlier. It was to have a vital posterity.

In the early eleventh century the bishop of Chartres, Fulbert, apparently thought of the Last Judgment as imminent,[113] and the chronicler Adhémer of Chabannes considered the heretics discovered in Aquitaine in 1020 as "ambassadors of Antichrist."[114] Perhaps the most extensive evidence for fears of the end at this time is found among Anglo-Saxon church leaders, though they too lay no stress on the calendar date of 1000.[115] Ælfric, abbot of Eynsham (c. 955–1020), and Wulfstan, archbishop of York (died in 1023), are rightly considered among the major figures of the early English church. Both showed great interest in apocalyptic themes, especially in Antichrist, and both appear to have been convinced that the end was near.[116] Although their teaching about the Antichrist is largely traditional, based as it is on Gregory the Great, the standard biblical commentators, and in Wulfstan's case on Adso's *Letter* (to be studied presently), they are important, for they indicate fears of Antichrist's imminence were present in the popular imagination, as reflected in the vernacular preaching they addressed to monastics, clergy, and large crowds of laity.

There can be no doubt that in the decades before and after the year 1000 some, both among ordinary believers and among the church leaders, lived in fear of Antichrist's coming. But there is no evidence that concerns about Antichrist and the endtime greatly increased at this time. Others, at least among the clerical intelligentsia influenced by Augustine's views, resisted such expectations.

ADSO'S BIOGRAPHY OF ANTICHRIST

From the perspective of the history of Antichrist, the real innovation came not around 1000 but shortly after 950, when a reforming monk named Adso, later abbot of Montier-en-Der, undertook the task of writing a full account of Antichrist in a letter addressed to Gerberga, sister of

Otto I (the German ruler who renewed the Western Empire) and wife of Louis IV of West Francia (one of the contemporary pretenders to the mantle of Roman supremacy). The popularity of Adso's work was immense: the critical edition uses 171 manuscripts and identifies no fewer than nine different versions of the text, many of them pseudonymously ascribed to the most noted of medieval authors.[117] Adso's success stems from two factors. First, his handy compendium fulfilled a real need in medieval culture, already noted by Agobard of Lyon—a summary of the traditional teaching about the Final Enemy. Second, the text was so successful in part because it is a form of "reverse" hagiography.[118] As medievalist Richard Emmerson says, the "establishment of a *vita* of Antichrist that closely parallels the structure of the popular saints' lives was a creative act with great ramifications for the later Antichrist tradition."[119]

By choosing a narrative rather than an exegetical basis for his presentation of the Antichrist legend, Adso did more than just summarize tradition. Although the most obvious sources for his picture are Western and have been much examined, several important details and, more tellingly, the structure of his account indicate that he injected the Western materials into an Eastern structure, the sevenfold pattern we have seen above in Pseudo-Ephrem and Pseudo-Methodius.[120] Yet his fusion of Eastern and Western materials is not without problems. Adso offers a lengthy account of much of the Final Enemy's career, mentions the Last Emperor and his surrender, then concludes with a second lengthy account of Antichrist that awkwardly repeats elements already mentioned in the first.[121]

A second problem in Adso, which seems to result from the conflation of various traditions, is the role of the Jews. In the second manifestation the Jews flock to Antichrist in Jerusalem "in the belief that they are receiving God"—a parallel to the ingathering of the Jews found in some of the Byzantine Daniel texts. But the account of the two witnesses that follows says that the preaching of the prophets "will convert the sons of Israel . . . and they will make their belief unconquerable among the elect in the face of the affliction of so great a storm" (a quotation from Bede's *Explanation of Times*).[122] Despite these contradictions, Adso's *Letter* provides the first full narrative of the Final Enemy, one that by turning the genre of saint's life on its head marks a major moment in the history of the Antichrist legend.

After a short explanation of the meaning of the name Antichrist as "contrary to Christ," the monk begins by discussing the many ministers of his malice, first the traditional prototypes like Antiochus, Nero, and

Domitian, and then, following the tradition of Augustine and Gregory, "anyone, layman, cleric, or monk, who lives contrary to justice and attacks the rule of his way of life and blasphemes what is good." But Adso's real concern is not with collective antichrists but with the final Antichrist, whom he asserts is to be born of the tribe of Dan and of a union of a father and a mother, "not, as some say, from a virgin alone." Following the standard Western view, Adso holds that Antichrist will be born in Babylon, but he turns to the Pseudo-Methodius by invoking two of the three woes of Matthew 11:21 to indicate that the enemy will be raised in Bethsaida and Corozain. Educated in wizardry, he will then go to Jerusalem, rebuild the temple, and "will circumcise himself and will pretend that he is the son of Almighty God."

A lengthy description of Antichrist's activities follows, some traditional (like sending out messengers and preachers), others more unusual (like his destruction of the Holy Places). Seven miracles are recounted, including his ability to raise the dead.[123] Adso follows the Carolingian writers Alcuin and Haymo in discussing how Antichrist "will lift himself up against the faithful in three ways, that is, by terror, by gifts, and by prodigies."[124] His brief mention of the kinds of torture used by Antichrist would be expanded upon in later presentations, both written and pictorial. This account of the first manifestation concludes with a reference to the forty-two-month reign and the shortening of the days.

Adso's section devoted to the Last Emperor is brief. In line with the ancient tradition, the necessary falling away or defection (*discessio*) of 2 Thessalonians 2:3 before the coming of Antichrist is interpreted as the departure of all political power from the Roman Empire. Adso says that although the empire is mostly in ruins in his day, as long as the kings of the Franks possess it, by right the dignity of Rome has not completely perished.[125]

> Some of our learned men say that one of the kings of the Franks will possess anew the Roman Empire. He will be in the last time and will be the greatest and last of all kings. After he has successfully governed his empire, he will come to Jerusalem and will lay aside his scepter and crown on the Mount of Olives. This will be the end and consummation of the Roman and Christian Empire.[126]

The monk's remarks on the end of Antichrist echo the Western confusion about whether Jesus will slay him directly or through the instrumentality of Michael.[127] The monk adheres to the tradition of Jerome in naming the Mount of Olives as the place of the Final Enemy's destruction, though he does not explicitly mention an attempted false ascension.[128] Also like Jerome, he allows for a period of respite: "the Lord will grant the elect forty days to do penance because they were led astray by the Antichrist." The anomalous forty instead of the usual forty-five days is probably to be explained by the attraction of the notion of forty days of Lent as a special time of penance. As medievalist Robert E. Lerner has shown, both Adso and Haymo, his source, significantly held open the possibility for an even further period of peace before the arrival of the judgment.[129]

The original text of Adso survives in twenty-three manuscripts, but this tally is just a portion of the witnesses—in both Latin and various vernaculars—that testify to the subsequent popularity of the work. As was so often the case with apocalyptic best-sellers, later editors felt free to alter the text, bringing it up to date and often enhancing its authority by ascribing it to well-known authorities. At least two of the eight Latin reworkings—the one ascribed to Alcuin, which couples the legend of Charlemagne's Jerusalem pilgrimage with the story of Antichrist, and the form ascribed to Methodius, which reflects the events of the First Crusade—contain interesting variations on the story of the Final Enemy.[130]

Adso's treatise was also translated into a number of vernaculars. The earliest of these is the Old English version, which was translated prior to the twelfth century.[131] Such vernacular texts show that the letter enjoyed great popularity. Given the wealth of versions in both Latin and vernacular, the number of manuscripts, and the creative manipulations evident in some of the reworkings, the later versions of Adso have central importance in the history of Antichrist.

What Did Antichrist Look Like?

One final dimension of Christian attitudes toward Antichrist in the centuries between 500 and 1100 deserves attention: the pictorial one. During these centuries—exactly when is disputed—the first attempts to create artistic depictions of Antichrist, especially the human form of the Final Enemy and not just his symbolic animal types, were created.[132]

The earliest pictures of Antichrist were based on biblical texts. Illustrators often chose the Apocalypse as their pictorial source, for although many of its images are quite bizarre, the Apocalypse is the product of an intense pictorial imagination. Images from the Apocalypse, especially from the heavenly court scenes (for example, Apoc. 4) were widely used in imperial Christian art as early as the fourth century.[133] It was not until illustrated Apocalypse manuscripts began to be produced, perhaps as early as the fifth or sixth centuries, that the possibility of picturing Antichrist, either in his animal (Apoc. 13) or human forms, became real. The earliest illustrations have not survived, though on the basis of later illustrated Apocalypses, art historians have argued for the existence of two early groups: a Roman cycle that influenced central and northern European Apocalypse illustration throughout the Middle Ages; and a North African and Spanish one, best known through the famous illuminated Beatus manuscripts.[134] It is mainly in the second group that pictures of a human Antichrist first appear.

A second biblical source that inspired early illustrators of Antichrist was the Psalms.[135] Again, these traditions of illustration probably go back to lost exemplars of late antiquity, but the earliest Western survivals date from the Carolingian period of the ninth century.[136] Artists drew on the practice of identifying certain negative figures in the Psalms as predecessors or types of Antichrist. In the Corbie Psalter of about 800, the initial illuminated letter Q of Psalm 51 pictures an enthroned figure (doubtless Doeg the Idumenean of the Psalm) riding two entwined beasts, perhaps Behemoth and Leviathan (Fig. 1). Given Cassiodorus's reading of Doeg as a type of Antichrist, as well as the fact that the Psalm text does not mention any beasts, it is likely that the illuminist had the Antichrist aspect of the character in mind.[137]

Even more revealing are the illustrations for Psalms 13 and 52 in the Utrecht Psalter, probably produced near Rheims in about 820. The illustration for Psalm 13 (Fig. 2) reveals an enthroned figure under a canopy, to whom two heads are being brought by retainers with swords. Underneath are scenes of torture and killing. Near the middle is a figure on a hill addressing the heavenly host, who look down from above. On the right a group of mounted warriors and supplicating women and children approach a warrior standing on another hill. It has been suggested that the scenes on the left can best be understood as an illustration of Antichrist enthroned, slaying the witnesses and persecuting true believers.[138] Although I have not been able to find this exegesis of the related Psalms in any of the surviving commentators,[139] the fact that these Psalms were interpreted in terms of evil persons, especially the Jews, traditionally seen as members of Antichrist, makes the interpretation at least plausible. If the central figure

FIGURE I
Doeg the Idumenean
as a type of Antichrist
illustrating Psalm 51.
Corbie Psalter (c. 800).
Courtesy of the
Bibliothèque
Municipale, Amiens.

is the psalmist addressing Christ in heaven, what is the meaning of the scene on the right? Given the relation of the whole ensemble to the Antichrist legend, it seems to me that the figure on the right might well be the Last Emperor about to surrender the imperial rule to God on either Golgotha or the Mount of Olives. This would make it the earliest illustration of that other potent legendary figure.

Better known are the illustrations of Antichrist in the illuminated Beatus manuscripts. The earliest surviving Beatus manuscripts come from the middle of the tenth century, about 150 years after the composition of the text. It seems likely, however, that the earlier lost manuscripts were

FIGURE 2   Antichrist and Last Emperor illustrating Psalm 13. Utrecht Psalter (c. 820). From
Ahuva Belkin, "The Antichrist Legend in the Utrecht Psalter," *Rivista di Storia e
Letteratura Religiosa* 23(1987), plate facing p. 280. Courtesy of Olschki Publishers,
Florence.

also illustrated and that these illuminations included figures of the Beasts
of Apocalypse 13, which were traditionally seen as Antichrist, as well as
human portrayals of the Final Enemy. In the surviving Beatus pieces,
Antichrist as a human figure appears in two contexts. The first is the
killing of the two witnesses of Apocalypse 11:7. Although the biblical text
ascribes this to the Beast from the Abyss, the exegetical identification of
the Beast with Antichrist allowed the illustrator to picture the Beast as a
giant human tyrant, a form fully in accord with Western views of "Titan"
as one of the traditional names of Antichrist (Fig. 3).[140] Other Beatus manuscripts illustrate the attack on Jerusalem found in Apocalypse 20:7–9
with a similar giant tyrant.[141]

Another early Apocalypse, the Bamberg Apocalypse, dating from
about 1000 C.E., also appears to portray a human Antichrist.[142] In any case,
it is clear that in the earliest biblical illustrations of Antichrist, his role as
persecuting tyrant is much to the fore. One of the best examples is found
in Lambert of St. Omer's *Flowery Book,* a medieval encyclopedia composed about 1120. On folio 62v of the Ghent manuscript the Antichrist appears in a magnificent, almost full-page picture (Fig. 4) as a king seated on
the Beast Leviathan.[143] The pictorial Antichrist, however, soon spread
outside the confines of biblical illustration, just as the Antichrist legend itself had. But these innovations occurred after 1100 and will therefore be
discussed in the next chapter.

FIGURE 3   Antichrist slaying the two witnesses (detail), illustration from the *Beatus of Liébana* (Apoc. 11:7), fol. 151r, Spain, mid–tenth century. Reproduced with permission of the Pierpont Morgan Library, New York, M.664, fol. 151.

Antichrist Established

The centuries between 500 and 1100 C.E. helped to give the Antichrist legend new dimensions and, in the West at least, a standard form. The imperial Christian apocalypticism that was established in these centuries is

FIGURE 4
Antichrist astride
Leviathan, from the
*Liber Floridus (Flowery
Book)* of Lambert of
Ghent (early twelfth
century). University
Library, Ghent, ms. 92,
fol. 62v. Reproduced
with permission.

proof that the mythic mentality was strongly at work in times of social, political, and cultural collapse. The legend of the Last World Emperor, a creation of Eastern Christianity, interacted with the Antichrist legend both in East and West for more than a thousand years. In the West, Adso's *Letter* had the effect of freeing the developing legend from its enmeshed location in apocalypses, exegetical treatises, and theological pamphlets to allow it a more independent life. The first freestanding biography of the Final Enemy had important consequences for later accounts and illustrated lives, though much new material also continued to be produced in the older forms.

Moralizing interpretations of Antichrist were still most often used during these centuries to identify present enemies of the Christian order—especially heretics, Jews, and increasingly Muslims—as agents of ultimate evil. The practice was deplorable, but it was a natural step in the evolution of the Antichrist legend. Such condemnations of perceived enemies remain a major part of the Antichrist legend's heritage even today. In the midst of conflict between good and evil, especially when that conflict is viewed in ultimate terms, Antichrist traditions offer unusually strong resources for group solidarity and action against threats, imagined or real. This is as true as we approach the year 2000 as it was at the turn of the first millennium.

APPENDIX: ANTICHRIST-LIKE FIGURES IN JUDAISM AND ISLAM

As the first chapter in this study has suggested, the mythic and legendary traditions that made possible the early Christian creation of the figure of Antichrist were rooted in Jewish speculation on angelic and human opponents of God and his messiah in the last days. This archaeological contribution of Judaism to the Antichrist legend is not the whole story, however. Some Jewish messianic texts of Talmudic and post-Talmudic times demonstrate an interesting interaction in which a Jewish "antimessiah" named Armillus takes on a more specific identity.[144] This may be partly due to the influence of the Christian Antichrist legend on Judaism.

Medieval Judaism

While Armillus is not a true Antichrist, he is certainly an Antichrist-like figure.[145] A basic problem one confronts when investigating Armillus is the context and dating of the materials that refer to him. For the sake of this presentation, I have used the passages found in Raphael Patai's *The Messiah Texts,* which, though they date from different epochs, reveal elements of a common scenario.[146] This scenario is structured around the distinctive rabbinic belief in two messiahs—the Messiah ben Joseph who leads Israel to many victories but is eventually slain, and the Messiah ben David who ushers in the definitive reign of God.

Historian of Judaism Gershom Scholem saw this doubling of the messiah as a logical outcome of the mingling of catastrophic and utopian currents in Jewish messianism.[147] Others have viewed the anomalous

Messiah ben Joseph as a reflection of the career of Bar Kochba,[148] the leader of the second-century Jewish revolt against Rome, or typologically connected him with the rabbinic tradition that the tribe of Ephraim (from which the Messiah ben Joseph was to come) had been defeated in its early attempt to conquer the Holy Land.[149] Armillus's story is intimately bound up with both messiahs, since it is he who slays the Messiah ben Joseph and is in turn slain by the Messiah ben David.

The earliest mentions of Armillus come from the seventh century C.E. in the Targum to Isaiah 11:4 and the Targum Jonathan on Deuteronomy 34:3.[150] More extended descriptions are present in other seventh-century texts, such as the apocalyptic *Book of Zerubbabel* of about 630 C.E., as well as in later messianic texts. Five of the eight texts translated by Patai (1, 2, 4, 5, 8) contain accounts of Armillus's birth from a female idol, and six (2, 3, 4, 5, 6, 7) contain physical descriptions that have affinities with the Christian Antichrist physiognomies.[151] The account in the T'fillat Rabbi Shim'on ben Yohai is typical:

> They say that there is in Rome a stone of marble, and it has the shape of a beautiful girl. She was created in the six days of the Beginning. And worthless people from the nations come and lie with her, and she becomes pregnant, and at the end of nine months she bursts open, and a male child emerges, in the shape of a man whose height is twelve cubits and whose breadth is two cubits. His eyes are red and crooked, the hair of his head is red like gold, and the steps of his feet are green, and he has two skulls. They call him Armillus.[152]

This birth appears to be both a condemnation of idolatry and a parody of Christ's virgin birth from Mary.

Concerning the name Armillus, several explanations have been suggested. Today, most scholars agree that Armillus is really Romulus, as the Pseudo-Methodius explicitly says.[153] But, as Jewish scholar David Berger points out, the connection of the antimessiah with Rome (referred to as Edom in Jewish texts) also involves a typological reference to Balaam, seen as the opponent of Moses, whose name, according to the rabbis, is interpreted as Eremolaos, that is, "destroyer of the people."[154]

In the T'fillat Rabbi Shim'on ben Yohai, Armillus goes to Edom-Rome, announcing himself as messiah and God. Other texts do not describe this action but do recount his battles against Israel and his killing of the Messiah ben Joseph, often called Nehemiah (see 2, 3, and 7). At this point some accounts (2, 4, 7) have Israel fleeing into the wilderness for forty or forty-five days to await the coming of the Messiah ben David.

> And thereafter will come Messiah ben David. . . . And he will kill the wicked Armillus. . . . And thereafter the Holy One, blessed be He, will gather all Israel who are dispersed here and there.[155]

Little is actually said about Armillus's deeds in these accounts, but one parallel with Christian legends is found in references to his ability (or inability) to perform various miracles.[156] The legend of Armillus, then, appears to have been influenced by Christian accounts of Antichrist but also to be a critique of Christianity, especially at a time when Edom-Rome had become a Christian Empire.

Islam

Given the connections, especially the shared apocalyptic mentality,[157] between Islam and both Judaism and Christianity, it is not surprising to find an Antichrist-like figure called the Dajjāl in the new monotheistic religion that came out of the Arabian desert in the seventh century.[158] It is quite likely that Christian Antichrist traditions, especially of Syriac provenance, were known in Arabia in the pre-Islamic period. Despite the Qur'an's emphasis on eschatology, the Dajjāl does not appear in it, though enterprising exegetes were able to find a veiled reference in Sura 108 (called Kauthar, or Abundance), which reads, "Surely We have given thee abundance; so pray unto the Lord and sacrifice. Surely he that hates thee, he is the one cut off" (Arberry translation). The notion of being cut off, or defective (root *BTR*), became one of the hallmarks of the Dajjāl, and some traditions give the name of the ass he is traditionally seated on as Abtar.

The development of the Dajjāl figure was a product of the *hadith,* the various traditions about the prophet and his sayings formed into collections in the first centuries of Islam. An interesting group of *hadith* concerns Ibn Sayyad, a Jewish youth in Medinah in Muhammad's time who converted to Islam and who died in 683 c.e. As Islamic scholar David Halperin argues, Ibn Sayyad was apparently a Jewish ecstatic mystic, perhaps a prophet of sorts, whom Muhammad apparently suspected of being the Dajjāl.[159] According to one *hadith,* when one of the companions, the future caliph 'Umar, offered to kill him, Muhammad said it would not be possible.[160] It would seem, then, that the Dajjāl tradition may have begun as a conception of a false last prophet, the last of a line of pretenders, not unlike the pseudoprophets of the Synoptic Little Apocalypse (for example, Matt. 24:24). The *hadith* are evidence of Muhammad's expectation of the imminence of the Dajjāl as one of the signs of the coming terrors of the end, especially in the traditions called the Prayer of Refuge. "Abu Huraira reported: The Apostle of Allah (may peace be upon him) said: 'O Allah! I seek refuge with Thee from the torment of the grave, the torment of hell, and the trial of life and death, and the mischief of Masih [Messiah] al-Dajjāl.'"[161]

From these relatively spare beginnings, the Dajjāl, like the Christian Antichrist, soon grew into a human monster with a bizarre appearance and complicated story. Some legendary elements are already present in the stories and accounts of Muhammad's companions, such as the belief that the Dajjāl will be a Jew[162] who will be sterile, one-eyed (both marks of defect), and unable to enter Medinah or Mecca.[163] It is also frequently asserted that he will come from the East. How much these legendary accretions may have owed to the internal religio-political struggles of early Islam, especially the wars against the extreme "Exaggerators" (*ghulat*) of the Shi'i version of Islam, is difficult to know.[164] By the ninth century, the famous fundamentalist Sunni scholar Ahmad ibn Hanbal, in summarizing the creed of Islam, gave the following succinct account of the basic Muslim belief in the Dajjāl:

> And belief that the False Messiah will rise up, with the word "Unbeliever" [*kafir*] written between his eyes, and in the hadiths that have come about this. And faith that this shall really be so, and that Jesus will descend from Heaven and slay him at the Lydda Gate.[165]

This is a creedal statement. Popular belief filled out the picture with a mass of legendary details. According to tradition, one Tamim al-Dari, an early Christian convert to Islam, met the Dajjāl chained in a monastery on an island in the sea, and the monster predicted he would soon be loosed upon the earth.[166] Islamic attempts to conquer Constantinople, such as the sieges of 673–78 and 717–18 C.E., were probably the source for the belief that the Dajjāl would arise either seven months or seven years after the Great City would be captured.

The description of Antichrist as a one-eyed monster riding on an ass as large as himself and leading the Jews against Islam appears to have been fairly widespread in both Sunni and Shi'i Islam from the eighth or ninth century c.e. Like the Christian accounts (and at least some Jewish ones), Muslim texts also speculate about the miracles that he will or will not be able to perform, especially whether or not he will be able to raise the dead. Many of the legal scholars thought yes, but this was denied by the Sufis, who usually took a dim view of the Dajjāl traditions. After a reign of forty days (like the Jewish Armillus!), he will be slain, usually by Jesus, or sometimes by the Mahdi assisted by Jesus.[167] As one account puts it: "When ad-Dajjāl sees Jesus and recognizes his voice, he will melt away like lead in a fire, or like suet in the sun, and had not Jesus said: 'Go gently' to that melting, there would have been nothing of him left. Then Jesus will leap at him with his spear, stab him between the breasts and kill him."[168]

In some late (sixteenth century) Ottoman imperial prophecies, we even find illustrations of the Dajjāl's career, including his destruction by Jesus—an interesting parallel to the Christian need to give visual expression to fears of the end.[169]

It would take a scholar with much greater knowledge of Judaism and Islam than I to do justice to Armillus and the Dajjāl. Despite the presence of these figures within Judaism and Islam, it seems fair to say that neither of them ever loomed as large in the history of their respective faiths as Antichrist did in Christianity. This is because Christianity was—and is—founded upon the Christ whose nemesis seems required by both doctrinal and symbolic symmetry.

CHAPTER FIVE

CHURCH REFORM AND ANTICHRIST'S IMMINENCE

(1100–1200)

Medievalists customarily make a division between the High Middle Ages of the twelfth and thirteenth centuries and the Late Middle Ages of the fourteenth and fifteenth. The latter period has often been seen as a time of crisis, even of decline. Whatever differences can be detected between the two periods, one thing they shared was a burning curiosity about Antichrist and a curiosity about him that resulted in the creation of a number of new roles for the Last Enemy. In some ways, these centuries can be seen as the period when the Antichrist legend flourished in its most exuberant fashion, not only in exegesis and theology but also in the general culture, as the appearances of the Man of Perdition in art and literature demonstrate. The sources on Antichrist from this period are so rich that here, even more than in the previous chapters, my selection leaves out much interesting material. I still hope to give a picture that will be true to the most important lines of development.[1]

It is impossible for us to know in any accurate fashion just how widespread and deep fears of Antichrist and his imminence were during these centuries. The surviving evidence for the Antichrist legend from this period is more extensive than for previous eras, but the same is true for almost every other aspect of historical research. Doubtless, many were indifferent to fears of Antichrist, but probably others regularly reminded them of their error! In the middle of the twelfth century the Benedictine monk Ralph of Flavigny provides an interesting witness: "Such is the state of the Church today that you see people who have perfect faith with whom, if you have a conversation about the final persecution and coming of Antichrist, it seems as if they hardly believe it will come, or, if they believe it, in a dreamy way they attempt to demonstrate that it will happen after many centuries."

Ralph, though he adhered to a quite traditional view, wrote to warn these deluded dreamers, convinced that there were "no more evident signs" of Antichrist's approach than comforting convictions that his coming was well in the future.[2]

Two major twelfth-century developments in Christian apocalyptic eschatology were fundamental to the new roles that Antichrist began to take. The first was the impact on apocalyptic expectations of the Great Reform movement. Although the papal attempt to free the church from the control of lay magnates and to reform the clerical life began in the mid–eleventh century, its real effects on expectations for the end appeared only near the twelfth century. Historians have identified a "reformist" mentality in much of later medieval apocalypticism, meaning that end-time speculation often involved hopes for a coming repristination of the clergy and through them of the whole body of the church.[3] This purifying urge took many guises and was shaped by a variety of understandings of reform, but its earliest stages were primarily an outgrowth of the papal Great Reform movement's attempts to purge the church of abuses such as simony, lay investiture, and clerical unchastity.[4] This is not to say that Pope Gregory VII and his immediate allies had provable apocalyptic motivation for their efforts to restore the church to what they saw as its original purity and purpose. But the partial success of their program—at least insofar as it gave the papacy a more central role in the ordering of Christian society and put the ideal of a purified clergy center stage—was to have profound effects on apocalypticism and hence also on the Antichrist legend.

The second development that profoundly affected much (though not all) later medieval apocalypticism was the thought of Joachim of Fiore (c. 1135–1202), a Calabrian abbot who was, without doubt, the greatest medieval apocalyptic thinker and the creator of one of the most influential of all Christian theologies of history. Joachim was a reformer in the sense that he looked forward to a coming better state of the church, but the abbot's specifically monastic reformism and the daring trinitarian vision of history in which he framed his expectations put him in a special category.

Joachim's apocalypticism involved important new developments in the story of Antichrist that will be spelled out later in this chapter.

Both these new types of apocalyptic eschatology implied an optimism about the historical future that contrasted with the pessimistic view of history enshrined in the mainline Augustinian eschatology. Optimism about a coming better state of Christian society was also present in the early medieval period, as we have seen in the previous chapter. In the early Middle Ages, however, these hopes were directed toward a period *prior* to the coming of Antichrist and were usually associated with a Last World Emperor who would usher in an age of triumph and material prosperity before the appearance of the Final Enemy. Such forms of pre-Antichrist millenarianism continued into the period 1100 to 1500 and beyond, but the reformist and Joachite scenarios of the end, as medievalist Robert E. Lerner has shown, emphasized a *post*-Antichrist millenarianism that became quite influential in the last centuries of the Middle Ages.[5] The intermingling of these optimistic hopes (pre- and post-Antichrist) with waves of intense fear about the imminence of the Final Enemy (or enemies) conceived of in a detail surpassing anything yet seen give these next centuries a distinctive place in the long history of the Antichrist legend.

Western Embellishments to the Traditional Image

While acknowledging the importance of the twelfth century as the initiating period for these new traditions, we should beware of exaggerating the originality of twelfth-century views of Antichrist.[6] The legend of the Final Enemy had acquired the weight of a deep and permanent structure of belief in Christianity after a thousand years of development, and this traditional scenario retained its continuity and centrality despite important new developments, accretions, and applications made between 1100 and 1200. The standard tradition of biblical exegesis played the major role in handing on this ancient Antichrist legend, so we can begin our survey of the twelfth century by looking at some examples of how exegesis was a vehicle for Antichrist beliefs.

The most important channel was the *Ordinary Gloss,* the great biblical textbook created in the nascent universities of the twelfth century.[7] In the words of Richard Emmerson, "The *Glossa* is particularly valuable in the study of the medieval Antichrist, for in its comments on the key texts of the tradition, it presents an orthodox and collocative statement that is detailed yet not colored by the more ingenious and sometime radical features that became associated with the tradition in its later development."[8]

Thus, for any of the usual scriptural bases for the legend (for example, Dan. 7–12, Mark 13 and parallels, 2 Thess., Apoc. 13, 1 John, and so on), as well as for a host of the texts typologically applied to Antichrist, the *Gloss* gives a good view of the standard interpretation.

The more traditional Apocalypse commentaries of the twelfth century, such as those of Berengaudus and Richard of St. Victor,[9] also conveyed the standard view of the Final Enemy to clerical audiences. The Pauline Epistles, given their difficulty of interpretation, were much commented upon by the early scholastics, such as Lanfranc and Peter Lombard. Interpretations of 2 Thessalonians were another source for the standard inherited materials.[10]

An example of how these traditional views could be handled in new ways, though without contemporary political reference, is found in the Antichrist writings of Honorius Augustodunensis, a monk from the British Isles who spent most of his career in southern Germany, where he died perhaps as late as 1145. Honorius treated Antichrist in at least four of his works: the *Elucidarium* (c. 1107), the *Gem of the Soul* (c. 1115), the *Mirror of the Church* (c. 1120), and the *Exposition on the Song of Songs* (after 1132).[11] The *Elucidarium* presents a fairly standard Antichrist portrayal;[12] the *Mirror of the Church* is more interesting for the emphasis it gives to hypocrites as the most obvious members of Antichrist identified as the Dragon of Apocalypse 12:3.[13] The *Gem* reads the events of the endtime, including Antichrist's career, as typologically revealed in the liturgy of Holy Week.[14]

Honorius's most original use of the Antichrist legend is in his remarkable *Exposition on the Song of Songs*.[15] The twelfth-century monk read the Song as a portrayal of the history of the love between Christ and the Church, seen as comprising the whole of humanity over the course of the four ages of salvation history. He identified four women found in the Song with the Church's historical permutations. In the first age of the patriarchs before the law *(ante legem)* she is the daughter of Pharaoh, coming from the East on her chariots (Song 1:8). In the age of the prophets under the law *(sub lege)* she is the Queen of the South (Song 3:1–6:9), while in the age of the apostles under grace *(sub gratia)* she is the Sunamite (or Shulamite) from the West mentioned in Song 6:10–7:10. Finally, Queen Mandragora from the North (that is, the mandrake root mentioned in Song 7:13) represents the church of the age of Antichrist *(sub Antichristo)*.[16] The mandrake signifies the Jews and pagans whose original head is Antichrist. After Antichrist's death this head will be replaced by Christ's own; that is, these peoples will be incorporated into the church.[17]

Honorius's text is also the source for a striking illustration of Antichrist. A number of South German manuscripts of the *Exposition* contain pictures of the four queens in which we see Christ placing his own head on Queen Mandragora's body while Antichrist's severed head is visible below (Fig. 5).[18] In its optimistic implications, Honorius's account of Antichrist is one of the more unusual of the Middle Ages. However, it makes good symbolic sense in the light of the Adamic myth contrasting good and bad "Adams," a symbolic opposition that has remained vital to the Antichrist legend, even when its presence is scarcely overt. The struggle between final good and evil is preeminently a struggle within the whole human race throughout its history. Antichrist falsely places his own head on Mandragora's body representing the fullness of humanity, only to have Christ, humanity's true head, replace him at the endtime. The ancient symbolism of the mandrake, a mysterious "human-shaped" plant that had long been the subject of speculation in Greek mythology and Christian legend, here reinforces the inner symbolism of the Antichrist legend.[19]

Another example of the imaginative power of the traditional form of the Antichrist legend comes from the end of the twelfth century. The *Garden of Delights* (*Hortus Deliciarum*) was a theological encyclopedia, not unlike Lambert's *Flowery Book,* put together and profusely illustrated at the convent of Mont Sainte-Odile between 1170 and 1205 under the direction of the abbess Herrad of Hohenberg. The original was destroyed in 1870, but fortunately not before a copy was made.[20] Antichrist texts, mostly dependent on Adso and Honorius, occur in several places in the *Garden.*

The real importance of the *Garden of Delights* is found in the illustrated cycle of Antichrist's life, which accompanies these texts on folios 241v to 242v. This is the earliest surviving narrative portrayal of the career of the Son of Perdition. It is based on Adso's popular *vita* but contains several new elements.[21] Seven scenes appear with identifying captions: (1) Antichrist slaying the witnesses; (2) his bribing the kings; (3) three of his miracles; (4) eight scenes of the various tortures he will inflict on the faithful; (5) his destruction by Michael on the Mount of Olives; (6) the consternation of his followers and their conversion; and (7) the baptism of the Synagogue, pictured as an old man rather than a woman (see Fig. 6 for illustrations 5 through 7). The *Garden* illustrations inspired many later renditions.

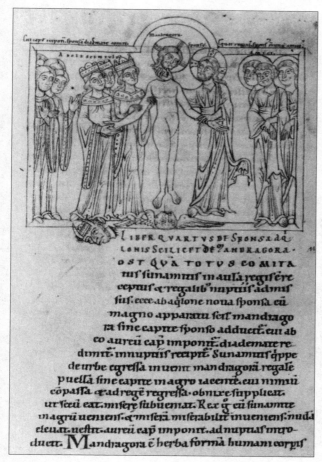

FIGURE 5
Christ places his head
on Queen Mandragora's
body with severed head of
Antichrist below. Honorius
Augustodunensis, *Exposition
on the Song of Songs* (twelfth
century). Reproduced with
permission of Österreichische
Nationalbibliothek, Vienna,
codex 942, fol. 92.

Antichrist and the Debates over Reform

The standard inherited materials, whether set forth in exegetical surveys
or reworked in various ways, could be richly amplified or applied in new
ways. Applying them to the understanding of current events and personalities, as we have seen, often resulted in important new additions to the
Antichrist legend itself. Increasing willingness to use apocalyptic imagery
in general, and Antichrist symbols in particular, as a means of understanding current conflict in the church and Christian society was closely
tied to the wrenching debates over the proper ordering of Christian society that followed the Great Reform movement. Scholars have sometimes
thought that using apocalyptic imagery to give meaning to present events

FIGURE 6
Antichrist's destruction and
the conversion of his Jewish
followers. Herrad of
Hohenberg, *Hortus
Deliciarum* (*Garden of
Delights*), fol. 242v
(late twelfth century).
Reproduced with permission
of the Warburg Institute
from Rosalie Green, et al.,
*Herrad of Hohenbourg.
Hortus Deliciarum* (Leiden-
London: Warburg Institute-
Brill, 1979), vol. 2, plate 136.

is tantamount to removing true apocalyptic dimensions from the inherited symbols.[22] But this does not seem correct. Interpreters need not choose between apocalyptic fears and contemporary historical application; people who used apocalyptic imagery both expected the end and used endtime symbols for their own present purposes. The process of understanding present conflicts in terms of symbols of the end can have apocalyptic significance even in the absence of definite prediction about the imminence of the last things.

We can, however, distinguish between what we might call Antichrist *language* and Antichrist *application*. Those who use Antichrist language use the term *Antichrist* and its equivalents only as a weapon to smear opponents, paying no attention to the general course of salvation history. Antichrist application occurs when a conscious and concerted effort is made to understand historical events, recent and contemporary, in the light of the Antichrist legend as part of an apocalyptic view of history. In the early days of the Gregorian Reform movement in the latter eleventh century we see mostly Antichrist language. In the twelfth century we begin to see new developments in Antichrist application.

The use of Antichrist language appears on both sides of the controversy that erupted over the actions of the monk Hildebrand, who reigned as Pope Gregory VII from 1073 to 1085. Gregory attacked Wibert, the Archbishop of Ravenna, who had been set up as Antipope by the German emperor, Henry IV, as "a plunderer of the holy church of Ravenna, an antichrist, and an archheretic."[23] On the emperor's side his supporter, Cardinal Beno, in his *Decree Against Hildebrand,* wrote, "Hildebrand is either a member of Antichrist, or Antichrist himself."[24] All of this rhetoric merely follows the pattern of previous centuries.

One interesting use of Antichrist motifs connected with the papal reform program is to be found in connection with the launching of the First Crusade by Urban II in 1095. Gregory VII had conceived the idea of a rescue mission to the East, and the use of the crusade, politically speaking, was the papacy's foreign policy—its attempt to reintegrate all Christian realms (not just the West) under the new papal model. One account of Urban's speech at Clermont that launched the crusade (the account given by Guibert of Nogent in his *Deeds of God Through the Franks,* c. 1110) has the pope inspiring his listeners by referring to the necessity that Christians retake Jerusalem and the East so that Antichrist will be able to attack them: "The end of the world is already near, even if the pagans are no longer being converted to God. . . . According to the prophecies, before the coming of Antichrist it is first necessary that the Christian Empire be renewed in those parts, either through you or through those whom God pleases, so that the head of all evil who will have his imperial throne there may find some nourishment of faith against which he may fight."[25]

It is doubtful that Urban actually used motifs from the Antichrist legend in his speech, but it is important to note that a papal supporter like Guibert could employ them to understand why it had been necessary for Christians to retake the apocalyptic city of Jerusalem. Some historians have stressed the role of apocalyptic elements in the great march to the East that resulted in crusader conquests of 1099. If apocalyptic motifs were used, they do not seem to have played a major role.[26] What was important was how the crusade and the subsequent fate of Jerusalem underlined the apocalyptic significance of the city and how the papally inspired crusade challenged the traditional understanding of a special bond between the Last Emperor and Jerusalem.

One could argue that a shift from Antichrist language to Antichrist application began to take place in some of the adherents of the papal reform program at the end of the eleventh century. A prime example is Rupert of Deutz, a reforming German monk who was compelled to flee his monastery in Liège by the emperor's adherents. About 1095 he wrote a poem entitled "The Calamities of the Church of Liège," in which he described the victory of Henry IV and his Antipope over Gregory and their occupation of Rome as the triumph of the first and second Beasts of Apocalypse 13, equated with Nero and Simon Magus.[27] In his later *Commentary on the Apocalypse* (c. 1119–21) Rupert did not go quite so far in applying apocalyptic symbolism to current events, but he did begin to break with the standard Tyconian moralizing interpretation, especially by identifying the seven heads of the Dragon (Apoc. 12) and of the first Beast (Apoc. 13) with seven kingdoms that represent the unfolding of Antichrist's reign.[28] Rupert's picture of Antichrist emphasized the view of the opponent of all good as the growing body of evildoers through history—a body that includes Jews, evil rulers, simoniacs (those who bought church offices), and the three sects of "magicians, poets and philosophers."[29] Rupert made no predictions about the time of the Final Antichrist, who would bring the accumulating weight of evil to completion, but by applying images of the Apocalypse to history he is an early witness to a twelfth-century shift in Antichrist speculation.

Rupert's pro-papal application of the Antichrist legend was further developed by Gerhoh of Reichersberg (1093–1169), a pugnacious Bavarian canon who lived at the time of the second great struggle between pope and emperor, the conflict between Alexander III and Frederick Barbarossa that raged between 1159 and 1177. Gerhoh was one of the major historical theorists of his time. His concern with the scriptural patterns that reveal the course of the church's history, and especially with the relations between Antichrist and the papacy, make him an important figure in our story.[30]

Gerhoh's major historical-apocalyptic writings are *The Investigation of Antichrist* (c. 1161) and *The Fourth Watch of the Night* (c. 1167). He uses a number of historical motifs, the most important one taken from the Gospel account of the four watches of the night, during which the apostles rowed on the Sea of Galilee until Jesus appeared to them walking on the waters (see Matt. 14:22–33).[31] Gerhoh saw the four watches as providing an overview of the history of the church. The first watch was the time of the Roman persecution featuring the *antichristus cruentus,* or "Bloody Antichrist," which ended in the tranquillity of Constantine's reign. The second watch was the era of heresy (the *antichristus fraudulentus,* or "Fraudulent Antichrist"), defeated by the confessors. The third saw the inner corruption of the church through simony and evil living (the *antichristus immundus,* or "Impure Antichrist"). The Roman pontiffs from Gregory I to Gregory VII labored against these perversions. Gregory VII's excommunication of Henry IV marked the culmination of this era. "From then, it appears that more dangerous times began, because then there arose a new avarice in the city of Rome. . . . In this fourth watch widespread avarice swollen with desire for gain rules the whole Body of Christ from head to foot."[32] This is the era of the *antichristus avarus,* the "Avaricious Antichrist." The German reformer saw the beginning of the conflict between *regnum* and *sacerdotium* in the time of Gregory VII and Henry IV as the loosing of Satan after his thousand years of captivity predicted in Apocalypse 20. Both priesthood and kingship had been hurt by this conflict, though Gerhoh left no doubt where his sympathies lay.[33]

Gerhoh's account of Antichrist, found primarily in *The Investigation* and *The Fourth Watch,* paradoxically points in two directions—backward toward the collective Tyconian view, and forward in the direction of greater involvement of the papacy with the Antichrist legend. A number of scholars have noted how Gerhoh eschewed much of the extrabiblical legendary material that had collected around the figure of the Final Enemy in the early Middle Ages.[34] The details of his presentation of Antichrist reflect a strongly spiritual view of the growth of the *corpus antichristi* during the history of the Church. To the traditional persecutors and heresiarchs of the first and second watches, he adds a reforming concern with simoniacs and married priests in the third and even in the fourth watch (all the evil aspects of the collective Antichrist continue to exist, carrying on into future historical eras). He attacks the simoniacs at the papal court as "new and modern antichrists,"[35] and in the *Fourth Watch of the Night* he asserts, "From the proliferation of such simoniacs, so prevalent in the last times, will come the Final Antichrist."[36] The buying and selling of sacred things found among simoniacs leads quite logically to the triumph of avarice, both within and without the priesthood, and in the fourth watch of the night the Church suffers the most severe buffeting, for this avarice affects even the present papacy.[37] Gerhoh's moralizing tendency has led some to view him as a fundamentally nonapocalyptic thinker who made Antichrist so present in current abuses that the legend had no real future referent.[38]

However, the other side of Gerhoh's application of the Antichrist legend to his reform ideas challenges this view from three perspectives.

The first is the German canon's repeated insistence on the historicity of the Final Enemy and his assertions that the time of his arrival is imminent.[39] The second is the way in which Gerhoh broke with the Augustinian-Tyconian tradition by linking apocalyptic symbols with contemporary issues, especially those involving the conflict of pope and emperor. One of the most striking of these applications occurs in chapter 19 of *The Investigation of Antichrist,* where Gerhoh establishes an elaborate concordance of three events: (1) the struggle between the Maccabees and Antiochus IV as a type of Antichrist; (2) a recent discomfiture of Barbarossa and his Antipope in Rome; and (3) the coming defeat of the Final Antichrist who will be slain by "brightness of the Lord's coming."[40] Gerhoh does not dwell on these concordances between current events and elements of the apocalyptic scenario as much as Joachim of Fiore was later to do, but his willingness to invoke them in a variety of contexts is a development of the important shift first noted in Rupert.[41]

The third innovative element in Gerhoh's thought is the way in which his reformist attitude focused on the place of the papacy, both within the present pessimistic ecclesiastical situation and in the coming better state of the Church on earth. Gerhoh believed that the Roman curia's venality was a sign that Peter, that is, the papacy, had begun to sink beneath the waves of the *antichristus avarus,* but the reformer was also convinced that Christ would help Peter into the boat, calm the sea of this world that had been stirred up by Antichrist, and bring the papacy safely to the shore of eternity. In his *Commentary on Psalm 64,* which Gerhoh personally delivered to Pope Eugene III in early 1152, he prophesied that "the high priest presiding over the Apostolic See [would be] crowned and exalted over all kingdoms."[42] In the *Investigation of Antichrist* he also spoke of coming reform of the Church through the agency of "spiritual men" (*spirituales*): "Before the final coming, the Church which is the true and living house of the living God, is to be reformed to its ancient practice of apostolic perfection in those who are called and ought to be spiritual men."[43] Thus Gerhoh, like Honorius, looked forward to a coming better state of the Church *after* the time of Antichrist, though he did not speculate about its length.[44] Even more, by putting the office of the papacy at the center of salvation history—a clear reaction to the enhanced status of the papacy, which was the most enduring part of the Great Reform movement—Gerhoh was a harbinger of a major development in late medieval apocalypticism, the growth of the legend of the *pastor angelicus,* the holy pope of the last days who would oppose Antichrist and reform the Church in head and members.[45]

Other pro-papal reformers of the mid–twelfth century also tried to understand current history in light of the symbols of the apocalyptic texts in Scripture. Perhaps the most noted of these was Anselm of Havelberg (c. 1100–1158), a canon of the reformed Premonstratensian order and a papal diplomat. Anselm's three books of *Dialogues* were written in 1149 at the request of Eugene III. The first book contains a sketch of the ages of the Church on the basis of the seven seals of the Apocalypse. Anselm was not the first to use the seven seals in this way, but in his attempt to apply them to concrete events and his willingness to allow for growth (*incrementum*) and diversity (*varietas*) in the Church's history he gave expression to the new historical interests of the twelfth century. He saw his own time as that of the fifth seal (Apoc. 6:9–11), making no prediction regarding the coming of the sixth seal, the time of Antichrist. He presented Antichrist as a traditional collective, an interpretation of a largely Tyconian cast.[46]

Reformers and Antireformers on Antichrist

Disputes within the movement for reform, particularly between hard-line Gregorians and those willing to take a more conciliatory position, were evident from the start. Especially when the Synod of Worms of 1122 brought a truce to the struggle between pope and emperor, the desire for reform in the Church and various movements of revitalization in the religious orders broadened and diversified. The papacy encouraged these more specialized reform movements, such as the groups of reformed canons (priests living a common life according to the Rule of St. Augustine) and the Cistercian mode of Benedictinism.

On the other side, many Christians and many clerics, even ones of goodwill and upright life, were suspicious of the reformers. They did not defend simony, of course, and clerical marriage was increasingly seen as an abuse, but they did not agree that lay investiture (the giving of the symbols of office to a cleric by a lay magnate) was wrong, pointing out that it had been done for centuries. They saw the reformers as revolutionaries who were trying to overturn a Christian society in which the emperor served as God's emissary on earth. They often viewed the reformers' claims to a higher standard of morality as hypocrisy—a mark of the agents of Antichrist! The debate over the nature of Christian society that burned through western Europe from the late eleventh through the twelfth century could use Antichrist language and Antichrist applications on many fronts and for very different purposes.

The Cistercians showed rather less interest in the apocalyptic dimensions of reform than many other groups. Bernard of Clairvaux (1090–1153) was not the founder of the new order, but his magnetic personality and literary gifts made him its foremost spokesman and the dominant figure in the religious life of the mid–twelfth century. The abbot used a fourfold division of the history of the church in which the present third era, that of internal hypocrisy, would be followed by the fourth time, that of Antichrist.[47] Bernard's many letters show a broad use of Antichrist language, especially against the Antipope Anacletus II and his followers in the early 1130s and later against Peter Abelard.[48] But an interesting letter from the 1120s in which Bernard recounts a conversation he had with Norbert of Xanten, the founder of the Premonstratensians, shows that the abbot of Clairvaux did not think the Antichrist was really near. According to Bernard,

> When I asked him [Norbert] what he thought about the Antichrist, he declared himself quite certain that it would be during this present generation that he would be revealed. But upon my asking, when he wished to explain to me the source of this same certainty, I did not think after I had heard his response that I ought to take it for certain. He concluded by saying that he would live to see a general persecution of the Church.[49]

While a few late texts of Bernard indicate that he may have become more willing to see Antichrist as imminent toward the end of his life, especially in the wake of the failure of the Second Crusade he had preached for the Cistercian Pope Eugene III,[50] his use of Antichrist remains on the language level alone. Later Cistercians, following in his wake, made relatively little contribution to the development of the Antichrist legend.

The Premonstratensian followers of Norbert were rather more apocalyptic in outlook. It is unfortunate that Norbert himself did not put into writing his reasons for believing in the proximity of Antichrist. Anselm of Havelberg, while not an innovator in Antichrist lore, showed a concern for the meaning of history, as noted above. Several other Premonstratensians were closer to the founder in their concern over the coming of Antichrist. For instance, in 1147 the priest Gerard of Poehlde wrote to Evermord, the prior of the Premonstratensian house in Magdeburg, claiming that the troubles of the times indicate that the thousand years of Satan's binding were ending ahead of schedule, so that the first Beast of Apocalypse 13 (that is, Antichrist's forerunners) is about to be loosed and Antichrist himself (the second Beast) must soon follow.[51] Eberwin of Steinfeld, a Premonstratensian who corresponded with Bernard of Clairvaux in the early 1140s, sketched a six-age view of the church's history based on an exegesis of the six waterpots of the Cana narrative (John 2). Perhaps under the influence of Rupert of Deutz, he saw the rise of heresy in his day as the mark of the fifth waterpot that was to be used "against the heretics to come at the end of the world." Only the sixth waterpot, which would refresh the faithful at the time of Antichrist, remained.[52]

A good example of the use of the Antichrist legend in terms of a reforming critique of current abuses in the church and Christian society can be found in the poetry of Walter of Chatillon (c. 1135–c. 1185). Walter was a sometime adherent of the court of Henry II of England but broke with Henry over the Becket affair. Walter's poems combine technical virtuosity and biting satire in a style similar to that of John Dryden, five centuries later. He employed Antichrist motifs in several pieces, notably in that entitled *"Dum contemplor animo,"* which is among the finest Antichrist poems of the Middle Ages.[53] Written in the early 1170s, the poem begins with Walter meditating on the sad state of humanity. He is then transported in spirit to a vision of a demonic assembly in Hell where Antichrist addresses the devil:

> Father! What delay prevents me from being born?
> Fate, what prevents me from coming into the world?
> Open gates, because if you hinder my going forth,
> I will leap over the wall in the power of God Beelzebub.[54]

After Antichrist enumerates the standard signs of his proximity, the Fury Allecto addresses the assembly in a more contemporary vein, showing how Henry II's assassination of Becket—"truly more Nero-like than Nero" (*re vera neronior est ipso Nerone*)—is a sign of Antichrist's coming. Her sister Tesiphone answers by pointing to the evil life of the clergy and the schism caused by Frederick Barbarossa as even better contemporary signs:

> Well do you know that Emperor Frederick
> Through whom you have sowed the seeds of schism,
> And therefore put in charge of that schismatic people.
> What better precursor of Antichrist is there? (stanza 24)

Finally, the devil himself ends the verbal strife between the Furies with a speech in which he says he alone knows the time when he will take on flesh as Antichrist, thus showing that the ancient belief in Antichrist as the devil incarnate was poetically alive in the twelfth century, despite centuries of theological objections.

> Behold the days are coming when I will become man
> In order to vanquish Enoch and Elijah with miracles.
> When I snatch away the path of truth from the earth
> Rachel [meaning Christianity] will serve me, and I will blind Lia
>   [meaning the Jews].

He goes on to boast that his control of the world is already almost complete:

> Mine the monasteries, mine the monks,
> Mine the schools, mine the nuns,
> Mine the scepters of kings, mine the Cardinals
> Through whom I put the Church up for sale.

The poem concludes with Satan's commission:

> Go forth, my accomplices, go forth, gods of the nations,
> Go forth and disperse through the corners of the world.
> I will follow you when I take on flesh—that I promise.
> And groaning they took flight. (stanzas 28–30)

What is remarkable about Walter's poem is not only its topicality but also the depth of its reforming pessimism about the current state of the church and the world.[55]

Hildegard of Bingen

Placing Hildegard of Bingen (1098–1179) among the reformers may seem questionable.[56] The aristocratic German abbess was in many ways a conservative who stressed a traditional form of Benedictinism and her own visionary version of monastic theology. She was no great proponent of new papal claims, since she expected the decay of both empire and papacy before the end. Hildegard's major concern was the moral reform of the laity and especially the clergy in light of the history of salvation. Clerical corruption, both sexual and pecuniary, upset her more than anything. Although she did not see Antichrist's arrival as imminent, she thought that Henry IV's attack on Gregory VII marked a new age in history, the beginning of the *tempus muliebre,* the "womanly era" of corruption and decline that set the apocalyptic scenario in action.[57] Hildegard was the first woman to make an important contribution to Antichrist traditions and also one of the more creative twelfth-century thinkers in drawing out the underlying symbolism of the ancient legend.

In her theological masterpiece, the *Scivias,* completed in 1151, Hildegard included a famous vision of the last times in which she saw five beasts standing in the north—a fiery hound, a tawny lion, a pale horse, a black pig, and a gray wolf. These represent the kingdoms or ages of the last times. Christ and a female figure representing the Church also appear.[58] The vision includes a graphic description of Antichrist's birth from the Church's body and his subsequent destruction:

> In her vagina there appeared a monstrous and totally black head with fiery eyes, ears like the ears of a donkey, nostrils and mouth like those of a lion, gnashing with vast open mouth and sharpening its horrible iron teeth in a horrid manner. . . . Lo, the monstrous head removed itself from the place with so great a crash that the entire image of the woman was shaken in all its members. Something like a great mass of much dung was joined to the head. Then, lifting itself upon a mountain, it attempted to ascend to the height of heaven. A stroke like thunder came suddenly and the head was repelled with such force that it both fell from the mountain and gave up the ghost.[59]

This account, which contains what appears to be the earliest direct reference to Antichrist's attempted ascension, was illustrated in the manuscripts of the *Scivias* with a colorful portrayal (Fig. 7).

It is important to note that Hildegard, like Honorius and Gerhoh, foresaw a time after Antichrist's death when his followers would be converted and the church would be renewed. At the vision's end she heard a voice from heaven saying:

> Even though all things on earth are tending toward their end, . . . nevertheless, the Spouse of my Son . . . will never be destroyed either by the heralds of the Son of Perdition or by the Destroyer himself, however much she

FIGURE 7
Antichrist's birth from the
Church and his destruction.
Hildegard of Bingen, *Scivias*
3.11, from Eibington Abbey
codex 1, a modern copy of
the lost Rupertsberg
manuscript (late twelfth
century). Reproduced from
*Hildegarde von Bingen. Wisse
der Wege. Scivias* (Salzburg:
Otto Müller, 1954), Tafel 32.

will be attacked by them. At the end of time she will arise more powerful and more secure; she will appear more beautiful and shining so that she may go forth in this way more sweetly and agreeably to the embraces of her Beloved.[60]

The explanation of this vision (the *Scivias* is structured according to visionary accounts that substitute for Scripture and subsequent exegetical explanations) includes a lengthy description of Antichrist and his reign.[61]

In her later *Book of Divine Works,* finished in 1174, Hildegard expanded on the earlier account. In the tenth vision of book 3 of this work, she identified her own time with that of the fiery dog, the *tempus muliebre* mentioned above.[62] Her virulent attack on clerical vices, especially those of venality and impurity, led her to advocate a disestablishment of many of the perquisites of the clergy.[63] But she envisioned her own era as being succeeded by the *tempus virile* of the lion, a millenarian time when the

Church would be cleansed and many Jews and pagans would be converted (3.10.17–20). Then would follow the age of the pallid horse, a time of sorrow and persecution in which both the empire and the papacy would fail (3.10.21–25). In the time of the black pig (3.10.26), heresy would flourish to lead the way for the time of the gray wolf, when Antichrist would devour the faithful (3.10.27–36). Once again, though, Hildegard ended by predicting a time of renewal *after* the Final Enemy's destruction (3.10.37).[64]

In examining the German abbess's two accounts of Antichrist, we find a presentation that depends on the standard Western view found in Adso's *Letter* but that also contains some new materials. Hildegard possessed one of the most fertile symbolic imaginations of the Middle Ages, and this is evident in her picture of the Final Enemy. The abbess's account needs to be understood in light of her whole view of salvation history in which the evil male figure of Satan envies and attacks humanity symbolized as female in the progressive manifestations of Eve, the Synagogue, Mary, and the Church.[65] But at the end of time, Satan works, not through himself but through his human agent, as the logic of the Adamic myth dictates: "The ancient enemy whom divine strength cast into the pit of the abyss like lead into raging waters, because he wished to establish iniquity. . . , since he had overcome the first man, thought that he would be able to complete what he had begun through another man, that is, Antichrist. . . ."[66]

The male-female symbolism in which Hildegard cast her understanding of the ancient oppositions allowed her to bring out new dimensions of the legend, specifically sexual ones. There are what medievalist Neal R. Clemens has termed "overtones of sexual violence" in Hildegard's account of Satan's assault on Eve, and she also presents the evil-living clergy who are Antichrist's forerunners as guilty of sexual assault on the Virgin *Ecclesia*.[67] Just as God willed his son to be born from a virgin mother for the salvation of humanity (*Scivias* 3.11.24), so Satan will see to it that Antichrist is born from an unchaste woman whose licentiousness parodies the purity of Mary in the traditional Gospel account of Christ's conception and birth.[68] Furthermore, Hildegard goes out of her way to emphasize that Antichrist's false teaching consists primarily in his attack on the Christian doctrine of virginity by means of a naturalistic argument regarding hot and cold bodies (*Book of Divine Works* 3.10.30). Antichrist is a sexual criminal, one whose very birth from his typological mother, the Church, is so violent and bloody (as recounted in the *Scivias* vision) that it can be seen as a kind of reverse rape.[69]

Several other innovations appear in Hildegard's presentation of Antichrist. He deceives his followers in various ways (3.11.28), especially through a pretended death and resurrection (3.11.29, and *Book of Divine Works* 3.10.32). In the *Book of Divine Works* 3.10.32 (more briefly in *Scivias* 3.11.31), the account of the false resurrection based on Apocalypse 13:3 is followed by a curious notation regarding the writing or inscription that Antichrist will place on the forehead of his followers (see Apoc. 13:16–17):

> Through it he will insert every evil into them, just as the ancient serpent did when he deceived humanity and afterward had them in his power by inflaming their lust. By means of this writing that is against baptism and the Christian name he will be so infused into them by magic art that they will not even desire to leave him. They will all be named after him, just as Christians are named after Christ.[70]

Hildegard conceives of this inscription in cosmic terms, as a writing discovered by Satan and hidden throughout history until he reveals it to Antichrist. Antichrist presents the inscription as a new nature, one contrasted with the writing that the Holy Spirit engraves on the hearts of the faithful (see 2 Cor. 3:3).

The other major novelty in Hildegard's account is her emphasis on Antichrist's attempt to ascend to heaven. The German abbess seems to have been the first to grasp the symbolic necessity that Antichrist's parody of this culminating event in Jesus' earthly life would also constitute the moment of his destruction. As she summarizes:

> For when that Son of Perdition would raise himself on high by diabolical art, divine power will throw him down and the stench of pitch and sulfur will receive him. The crowds standing about will flee to take refuge in the mountains. Such great terror will capture those who see and hear this that they will renounce the devil and his son and will be converted to the true faith of baptism.[71]

Hildegard's rich account of Antichrist demonstrates that the mythological oppositions at the heart of the legend were still capable of considerable development in the twelfth century.[72] The abbess's views were well known in the later Middle Ages, not so much through her own writings as through the selections made from them by a Cistercian monk, Gebeno of Eberbach, about 1220. Gebeno's *Mirror of Future Times,* or *Pentachronon,* was put together as an answer to claims from the followers of Joachim of Fiore that Antichrist was already born.[73]

Antichrist in Twelfth-Century Politics

A contemporary of Hildegard who can be thought of as a reformer, but of a special sort, is Otto of Freising (c. 1111–1158), uncle of Frederick Barbarossa, Cistercian monk, bishop, and diplomat. Otto's major work, *The Two Cities,* is a neo-Augustinian universal history extending down to 1146 C.E. Though he supported the justice of Gregory VII's excommunication of Henry IV, seeing the Church's growing power in relation to the empire as the fulfillment of the Danielic prophecy about the stone not cut by hands that destroys the idol (Dan. 2:34), he viewed the conflict between Church and empire as a sign that "the times were passing from perfection to overthrow."[74] The German prelate's historical pessimism (he was convinced the end was near, though he did not predict the actual date) is evident in the seventh book of *The Two Cities,* an important account of the events of his own lifetime, as well as in book 8 where he discusses the last things.[75]

Contemporaries of Otto of Freising used the Antichrist legend to critique reformers' attacks on the imperial office. Their words provide evidence that the legend had not lost its imperial connections. The famous *Play of Antichrist* (*Ludus de Antichristo*) is the earliest and the best of the many dramas devoted to the Final Enemy.[76] It survives in only one manuscript from the south German abbey of Tegernsee and appears to date from shortly after the mid–twelfth century. It has been suggested that the play was composed and put on for Frederick Barbarossa—an attractive idea, though not proven.[77] The Tegernsee drama was written by someone who had a good knowledge of the major texts of imperial apocalyptic, especially the Pseudo-Methodius, but it is not its learning as much as its panache that makes it one of the most convincing artistic versions of the Antichrist legend.

The *Play of Antichrist,* like much early medieval drama, is liturgically stylized. What sets it off from other early medieval plays is its overt political agenda. At a time when German imperial claims were under attack both from papal reformers and from the rising national monarchies, especially in France, the play insists that the fate of Christianity rests in the hands of the emperor; he alone controls the destiny of all Christians until the Antichrist (whom no human power can withstand) appears. The French king appears as a weakling; other monarchs have bit parts. The pope has nothing more than a walk-on role, as befits the emperor's chaplain, though hypocritical clerics who represent the reformers are important in Antichrist's retinue. With a cast and subject matter embracing the whole world and its destiny, the Tegernsee *Play of Antichrist* cries out for large-scale Hollywood production.[78]

The *Play of Antichrist* opens with an assembly of kings, Christian and non-Christian, seated in a circle disputing the leadership of the world.[79] Paganism (*Gentilitas*), represented by the king of Babylon, and Judaism (*Synagoga*) plead their cause, but the Church (*Ecclesia*), accompanied by Mercy and Truth (see Ps. 84:11) as well as pope and emperor, wins the day. The emperor then demands fealty of the other Christian rulers. The French king resists with proud boasts but is soon defeated in battle (a scene that doubtless was received with cheers by the original audience). The king of the Greeks and the king of Jerusalem follow suit, and even the king of Babylon is defeated after attacking Jerusalem. Having established German hegemony over the world, the play then shifts to an apocalyptic scenario.

In accordance with tradition, the German emperor fulfills his apocalyptic function by laying down his crown in Jerusalem. He does not die, however (as in the Pseudo-Methodius), but retires to his position as king of Germany. This is the signal for Antichrist's entry (with a change in meter), marking the beginning of the second part of the play. The stage directions read:

> Then, while *Ecclesia, Gentilitas,* and *Synagoga* sing in turn, as above, the Hypocrites come forth in silence with the semblance of humility, bowing down on all sides and winning the favor of the laity. Finally, all come before *Ecclesia* and the throne of the King of Jerusalem, who receives them fittingly and submits himself totally to their advice. Immediately, Antichrist enters with a breastplate under his other garments. Accompanying him are Hypocrisy on the right and Heresy on the left.[80]

When the Hypocrites hail Antichrist as the "reformer" of the Church, the cat is out of the bag—the author is painting the reform party as Antichrist's adherents who falsely claim to be the only true Christians.[81]

The Hypocrites depose the king of Jerusalem (just as Gregory VII had claimed power to depose rulers) and then crown Antichrist. The former king goes to the king of the Germans, telling him that his abdication (*discessio,* see 2 Thess. 2:3) was wrong because it has let loose "the law of superstition." But Antichrist is ready for this challenge and sends messengers to all the kings of the earth, gaining their obedience. Only the king of the Germans resists, confuting the Hypocrites (as the German emperors had resisted the reformers) and defeating Antichrist's army. With a foretaste of Bismarckian "Blood and Iron" the triumphant German king sings:

> Bloodshed must preserve a country's honor,
> And valor drive out all her enemies.
> Blood alone redeems a tainted name,
> And blood will keep the Empire free from shame.[82]

What force cannot achieve, guile may. Antichrist performs three miracles, including raising a man from the dead, at which the king of the Germans acknowledges him as God and gives him homage. Then the German king leads Antichrist's army forth to conquer the king of Babylon and *Gentilitas,* and the Jews are converted by the Hypocrites. Antichrist is now Lord of the world.

At this point the final part of the play, marked by another change in meter, begins, with the entrance of the two witnesses. They denounce Antichrist, strip off the veil that has blinded *Synagoga* (i.e., the Jews) up till now, and convert them to the true faith. When they are brought before Antichrist, they denounce him:

> You root of evil, foe of truth,
> False Antichrist, corruptor of the faith,
> Blaspheming author of iniquity,
> Liar in the mask of deity.[83]

The witnesses are slain and Antichrist calls all the kings of the earth together to worship him (there is no mention of an attempted ascension). "Suddenly there is a sound over Antichrist's head," the stage direction reads, "and he falls and all his men flee." *Ecclesia* closes with a hymn signaling universal return to the faith. The *Play of Antichrist* is as remarkable for its dramatic power as for its political tendentiousness. It illustrates just how varied and creative the use of Antichrist rhetoric was in the twelfth century.

Joachim of Fiore on Antichrist

The most original and influential of all medieval apocalyptic authors was the twelfth-century monk Joachim of Fiore.[84] Joachim became a monk at a mature age, after some years as a wandering preacher. His early commitment to the Cistercian order began to waver in the 1180s, when his visionary experiences led him to a new theology of history and soon to a break with the Cistercians so that he could found his own order of Fiore in the remote mountains of his native Calabria. In the last two decades of the twelfth century, Joachim, who achieved notoriety in his time as a prophet, worked on a series of major scriptural commentaries, especially the *Book of Concordance* (which gives an introduction to his theory of exegesis and a commentary on parts of the Old Testament), the *Ten-Stringed Psaltery* (exegeting the Psalms and the liturgy), and the *Exposition on the Apocalypse,* his masterwork. An unfinished *Treatise on the Four Gospels* as well as a number of shorter tracts survive. Of special import is the *Book of Figures,* a series of diagrams and symbolic presentations of the major images of the abbot's thought, which seems to have been begun by him but was probably completed by his disciples.

Joachim was typical of the twelfth century in his reformist outlook. The Calabrian abbot believed that the Church had fallen away from its original ideals, both in head and members, but he did not look to institutional reforms for its betterment. He felt that in the conflicts between pope and emperor, the papacy should play the role, not of political and military opposition but of the suffering servant attacked by the minions of Antichrist. Unlike the other reformers we have considered, Joachim did not hark back to the primitive church and seek to revive its practices and morals. His progressive view of history placed the magnet of reform in the future, not the past—in the coming era of the Holy Spirit. The prime agent of reform for him was the monastic life. Under divine guidance, monasticism would gradually progress to higher stages until, in the coming era (*status* was his usual term), the papacy and Christian society itself would be fully monasticized and spiritualized. Joachim was a loyal subject of the papal church of the second *status,* but his apocalyptic mode of spiritual reform was new and distinctive. It implied a very different model of reform from what most late medieval popes were willing to allow.

Joachim did not write a separate treatise on Antichrist. His view of the Last Enemy is presented in his analyses of Scripture, as had been customary for many centuries. The Calabrian's contribution to the Antichrist legend can be understood only in light of his general theology of history, so we must begin with a few remarks on this.

What makes Joachim of Fiore so significant in the history of apocalypticism? First, the tendency to link apocalyptic symbolism with concrete past and present events reached a new level in the Calabrian abbot. Despite his politeness toward Augustine, Joachim's theology of history is fundamentally at odds with that of the bishop of Hippo in its conviction that God has revealed history's plan in Scripture and that the gift of "spiritual understanding" (*intelligentia spiritualis*) of the Bible allows one to read the meaning of all events—past, present, and future. The abbot of Fiore also broke with Augustine and the Tyconian tradition in his return to millenarianism, that is, in his conviction that history was not just an inexorable accumulation of ills until the final and worst of all, Antichrist's persecution, but rather that God's plan included a new and better stage of the church on earth before the dawn of eternity. Like a number of other twelfth-century authors (Honorius, Rupert, and Hildegard, all of whom built on the ancient motif of the forty-five days after Antichrist based on the discrepancies in Daniel), Joachim held that this blessed period would come *after* the defeat of Antichrist (at least the Antichrist of this era). But he differed from his predecessors in the grounds on which he argued for this *post*-Antichrist millennium.[85] Finally, Joachim was unusual, from the theological point of view at least, in that the basis for his new apocalypticism was not so much a reworking of tradition as a new creation based upon his attempt to give a trinitarian grounding to historical process.[86]

Beginning from this trinitarian perspective will help us understand one of the most distinctive aspects of the abbot's view of Antichrist—his reinvention of the dual Antichrists of the patristic era. For Joachim the meaning of history *is* exegesis; that is, God's judgment over history is grasped only through the interpretation of the Bible. The Bible reveals that God is a Trinity of Father, Son, and Holy Spirit. For Joachim this meant that the inner life of the Trinity must be inscribed in the world the Trinity has created. Joachim was not interested in cosmology, that is, the world as created object, but in eschatology, that is, in the world as a process of historical development whose inner connections were expressions of the life of the Trinity.

The interconnection between Trinity and history, according to Joachim, is revealed in the Scriptures in two ways—the pattern of "Alpha," by means of which the three persons of Father, Son, and Holy Spirit each have a particular *status* reserved for them; and the pattern of "Omega," through which the persons of Father and Son are the joint source of the Holy Spirit, so that the letter of the Old Testament (ascribed to the Father) and that of the New Testament (ascribed to the Son) must eventually produce the flourishing of the spiritual understanding of both Testaments in a coming time of exegetical and historical fulfillment.[87] Joachim's calculations of the concordances—the agreements or parallels between events and persons in the Old Testament and events and persons in the time of the New Testament (this was a part of Scripture's literal sense for him)—led him to see his own time as marking the final years of the second *status* and the dawning of the third. Though he was careful not to make precise predictions (probably more hesitant in writing than in his preaching and conversation), the inner logic of his thought demanded that the end of the second *status* be realized soon after 1200. "This [the crisis of the second *status*] will not take place in the days of your grandchildren or in the old age of your children, but in your own days, few and evil."[88]

Within this new apocalyptic theology of history, Antichrist—both collective, multiple, and individual—played a key role. In one of his key presentations of Antichrist, the "Dragon Figure" of the *Book of Figures* (Fig. 8), the abbot noted:

> John and John's Master [Christ, see Matt. 24:4] say many Antichrists will come. Paul, on the other hand, foretells that there will be one. Just as many holy kings, priests, and prophets went before the one Christ who was king, priest, and prophet, so likewise many unholy kings, false prophets, and antichrists will go before the one Antichrist who will pretend that he is a king, a priest, and a prophet.[89]

This text introduces us to the way in which Joachim put together the collective and individual aspects of the Antichrist legend as well as how he strove to bring out new elements of the underlying opposition between Christ and Antichrist. Though the abbot's teaching on Antichrist was original, he insisted that his doctrine was based solely on the Bible, and he eschewed "the useless things drawn from apocryphal writings about the origin and deeds of Antichrist and the end of the world."[90]

Like many of his twelfth-century predecessors, Abbot Joachim distinguished a number of times or eras (*tempora* is his usual word) in the history of the Church during the New Testament era of the Son. The seven seals of the Apocalypse, the book that contains the "fullness of history" (*plenitudo historiae*), provided him with his favorite pattern.[91] On the basis of concordances, he argued for a parallel between seven persecutions of the Jews in the Old Testament and seven times of persecution in the New. This pattern was set forth with symbolic power in the figure of the seven-headed Dragon from Apocalypse 12: "The seven heads of the Dragon signify seven tyrants by whom the persecutions of the Church were begun."[92] In the figure he numbers these antichrists as Herod and the persecution of the Jews,

FIGURE 8   Seven-headed dragon figure illustrating Apocalypse 12. Joachim of Fiore, *Liber figurarum (Book of Figures),* early thirteenth century. Reproduced from Leone Tondelli, Marjorie E. Reeves, Beatrice Hirsch-Reich, *Il libro delle figure dell'Abate Gioachino da Fiore* (Turin: SEI, 1953), Tavola 14.

Nero and the persecution of the pagans, Constantius and the persecution of the heretics, Muhammad and the persecution of the Saracens, "Mesemoth" and the persecution of the sons of Babylon, Saladin and the sixth persecution, and "the Seventh King, who is properly called Antichrist, although there will be another like him, no less evil, symbolized by the tail."[93] The abbot speaks of this individual as the "great, or greatest Antichrist" (*magnus Antichristus, maximus Antichristus*—terms he seems to have invented), and he was convinced that the signs of the times indicated that he was imminent, indeed, that he was already born and present in the world. Three separate accounts of interviews with Joachim—one with Pope Lucius III in 1183 or 1184, another with Richard the Lionhearted in the winter of 1190–91, and a third with the Cistercian Abbot Adam of Perseigne in 1195—all indicate that Joachim made such claims. In the *Exposition* he also refers to "that great Antichrist whom I think is present in the world."[94]

Before we investigate what Joachim says about this Antichrist and why he was convinced that he was already present, we must reflect on why the abbot refers to "another like him, no less evil, figured in the tail."[95] The need for two special Antichrists, one before and one after the millennial third *status* of the Holy Spirit, as Robert E. Lerner has shown, was demanded both by Joachim's reading of the Apocalypse and by the dynamics of his trinitarian view of history.[96]

I have elsewhere characterized Joachim's exegesis as "simultaneously world-historical, 'ordinal' (in the sense of comprising a history of religious *ordines*), apocalyptic, utopian and trinitarian."[97] Joachim's complex exegesis of the Apocalypse considered the book as both *recapitulative* in the sense that it kept repeating the same message (and hence the seven seals told of the seven persecutions) and also *successive* since the whole book gave an extended history of the same seven persecutions. This meant that the Apocalypse's sixth part (Apoc. 16:18–19:21 in Joachim's view) needed to be carefully studied in order to understand the present dangers to the church and the future course of history. From this perspective, the seven-headed Beast who reappears in Apocalypse 17:8–18 once again symbolizes the seven Antichrists who persecute the church through its six times (*Exposition,* fols. 196ra–198rb). However, after the Beast and his allies are defeated (Apoc. 19:11–21), the description of the millenarian reign of Christ and the saints on earth follows in Apocalypse 20:1–6. For Joachim this can be nothing else but the coming seventh *tempus* of the church, which is also the third *status,* the era of the triumph of the Holy Spirit (*Exposition,* fols. 209va–214va). After the thousand years (which Joachim does not take as a literal millennium, but as nonetheless a real historical period of uncertain duration), Satan is loosed and mobilizes Gog and Magog for the final battle (Apoc. 20:7–10). For the abbot of Fiore, then, Gog can be none other than a Final (*ultimus*) Antichrist who will perform a similar function at the end of the third *status* as the Antichrist of the second *status* represented by the seventh head. Although Joachim only gradually and to some degree hesitatingly worked out this novel exegesis,[98] by the time of the *Book of Figures* he was prepared to argue for the necessity of two Antichrists on the basis of a new application of the ancient theme of the complete opposition between Christ and Antichrist that had always fueled the legend's growth. Just as Christ has two historical manifestations, the first hidden and the other open at the end of time, so too Satan will do his work first secretly through the lies and deceit of the "Seventh-Head" Antichrist and then openly through the assault of the "Tail-Gog" Antichrist. According to Robert E. Lerner, "The Antichrist of the tail was Joachim's greatest novelty, for no one hitherto had posited a final Antichristian persecution coming after an ultimate earthly Sabbath."[99]

Joachim's teaching about the seventh-head Antichrist was also highly original and was to make an important contribution to the legend. The way in which the abbot tied the advent of this persecutor to major contemporary events represents a culmination of a tendency going back a century. On the basis of his concordances, Joachim insisted that the sixth time of the Church would see a double persecution—one that had already begun with Saladin and his reconquest of Jerusalem, the other soon to come from Antichrist. Indeed, he often treated them as two sides of the same tribulation:

> In that time also the seventh head of the Dragon will arise, namely, that king who is called Antichrist, and a multitude of false prophets with him. We think that he will arise from the West and will come to the aid of that king who will be the head of the pagans. He will perform great signs before him and his army, just as Simon Magus did in the sight of Nero.[100]

Joachim was unsure whether the pagan ally of the seventh head would be Saladin or another Muslim ruler soon to follow, but he knew the time was short. For the Calabrian abbot this all meant that the seventh head would not be a Jew born from the tribe of Dan but a false Christian from the West.

As mentioned above, Joachim saw the seventh head as imitating Christ's salvific roles as priest, king, and prophet. This triple formula provides the key to the Calabrian's thought on the nature of the seventh-head Antichrist and also an explanation for some of the problems found in his presentations. Antichrist is certainly a king, but Joachim rarely spends much time discussing the royal aspect. At times he falls into a kind of prophetic ambiguity, as in the discussion of the two Beasts of Apocalypse 13 (*Exposition,* fols. 162ra–168rb), where he begins by suggesting that these represent the two aspects, king and priest, of the Antichrist but then shifts to talking about the kingly aspect more in terms of the Saracen threat (the sixth head) who will ally with Western heretics (fol. 167vb).[101] This passage goes on to mingle both aspects of the imminent danger:

> Just as the Beast from the Sea is held to be a great king from his sect who is like Nero and almost emperor of the whole world, so the Beast ascending from the earth is held to be a great prelate [*magnum prelatum*] who will be

like Simon Magus and like a universal pope [*universalis pontifex*] in the entire world. He is that Antichrist of whom Paul said he would be lifted up
and opposed to everything that is said to be God, or that is worshipped, and
that he would sit in God's temple showing himself as God [2 Thess. 2:4].[102]

Joachim always identified God's temple not with a rebuilt Jerusalem
structure, but with the temple of the Church, so in this passage he hints
that the "priestly" aspect of Antichrist implies that he will be a false pope
(in reality a member of a heretical sect) who will deceive the faithful as
well as the Jews.[103] Joachim's thought thus seems to represent a step on the
road to the full-blown conception of a papal Antichrist, though it must be
stressed that he also emphasized the role of a true and holy pope of the
time of the crisis of the second *status,* who, like Gerhoh's successor of
Peter, would not waver but would be strengthened by divine aid to preach
against the Enemy.[104]

A distinctive meaning is given to the "prophetic" role of the seventh-
head Antichrist in Joachim, though it is present more by implication than
direct assertion. Christ's role as true prophet or teacher, says Joachim, was
connected with the revelation of the spiritual understanding of Scripture.
Since the inner meaning of all history is the growth of this spiritual understanding,[105] Antichrist, the false teacher who performs only outward
wonders, is contrasted with Christ, who reveals the inner, spiritual understanding that is to be completed by the coming of the Holy Spirit. Commenting on Apocalypse 5:7, where the Lamb takes the scroll from the
hand of the Ancient of Days, Joachim notes that Christ's opening of the
seven seals signifies the uncovering of the mysteries of the spiritual understanding from the time of his resurrection. He goes on to say, "Just as
Jannes and Mambres performed signs through incantations [see 2 Tim.
3:8], and Antichrist will do many similar deeds of error, there is always a
worry that the disciples see only the external signs and do not correctly
assess interior matters in spiritual understanding" (*Exposition,* fols. 111vb–
112ra). In other words, Antichrist gives false instruction by external signs,
while Christ reveals inner spiritual understanding.

Joachim of Fiore's new view of Antichrist was to prove influential
over many centuries. By placing it within the context of twelfth-century
debates over the nature of apocalyptic reform and its attendant fears of
Antichrist, we can judge the roots of its power on later ages. The Calabrian abbot summed up a century of debate over the meaning of the last
events and their relation to the current state of the Church.

CHAPTER SIX

COUNTERFEIT HOLINESS

THE PAPAL ANTICHRIST (1200–1335)

P oets and artists made as great a contribution to the Antichrist legend in the later Middle Ages as did theologians and polemicists. Important innovations, of course, took place among the apocalyptic propagandists, but the theological component of the Antichrist legend in the late Middle Ages built upon the past more than it took off in new directions. In this chapter I will look at the major strands of Antichrist traditions during the period from 1200 to 1335 and will also try to introduce the literary and pictorial presentations that reveal how much Antichrist haunted the late medieval imagination.

Through the Great Reform movement and its aftermath, the papacy had become the central religious institution of Western Christianity. Innocent III (1198–1216), arguably the most able and powerful of the medieval successors of Peter, was the pope to whom Joachim of Fiore wrote his respectful "Testament" in 1200, asking for papal correction of his apocalyptic writings. More than a century later, the imperious John XXII (1316–1334) was widely identified as Antichrist by Joachim's followers. During the tumultuous years between these two popes, Western Christianity and the papacy passed from a period of expansion, confidence, and great hopes for reform to a time of crisis and adversity marked by the Avignon Captivity of popes like John, who were seen as enemies of reform for abandoning their true home in Rome. Antichrist traditions reflected many historical currents during these years—none more so than those connected with the papacy and its relation to reform.

Antichrist—individual and collective, single and double, tyrant and deceiver—is found in many forms and permutations during this period. To bring some order into this presentation we can distinguish three broad traditions of Antichrist in the later Middle Ages: (1) the standard view dependent on scriptural exegesis and very often also on Adso's *Letter;* (2) the "applied" standard view that connected Antichrist traditions, often in a reformist way, to current historical events and often to expectations of the imminence of the Final Enemy; and (3) Joachite views of Antichrist, which in most cases were also applied to contemporary events and fears of an imminent end.

The Legacy of Adso

The Scholastic thinkers of the thirteenth century accepted the standard view of Antichrist with few exceptions. The most influential theological presentation came from the pen of a Dominican contemporary of Thomas Aquinas, Hugh Ripelin of Strassburg. His *Compendium of Theological Truth,* written about 1265, was a simplified handbook that often circulated under the names of better-known teachers, like Albert the Great, Thomas, and even Bonaventure. Its seventh book includes a succinct account of the Final Enemy dependent on the *Gloss,* Adso, and other authorities.[1] Noteworthy is the lengthy description of the four ways by which Antichrist will deceive the world: "by cunning persuasion, by the working of miracles, by giving of gifts, and by displaying tortures." Hugh clearly describes Antichrist's triple parody of the major events of salvation history—making fire descend on his followers in imitation of Pentecost, pretending to arise from the dead in a false resurrection, and trying to ascend into heaven.[2] Hugh makes no attempt to relate any of his material to current events, let alone to make predictions about the future. The same is true for other popular compendia of traditional Antichrist teaching from later in the period under review, such as that of the Franciscan Scotist Hugh of Novocastro.[3]

The reluctance of many adherents of the standard version of Antichrist to view current events as signs of his advent was underscored by the Apocalypse interpretation of the most influential of late medieval exegetes, the Franciscan Nicholas of Lyra, writing in 1329.[4] Nicholas used a linear historical reading of the last book of the Bible pioneered by two other Franciscans, Alexander of Bremen in the 1240s and Peter Aureol in 1319. This interpretation saw John's prophecy as a straightforward account of the history of the church. In reaction to contemporary disputes over the applied apocalyptic readings of the Franciscan Spirituals (more on these below), Nicholas made a strict division at the end of Apocalypse 16. Everything described prior to that he held to have already been fulfilled in history. For example, the two Beasts of chapter 13 do not refer to Antichrist and his prophet but to two seventh-century persecutors, the Persian king Chosroes and Muhammad. From chapter 17 on, however, everything John wrote pertains to true prophecy and cannot be known with security. Adopting an ironical stance, Nicholas prefaced his commentary on these chapters with the words:

> Because "I am not a prophet, or the son of a prophet" [Amos 7:14], I will not say anything about the future, except what can be taken from Scripture or the words of the saints and the established teachers. Therefore, I leave the interpretation of this to the wise. Were the Lord to grant me its understanding, I would be happy to share it with others.[5]

He explicitly denied that the arrival of Antichrist was near.[6]

The popularity of the Adsonian view of Antichrist is evident from the literature, especially the vernacular poetry, of the period 1200 to 1335 C.E. Much of this didactic verse, which often combines an account of Antichrist's life with the "Fifteen Signs of Doomsday," is of minor artistic value, but it does indicate the growing vernacular popularity of the legend.[7]

The most original French version of the standard picture of Antichrist is found in Huon de Méry's romance, *The Tournament of Antichrist,* a transposition of the Antichrist legend into a courtly genre. A monk from near Troyes, Huon wrote his poem of 3544 lines sometime about 1240.[8] Medievalist Richard K. Emmerson has provided a good discussion of Huon's treatment of the Antichrist legend as psychomachia, that is, an internal warfare between virtues and vices in the soul.[9] The poet presents the tournament under the guise of an adventure he experienced as a young knight while on an expedition to Brittany. He is invited by Bras-de-Fer, Antichrist's Moorish chamberlain, to witness the tournament between Antichrist and his forces and those of Christ, the Lord of Heaven. There is a lengthy description of the combatants (on the one side vices, demons, pagan gods, heretics, and enemies of France like the English; on the other virtues, angels, and French heroes like Gawain). Then the battle begins and Huon is wounded by Venus. Antichrist and his horde are defeated and agree to retire to their castle of *Desesperence* (Despair), while Huon, who had arrived with Antichrist's army, is healed by Contrition and Confession and departs with Christ's forces. Later Antichrist and his minions escape to continue ravaging the world. Huon wisely decides to enter the monastery of Saint-Germain-des-Pres.

This moralizing interpretation takes its worthy place in the long line of internalizations of the Antichrist legend stretching back at least to Origen. In contrasting Christ as perfect knight with Antichrist, the anti-knight, Huon, as Richard Emmerson puts it, "does not develop the tradition for its own sake but for his special purposes, as a popular way to describe a cosmic conflict over the soul of an individual Christian."[10] While the internalization of Antichrist traditions was not new, the presentation of it in courtly guise was distinctive.

The Adsonian tradition is also present in Middle English literature of the period. The *Cursor Mundi* is a long poem of the early fourteenth century giving a biblical account of world history from creation to the end.[11] Under the sixth age of the world, 450 lines are devoted to a poetical rendition of the "Alcuin" version of Adso's *Letter*.[12] The didactic purpose of the work is enlivened by considerable legendary accretions found in the Alcuin text and sometimes expanded upon in the *Cursor*. Broad scatological humor is displayed in the passage where the poem expands upon the brief Alcuinian reference to Antichrist shitting in fear at Christ's sudden appearance:

> For crist com sal be sa bright
> That thoru that mikel lorde light
> Him [Antichrist] sal of stand so mikel awe,
> That all the filthes of his maugh
> Sal breste out atte his fondament
> For drede of crist he sal be shent,
> Sua sal he peris al be-shetin
> Bath with drede and soru beten. (lines 22, 391–98)

The *Cursor Mundi,* like the French literature noted above, shows how the traditional picture was transmitted and adapted to the vernacular audiences of the later Middle Ages.

The standard view also served as the basis for most of the pictorial Antichrist materials of the period. These images rarely provide any clues to indicate they were meant to have direct applications to current events. Two major groups of Antichrist manuscript portrayals as well as several minor ones[13] were created in the period beginning at the end of the twelfth century.

The first major collection is found in the Moralized Bibles (*Bible Moralisée*), vast picture Bibles containing excerpts from the Scriptures and glosses providing moral and typological interpretations of scriptural figures and events.[14] Over five thousand illustrations are found in the complete versions of these manuscripts, which were originally produced for the French royal family between about 1220 and 1235.[15] The Moralized Bibles are rich in Antichrist imagery, based both on his Old Testament types[16] and on the New Testament passages traditionally taken as referring to him, especially in the Apocalypse. Nine different classes of scenes of the Final Enemy are found.[17] Particularly interesting are the portrayals of Antichrist as a three-headed human tyrant, apparently the artists' way of underlining his claim to be God, that is, the Trinity (Fig. 9).

Among the hundreds of illustrated Apocalypse manuscripts of the Middle Ages, the most plentiful are the Anglo-French group.[18] They usually include the text of the Apocalypse in Latin or in French, a commentary,[19] and eighty to a hundred illustrations. These richly decorated manuscripts (which are probably related to lost Romanesque predecessors) began to appear in England around 1240 and soon spread to northern France and beyond. They were popular in the fourteenth century and lasted into the fifteenth, influencing much subsequent Apocalypse and Antichrist iconography. The Anglo-French apocalypses appear to reflect reformist clerical concerns that soon also became popular in courtly aristocratic circles, where the Apocalypse came to be viewed as an adventure or romance containing a moral message about the conflict of good and evil in human life (not unlike what we have seen in Huon de Méry).[20] These illustrated Apocalypses are little concerned with the course of history and the imminence of the end; their very arrangement of picture and gloss disturbs the narrative flow of the text and instead promotes contemplation of the Apocalypse's moral message.

Art historian Jessie Poesch has studied the extensive Antichrist imagery found in these Apocalypses.[21] For Antichrist iconography the most important development is the series, included in some Anglo-French Apocalypses, of pictures of Antichrist's career incorporating materials from 2 Thessalonians and Adso's *Letter*. These constitute a "minilife" of the Final Enemy.[22] The full version of this cycle has five scenes: (1) the two

FIGURE 9   Antichrist as three-headed tyrant (detail), illustration from the *Harley Manuscript 1527*, fol. 127r (mid–thirteenth century), (Apoc. 9:1–3). Courtesy of The British Library.

witnesses preach before Antichrist; (2) Antichrist seated on his throne orders the execution of the two witnesses; (3) Antichrist's tree miracle and the slaughter of the faithful; (4) Antichrist seated in the temple as God with Christians being bribed and threatened; and (5) Antichrist's destruction in the temple (see Figs. 10–11).

The symbolic opposition between Antichrist, the false judge who orders the death of the two witnesses, and Christ, who justly condemns Antichrist to death, is also taken up in the few monumental portrayals of the Final Enemy from the High Middle Ages. Two scenes of Antichrist (with Old French inscriptions) in the North Rose of Notre Dame in Paris, dating from about 1260, portray this contrast.[23] About 1330 the Church of Santa Maria in Porto Fuori outside Ravenna was decorated with a large fresco (since destroyed) of the Last Judgment and history of Antichrist. In

FIGURE 10

The two witnesses preaching before Antichrist (Apoc. 11:1–6). Paris, Bibliothèque Nationale, ms. fran. 403, fol. 17r (mid–thirteenth century). Reproduced from L. Delisle and P. Meyer, *L'Apocalypse en français au XIIIe siècle. Reproduction phototypique* (Paris: Firmin-Didot, 1900).

the middle of the arch over the altar, Christ, the true judge of humanity, sits enthroned. On his right hand is a scene of Antichrist as tyrant commanding the death of the two witnesses. On his left, Michael slays the enthroned (not the ascending) Antichrist with his sword (Fig. 12). Theologically, the clear contrast between the true and false judgments makes this among the most satisfying of all Antichrist portrayals.[24]

Identifying Antichrist in the Thirteenth Century

Although many refrained from imbuing inherited Antichrist views with specific apocalyptic intent, it was also possible to use these traditional materials for more than theological education about distant end events. Some writers applied standard Antichrist rhetoric to contemporary events between 1200 and 1335, often for reformist purposes.

FIGURE 11
Antichrist's death and the
ascent of the two witnesses
(Apoc. 11:11–13). Paris,
Bibliothèque Nationale,
ms. fran. 403, fol. 18r
(mid–thirteenth century).
Reproduced from Delisle
and Meyer.

We can begin with Pope Innocent III himself. Although not usually thought of as an apocalyptic propagandist, Innocent was certainly willing to appeal to Antichrist traditions in his crusading efforts. In a letter written to the diocese of Mainz in 1213 but also circulated elsewhere, he encouraged support of a new Crusade through denunciation of Muhammad as the "Son of Perdition" whose reign had been prophesied to last only 666 years, "of which almost six hundred are now complete."[25] Innocent's appeal may be merely a rhetorical device, but some of his contemporaries and successors saw in events in the East definite signs of the approach of Antichrist.

One piece of evidence is the "Prophecy of the Sons of Agap," a text connected with the Fifth Crusade (1217–21 C.E.) known in both Latin and French versions. Supposedly derived from Arabic, the prophecy was a production of supporters of the Cardinal Legate Pelagius who is praised as the "thin man" who will be responsible for a major defeat of the Muslim

FIGURE 12   Antichrist and Last Judgment. Ravenna, Santa Maria in Porto Fuori, arch fresco
(c. 1300). Reproduced from F. Bisogni, "Problemi Iconografici Riminesi," *Paragone* 26,
no. 305(1975), illus. 11. Courtesy of Sansoni Publishers, Florence.

forces (wishful thinking because the Crusade ended in disaster). It predicted a series of victories for Christianity over Islam, including the conquest of Mecca, before the coming of "Mexadeigan, that is, Antichrist,
[who] will appear and will overthrow as many nations as had previously
existed."[26] This prophecy does not predict the number of years until Antichrist's coming, but it is a good example of how events in the East (remember, Antichrist was to be born in Babylon) were given meaning in
light of the apocalyptic scenario.

The role of Antichrist in prophecies about the East, however, did
not form a major new component in the legend but rather indicated how
current events that seemed to presage the end always involved Antichrist.
For example, as Robert E. Lerner has shown, the "Cedars of Lebanon
Prophecy," composed originally about 1239 in light of the Mongol onslaught on Europe, contained no reference to Antichrist, but when the
prophecy was rewritten about 1290 as a history disguised as prophecy of
the fall of Tripoli to the Muslims, it predicted the eventual reconquest of
the Holy Land and a time of messianic peace.[27] Other texts saw the unexpected invasion of the Mongols from distant Asia as a sign of Antichrist.

The earliest appearance of a famous verse about the coming of Antichrist (often ascribed to Joachim of Fiore) appears in Matthew Paris's *Great
Chronicle* under the year 1242 in connection with fear of the Mongols:

In those times because of terrible rumors of this sort these verses announcing Antichrist's coming were often recited,

> When twelve hundred years and fifty
> After the birth from the dear Virgin are completed,
> Then will be born demon-filled Antichrist.[28]

The learned Franciscan Roger Bacon provides another example. Bacon mingled astrological predictions and wide reading of prophecies with
a concern for recent events in the East as indicative of the approaching
end.[29] In his *Large Work (Opus majus)* written in 1266 and 1267 he included such materials under the heading of "Mathematics," trying to convince Pope Clement IV that Arabic astrological predictions conformed
with the number of the Beast (Apoc. 13:18) in predicting the imminent
end of the Saracens, which had already begun with the Mongol destruction of Baghdad. While the friar saw the Final Enemy near, rather than
expanding upon the legend, he used it primarily to understand the present
world situation.

The Apocalyptic Career of Frederick II

One historical conflict of the thirteenth century not only was understood as
a struggle against Antichrist but also molded and expanded the legend in
the light of current events: the great quarrel between the papacy and
Emperor Frederick II Hohenstaufen (1194–1250) and his heirs. It is among
the most dramatic chapters in the history of the medieval Antichrist.

The reasons for the peculiar heightening of apocalyptic rhetoric in
this great struggle between papacy and empire is probably due to the combination of competence and intransigence on the part of the opposed parties. Frederick II was an intelligent and able monarch, the last real
medieval claimant for an effective universal imperial position. But his
pride and cruelty (remarkable even by medieval standards), as well as his
reputation as a nonbeliever (deftly encouraged by his papal opponents),
seemed to fulfill twelve centuries of speculation about Antichrist as a combination of persecuting tyrant and arch-heretic. His papal opponents—
less cruel, if no less devious—introduced a new dimension into papal
politics that was to prove disastrous in the long run. Former quarrels between popes and emperors had mostly been settled by arbitration. In this

thirteenth-century struggle, ill-advised pontiffs decided on solution by elimination—a dubious choice for a spiritual power.

Another element that gave the quarrel between Frederick and the papacy a special new apocalyptic valence was the presence of strong Joachite expectations among the emperor's opponents. Indeed, a look at applied understandings of the Antichrist legend in the later Middle Ages shows that few had not been at least touched by Joachite themes. Joachim of Fiore's earliest reputation had been as a prophet of Antichrist's imminence, probably because few could understand the more complicated aspects of his thought.[30] In France there is evidence that the heretical Amalricians at Paris in 1210 were influenced by Joachim in their claims that the pope was Antichrist, the prelates of the Church his members, and Rome was Babylon.[31] But the first major application of Joachim's apocalyptic thought to a historical crisis—one that changed Joachimism and its view of Antichrist—came during the struggle with Frederick II.

Probably even before his coronation in 1220 the young Frederick had planned to restore the power and prestige of the imperial office. His position as both emperor and ruler of Sicily made him a serious threat to papal territorial independence, something that the medieval popes thought of as absolutely necessary for their position in medieval society. Conflict broke out in the 1220s, when Frederick was excommunicated for his failure to fulfill his Crusade pledge, but the real struggle began in 1236 and continued for over thirty years, long after the emperor's death in 1250. The apocalyptic dimensions fall basically into two periods: first, 1239 to 1245, when a circle in the papal court led by Cardinal Rainer of Viterbo, a former Cistercian, traded apocalyptic insults with the imperial propagandists; and second, from about 1245 down to about 1270, when Franciscan publicists heavily influenced by Joachim created a new chapter in the Antichrist legend reflecting the figure of the fearsome Frederick.[32]

On June 21, 1239, Gregory IX issued a letter (composed by Rainer and his circle) attacking Frederick as the "Beast arising from the sea" of Apocalypse 13:1–2, one of the traditional symbols of the Antichrist. Frederick's own propaganda team was not slow to take up the challenge, responding in a public letter that identified the pope with no less than three of the dread figures of the Apocalypse—the red horse (Apoc. 6:4), the dragon (Apoc. 12), and the angel from the abyss (Apoc. 16:1–3). Gregory's response was to make more explicit the identification of the emperor with the Final Enemy: "What other Antichrist should we await, when, as is evident in his works, he is already come in the person of Frederick? He is the author of every crime, stained by every cruelty, and he has invaded the patrimony of Christ, seeking to destroy it with Saracen aid."[33]

After Gregory's death, the struggle was continued with greater intransigence by Innocent IV (1243–54). The emperor's power in Italy compelled the pope to flee to southern France in 1244, and in the spring and summer of 1245 a series of three apocalyptic broadsides composed by Rainer was launched against Frederick by way of preparation for the papal deposition of the emperor, which took place at the First Council of Lyons on July 17, 1245. Making use of a wide variety of apocalyptic images, including some themes that seem to have been taken from Joachim of Fiore, these letters and pamphlets are examples of extreme apocalyptic rhetoric. Comparing Frederick to Herod, Nero, Julian the Apostate, Nimrod, and Lucifer himself, Rainer once again identifies Frederick with the Beast from the sea: "Since Frederick has in his forehead the horn of power and a mouth bringing forth monstrous things, he thinks himself able to transform the times and the laws and to lay truth in the dust." Though Rainer continues to speak of Frederick as the "foreteller of Antichrist" (*prenuntius Antichristi*), he so blends the precursor with the Final Enemy that there is little if any difference between the two. Hence, the call to apocalyptic destruction:

> Have no mercy on the impious one. . . . Do not spare the darts, because this proud king has sinned against the Lord more than all the other sons of pride who have attacked the churches down through the ages. . . . Cast him forth from the sanctuary of the Lord so that he may not reign over a Christian people. . . . Destroy the name and the remains, the seed and the sapling of this man from Babylon! Let mercy forget him, since he is merciless and cruel without end![34]

Not to be outdone, Frederick's publicists also continued to use Antichrist language about the popes. From the point of apocalyptic ingenuity, one anonymous pamphlet gained an advantage by showing how the numerical value of the name *Innocencius papa* was 666, concluding that there can be no doubt that Innocent IV is the "true Antichrist!"[35]

This polemical clash of pamphlets succeeded in making Frederick more of an Antichrist than any ruler since Nero. Thus began the second stage of the apocalyptic history of the quarrel (c. 1245–70), in which the movement was reversed: that is, aspects of Frederick's life, or at least afterlife, were transferred into the Antichrist legend itself. This was primarily the work of Franciscan opponents of Frederick, heavily influenced by the ideas of Joachim of Fiore.

It is difficult to know exactly when and where the Franciscans began reading Joachim. Ironically, Frederick himself was responsible for at least one early encounter, when a Florensian abbot fleeing the advance of his armies in 1247 brought Joachim's works to the Franciscan convent in Pisa,[36] but Franciscan Joachitism probably began a few years earlier. The Franciscan Joachites found in the works of the Calabrian abbot a handy prophecy of the apocalyptic importance of their order as one of the two groups of "spiritual men" (*viri spirituales*) who would resist Antichrist at the crisis of the end of the second *status*. They also found a way of reading the events of the time that clearly indicated who the seventh head of the dragon was (Frederick, of course) and just how long his persecution was to last according to Joachim's calculation of generations (not beyond 1260, the forty-second generation of the second *status*). Under the minister general John of Parma (1247–57), a convinced Joachite, many in the order took up apocalyptic prophecy with enthusiasm, as we learn from the *Chronicle* of Brother Salimbene, and especially from a series of apocalyptic writings produced during this time, many pseudonymously ascribed to Joachim. Most of these appear to come from Franciscan circles, or at least to have been reworked by Franciscans. The various forms of history disguised as prophecy found in these tracts did much to enhance Joachim's status as a prophet. They also were responsible for significant additions to the Antichrist legend.

The most important of these texts was the *Commentary on Jeremiah*, which pretended to have been sent by Joachim of Fiore to Henry VI, Frederick's father, in 1197. It is possible that a portion of the work does go back to Joachim, but the various manuscript versions indicate that the work as we presently have it was basically the creation of the abbot's followers during the 1240s. It may have been begun by Florensians or Cistercians, but it was certainly taken up and expanded upon by Franciscans.[37] The longer version predicts a threefold persecution of the Church by a corporate Antichrist to last down to the year 1260. The first persecution is that of the "new Chaldaeans," or Germans, led by the basilisk (Frederick II) who will arise from the serpent (Henry)—an interpretation of Isaiah 14:29—and who will wound the Church, causing the pope to fall. This persecution is prefigured in the first horn of the second Beast from the Apocalypse, that is, the Beast from the earth (Apoc. 13:11). The second persecution is that of heretics symbolized by the second horn of the same Beast. The third persecution is that of Saracens. The prophetic basis for this is found in the first Beast of the Apocalypse, the Beast from the sea (Apoc. 13:1–7), who is said to be joined to the imperial persecutor (probably a reference to Frederick's use of Muslim troops in his army). There is some ambiguity over whether Frederick or his heirs will be the final Antichrist of the second *status*. "Doubtless the basilisk himself will fly higher and farther so that he may afflict the Church throughout the whole breadth of the empire. As if to swallow the bird [the Church], he will sit like God in the temple [2 Thess. 2:4], *either in his own person or in his seed*."[38]

We can well imagine the apocalyptic fears as well as the hopes for the coming messianic third *status* that moved these ecclesiastical opponents of Frederick as the year 1260 drew nearer. In December 1250, however, the dread emperor suddenly died, to provide just another failed identification of Antichrist, we might suppose. But Frederick's death was a beginning, not an end. Frederick's heirs continued his struggle against the papacy, the popes were increasingly resolved to pursue the "basilisk's seed" to complete destruction, and apocalyptic publicists interpreted Frederick's unlikely death as an apocalyptic secret. Just as rumors about *Nero redivivus* had been responsible for the Apocalypse's picture of the head of the Beast that had the fatal wound but was brought back to life (Apoc. 13:3, 17:10–11), so now legends began to circulate that Frederick II was not dead. A number of sources repeat versions of a mysterious prophetic verse:

His death will be hidden and unknown.
Among the people will resound: "He lives," and "He does not live."[39]

Joachite fears for the coming of the "Great Antichrist" before 1260 were also responsible for the shift in the famous ditty noted above, that Matthew Paris first recorded as specifying the date 1250. In the prophetic literature of the time, especially that of Joachite provenance, there is ample evidence for a wide circulation of this verse bearing the new date of 1260 for the events of the end.[40]

Continuing fears about Frederick soon expanded. In 1258 the English Franciscan Thomas of Eccleston reported a story brought from Italy that a Sicilian Franciscan had seen Frederick shortly after his death along with five thousand burning spectral warriors enter the sea on their way to refuge in Mount Etna, traditionally the opening to hell.[41] So Frederick was *the* Antichrist after all—either in himself when he would return from hell, or when he would be "resuscitated" in one of his seed, such as his bastard son Manfred and later his legitimate grandson Conradin, both of whom continued the fight against the papacy in the 1250s and 1260s. In the *Book of the Prophets' Afflictions,* ascribed to Joachim but written by an Italian Franciscan about 1255, we have the first appearance of a *Fredericus tertius,* or "Frederick the Third," as an imminent Antichrist figure, possibly a reference to Frederick of Antioch, another bastard of the emperor who joined with Manfred in attacking the papal legate in Apulia.[42] Another Pseudo-Joachim work, the *Commentary on Isaiah,* probably written in the 1260s, portrays Frederick, both as the seventh head of the Dragon and seventh head of the first Beast, being restored to life in Gog, the Dragon's tail. Yet another witness to Joachite redatings of the coming of Antichrist in relation to Frederick II's death and the failure of the year 1260 is to be found in the "Brother Columbinus Prophecy," which apparently was written in Italy between 1260 and 1275.[43] According to this text, "Saint Columbinus asserted that when the year 1316 has been completed Antichrist will appear in Jerusalem with his evil generations, Gog and Magog, and preach there. . . ." He will be killed on Mount Sinai (an unusual location), and the millenarian period of the seventh seal will follow.[44]

Thus a distinctive "Frederician" subplot in the Antichrist legend was formed in the mid–thirteenth century. This never became a major strand, but its vitality for some three centuries demonstrates the continuing interaction between history and mythic structures in the story of Antichrist. The tendency to demonize one's opponents, especially in times of unusually threatening conflict, has been a major engine in Antichrist's ongoing career. This is doubtless linked with another tendency, perhaps more obvious in our time than in the thirteenth century—eagerness to heighten the importance of a contemporary event by using heightened rhetoric ("This week's game of the century!"). Though the Frederician Antichrist legend built upon the past, in its identification of the Antichrist as a German emperor named Frederick (usually Frederick the Third) and its emphasis on his role as a scourge of the clergy, it elevated history into legend, as Antichrist had been doing for almost fifteen centuries.

Conflict Between Popes and Mendicants

The Franciscan involvement with Joachite ideas in the middle decades of the thirteenth century also produced another development in applied Antichrist traditions in the later Middle Ages, one that paradoxically viewed the mendicant orders themselves (primarily the Franciscans) as evidence for the proximity of the Son of Perdition. This story (part of the wider history that recent investigators have spoken of as the antifraternal tradition) was especially important for its influence on late medieval literature.[45]

The new mendicant, or begging, orders were the great success story for the reform of religious life in the thirteenth century. They were living proof that the papacy was still arbiter of reform, at least in the early 1200s. But papal support for the Franciscans and Dominicans soon produced tensions between these new urban orders and the local clergy, who were mostly less well educated and often less fervent. Franciscan involvement with Joachite ideas about the approach of Antichrist and the end of the present stage of church history provided some clever clerical opponents of the mendicants with ammunition to launch a major attack. The continuing use of antifraternal apocalyptic rhetoric says much about how the gap between Franciscan claims to be leading the highest form of Christian life and public perception of the friars' human failings fueled the fire of reformist ideas that grew progressively stronger in the centuries between 1200 and 1500.

The spark that lit the fire of controversy was ignited by a young Franciscan, Gerard of Borgo San Donnino, a convinced Joachite sent from his native Italy to Paris about 1250 to study theology. As a student, Gerard was in good company (these were the years when Thomas Aquinas and Bonaventure were finishing their studies or beginning their careers as junior professors), but Gerard's contribution was not a famous *summa* but an odd work, now surviving only in fragments, known as the *Introduction to the Eternal Gospel*. This was an edited version of Joachim of Fiore's major writings with appropriate comments, proving that the Antichrist of the second *status* was now active, that the present Church would be destroyed in 1260, and that the new spiritual Church of the third *status* would basically be a Franciscan-run operation whose sacred Scripture would be Joachim's writings collectively known as the Eternal Gospel. Such radical views were grist for the mill of the secular Paris Master William of St. Amour and his followers, who attacked the novel teaching of the mendicants as evidence of their heresy—and therefore their role as forerunners of Antichrist—rather than heralds of a new and better Church! How far William and his associates, such as Nicholas of Lisieux, were real apocalypticists is subject to dispute;[46] but in painting the Joachite mendicants as heretical proponents of the end of the present papal order of Christendom, they brought on an ecclesiastical crisis of no small moment.

One cannot but admire the political skill with which the popes of the time extricated themselves from this dilemma, though the solution proved temporary. Papal support for the mendicants could not be destroyed by the vagaries of a few extremists. Gerard's *Introduction* was investigated by a papal commission and condemned as heretical in 1255. He himself was imprisoned for life. But William's work against the mendicants, *The Dangers of the Last Times,* was also censured in 1256, though this did not prevent it from being widely read by later opponents of the friars.[47] The young theological giants of the mendicants, Aquinas and Bonaventure, were called upon to rebut the attacks on their orders, and in 1257 John of Parma, the suspect Joachite head of the Franciscans, was compelled to resign his office in favor of Bonaventure.

Even Bonaventure, though he rooted out the radical Joachites from the Franciscan order, showed himself to be a modified follower of the Calabrian abbot in his unfinished *Collations on the Hexaemeron* delivered to the Paris community in 1273. The Seraphic Doctor's view of Antichrist's signs centered not so much on persecuting tyrants as on the danger of false teaching, especially the Aristotelian errors he found rife in the University of Paris.[48] It was left to some of Bonaventure's more radical students to develop the next stage of Joachite applied Antichrist ideology, and to that story we now turn.

It is scarcely correct to speak of a true "Spiritual" party among the Franciscans until the struggles of the last two decades of the thirteenth century brought long-simmering tensions to the surface. Bonaventure had tried to unite the more rigorous and often Joachite wing of the Franciscans, who claimed adherence to St. Francis's own unyielding "Testament," with the majority group who saw no harm in a more lenient practice of poverty as long as this received papal approval. Bonaventure's theological solution, demonstrating how the Franciscans were the true heirs of the absolute poverty of Christ and the apostles, was canonized by a papal bull in 1279. Life proved to be more complicated than theology. The ongoing tensions within the order over the issue of poverty became increasingly pronounced in the 1280s, as the Spirituals within the order, especially in southern France and central Italy (Tuscany, Umbria, and the Marches), began to fuse the ideal of poverty and Joachite apocalyptic expectation into potent new configurations that included some original thoughts about Antichrist.

The key figure was Peter Olivi (c. 1248–1298), a Provençal student of Bonaventure who was a remarkable combination of Scholastic theologian, apocalyptic propagandist, and charismatic leader. Olivi was the great theologian of the "poor use," the interpretation of the Franciscan way of life that insisted that strict poverty in practice was a necessity and not just an ideal. He also firmly believed in Joachim's theology of history and its seeming confirmation of the historical importance of Francis and the order he founded. Olivi's interpretation of Franciscan Joachitism was far more subtle and therefore more dangerous to the papal institutional Church than poor Gerardo's had ever been. Given the effect of his ideas, we might say that Olivi was one of the few revolutionary ideologists of the time, though this was scarcely his intention. Like so many late medieval apocalypticists, he was really an ecclesiastical and clerical reformer, but one who had lost hope in attaining true reform without imminent apocalyptic change.

A good part of what made Olivi so dangerous was his convictions about Antichrist. In his *Commentary on Revelation,* written in the last two years of his life, he sketched out a theology of history based largely on Joachim, though with Franciscan modifications developed from his mentor, Bonaventure. Salvation history, for Olivi, can be understood both according to a pattern of double-seven ages (seven in the Old Testament mirroring seven in the New), and also according to Joachim's three *status*. In the seven ages of Church history (his usual pattern), the fifth age of laxity overlaps with the sixth age of renewal begun by Francis. This is the present era of struggle between good and evil forces in Christian society, one that Olivi saw as reaching a culmination in the year 1300.

From the time of Francis, a series of persecutions against the evangelical life—such as that of the Paris Masters against the mendicants and that of Frederick II against the Church generally—all pointed toward the imminent coming of Antichrist at the end of the sixth age. Building on Joachim and also upon earlier Franciscan exegesis of the Apocalypse, Olivi interprets this Antichrist as twofold—the *Antichristus mysticus* and the *Antichristus magnus*.[49] The terms *magnus* and *maximus Antichristus* are found in Joachim, but Olivi appears to have been the first to speak of an *Antichristus mysticus* or *misticus*.[50] Basically, Olivi argues that the two Beasts of Apocalypse 13 signify both Antichrists or rather the dual aspect of each Antichrist: "Know that anywhere in this book [the Apocalypse] where it treats of the Great Antichrist in prophetic fashion, it also implies the time of the Mystical Antichrist preceding him." The Mystical Antichrist, whose persecution Olivi sees as active in the present moment, is the body of evildoers within Christianity, consisting of both evil laity (carnal Christians and their leaders) and also wicked clergy (false religious and false prophets). It will soon reach a culmination in two evil leaders:

They [his prophetic authorities] think that Frederick with his seed is like the slain head in this age, and that he will revive at the time of the Mystical Antichrist in someone from his seed in such a manner that he will not only obtain the Roman Empire, but will conquer the French and take their kingdom. . . . He will set up as pseudopope a certain false religious who will contrive something against the Evangelical Rule [the Franciscan Rule].[51]

The Mystical Antichrist prepares the way for the Great Antichrist who will also have a dual aspect symbolized by the two Beasts, in this case a "gentile," that is, a Muslim side (the Beast from the sea representing revived Islamic power under a conquering ruler), and a Christian one, the Beast from the land representing the "false prophets" who will be led by another false pope. The Franciscan's view of Antichrist thus includes Christian/non-Christian, clerical/lay, individual/collective, and tyrant/heretic models all in one complex picture.[52] It is noteworthy that there is no Jewish component. He seems to have recognized how obscure and perhaps how tentative this all was when he said, "I don't really care all that much whether the one who will be Antichrist in the proper sense . . . is a king or false pope, or both together. It's enough for me to know that he will be against Christ."[53]

Olivi's Antichrist views were of major moment for a number of reasons. Although Joachim had hinted at a papal aspect to Antichrist and some of the Joachite works, such as the *Commentary on Jeremiah,* had also mentioned it, Olivi was among the first to give the papal Antichrist a central role. Furthermore, in predicting that the *Antichristus mysticus* "will heretically err against the truth of evangelical poverty and perfection," he was a better prophet than he knew. Two decades later, when Pope John XXII attacked the followers of Olivi within the order and then even condemned the previously approved Franciscan teaching about the absolute poverty of Christ and the apostles, it was difficult for many Franciscans and their followers not to think that Olivi was dead right. Finally, we can note that the emphasis of Olivi and the Spirituals on the issue of poverty brought a new dimension to the figure of Antichrist, or at least to the *Antichristus mysticus.* Antichrist as tyrant, heretic, and deceiver were all traditional. New is the note that Antichrist will be the enemy of poverty both in theory, because of his attack on the Rule of Francis, and presumably in practice, that is, in the opulence of his lifestyle.[54] The heavy taxation policies and wasteful court of John XXII and many of the Avignon popes were to make them look more and more like Antichrists to their opponents.

In the same decade in which Olivi penned his *Commentary,* others were also speculating on papal Antichrists.[55] A good deal of the stimulus for this came from the unusual history of Celestine V, the model for the *pastor angelicus* legend (at least in part), and from the career and quarrels of his successor, Boniface VIII (1294–1303), whose temper and tactics considerably influenced developing views of the papal Antichrist (though not Olivi's).

In July 1294, in order to break a stalemated papal conclave, an aged, holy, and simple hermit was unwillingly elected pope, taking the name Celestine V. His choice was greeted by some as a seeming fulfillment of the growing hopes for a holy pope of the last days who would introduce a period of reform and messianic peace before the end.[56] Celestine's pontificate, however, was a disaster, and he shortly abdicated. He was followed on the papal throne by the able but ambitious and tyrannical Benedetto Caetani (Boniface VIII), who promptly imprisoned Celestine until the latter's convenient death not long after. Celestine had shown favor to the Spiritual party among the Franciscans; Pope Boniface moved against them as rebellious troublemakers. It is not surprising that a number of the Spiritual party in Italy joined Boniface's ecclesiastical and political enemies, declaring that Celestine's abdication was illegal (Olivi did not agree with this). Growing interest in the apocalyptic role of the papacy is found in a number of texts produced at the end of the thirteenth and the beginning of the fourteenth centuries.

An important Pseudo-Joachite text, probably the work of Franciscans, reflects this concern. The *Angelic Oracle of Cyril* pretends to be a prophecy given to a Carmelite during Mass. According to legend, the worthy father sent the obscure text on to Joachim of Fiore for interpretation. The *Oracle* and the *Commentary* appear to have been composed in the 1290s. They were among the most popular of all the Pseudo-Joachite works, possibly because their puzzling language and symbolism were such an attraction for subsequent prophetic ingenuity. Cast in the form of a history disguised as prophecy, the *Oracle* contains references to the confrontation between a coming *orthopontifex* (correct pope) and an evil *pseudopontifex* (false pope) that reflect the history of Celestine and Boniface. The *Oracle of Cyril* does not identify the false pope with Antichrist, but it would have been an easy transition to make for those so inclined.

The growing interest in the apocalyptic role of the papacy, reflecting the contrast between Celestine and Boniface, is also evident in the illustrated *Prophecies Regarding the Supreme Pontiffs (Vaticinia de summis pontificibus*), also usually ascribed to Joachim. These are among the most influential and enigmatic of medieval apocalyptic texts. Many readers in the late Middle Ages would have associated Joachim more with these *Vaticinia* and works like the *Commentary on Jeremiah* than with his authentic writings. (The *Prophecies* survive in more than sixty manuscripts and twenty-four early printings between 1505 and 1670.)[57]

The original Latin *Vaticinia* were based on Greek prophecies (the "Leo Oracles") concerning future emperors, probably dating from the twelfth century. The earliest series of fifteen prophecies, which take the form of titles, brief texts, and accompanying illustrated figures (lacking in some manuscripts), probably appeared sometime during the reign of Boniface VIII (1295–1303) or shortly thereafter.[58] In this version the first six are *vaticinia ex eventu* of popes from Nicholas III to Boniface. Several enigmatic scenes follow (often in varying order in the manuscripts) and then a series of five pictures and texts that apparently illustrate the career of a holy pope of the last days (the term *pastor angelicus* does not appear, but the pope is crowned by accompanying angels). In the final picture the holy pope often holds his mitre over a crowned or horned animal figure with a human head—a scene that appears to represent papal abdication at the coming of Antichrist (see Fig. 13).

Many investigators think that the *Prophecies* come from Franciscan Spiritual circles. Though they were disseminated under Joachim's name, they have little connection with the main lines of his thought, such as the three *status* theory. Rather, they emphasize a new version of pre-Antichrist millenarianism in which the holy pope of the last days takes the place of the Last World Emperor. They are evidence of growing apocalyptic interest in good and evil popes, though only the subsequent additions (to be discussed presently) deal with Antichrist in any detail. The *Vaticinia* suggest that a major shift in Western apocalypticism was in the making around the year 1300 C.E., one that held important developments for Antichrist as well as for the wider scenario in which he (they, actually, since we are dealing with multiple Antichrists) participated. The new scenario involved the mingling of the centuries-old imperial legends of the Last Emperor with Joachite apocalypticism and the developing positive and negative roles for the papacy in the last days. This took place under the impact of Franciscan ideology, as well as through nationalistic fervor originating in France and later also in Germany.

The role of Boniface VIII in the creation of the papal Antichrist is clear in some of Olivi's friends and followers. Ubertino of Casale

FIGURE 13
Crowning of Antichrist
Beast. Rome, Vatican
Library, ms. lat. 3819, fol.
149r (early fourteenth
century). Courtesy of the
Vatican Library.

(c. 1259–c. 1330) was a Spiritual from Tuscany who had known John of Parma and taught with Olivi. Suspended from preaching because of his attacks on the carnal church, he retired to Monte Alverna where St. Francis had received the stigmata. Here in 1305 he finished his *The Tree of the Crucified Life of Jesus,* the fifth book of which is a lengthy commentary on the Apocalypse, following in the footsteps of Olivi. But Ubertino was more direct than Olivi in precisely identifying the two aspects of the *Antichristus mysticus:* The first is the tyranny of Boniface VIII, the second the hypocrisy of his successor, Pope Benedict XI (1303–4).[59] Ubertino shows that the identification of individual popes with Antichrist was well established by the early fourteenth century.

Olivi dead was more dangerous than Olivi alive. His *Commentary,* though burned by his Franciscan enemies and later condemned by John XXII in 1326, proved widely popular and was translated into Provençal. Meanwhile, Clement V (1305–14) tried to work out a compromise between the Spiritual party and the majority Conventual Franciscans, but to no avail. A native of southern France, Clement had fled the disorders and dangers of Italy to settle in Avignon. His successor at Avignon, John XXII, resolved to settle the Franciscan question once and for all.

John's peremptory action was facilitated by the increasing intolerance and rigidity evident in the late medieval papacy. In response to widespread movements of heresy, especially the dualist Cathars of southern France active from the mid–twelfth century, the powers of both Church and state had responded at first with confusion and fear and subsequently with organized repression.[60] The papal Inquisition, a legal institution designed to hunt out and exterminate heresy, was largely successful against Catharism. In the latter part of the thirteenth and the early fourteenth centuries, the popes would use the Inquisition to stamp out a wide range of heresies, which, according to medieval definition, meant willful adherence to something the papacy defined as incorrect belief. Thus, when Pope John XXII decided that all Franciscan views about poverty were incorrect—both those of the Spirituals and those of their opponents, the Conventuals—anyone who continued to uphold the rejected opinions could be considered a heretic.

John first moved against the Spirituals. In the bull of 1317 entitled *Quorundam exigit* he condemned two of the key aspects of the "poor use" defended by Olivi and others: shorter habits and refusal to store food. Dissident Spirituals who did not give in were hauled before the Inquisition, and four who refused to obey were burned as heretics in May 1318. In a bull of 1317 Pope John also closed the houses of the Fraticelli, as the followers of Peter Olivi had come to be called. A more formal condemnation of their doctrinal errors followed in the constitution *Gloriosam ecclesiam* in 1318, including "the much they publish about the coming of Antichrist whom they assert is now threatening." During the following decades many Fraticelli, who were also often called Beghini, were hunted down by the Inquisition.[61] In his famous *Inquisitor's Manual* of 1324, Bernard Gui summarized Fraticelli errors, including those about Antichrist:

> They teach that Antichrist is dual, that is, there is one who is spiritual or mystical, and another, the real, greater Antichrist. The first prepares the

way for the second. They say, too, that the first Antichrist is that pope under whom will occur and, in their opinion, is now occurring the persecution and condemnation of their sect.[62]

Pope John had enjoyed the cooperation of the Conventual Franciscans in putting down the Spirituals. In 1322, however, he decided to reopen the question of apostolic poverty, the theological teaching that the Franciscans had renewed the absolute poverty of Christ and the Apostles. This was the cornerstone of Franciscan claims for the superiority of their order, and so it was devastating when Pope John reversed earlier papal teaching in 1323 with the bull *Cum inter nonnullos,* which said that it was heretical to claim that Christ and the Apostles had owned nothing. A number of important Conventuals, including the minister general, Michael of Cesena, accused the pope of heresy for attacking the Franciscan rule and fled to his enemy, Lewis of Bavaria. They too became known as Fraticelli and soon were also attacking Pope John as Antichrist. These two groups of dissident Franciscans were the most energetic proponents of the identification of a false pope with Antichrist thus far in the history of Christianity.

Theologians and Poets Discuss Antichrist

The convictions of the Spiritual Franciscans about the proximity of Antichrist became mixed up with a theological debate over Antichrist that disturbed the University of Paris in the early years of the fourteenth century. The initiator of this debate was Arnold of Villanova (c. 1240–1311), a Catalan layman and one of the most famous physicians of the day (he included three kings and Pope Boniface among his patients).[63] Arnold apparently developed his interest in Antichrist, independently of Spiritual influence, about 1290. On the basis of his own reading of the Bible and prophetic authorities (he was much influenced by Joachim), he produced a treatise, *The Time of Antichrist's Coming,* that he continued to revise over the years. The work sought to show that while human ingenuity could not discover the time of the Final Enemy, God could and had revealed it. Specifically, the 1290 days between the removal of the daily sacrifice and the setting up of the Abomination of Desolation in Daniel 12:11 signified that Antichrist would come 1290 years after the destruction of the temple of Jerusalem. Hence, Antichrist was due in the decade 1366–76 (Arnold seems to have varied the date in different editions).

In 1299 Arnold was sent to Paris by King James II of Aragon as part of a diplomatic mission, and while there he took the opportunity to submit his treatise to the Paris theologians. An uproar ensued among the Augustinian-minded masters, not only that a layman would try to do theology, but that he would get things so wrong! Arnold was condemned as a heretic and his book burned, but he escaped due to diplomatic immunity. Undaunted, he made the unwise decision of appealing to the pope—none other than Boniface VIII. Arnold's good luck held, however, because he turned out to be too valuable to the pope in his medical capacity to be awarded the fate that his apocalyptic speculations alone would have probably merited for him.

Arnold continued to write apocalyptic treatises during and after Boniface's reign. His commentary on the Apocalypse shows the growing influence of the ideas of the Franciscan Spirituals on his thought. His trial in Paris was the stimulus for two important theological treatments of the Antichrist theme by well-known theologians—an attempt at a mediating position by the Paris Dominican John Quidort (died 1306),[64] and a strongly Augustinian attack on any attempt to predict Antichrist's time in a *quaestio* by Henry of Harclay, chancellor of Oxford.[65] Although John did not dismiss Arnold and other prophets out of hand, trying instead to qualify their predictions,[66] Henry believed that any attempt to precisely calculate the time of the end was either erroneous or heretical. As he put it, "All investigators of the end of the world, even if they were saints, were mistaken in their conjectures."[67]

Developments in the applied views of Antichrist, mostly of a Joachite variety (though the abbot's followers had gone far beyond what he would have been comfortable with), also had an impact on presentations of the Antichrist in literature. As mentioned above, Antichrist iconography between 1200 and 1335 shows little that can be directly related to imminent hopes of the Final Enemy in relation to current history. The same is not true for literature, especially poetry. A brief glance at three of these poets—Jean de Meun (writing c. 1275), Jacopone da Todi (c. 1230–1306), and finally Dante Alighieri (1265–1321)—reveals the varied ways applied views of Antichrist were presented.

The *Romance of the Rose* is one of the greatest products of medieval courtly literature. The poem was begun by Guillaume de Loris in about

1230, but most of its nearly 22,000 lines come from Jean de Meun. Like the works of Dante and Chaucer, it has been the subject of an immense scholarly literature, one made more complex by the dual authorship. Though many read Jean's part of the poem as a naturalistic defense of the necessity for procreative sexuality, lately a strong case has been made that Jean was really writing a moral work about the delusion of self-love in the apocalyptic age of hypocrisy leading to Antichrist.[68] A key to this interpretation is the long section on "Faus Semblant" (lines 10,467–12,380), which many readers have dismissed as a distracting interlude in the midst of the major story of the Lover's pursuit of the Rose. Richard Emmerson and Ronald Herzman, on the other hand, argue that the "Faus Semblant episode is not an atypical episode in the poem where moral criteria cannot be ignored, but rather an episode that helps provide the criteria that illuminate the moral dimensions of the entire poem."[69]

Faus Semblant (False Seeming) is described as "one of Antichrist's boys" (line 11,713). The personification of hypocrisy, he functions as one of the barons who help the Lover storm the castle and deflower the Rose. His own account is cast as a pilgrimage in which he disguises himself as a friar in the company of his girlfriend, "Astenance Contraint" (Constrained Abstinence), who masquerades as a Beguine (see Fig. 14). In the description of their journey, Jean makes considerable use of the apocalyptic attacks on the Franciscans of "Master William of St. Amour," who is named on several occasions.[70] The pilgrimage ends with the grisly murder of "Male Bouche" (Foul Mouth) by Faus Semblant during confession. Here the personification of hypocrisy pretends to be a priest who has the whole world in his charge (just like Antichrist). Later in the poem, the Lover praises these two accomplices as follows:

> There was the traitor False Seeming,
> Son of Fraud and false minister of Hypocrisy,
> His mother, who is so bitter toward the virtues;
> There too was Lady Constrained Abstinence,
> Pregnant by False Seeming
> And ready to give birth to Antichrist,
> As I find it written in a book.
> Without fail, these were they who overcame the gate.
> Therefore, I pray for them, for whatever that is worth.
> My lords, he who wants to be a traitor
> Should make False Seeming his master

FIGURE 14   Antichrist ("False Seeming") disguised as friar with his consort, "Constrained
Abstinence," *Roman de la Rose,* lines 14, 740–52. From Oxford, Bodleian Library,
Ms. Douce 195, f. 86v (late fifteenth century). Reproduced with permission of the
Bodleian Library.

> And take Constrained Abstinence,
> He may then practice duplicity and pretend simplicity.[71]

A moral and apocalyptic reading of the poem, then, suggests that the whole action is taking place in the final age of hypocrisy and that the pilgrimage of the Lover to his rape of the Rose is another violent and hypocritical demonstration of the imminence of Antichrist.[72] Though Jean de Meun does not bother with the details of Antichrist's career, we can describe his poem as one of the most incisive moral uses of the legend in medieval literature.

Jean de Meun's relation to apocalyptic speculation on Antichrist remains controversial, but there can be no question that Jacopone da Todi was a convinced apocalypticist of the Franciscan Spiritual party. After the death of his wife in 1268, the lawyer Jacopone was converted to a life of severe asceticism and began composing religious poems, called *Laudi* ("Songs of Praise"). In later life he became a Franciscan, a staunch upholder of the Spiritual cause, for which he was imprisoned by Boniface VIII. A number of his poems, such as *Lauda* 50 on "The Great Battle of the Antichrist," apply Antichrist imagery to the Spirituals' current struggle against Boniface's attempt to mitigate the Rule of Francis, depicting the struggle as an apocalyptic battle.[73]

Dante is the supreme poet of the Middle Ages and a supremely difficult poet to write about. Everyone admits that he used apocalyptic themes extensively in the *Divine Comedy,* but since they are transmuted for his own purposes, there remains much debate over what ideas and symbols he used and for what ends. It is clear, both from his personal history and from recent study of the *Comedy,* that Dante was acquainted with Joachim's *figurae* and with the thought of some of the Franciscan Spirituals, such as Ubertino, but it would be going too far to call him a Joachite or a Spiritual. Dante's apocalypticism reflects current events only in an ambiguous fashion, and he does not calculate the time of the end; but, for all that, he is still a good witness to the medieval sense of living in the last times and seeing present evidence of the signs of Antichrist.[74]

Antichrist traditions are strong in at least two contexts in the *Divine Comedy,* Inferno XVI–XIX and Purgatorio XXXII–XXXIII. One might argue that the Inferno appearances represent the poet's use of the *Antichristus mysticus* and the Purgatorio the *Antichristus magnus,* but this seems to put constraints on a complex and fluid presentation.[75] The strange beast Geryon, summoned by Vergil at the end of Canto XVI to carry Dante and his guide down to the "Malebolge" in Canto XVII, has many Antichrist reminiscences, as medievalist John Friedman has shown. A Dracopede, or serpent with human face, it also bears a scorpion's tail— Dante's appropriation of the animal images of Antichrist found in Scripture and tradition. When Dante and Vergil are deposited in the eighth circle, they reach the realm of fraud, where Satan and Antichrist reign. Canto XVIII describes the simple fraud of Panderers, Seducers, and Flatterers, while Canto XIX contains those guilty of sacred fraud, the Simoniacs, whom tradition had long associated with Antichrist and his predecessors. This canto might be called the "inversion" canto, suffused as it is with images of the reversal of values and historical types long associated with Antichrist, as R. Emmerson and R. Herzman have shown.

Foremost among these images of reversal is Simon Magus, whose fall from heaven at Peter's behest had been considered a type of Antichrist for centuries:

> O Simon Magus, o wretched followers,
>> who rape the things of God
>> that should be wedded to goodness
> For gold and silver!
>> Now must the trumpet sound for you,
>> because you are in the third chasm.
> (Inferno XIX.1–6)

In this canto Dante's wrath against the simoniac popes Nicholas III, Boniface VIII, and Clement V boils over. It can scarcely be an accident that these popes, especially the first two, were also targets of the attacks of the Spirituals. Dante shows them inverted in narrow holes with their feet tortured by flames, images of the false Simon Magus falling from heaven—himself a figure of the Antichrist who will bring down fire upon his followers in a parody of Pentecost (XIX.22–30). In this context, Dante and Vergil seem to act typologically as the two witnesses, accusing the Antichrist(s) before the world.

Inferno XIX contains a reference to the Whore of Babylon of Apocalypse 17 as a symbol of the corrupt present church (XIX.103–17). This provides a transition to the other major Antichrist appearance in Purgatorio XXXII–XXXIII, the vision of the history of the church that Dante beholds in the earthly paradise at the end of his ascent of the mountain of Purgatory. Medievalist Robert E. Kaske has provided important insights into this complex allegory in which the chariot of the Church is first presented in its ideal state and then in its present corrupt situation.[76] The exact details of the chariot's troubles (XXXII.109–60) need not delay us. The last and worst, however, is when the cart is commandeered by a "shameless harlot" (see Apoc. 17) and a lustful giant:

> Securely, like a fortress on a high hill,
>> there appeared to me a shameless harlot seated on it,
>> with her eyes glancing about her.
> And, as if because she did not want to be taken from him,
>> I saw a giant standing at her side,
>> and from time to time they kissed each other.
> (Purgatorio XXXII.148–53)

FIGURE 15   Antichrist and harlot in the chariot of the Church, illustrating Dante's Purgatorio
XXXII.148–60. Ms. Holkham misc. 48, p. 110 (late fourteenth century). Reproduced
with permission of the Bodleian Library.

The usual interpretation of this is a political one that sees the giant as
the French king stealing the corrupt papacy away to Avignon. But a political reading does not preclude an apocalyptic one in which the giant is
none other than the great tyrant Antichrist (often pictured as of giant
stature—see Fig. 15). The harlot Church shamelessly gives herself to him,
and he rewards her by scourging her and dragging her off until the mysterious messianic figure of the DXV (515) comes to rescue her and slay the
whore and the giant in Canto XXXIII.31–45.[77]

These poetic renderings of Antichrist from the late thirteenth century and the early fourteenth highlight what was perhaps the most
distinctive contribution of this period to the Antichrist legend—the increasing involvement of the papacy. Many still think that the notion of a
pope as Antichrist was the creation of Martin Luther and was spread by
the Reformation. But the connection between the papacy and Antichrist
was of long standing, being rooted in the Son of Perdition of 2 Thessalonians 2 who takes up his blasphemous position in the temple. It was also in
conformity with the inner logic of the Adamic myth always at work in the
core of the legend. If Antichrist is to be the most deceptive of humans, the
one who will put on the best counterfeit of holiness to perform the worst
evil, what position would he more likely occupy than that of the spiritual
leader of Christendom? From before the year 1000 such fears had been
growing, but it was only in this period that they reached full flowering.

CHAPTER SEVEN

ANTICHRIST ON THE EVE OF THE REFORMATION

(1335–1500)

The situation of the Church and Christian society deteriorated rapidly after the death of John XXII in 1334. The papacy became mired in the tragedy of the Avignon captivity, despite the attempts of some popes and others to rescue it. Criticism of the papal antichrists, both from the surviving Fraticelli and from others, like the poet Francesco Petrarch, continued.[1] Within a few years, western Europe was plunged into a medically apocalyptic situation with the outbreak of the Great Plague in 1348–49, which probably killed a third of the population and caused immense disruptions in society. Recovery was slow, both in the Church and elsewhere. The remainder of the fourteenth century and a good part of the fifteenth were years filled with fears of Antichrist. Predictions of the time of his coming were rife: the years 1346, 1347, 1348, 1360, 1365, 1375, 1387, 1396, 1400, 1417, and 1418 were just some of the dates announced for his advent prior to 1450.[2]

This period might well be called the great era of Antichrist application rather than of innovation. Little was added to the established scenario, but much was made of how the events of the day demonstrated the proximity of the Son of Perdition. Perhaps the most interesting new Antichrist materials at this time relate to iconography, but I will begin with a look at learned and popular texts and treatises.

Late Medieval Pessimism

The standard view of Antichrist, based on traditional biblical exegesis and also often dependent on the Adsonian biography, is well attested in the late Middle Ages, especially in vernacular texts. But the twelfth and thirteenth centuries had supplied such good summaries that little was left to do except the work of translation.[3] Much more important was reading the signs of the times as indicating Antichrist's coming, either from a standard Adsonian perspective or from one tinged by varieties of Joachite speculation. Many apocalyptic texts of the time also looked forward to some kind of millenarian period on earth as a respite from the trials and horrors of the present. Those of the pre-Antichrist variety, springing from the Last World Emperor tradition, usually included little on Antichrist, since the *Tiburtine Sibyl,* Methodius, and others had said it all. Those of the post-Antichrist variety, either connected with the forty-five days after his death or with newer Joachite understandings of a third age of the Holy Spirit, often offered more extensive observations.

Roberto Rusconi, a scholar of medieval apocalypticism, has noted that around the middle of the fourteenth century certain key themes came to the fore in much of the prophetic literature of the time: (1) the identification of the Avignon papacy with Babylon of the Apocalypse and the attendant notion of a "Babylonian Captivity" of the Church; (2) expectation of a coming false pope, the *Antichristus misticus;* (3) fear of an imminent schism; (4) expectation of a heaven-sent *pastor angelicus;* and, finally, (5) conviction that the persecution of the *Antichristus magnus* could not be far behind.[4] While these elements all had a considerable prehistory, the sad state of both Church and society as well as one of the greatest natural disasters of all time contributed to a general sense of pessimism.

Concrete evidence for connections between endtime expectations and the Great Plague, which did its worst in 1348 and 1349 and recurred several times in subsequent decades, is not as plentiful as a crude model of the relation between apocalypticism and societal crisis might suggest.[5] Nevertheless, the Plague apparently confirmed for many what they already sensed—that the end was near—and those tried to move others toward a more apocalyptic frame of mind.

One influential prophet who mentioned the Plague was John of Rupescissa (Jean de Roquetaillade, c. 1310–c. 1365), who can be called the foremost apocalypticist of the fourteenth century. John was from southern France (along with Calabria always a seedbed of prophets). Influenced by

Olivi's writings, he became a Franciscan in the 1330s.[6] By 1344 he had been taken into custody by his superiors for his apocalyptic views. Such an incarceration (many religious orders now had some form of prison for recalcitrant members) highlights the increasing danger many sensed in apocalyptic expectations in the later Middle Ages—at the very time when such beliefs experienced considerable growth.

In 1345, while in prison, John received a further prophetic illumination, which he claimed was crucial to complete his understanding of the last times. Although he suffered terribly during his many years in jail, this strange Franciscan managed to write an astonishing amount, all the while avoiding final condemnation. Many of his most important works, such as the *Book of Secret Events* and the *Commentary on the Angelic Oracle of Cyril,* have not been edited; others, such as his *Companion in Tribulation* (c. 1356), are known only in poor early editions.[7]

John was well informed about the late medieval prophetic tradition, especially the Francophile Joachite scenario of the end that had begun to develop a generation before him. The *Book of Secret Events,* completed in 1349, sets out a scenario for the last times based on the Apocalypse as read by Olivi and Arnold of Villanova as well as on John's own revelations. According to the imprisoned friar, a series of trials beginning with a famine in 1347 and a "piling up of unnumbered corpses" in 1348 (obviously the Great Plague) would preface the great crisis of history to come in the decade between 1360 and 1370. John's different works provide a series of variations on this plot and the role of various Antichrists within it. He continued to adhere to the Spiritual Franciscan distinction between *Antichristus mysticus* and *Antichristus magnus* but thought of the former more as a political than a religious figure, sometimes identifying him with the German Emperor Lewis of Bavaria and his struggle against the Avignon popes. The Great Antichrist would come from the seed of Frederick II and rule over Sicily (early works identify him with Louis of Sicily, later ones with another Sicilian ruler, Frederick IV).[8] In a late work, the *Companion in Tribulation,* we are told that "The eastern [mystical] Antichrist will publicly appear before we come to 1365, and his disciples will preach openly in the area of Jerusalem. . . ."[9] Later, the Western Antichrist, seen as a new imperial Nero, will manifest himself. John writes much about the reforming Franciscan pope (a *pastor angelicus*) and his companion, a king of France who will become Last Emperor. They will lead the struggle against the imminent dual Antichrists until the destruction of the *Antichristus magnus,* which John believed would come by 1370. After a forty-five-year period of some confusion, the true significance of Antichrist's death would become evident in a thousand-year stretch of earthly happiness before the end of the world in 2370 c.e. It is evident that John of Rupescissa was a *literal* millenarian of a type virtually unknown in Christianity since the second century.[10]

The appearance of prophets and prophetic texts of both non-Joachite and Joachite types are evidence of apocalyptic anxiety over the Babylonian captivity of the church. An example of the former is found in Birgitta of Sweden (c. 1303–1373), who was commanded by Christ to go to Rome in the 1340s and to offer the pope and emperor "revelations for the reformation of the Church." For years Birgitta upbraided the pope and the curia about their moral failings and the necessity of returning to Rome. She acquired a wide reputation as a visionary, including the accolade of having pseudonymous revelations circulated in her name. The authentic *Revelations* collected during her life and afterward put together by members of her circle are generally expressions of present divine judgment rather than predictions of the imminent last events, but the sixth book includes some prophecies regarding Antichrist, though of a traditional kind.[11] The record concerning applied Joachite expectations of Antichrist is more plentiful.

The Fraticelli, both of Spiritual and non-Spiritual origin, continued to be strong in parts of Italy where they pressed their attacks on the papal Antichrist, now including both John XXII and his successors (Fig. 16).[12] In a letter sent from some southern Italian Fraticelli to the citizens of Narni about 1354 we read: "These errors and heresies listed above [the condemnations of apostolic poverty], along with others invented, set forth, preached and defended by Pope John XXII, and confirmed and approved by his successors, are without doubt that Abomination of Desolation standing in the holy place (the Church) that Daniel prophesied and Christ predicted and spread abroad so that faithful Christians might vigilantly and diligently beware of it."[13]

Cola da Rienzo, the leader of the brief Roman Republic between 1347 and 1354, was influenced by Fraticelli ideas in his expectations for a coming Holy Pope and Last Emperor, though he wrote little about Antichrist. Another place where Fraticelli ideas were found was in Spain, as the witness of the Joachite *Breviloquium* of about 1350,[14] and the writings of the Franciscan Peter of Aragon, active as a prophet between 1360 and 1380, indicate.[15]

The Great Schism

Ever since the 1290s, prophetic authorities had been darkly or openly speaking of a coming schism that would pit a holy *pastor angelicus* against a papal Antichrist, usually conceived of as the *Antichristus mysticus*. Once again, history seemed to fulfill prophecy as the Western church confronted the trial known as the Great Schism.

In 1377 Gregory XI had finally returned from Avignon to Rome. His death in 1378 resulted in a split papal election. Under pressure from the Roman mob, the cardinals chose an Italian who took the name Urban VI. The cardinals soon repented of this choice, and a majority of their number, claiming an election conducted under duress was invalid, then elected a Frenchman, Clement VII, who returned to Avignon. Western Christendom split along political lines, with France and its allies supporting the Avignon popes and most of the rest of Europe defending Urban and the Roman line. Both popes were better qualified for the role of Antichrist than for that of *pastor angelicus*,[16] and apocalyptic propagandists throughout Europe found in the schism, which lasted down to 1417, a clear sign that the end was imminent.

The most important prophetic text to incorporate the schism into an apocalyptic scenario was the work of someone calling himself Telesphorus of Cosenza (probably a pseudonym); it was entitled *The Great Tribulations and the State of the Church*.[17] The Telesphoran treatise, which Roberto

Rusconi has justly called "the ultimate development of the Joachimite prophetic tradition,"[18] is difficult to interpret because the text as we have it appears to be a conflation of two versions—a prophetic work originally written between 1356 and 1365, which predicted an "imminent schism" (*instans scisma*), and an updating done between 1378 and 1390, which speaks of the "present schism" (*praesens scisma*). According to Telesphorus, the Mystical Antichrist (a German) was to be born about 1365 and would be crowned by a false German pope as Frederick III. Satan would then be released, and a convulsive struggle between the forces of good and evil to last down until 1409 would ensue. The good would be led by a *pastor angelicus* who would crown the French king Charles as the true Last Emperor. They would defeat the Mystical Antichrist and his papal ally but then would have to face the *Antichristus magnus*, who would appear about 1378 and lead the Church into schism. After victory over the *Antichristus magnus* in 1393, a succession of holy popes would rule in a messianic era down to 1433, when Gog, the *Antichristus ultimus*, would arrive after the emperor Charles had laid down his crown in Jerusalem. A second messianic era, however, was to follow the defeat of this final Antichrist. This scenario, with its odd triple Antichrist, used both Joachite and imperial apocalypticism in attempting to locate the crisis of the schism within God's total plan for history. The Telesphoran program remained popular in the fifteenth century and into the sixteenth. A number of illustrated versions were produced. These contain important additions to the Joachite tradition of Antichrist iconography, such as the scene of the false German pope (with accompanying devil) crowning Frederick III, the Mystical Antichrist (Fig. 17).

The era of the Great Schism was also marked by public movements of penance often connected with preaching about the imminent coming of Antichrist as well as his present immanence in the hearts of sinners.[19] The most important example is found in the Dominican preacher and supporter of the Avignon papacy, Vincent Ferrer, later canonized despite his adherence to Avignon.[20] Vincent (c. 1350–1419) was a traditionalist in his view of the Final Enemy, but the sad events of his time convinced him that the end was very near, and he made this conviction a central element in his influential penitential preaching throughout Europe in the early years of the fifteenth century.[21]

On the basis of the proper interpretation of Scripture and a number of private revelations (including one he himself received in 1398), Vincent

FIGURE 17   A false German pope crowns Frederick III, the Mystical Antichrist. Telesphorus of
Cosenza, *Liber de ultimis tribulationibus* (*The Great Tribulations and the State of the
Church*) in Munich, Bayerische Staatsbibliothek, ms. Clm. 313, fol. 26r (Salzburg,
1431 C.E.). Reproduced courtesy of the Bayerische Staatsbibliothek.

preached that Antichrist had been born in 1403. In a report he sent to the
Avignon pope Benedict XIII in 1412 he claimed:

> The conclusion stands through another clear revelation which I heard in
> Piedmont by the report of a Venetian merchant very worthy of faith, I be-
> lieve. He said that when he was overseas in a Franciscan monastery he
> heard Vespers on a feast day. At the end of the service, when they usually
> say "Benedicamus Domino," two small novices of the monastery were

immediately and visibly put in a trance before the eyes of all for a long space of time. Then they cried out together in a terrible voice: "Today, in this hour, Antichrist, the destroyer of the world, is born." When I inquired and asked about the time of this vision, I found out that it was only nine years ago. . . .[22]

The crisis of the schism led many leaders in western Europe to the conviction that only a General Council could solve the split between the competing popes of Rome and Avignon. In 1409 cardinals from both camps met in Pisa and elected a new pope, but since neither Rome nor Avignon yielded, this only made things worse. Finally, a larger council supported by the German emperor Sigismund met in Constance from 1414 to 1418. The Roman pope resigned, the Avignon and Pisan popes were deposed, and a new pope, Martin V (1417–31), was elected, who eventually restored ecclesiastical unity to Western Christendom.

These political shifts had many repercussions on Antichrist traditions.[23] Among these was a decline in popular preaching about Antichrist's imminence after 1417. Bernardino of Siena (1380–1444), the most famous preacher of his day, offers a good example of the shift.[24] From 1413 to 1417 the Franciscan preached almost exclusively on the Apocalypse, making considerable use of the pessimistic commentary of Matthew of Sweden, one of Birgitta of Sweden's followers. At this time, he insisted that Antichrist was near, especially because of the "triple silence" he discerned in the contemporary Church—*silentium praedicationis, silentium devotionis, silentium timorationis* (silence of preaching, of devotion, and of fear of God). Between 1418 and 1423, however, Bernardino shifted his message. Antichrist was still a part of his preaching, but he emphasized a moral message (for instance, combating the evils that make us part of Antichrist's body, like usury), and he also adopted a more positive attitude toward the present situation of the Church.[25] In his later sermons (after 1423), he dropped all references to the proximate coming Antichrist, and, as is typical of disillusioned apocalypticists, he attacked the dangers of false speculations on Antichrist's advent.[26]

To be sure, this overview of Antichrist expectations between 1335 and 1435 does not tell the whole story. Although many of the authors we have considered were controversial (and some were condemned as heretical), they all believed in the divine foundation of the medieval church, even when they were intensely critical of individual clerics and popes. It is a mark of the respect that the Franciscan Spirituals and later the Fraticelli had for the papacy that they gave it so central an apocalyptic role. In their scenario of the end it was always necessary that a *pastor angelicus* undo the evils wrought by a papal Antichrist to vindicate the religious value of the highest office in Christendom.

Another dimension of Antichrist rhetoric during this period also began by applying the Antichrist legend to the current situation of the Church, especially in relation to the papacy. This form, however, focused not so much on a colorful legendary agenda, typical of the Joachites, but on the core significance of the use of Antichrist rhetoric against the papacy—the sense that no one was a more obvious member of Antichrist, or even possibly the Final Enemy himself, than an immoral occupant of Christendom's supreme spiritual office. In the development of this tradition, however, the notion of what constituted the essence of "Antichristianity" came to center more on the papal office itself and less on individual evil popes. Though the distinction between attacking the office as emblematic of Antichristianity and criticizing particular occupants of the office was not always clear in the midst of heated rhetoric, this tendency represented a far more subversive use of Antichrist language than that found in the Spirituals and Fraticelli.[27] The new trend began in England with John Wycliffe (c. 1330–1384) and his followers. It was developed in Bohemia in the first two decades of the fifteenth century, eventually reaching maturity in the reformers of the sixteenth century.

Radical Denunciations of Papal Antichristianity

It was only after the condemnation of some of his views by Pope Gregory XI in 1377 that the prolific English theologian John Wycliffe began his major use of Antichrist rhetoric as a weapon to belabor the papacy. Many were doing so at the time, as we have seen, but Wycliffe's use of Antichrist language was distinctive.[28]

Wycliffe's reaction to the troubled ecclesiastical situation of his day was based upon a sharp distinction between the invisible church of the saved and the visible church of the present. The visible church—sunk in vice, loaded down with endowments, beset by hypocritical friars—was clearly opposed to Scripture (the ultimate criterion for true Christianity for Wycliffe) and hence had lost all authority. This led the Oxford theologian to a radical attack upon the whole ecclesiastical establishment. In the words of medievalist Gordon Leff, "Wycliffe accordingly saw the conflict between Christ and Antichrist primarily as one between the truth of the Bible and the pretensions of the modern hierarchy."[29] Though he at times waffled on the question of whether there could be such a thing as a true and holy pope, especially in the present evil time, the thrust of Wycliffe's incessant rhetoric was to see the papacy itself, not just any individual pope, as the culmination of the power of the Son of Perdition.

This teaching is pervasive in his late works, especially *On Apostasy, On the Pope's Power,* and the commentary on the apocalyptic discourse of Matthew 23–25, which he incorporated as books 3 and 4 of his unfinished *Evangelical Work.*[30] Wycliffe refused to calculate the time of the end, scorning Joachim and others who did,[31] but he remained a true apocalyptic thinker who was convinced that the end was near and that the signs of the last two centuries made this crystal clear.[32] He believed that Innocent III's papacy, which saw the beginnings of the friars and false eucharistic teaching (i.e, the doctrine of transubstantiation), signaled the loosing of Satan (Apoc. 20:7). Gog signified Antichrist (the papacy) and Magog his followers, especially the hypocritical friars whom the English theologian scolded so often in his last years.[33] Closer to his own time, he thought that the Great Schism (both popes were Antichrist for him) and contemporary wars were also signs of the imminence of the end. Wycliffe conceived of Antichrist fundamentally in corporate terms. Rejecting the argument of those who said that the pope could not be Antichrist because he did not perform the miracles of the Adsonian tradition, Wycliffe summarized his position thus:

> From this supposition, depending on the way of life of Christ and the way of life of the pope, it will appear to the knowledgeable faithful that the pope is the evident [*patulus*] Antichrist, not just the individual person who sets up more laws that are against Christ's law, but the multitude of popes from the time of the Church's endowment—and of cardinals, bishops, and their other accomplices. The person of Antichrist is a monstrous composite one.[34]

Wycliffe's radical position on the papacy itself as Antichrist became a central tenet of the Lollard movement that took its inspiration from him. The Lollard "Twenty-Five Points" of 1388 began with the assertion that the pope is Antichrist, and the same teaching is evident in all the major leaders, such as John Purvey (Wycliffe's secretary), and later Sir John Old-castle, their aristocratic defender. A good example of Lollard vernacular teaching in the matter of the papal Antichrist is to be found in the treatise called *The Lantern of Light,* which was written in about 1410.[35]

The Hussites

Wycliffe's militant insistence on the necessity of the disendowment of the Church had radical implications, though his hope that this could be done through royal power was quite conservative. More revolutionary in implication and eventually in action was the Hussite movement, which arose in Bohemia in the first two decades of the fifteenth century. For the Hussites neither pope nor king possessed unquestionable divine authorization.

The generally bad condition of the Church in the fourteenth century, exacerbated by the Avignon captivity and the Great Schism, led to calls for reform with an apocalyptic ring in many parts of Europe. Not least of these was Bohemia, especially in the capital of Prague. An Austrian Augustinian named Conrad Waldhauser apparently began the reform preaching, but the main figures were two native Czechs, John Milič, who began preaching about 1364 and died in 1374, and Matthew of Janov, who went to Paris to receive a theology degree but returned to Prague and preached there from 1381 to 1394. Both men were obsessed with Antichrist and the evidence of his presence in the world, although neither departed from the usual applied Antichrist views prevalent in the fourteenth century.[36]

Matthew of Janov compiled a large work under the title *Rules of the Old and the New Testament* to provide a theological foundation to the Czech reform program. The third book of five contains one of the longest treatises devoted to Antichrist in the Middle Ages. Matthew's tract is largely biblical, but he had read widely in prophetic literature.[37]

Matthew's theme is the "mystical body of Antichrist" (*corpus mysticum Antichristi*), that is, the study of how Antichrist had come to dominate the Church and the world since the year 1200. His list of the characteristics of "antichristianity" (*antechristietas,* a term that may be his own coining) is a standard one—hypocrisy, avarice, concupiscence, and the like. He finds the schism a clear sign of the divided body of Antichrist and points to Clement VII as an antichrist if not perhaps the final Antichrist.[38] The last Antichrist (*Antichristus summus*) must be a Christian, not a Jew or Muslim, and a Christian who possesses the "state of the highest priesthood" and "fullness of power," that is, a pope.[39]

But Matthew did not think that the papacy itself was the essence of Antichrist. Rather, the Final Enemy had been invading the whole Church gradually for almost two hundred years, so that the present time (Matthew was writing about 1385) was the critical moment when the forces of good, that is, of moral and ecclesiastical reform, and those of antichristian evil were engaged in the ultimate battle.[40]

Jan Hus (c. 1372–1415) began from a similar traditional position, but in the 1390s he, like other contemporary Czech theologians, was influenced by reading Wycliffe. His teaching at the University of Prague, and especially his vernacular preaching at the Bethlehem Chapel after 1402, reemphasized the message of antichristian corruption of the Church. Hus went beyond his Czech predecessors, but it seems doubtful that he was ever quite as radical as Wycliffe, despite his unfortunate fate of being burned as a heretic at the Council of Constance in 1415.

Hus had a keen sense of the Church's corruption, under way since the legendary Donation of Constantine of the fourth century, which had given the Church wealth and power. He was critical of the powerful medieval papal establishment, as were many apocalyptic writers from the thirteenth century, but I would agree with medievalist Howard Kaminsky that "when the chips were down, . . . he was not prepared to repudiate the actual Church as the body of Antichrist."[41] In his major theoretical work, *On the Church,* Hus used ideas taken from Wycliffe, but in a more moderate way, giving, for instance, four signs by which one can recognize a pope who is really an Antichrist, but not claiming that the papacy itself is the Final Enemy.[42] Events would push his followers in a more radical direction.

Hus was excommunicated in 1411. In 1412 three of his lay followers were executed and he had to flee from Prague. At this time some of his associates, especially the Czech Master Jakoubek of Stříbro and the German Master Nicholas of Dresden, moved the Czech reform decisively in the direction of subversive Antichrist views similar to those of Wycliffe. According to Kaminsky, "The ideology of Hus encouraged others to revolt, but it led him to Constance—to submission and martyrdom. It was the ideology of men like Nicholas of Dresden and Jakoubek that actually justified schism with the Roman church as the mystical body of Antichrist."[43] In January 1412, Jakoubek publicly defended the assertion that Antichrist had already come personally into the world, leaving no doubt that this was in the person of the pope.[44]

In the same year, Nicholas issued a work called *The Old Color and the New,* which turned out to be perhaps the most influential of the Hussite Antichrist treatises. The ancient symbolic oppositions between Christ and Antichrist took on a new form here in relation to the contrasts between the poor and humble Christ of the Gospels and the wealth and power over

which claimants to the throne of Peter were then struggling.[45] His somewhat pedantic lists of church authorities, contrasting the "old color" of the
apostolic church and the "new color" of late medieval papal Christendom,
were intended not just for learned divines. They were meant to be illustrated for popular consumption. Evidence indicates that banners or plac-
ards picturing the contrasts between Christ and Antichrist based on this
treatise were part of the ceremonies connected with the preaching at the
Bethlehem Chapel. These have not survived, nor do the remaining manuscripts of the work contain illustrations. Nevertheless, later (c. 1500)
manuscripts of antipapal antitheses from Jena and Göttingen have been
recognized as related to these visual aids of early Hussitism, as is evident
from a picture of the papal Antichrist being adored by monks found in the
Jena manuscript (Fig. 18).[46]

During the time Hus spent in exile, we have evidence for a heightened degree of Antichrist rhetoric against the papacy and his other opponents.[47] But the Czech master did not change his basic position.
Summoned to the Council of Constance, he rejoiced in the possibility of
putting his case to the assembled fathers. When his safe conduct was
treacherously revoked, he continued to defend the orthodoxy of his views
in 1414 and 1415. In response to the accusation that he claimed that the
pope was Antichrist, his response was qualified but not dishonest: "I did
not say this, but I did say that if the pope sells benefices, if he is proud,
avaricious, or otherwise morally opposed to Christ, then he is the Antichrist. But it should by no means follow that every pope is Antichrist; a
good pope, like St. Gregory, is not the Antichrist, nor do I think he ever
was."[48] This was not enough to save him. Hus was burned as a heretic on
July 6, 1415.

Hus's death by the hand of Antichrist's church, now headed by a
new papal Antichrist, supported the swing among his followers to a view
indistinguishable from that of Wycliffe. But Hus's radical adherents went
beyond the Oxford don in their conviction that not only the pope but the
whole fabric of late medieval Christendom reeked of the stink of Antichrist. The Hussite revolution, which began its militant phase in 1419, is
the best example of revolutionary apocalypticism in the Middle Ages.

The role that Antichrist played in facilitating the transition from
calls for reform to armed revolt had been set out already by radicals like
Nicholas and Jakoubek. Antichrist rhetoric functioned as an integral part
of a broad apocalyptic appeal used to galvanize marginal peasants and
some city dwellers into recognizing that not only the pope (whoever he

FIGURE 18
Papal Antichrist adored by
monks. Prague, National
Museum, ms. IV.B 4, fol. 35a
(c. 1500 C.E.). Reproduced
from Karel Stejskal,
"Poznámky k současnému
stavu bádáni o Jenském
kodexu," Umění 9 (1961): 11.

might be!) but the whole late medieval system was the dread oppressor
and enemy of God. An early radical Hussite manifesto of 1419 demonstrates a generic use of Antichrist language within a truly revolutionary
context:

> We also ask God, now that we have recognized the cunning and the dam-
> aging seduction of our souls by false and hypocritical prophets, guided by
> Antichrist against the Law of God, that we may beware of them and dili-
> gently be on our guard against them. . . . For we now clearly see the Great
> Abomination standing in the Holy Place, as prophesied by the prophet

Daniel: the ridicule, blasphemy, suppression, and repudiation of all God's truth, and the enormous glorification of all Antichristian hypocritical evil. . . .[49]

Antichrist language was widely used during the course of the Hussite movement, not only against the papacy and those who opposed the now-militant reformers but also among the various factions themselves as the split between moderate activists centered in Prague and radicals of different shades connected with the utopian society of Tabor developed between 1419 and 1421. As in the Reformation debates to be considered in the next chapter, the more widespread the use of Antichrist rhetoric, the more jejune it became in the later history of Hussitism. But the Hussites played a key role in the history of the Antichrist legend. Though Wycliffe was the first to identify the papacy itself with Antichrist, it was among the radical Hussites that this new moment in Antichrist's story became a part of a revolutionary ideology that encouraged overthrowing the social and religious order.

Antichrist in the Later Fifteenth Century

The radical days of the Hussite movement ended in the 1430s, to be succeeded by a national church of a fairly conservative sort. In other parts of Western Christendom, the cooperation between the revived papacy and rulers was less conducive to Antichrist speculation than the time of the Great Schism had been. This is not to say that fears of Antichrist died out during these years, but they appear somewhat muted.

In Italy, for instance, late fifteenth-century preachers still appealed to Antichrist's imminence to frighten their congregations. In December 1461, the Franciscan Michael Carcano of Milan preached for four days on Antichrist at Florence, while in 1473 two wandering hermits announced a message of repentance in the face of Antichrist's coming in the towns and cities of central Italy. In 1484, a conjunction of Jupiter and Saturn was seen as a sign of the end, and in 1489 a Franciscan preaching in Bologna announced that Antichrist would be born on September 12, 1506, at 5:00 P.M. Although we customarily think of this period in Italian history as replete with Renaissance hopes for a new golden age, such hopes often paradoxically existed alongside fears of Antichrist's coming. Not all the prophets and apocalypticists of the time were Joachite in inspiration, but the well-known scholar of apocalypticism Marjorie Reeves is right to claim that "the Joachimist marriage of woe and exaltation exactly fitted the mood of late fifteenth century Italy, where the concept of the humanist Age of Gold had to be brought into relation with the ingrained expectation of Antichrist."[50]

The best-known prophetic voice of the time was that of Girolamo Savonarola (1452–1498), the Dominican preacher of the San Marco convent in Florence.[51] In the 1480s and 1490s he preached the coming of a severe chastisement on sinful Italy as the necessary prelude to reform. Savonarola was more interested in this proximate *flagellum Dei* and the succeeding renewed Christianity than he was in Antichrist, but he did expect a confrontation between the revitalized church and the Final Enemy in the coming Fifth Age and a millennial period that would succeed this struggle.[52] The Dominican's message of imminent crisis was fulfilled by Charles VIII's invasion of Italy in 1494 and his sparing of Florence. For a time Savonarola was the master of the city and was given the opportunity to try to build a new millenarian society there. But his reformist ideas brought him increasingly into conflict with the corrupt Alexander VI and the papal curia (though he never denounced the pope as Antichrist). After being excommunicated in 1497 and losing support in Florence, he was arrested, tortured, and burned as a heretic on May 23, 1498.

Interestingly enough, although the controversial prophet himself said little about Antichrist, many of his enemies denounced *him* as Antichrist for his hypocrisy and sedition (as they saw it). The Augustinian Leonardo of Fivizzano called the friar an agent of Antichrist, as did humanists such as Giovanni Francesco Poggio Bracciolini, and especially Marsilio Ficino, who had once been among his followers.[53] But Savonarola's fate did not prevent some of his followers from continuing to announce apocalyptic messages involving Antichrist's imminence, as we know from the cases of the Francesco of Montepulciano who preached in Florence in 1513, and from the condemnation of the lay prophet Francesco of Meleto in 1517.[54]

Evidence for continuing importance of Antichrist beliefs in the late fifteenth century is also found north of the Alps, especially in Germany.[55] An important treatise known as the *Wonderful Pamphlet on the End of the World,* often ascribed to Vincent Ferrer but probably from the mid–fifteenth century, was printed seven times in Germany before the Reformation.[56] The pamphlet did much to spread the new term *Antichristus mixtus,* while it also pictured a Holy Last Pope, dressed in white linen, who would effect the final reform of the Church.

Although some measure of peace and stability had been restored to Christendom by the end of the schism, the middle of the fifteenth century saw increased consciousness of an external danger, the growing threat of Turkish power made evident by the conquest of Constantinople in 1453 and Turkish advances in central Europe. Evidence of this concern is found especially in Italy and Germany, where some thinkers began to investigate prophetic classics, like the Methodian *Revelations,* to discover the apocalyptic meaning of the Turkish threat.[57]

Antichrist lived on in a variety of guises during these decades. For many, he was the standard Final Enemy, however near or far off. For others he was one of several players on a confusing apocalyptic stage. Still others were fed up with useless speculation about the end. The decree *Supremae majestatis praesidio* of the Fifth Lateran Council, adopted on December 19, 1516, condemned all attempts to fix the time of Antichrist's coming and the end of the world. The irony in this was that within a decade many in Europe would be convinced that there was indeed no need at all to speculate about *when* Antichrist would come—he was already present in the papacy!

Pictures, Plays, and Poetry

Not every appearance of Antichrist in literature and art between 1335 and 1500 need be noted here, because much of the material was unoriginal and of mediocre quality. The most important innovations were iconographic; the late Middle Ages saw the creation of extensive pictorial cycles of Antichrist. But some literary uses deserve mention. The most important are to be found in Middle English literature, *Piers Plowman* and the Chester *Play of Antichrist.*

Antichrist appears in many places in Middle English poetry, such as the *Pricke of Conscience* (c. 1350) and in John Gower's poems, but in no place is he as central to the action and meaning of a poem as in *Piers Plowman.* William Langland, a cleric in minor orders, composed the poem in three versions in the period from about 1365 to 1390.[58] The work might be described as a poetic "epic" on the necessity for reform in the late Middle Ages.[59] The action of the poem, as is typical of medieval dream visions, has both progressive and recapitulative elements.[60] The opposition between good and evil, between the Tower of Truth and the Dungeon of Hell, is presented in a variety of ways, all suggesting the growing dominance of evil typified by Lady Mede (that is, payment) and Falsehood. Among the most evident signs of Antichrist's imminence are the wickedness and corruption of the clergy, especially the hypocritical friars.[61] Passus XX contains a telling description of Antichrist's assault on the Church:

> Whan Nede hadde undernome [reproached] me thus, anoon I fil aslepe,[62]
> And mette ful merveillously that in mannes forme
> Antecrist cam thanne, and al the crop of truthe
> Torned it (tid) up-so-doun, and overtilte [upturned] the roote,
> And made fals sprynge and sprede and spede [prosper] mennes nedes.[63]
> In ech a contree ther he cam he kutte awey truthe,
> And gerte [made] gile growe there as he a god weere.
> Freres folwede that fend, for he gaf hem copes,
> And religious reverenced hym and rongen hir belles,
> And al the covent cam to welcome that tyraunt,
> And alle hise as wel as hym—save oonly fooles;
> Whiche fooles were wel gladdere to deye
> Than to lyve lenger sith Leute [Fidelity] was so rebuked,
> And a fals fend Antecrist over alle folk regnede. (XX.51–64)

Langland shows little interest in the details of Antichrist's career. Like the poets Jean de Meun and Dante, he goes straight to the heart of the late medieval contribution to the long history of the Antichrist legend—the emphasis on how the hypocrisy and deceit of the Final Enemy marshal the army of vices with which he attacks the Church.

Debates over Langland's apocalypticism center on two issues. The first is whether the poem is essentially optimistic, and perhaps therefore Joachite in inspiration, looking forward to a post-Antichrist repristination of the Church,[64] or rather fundamentally pessimistic, seeing current abuses as so powerful and pervasive that they indicate Antichrist is here and the Last Judgment will soon follow.[65] The question implies a second issue of how much ecclesial and social reform Langland felt was really possible—little at all, if the pessimists are correct. The final Passus of the poem is indeed very pessimistic in tone, but it ends with Conscience becoming a pilgrim and going in search of Piers the Plowman, the mysterious Christ surrogate who surfaces throughout the poem and whom some have thought includes elements of a Last Emperor or even a Holy Pope. A series of prophecies (for example, Passus III.284–330) has been used, on the other hand, as evidence for an optimistic reading about a coming millennial time after Antichrist's defeat.[66] While I see little evidence for any strong Joachite influence on the poem, not every form of optimistic apocalypticism need be Joachite in inspiration. Indeed, since all Christian beliefs about the end are mixtures of optimism and pessimism, it is a sign of Langland's artistry that the recipe he mixed in his great apocalyptic poem is such a subtle combination of both elements that the critics will possibly never be able to agree about it.

Plays about Antichrist proliferated in the late medieval world. Examples are known from France and Italy, but the majority (at least eleven) come from Germany.[67] Perhaps the most interesting example, however, is the sole English version, the Chester *Play of Antichrist*.[68] The *Play of Antichrist* takes its place in a well-planned presentation of the last things contained in the final three pieces of the Chester cycle. First, the *Prophets of Antichrist* (more correctly, *Prophets Before the Day of Doom*) introduce the final events with a tableau of four prophets and an account of the well-known fifteen signs of the end. After this "sermon on eschatology," the *Play of Antichrist* and the *Last Judgment* play that concludes the whole cycle serve as two typologically related acts in the great scenario of the end.[69] Seen within the context of the history of the Antichrist legend and its connections with the rest of sacred history, the Chester play reveals considerable knowledge and a deft reshaping of elements for dramatic presentation.

The Chester play contains elements of broad humor that must have been crowd pleasing, especially in the long "flyting" (abusive argument) between Antichrist and the two witnesses. But the essential message focuses on fear of Antichrist's hypocrisy. A new note, one that may be related to late medieval emphasis on the sacrament of penance, is found in the key role given to the four kings who are at first converted by Antichrist's false miracles but who, after the preaching of the two witnesses, see the error of their ways, do penance, and receive martyrdom along with the witnesses. The final lines, where two demons drag Antichrist down to hell while the slain witnesses ascend to heaven, form an admirable summary of the opposition between humble martyrs who rise to life and all proud and tyrannical deceivers, whose head is Antichrist and who will meet a very different fate.[70]

Antichrist iconography flourished as never before between 1335 and 1500. Especially significant was the rich development of the illustrated cycles of the life of the Final Enemy in manuscripts and early printed books. The period closed with the supreme monumental presentation of Antichrist in art, Luca Signorelli's fresco in the San Brixio Chapel in Orvieto.

Illustrated Bibles, as well as illustrated Apocalypses, continued to include portrayals of Antichrist. Among the latter, we can single out the magnificent Flemish Apocalypse from the early fifteenth century now in the Bibliothèque Nationale in Paris.[71] The most comprehensive picture Bible of the mid–fourteenth century, the Velislaus Bible from Prague, was important for breaking new ground in the presentation of the Son of Perdition.

Velislaus was a canon connected with the court of Charles IV. Though some have argued for an ideological basis to his work as a forerunner of Hussite biblicism and antipapalism, there is no evidence for this in the text.[72] The 747 illustrations contained in this huge Bible include an incomplete cycle of twenty-two pictures based on Hugh of Strassburg's handy compendium of the Adsonian Antichrist tradition. These include a scene of Antichrist's conception and birth, the first appearance of this motif (folio 130b, see Fig. 19). Antichrist later appears as a young Christ lookalike in the scenes of his arrival in Jerusalem, his circumcision, and his preaching to the Jews. Soon he sports a beard as he marks the kings as his followers. There is a scene of the false pentecost and of Antichrist raising the dead by diabolical power. Antichrist disputes with theologians and bids them to be beheaded, even burning their books—a unique scene (see folios 134b bottom and 135a). Finally, he rebuilds the temple and is adored as God. The cycle ends there, with no portrayal of the false ascension and his destruction.

A number of other fourteenth- and early fifteenth-century manuscripts display original pictures of the legend of Antichrist. What survives is doubtless only a part of what once existed, but such manuscripts as those in the Bibliotheca Casanatense at Rome and the Wellcome Museum Library at London, both German from about 1410 to 1440,[73] give some idea of the innovations of the time. But the major developments came in the fifteenth-century blockbooks. Blockbooks belong to the gestation period of printing—halfway between the manuscript and real printed books. Reproduced from wooden blocks carved with text and picture, they allowed for multiple copies, but without movable type, and they often included many of the details of manuscript reproduction, such as hand coloring. This intermediate technology was in experimental use by the end of the

FIGURE 19
Antichrist's conception and
birth. Velislaus Bible, fol.
130b (second half of the
fourteenth century).
Reproduced from Karel
Stejskal, ed., *Velislai Biblia
Picta* (Prague: Pragopress,
1970).

first quarter of the fifteenth century. Among its earliest products (c. 1440?) were illustrated Apocalypses that contained crude versions of the Anglo-French cycle of Antichrist's life connected with the eleventh chapter of the Apocalypse.

In the second half of the century, however, a series of blockbooks and early printings (*incunabula*) devoted specifically to Antichrist and the Fifteen Signs were produced in Germany. They are the most detailed, and among the most effective, of all portrayals of the Final Enemy. Adhering to the standard Adsonian view (with a few embellishments), these books are difficult to tie to any applied uses of the Antichrist legend. Still, how are we to know what the readers (or rather viewers, since the blockbooks are meant to have a visual effect) took from these volumes?[74]

In the absence of agreement among authorities about the exact dating of these volumes, we can only say that the blockbooks were most likely produced between 1455 and 1480. Several have been reproduced in facsimile versions in recent years.[75] Full versions of these Antichrist books contain as many as seventy pictures with brief German captions, by far the

Der Ennokrist wirt geborn in einer stat genant grofs babilonie Vnd er würt aller vntugent vnd bofheit vol · Wenn der tüfel tüt alles fin vermügen dar zü· Vnd das wepst das büch/das da heist Compendium Theologie·in dem fibenden Capitel·

Hye würt der Ennokrist sich vnder stan der vnkeüsch vnd vn: ordenlicher lieb der frowen/ vnd das geschicht in der stat Beth: sayda· Also sagt ouch Compendiu· Vnd vnfer herr flücht der sel: ben stat/in dem ewangelio/Do er spricht wee dir Bethsayda·

FIGURE 20
Antichrist's birth and
education. Strassburg
Antichrist Book, fol. 4v
(c. 1480). Reproduced from
K. Boveland, C. P. Burger,
and R. Steffan, *Der Antichrist
und die fünfzehn Zeichen vor
dem Jüngsten Gericht.
Faksimile* (Hamburg: Wittig,
1979), with the permission of
the publisher.

most complete pictorial presentations of Antichrist before or since. They also show some important innovations in the standard iconography. Among the most interesting is that relating to Antichrist's birth. After scenes of the Final Enemy's conception, he is portrayed as born by caesarean section (often with an assisting demon) as a mark of his perverse nature (Fig. 20).[76]

The remaining scenes expand upon what we have already seen in the Velislaus Bible. Following the Nuremberg blockbook, which may date from 1465, we note the following interesting details. First, Antichrist appears throughout as a handsome young man with curly blond locks, not a

FIGURE 21
Antichrist's miracles.
Nuremberg Blockbook,
fol. 5v (c. 1465). Reproduced
from H. T. Musper, ed., *Der
Antichrist und die fünfzehn
Zeichen* (Munich: Prestel,
1970), with the permission of
the publisher.

Christ look-alike. After completing his education in lechery and magic, he goes to Jerusalem to be circumcised and to rebuild the temple. But then (as contrasted with the Velislaus Bible) Enoch and Elijah appear. Pictures of Antichrist's miracles follow, most based on the expanded Adsonian tradition. One, however, represents a peculiar and still untraced popular view; it shows the supreme magician producing a stag from a rock and a giant from an egg and hanging a castle in the air (Fig. 21)! The blockbook cycle and its typographical successors reach their culmination in Antichrist's pretended death and resurrection, immediately followed by the fire miracle or false pentecost, and his attempt to ascend to heaven (Fig. 22). Earlier written versions of the triple parody had tended to weaken its force by dividing the incidents. In placing them together at the very culmination of the Final Enemy's life, the blockbook tradition showed that visual logic is often more effective than that found in texts.

Der Ennckrift heift fich die tüfel vff füren. So fchlecht in vnfer
herr mit de geift fins mundes. Vnd fpzicht die glofz vber Appo
calipfis an dem·xiij·capitel· Michahel fchlach in zu tod· Wan ich
wil des vnrechten nit lenger veztrage· In compendio theologie·

FIGURE 22
Antichrist's false ascension.
Strassburg Antichrist Book,
fol. 24v (c. 1480). Reproduced
from Boveland, et al., *Der
Antichrist,* with the
permission of the publisher.

The greatest of all monumental Antichrist portrayals was the fresco
executed by Luca Signorelli in the San Brixio Chapel in the cathedral of
Orvieto about 1500 C.E. Although attempts to link Signorelli's presentation of the last events to particular historical events or diverse tendencies
in the Antichrist tradition have not been successful,[77] no single work of art
provides a better sense of the general medieval Christian scenario of the
end and the role of Antichrist within it. As in the cases of literary artists
like Dante and Langland, Signorelli's presentation of the Antichrist legend exceeds the sum of its parts; pedantic attempts to tie it to particular
sources and contexts have been unsuccessful.

FIGURE 23   Sermon and Acts of Antichrist by Luca Signorelli, Duomo, Orvieto, Italy (c. 1505).
Photo: Alinari/Art Resource, New York.

Signorelli's frescoes were designed to complete an earlier program
begun by Fra Angelico portraying the whole range of the Last Things—
Antichrist's coming, the destruction of the world, the general resurrection,
Last Judgment, and heaven and hell, the ultimate fates of humans. Immediately upon entering the chapel, one sees the vast fresco picturing Antichrist's life and death to the left (Fig. 23). Behind, on either side of the
doorway arch, is an equally impressive scene of the destruction of the
world, foretold by sibyl and prophet. Proceeding around the chapel are
scenes of the resurrection of the dead and of hell on the right wall and
heaven on the other panel of the left wall.

Although Signorelli's fresco pictures the whole life of Antichrist, it centers more on the falsity of his preaching than on his ultimate destruction. What dominates is the figure of the *pseudochristos* mounted on a pedestal, his face a demonic parody of the usual Renaissance portrayal of the majestic Christ. The devil whispers in his ear as the standard events of the Adsonian life of Antichrist are played out in the vast space that surrounds him. In the foreground, an eager audience listens to his preaching, piling up gifts in his honor. Those who do not accept him are slaughtered on the left. In the middle ground, friars debate his coming, one pointing toward a scene of false resurrection. A splendid Renaissance version of the rebuilt temple of Jerusalem looms in the right background, with the execution of the witnesses taking place before its steps. On the right, immediately above those who have fallen at Antichrist's command, the Final Enemy is being struck down by Michael while numbers of his followers are also destroyed by rays from heaven. To a modern viewer, Signorelli's great fresco is impressive but perhaps confusing. To a late medieval audience, it would have provided a marvelously synoptic portrayal of the Antichrist legend.

The Meaning Behind the Symbol

Having surveyed, in these last three chapters, the centuries from 1100 to 1500, it is time to address, if only briefly, the question of what the ingredients added to the Antichrist legend during this time implied for its inner meaning—the symbolic presentation of ultimate human evil. Most importantly, Antichrist's iniquity came to be seen more and more as religious evil, specifically hypocrisy and corruption in the Church. Tyranny and persecution remained important themes, but a new concentration on doctrinal and moral falsity was apparently aided by the multiplication of final Antichrists that first became evident in Joachim and was later canonized by the distinction between the Mystical and the Great Antichrist and other similar terms. Even according to the standard view of the Final Enemy, however, hypocrisy was often given greater weight than tyranny. Ultimate evil was increasingly seen as the most subtle religious duplicity.

To be sure, hypocrisy was not a new theme in the Antichrist legend. What was new was the emphasis on its ecclesial character: clerical, fraternal (related to the friars), and especially papal. *Corruptio optimi pessima est* ("The corruption of the best is the worst") was the underlying principle of this growing association between Antichrist, both collectively and individually conceived, and corrupt ecclesiastics. To work for the reform of the Church in head (that is, the papacy) and members was to take part in the struggle against Antichrist—though others might always judge *your* particular idea of reform as a new and more insidious type of religious hypocrisy and therefore as part of the Antichrist's mystical body!

How far did understandings of Antichrist during these centuries continue the externalization of the legend, that is, the projection of ultimate evil onto groups of outsiders, especially Jews, Muslims, and heretics? The record here is mixed. Muslims remained very much part of Antichrist's party, but the Final Enemy understood in an individual sense was only rarely taken to be a Muslim. The Antichrist was often seen as a heretic, and leader of heretics, but the persecutors of specific groups of heretics, for whom these centuries later became infamous, rarely appealed directly to Antichrist rhetoric as a part of their persecuting mentality. While the traditional view still held that Antichrist would be born a Jew and would initiate a revival of Judaism, the new Antichrist motifs created in the twelfth century and developed during the next three hundred years often dropped the Jewish dimension, insisting that Antichrist must be a Christian in order to assume the role of false pope or imperial persecutor. Thus, an important internalization process was evident in the later medieval Antichrist, often a corporate internalization centering on religious hypocrisy.

CHAPTER EIGHT

ANTICHRIST DIVIDED

REFORMERS, CATHOLICS, AND PURITANS DEBATE ANTICHRIST (1500–1660)

Antichrist was a legendary projection of ultimate human evil forming the reverse image of the Christian Redeemer. In the previous chapters we have seen how historical personalities from Nero to Pope John XXII as well as events from the fall of Jerusalem to the Great Schism helped shape the legend's development. The last chapter has also shown how the Antichrist legend took on an increasingly ecclesial, even a clerical and papal, tone in the later Middle Ages as the identification of the Final Enemy with a persecuting emperor faded into the background and Antichrist as the power of deception and hypocrisy within the Church itself came to the fore.

These changes set the stage for a striking new polarization of the legend in the sixteenth century, when within Western Christendom the great split we call the Reformation produced a distinctive polemical division within Antichrist traditions. This was no longer a question of multiple forms of Antichrist beliefs (Antichrist as one or many, as present or future, as mystical or great) coexisting within a common frame of reference; it was rather a sundering of mutually exclusive conceptions fundamentally at odds with each other. Roman Catholic Christianity largely continued the medieval traditions, though generally abandoning the notion of a papal Antichrist. Protestant Christianity from the start made identifying the institution of the papacy with Antichrist a fundamental tenet of belief, though Protestant divisions soon broadened Antichrist rhetoric to include other claimants as well. Truly, this was the age of Antichrist divided. The great debate over Antichrist continued down through the late seventeenth century, when the end of the wars of religion and the influence of the Enlightenment brought it to a close. Though Antichrist rhetoric continued to be used during the next two hundred years and more, its employment tended to be repetitious.[1]

The extent to which the Reformation begun by Martin Luther (1483–1546) was or was not a medieval event has been much debated by historians over the past century. While historian Wilhelm Dilthey argued the traditional case that the Renaissance and Reformation were the twin foundations upon which the modern Western world was built, his contemporary, the theologian Ernst Troeltsch, claimed that the Lutheran Reformation was really medieval in its religious vision, however much it began the breakup of the earlier world.[2] What is clear is that Luther himself was a deeply medieval figure, obsessed with the devil, with Antichrist as his human agent, and with the imminent end of the world. As the historical theologian Heiko A. Oberman has reminded us, "Luther was proclaiming the Last Days, not the modern age."[3] Still, Luther's view of Antichrist reflects the ambivalence that surrounds so much connected with his epochal figure: He is both in continuity with late medieval Antichrist traditions and yet also a powerful originator.[4]

Luther on the Antichrist

As he always insisted, Luther began his career as a pious monk and typical late medieval theologian, and it is well to remember, as Luther scholar Scott Hendrix puts it, "There was no overnight metamorphosis from monk to Protestant."[5] The stages in Luther's mental and spiritual journey are complex and have been much studied, not least because we have such a mass of primary material, both from Luther himself and from his friends and opponents. The reformer's growing conviction that the office of the papacy itself—not merely some evil-living or erroneous pope—was to be identified with the Antichrist because of its opposition to the preaching of the gospel was an important part of his breakthrough to a full-fledged Reformation position, though he became aware of it only gradually over the course of several years. Once he accepted it, Luther maintained this

view until his death with a fierce conviction that was not above scatological
invective. Through him the identification of the papacy with Antichrist
became a central element in early Protestant belief, one that still survives in
our ecumenical era among some of Luther's more literal-minded successors.[6] In order to assess what Luther owed to medieval views of Antichrist
and where he went beyond them, it is necessary to take a look at the
progress of the reformer, especially during the years 1517 to 1521.

The young Luther entered the Augustinian Hermits in 1505 and
was ordained in 1507. He received his doctorate in 1512 and that same
year began to teach at the new Saxon university at Wittenberg. Whether
or not his early sermons and scriptural commentaries show the germs of
his later reformed theology in some particulars (a much-debated issue),
they display little interest in Antichrist and no originality in this area.[7] In
October 1517, however, when the young monk issued the invitation to a
debate over the papal indulgences being hawked through Germany (the
famous *Ninety-Five Theses*), he set himself in a direction that would lead
him to conclusions he could not have foreseen. Reminiscing over these
events in 1537, Luther said,

> After the pope, with force and cunning, usurped all power and authority,
> so that he could not be humiliated either by emperor or king, then it was
> fitting that by the power of the word the Son of Perdition should be re-
> vealed [2 Thess. 2:3]. However, I came upon it quite innocently; for I never
> would have dreamed this twenty years prior to that day. Rather, if someone
> else had taught such a thing, I would have damned and burned him. But
> God is the cause, because he did such things miraculously.[8]

Luther's original struggle, however, had nothing to do with Antichrist. It was only as Rome's opposition to his attack on indulgences compelled him to think hard about the papacy and its role in Christianity that
he began to sense an anti-Christian character to this opposition. Luther's
sense of this anti-Christianity remained muted, hypothetical, and pri-
vately expressed in 1518 and 1519, but in 1520 it burst upon the scene with
tremendous force in the first great series of Reformation treatises.

In a letter of December 1518, for example, shortly after Luther had
encountered the papal champion Cardinal Cajetan at the Diet of Augsburg, we find him writing to his friend Wenceslaus Link wondering
whether "the true Antichrist according to Paul is reigning in the Roman
curia."[9] At this time, Luther was still appealing to Pope Leo X himself, directly attacking only his curial spokesmen, such as Cajetan and Sylvester

Prierias, who tried to bring the rebellious monk to heel. In 1520 further reflection and the course of events shifted the Antichrist accusation directly onto the papacy itself, not just the shoulders of Leo X.

Some of this shift had to do with Luther's increasing knowledge about the history of the papacy and its activities. For instance, by March 1519 his study of papal decretals had led him to whisper to George Spalatin that the pope himself may well be Antichrist.[10] In late 1519 he was astonished on reading the condemned Hus at how correct the Bohemian theologian had actually been,[11] and in early 1520 his perusal of Ulrich von Hutten's edition of Lorenzo Valla's attack on the *Donation of Constantine* led him to exclaim, "I am so tormented, I scarcely doubt that the pope is properly that Antichrist which by common consent the world expects; everything which he lives, does, speaks and establishes fits so well."[12] The stage was set for the public proclamation.

Still, it was primarily the pressure of events rather than scholarly study that moved Luther to the point of rejecting the papacy for its fundamental opposition to Christ and Christ's saving message. The pope's tyranny over the word of God as well as over God's appointed worldly powers of kings and emperors had gone too far in Luther's view for any further hesitation. The reformer was already preparing his attack before his excommunication by the papal bull *Exsurge Domine* in June 1520. A series of ringing pamphlets confronted the papal Antichrist head-on. The most important of these was the *Address to the Christian Nobility,* Luther's most popular treatise, which first appeared in August.[13] In this pamphlet Luther stormed the "three walls" the Romanists built around themselves in order to expose the Antichrist hidden within: "Now the Romanists make the pope a vicar of the glorified Christ in heaven, and some of them have allowed the devil to rule them so completely that they have maintained that the pope is above the angels in heaven and has them at his command. These are certainly the proper works of the real Antichrist."[14]

The same message is found in *The Babylonian Captivity of the Church,* Luther's condemnation of the Catholic sacramental system issued in October 1520, which asserts, "The papacy is indeed nothing but the kingdom of Babylon and of the true Antichrist."[15] In November Luther issued his attack on the bull of excommunication entitled *Against the Execrable Bull of Antichrist,* which contained an equally strong denunciation of the papacy as the seat of the Final Enemy.[16] Luther was never to have any doubts on the issue—or to modify his attack—for the remainder of his life.

FIGURE 24   Christ casting out the moneychangers contrasted with the papal Antichrist receiving indulgence money. Martin Luther and Lucas Cranach, *Passional Christi et Antichristi* (*Passional of Christ and Antichrist*), 1521. Reproduced from *D. Martin Luthers Werke* (Weimar: Böhlau, 1893), vol. 8.

The popular side of this denunciation of the papacy as Antichrist can be seen in the illustrated *Antitheses,* or *Passional of Christ and Antichrist,* which was drawn up by Luther's collaborator, the artist Lucas Cranach the elder, in early 1521. Taking a cue from the earlier Hussite pictorial attacks on the papacy, Cranach and Luther's friend Philipp Melanchthon portrayed the contrast between Christ and the papal Antichrist in thirteen sets of aptly captioned double pictures.[17] This "illustrated morality play" was an effective salvo in the Reformation propaganda war against the papal Antichrist.[18] A good example of its power can be found in the picture that contrasts Christ driving the money changers from the Temple (see John 2:13–25) with the pope receiving the gold of indulgence money at the altar (Fig. 24). The pamphlet closes with an illustration cleverly adopted from the late medieval portrayals of Antichrist's demise. On the one side Christ ascends to heaven from the Mount of Olives, while on the opposite the papal Antichrist is dragged down to hell by a host of devils (Fig. 25). No wonder Luther was well pleased with the book.[19]

It would be tedious to take up all the texts from the later Luther that return to this central motif of his teaching, but several further issues are

FIGURE 25
Destruction of the papal
Antichrist. Luther and
Cranach, *Passional* (1521).
Reproduced from *D. Martin
Luthers Werke,* Böhlau, vol. 8.

worth a comment in order to demonstrate his contribution to the history of
Antichrist. As Reformation scholar Hans Preuss has stressed, the papacy
proved itself to be Antichrist for Luther primarily due to its opposition to
the word of God both in Scripture and in preaching.[20] The biblical basis
for Luther's view of the papal Antichrist was deepened by his developing
understanding of John's Apocalypse. At the beginning, the reformer had
little sympathy for the book, dismissing it in his 1522 translation of the
Bible with the remark "My spirit cannot fit itself into this book" because
"Christ is not known or taught in it."[21] But by the time he rewrote the
preface to the Apocalypse in 1530, he had changed his mind.[22] Adopting a
historically progressive view of the text somewhat like that popularized by
Nicholas of Lyra, Luther argued that the imagery of the Apocalypse conformed to the history of the trials and tribulations of the "one, holy Christian Church." Specifically, the three woes announced in Apocalypse 8:13
are taken as prophecies of the persecutions of Arius, Muhammad, and, finally, "the papal empire and imperial papacy," which is identified with the

Second Beast of chapter 13. In chapter 14, then, "Christ first begins to slay his Antichrist with the breath of his mouth, as Paul says in 2 Thessalonians 2." Therefore, Luther now praises the Apocalypse as an effective warning against the error of those who call the papacy "the Christian Church," since it is really the Christian Church's worst enemy.[23]

Luther came to view the papal Antichrist both as a developing evil and also as one associated with the Turkish threat in his own time. On the former issue, we can ask if Luther thought that the papacy had always been the Antichrist. The answer seems to be based on a distinction between some earlier good bishops of Rome, like Gregory I, whom Luther praised as a true preacher of the gospel, and the institution of the anti-Christian papacy, which the devil had begun to build up within the church from the seventh century C.E.[24] While preachers like Hus and Savonarola, and now Luther and his followers, had protested against Antichrist throughout history,[25] Luther's pessimistic apocalyptic views convinced him that only the return of Jesus Christ to judge the world would end the depredations of the savage Oppressor. (Following Augustine and Bernard, however, Luther generally avoided attempts to fix a date for the end.)[26]

Luther resembled many late medieval apocalypticists in viewing Muhammad and his religion as a force associated with Antichrist.[27] It is clear, however, from a number of comments to be found especially in his "Table Talk" and elsewhere that he did not believe that the Turkish threat was Antichrist in the same true and proper sense that the papacy was.[28] It was Luther's followers who really introduced the dual Antichrist of pope and Turk.

The depth of the older Luther's opposition to the papacy can be judged from his final contribution to Antichrist lore, two related treatises published in 1545. The first of these was entitled *Against the Roman Papacy: An Institution of the Devil;* the second was a scurrilous pamphlet with nine mostly scatological illustrations and captions called *The Depiction of the Papacy.*[29] An example of their sophomoric level can be seen from the picture of the birth, nourishing, and education of the little papal Antichrist by the three Furies (Fig. 26). Luther allowed for the modification of some of these pictures to avoid offending women, but he did not apologize for the acerbity of his language, noting in *Against the Roman Papacy* that "those who now live and those who will come after us should know what I have thought of the pope, the damned Antichrist, so that whoever wishes to be a Christian may be warned against such an abomination."[30]

FIGURE 26
Birth and infancy of
papal Antichrist. Martin
Luther, *The Depiction of the
Papacy* (1545). Reproduced
from *D. Martin Luthers
Werke* (Weimar: Böhlau,
1928), vol. 54.

Hie wird geborn der Widerchrift
Megera fein Seugamme ift:
Alecto fein Kindermeidlin
Tifiphone die gengelt m.
Mart. Luth. D.

The association of farting and shitting with Antichrist in these treatises
(not absent in the earlier Antichrist tradition, as we have seen) was part of
a conscious program of insult by inversion of values meant to unmask the
ultimate human evil found in Antichrist.[31]

What was Luther's real originality in the history of Antichrist traditions? The reformer's rejection of the legendary accretions to the scriptural picture of Antichrist and his adherence to a totally collective
interpretation of the Final Enemy distinguish him from any medieval
view, even those that identified the institution of the papacy with the Last
Enemy. This is not to deny important connections between his beliefs and

some late medieval perceptions, though the later Luther took pains to distinguish his view of the papal Antichrist from those of his medieval forebears.[32] The late medieval context shaped him, but he also did much to destroy that world. It was the reformer's uncompromising denunciation of the papacy as true and final Antichrist present in the world that initiated the divided Antichrist of the next two centuries.

Antichrist in the Hands of Protestants and Radicals

Luther's apocalyptic mentality provided a strong impetus for his followers' "powerful sense of eschatological expectancy," as historian Robin Bruce Barnes has claimed.[33] Not only Lutherans, however, but a wide variety of the other reformers who broke away from medieval Christianity in the first half of the sixteenth century shared vivid expectations of the end as well as the identification of the papacy with Antichrist. Differences in emphasis existed among the reformers, and even diverse viewpoints. Despite considerable recent literature, there is still much that we do not know about the main contours of Reformation apocalyptic beliefs.[34] Fortunately, we need not here survey the whole of Reformation apocalypticism; only those aspects that refer to Antichrist or directly impinge on Antichrist beliefs will concern us.

LUTHER'S FOLLOWERS

Luther's partners in reform and his immediate followers display fundamental agreement with his view of Antichrist as the institution of the papacy.[35] Most Protestants would have sided with the English reformer John Jewel (1522–1571), whose *Exposition upon the Two Epistles of St. Paul to the Thessalonians* dismissed the medieval legendary accretions to the history of Antichrist by noting that "these tales have been craftily devised to beguile our eyes, that, whilst we think upon these guesses, and so occupy ourselves in beholding a shadow or probable conjecture of antichrist, he which is antichrist indeed may unawares deceive us."[36]

Nevertheless, elements of the medieval Antichrist sometimes crept back into the apocalyptic scenarios of many reformers. Among these holdovers were attempts to determine the exact date of the end, speculations about the significance of the number 666, the conception of a time of peace after Antichrist, and, most ominously, the willingness to find Antichrist present not only in Rome but also in the Reform party itself.

The lunatic fringe of early Lutheran apocalypticism is evident in Michael Stifel, a fellow Augustinian who was one of Luther's early supporters.[37] Stifel, to his discredit, maintained that "Leo X Decimus" (Pope Leo X) was the numerical equivalent of 666, and he went even further in causing a scandal among the new churches by preaching to his congregation that the end would arrive at 8:00 A.M. on October 19, 1533. After the eschaton failed to arrive at the predicted date and the preacher was run out of town, Luther himself intervened to find Stifel another position.

A more serious example of early Lutheran fascination with Antichrist and the apocalyptic scenario may be found in Andreas Osiander (1498–1552). Luther had found in Hussite texts proof that evangelical opposition to the papal Antichrist was not an innovation; Osiander mined a wide variety of medieval apocalyptic writings, including those of the Joachite variety, to underline this message and to predict the time of the end.[38] During the controversial Interims of Augsburg and Leipzig of 1548 (these were doctrinal formulas designed to promote agreement between Protestants and Catholics in Germany), Osiander's apocalyptic ideas reached fever pitch. As a member of the strict party (called "Genesio-Lutherans"), he rejected the Interims, which had been sponsored by the party of Melanchthon (the "Philippists"), identifying them with the three and a half year-days of Apocalypse 11:11, the time before the pouring out of the vials upon the wicked and the destruction of Antichrist.[39] Osiander held that compromise with Rome among Lutherans indicated that Antichrist could taint even the reformers.

Other conservative Lutherans took a similar tack, such as Nicholas von Amsdorf in his *Five Principles and Certain Signs to Come Shortly Before the End* (1554).[40] The quarrel over the Interims, then, saw the beginning of fears within the Lutheran camp that Antichrist was not just to be found within papal Rome, but that he might be present even in Protestant Germany. This belief found pictorial expression in the popular illustration of Christ triumphing over a three-headed Antichrist Beast, one head of which represents the pope, a second the Turk, while the third with the deceptive face of an angel is actually the devil deceiving the faithful by means of the Interims.[41]

The Reformation debates, aided by the spread of printing, produced an unprecedented outpouring of popular tracts, pictures, and poems driving home the message that the pope was Antichrist. The illustrations that accompanied Luther's translation of the Bible often assumed an antipapal tone, especially in the full Bible issued in 1535, where the Great Whore of

FIGURE 27   Papal Antichrist as wild man. Melchior Lorch (1545). Reproduced from H. Grisar and F. Heege, *Luthers Kampfbilder,* vol. 4, Tafel II.

Apocalypse 17, for example, is unmistakably papal. In a famous picture that Melchior Lorch dedicated to Luther in 1545 (Fig. 27), the pope appears as the "wild man" of medieval legend with two heads, a monstrous hairy body, a destructive tail, and the papal symbols—the tiara, the keys, and the triple cross, here recast as a savage club.[42] This is surely one of the most effective of all representations of Antichrist, testifying to the imaginative force of Reformation fear of the papacy. Other pictures were more

FIGURE 28
Reviving the papal
Antichrist. *The Origin and
Heritage of Antichrist* (1540s).
Reproduced from H. Grisar
and F. Heege, *Luthers
Kampfbilder,* vol. 4, Tafel III.

amusing than terrifying. For example, the broadsheet published under the title "The Origin and Heritage of the Antichrist," probably from the 1540s, shows two devils breathing life into a fat, naked pope by means of black magic. In the background other devils are crushing priests, monks, and religious in a huge vat, preparing the raw material for the formation of the *imago diaboli,* that is, the papal Antichrist (Fig. 28).

A multitude of pamphlets spread the message to the Protestant faithful.[43] A good example can be found in Henry of Kettenbach's popular *Little Book of Antitheses (Antithesenbüchlein)* of 1523, which expanded upon the Hussite antitheses and the *Passional* to portray sixty-six contrasts between Christ and the papal Antichrist. Luther's scatological invective

against the papacy not surprisingly continued to be present in this literature, both in German and Latin.[44] Particularly important were the Antichrist plays written by the reformers.

Pamphilus Gegenbach had composed a medieval Antichrist drama
in 1517, the *Brother Nollhart,* consisting of a series of prophets announcing
the events of the end, including those of Antichrist's life. This was later
reworked to include a critique of the papacy as Antichrist. Gegenbach
himself, an early adherent of Luther, appears to be the author of the play
The Devourers of the Dead (Die Totenfresser), which in 1521 set out the
Lutheran critique of papal masses for the dead and other abuses.[45] At least
fourteen other Antichrist dramas of the sixteenth century in Latin, German, English, and Italian attacked the pope as the Final Enemy.[46] Most of
these were morality plays based on antitheses of Christ's virtues and the
vices of the papal Antichrist. The most famous was the 1538 Latin play
Pammachius of Thomas Kirchmaier (usually known by his Latin name,
Naogeorgus), which literary scholar Klaus Aichele describes as "a mixture
of a medieval morality play with humanistic tendencies and the polemical
interest in the history and development of the papacy enkindled by
Luther."[47] The emphasis on political actuality in these works (which
might be better called dramatic tableaus than real dramas) reached its culmination in the English *King John* of John Bale (1538, revised in 1563),
where King John loses control over England to the papal Antichrist only
to have Henry VIII regain it.

Luther's original protest, beginning in 1517 and fully antipapal by
1520, was the first of many movements of revolt against medieval Christianity in the third decade of the century. A number of the new Protestant
leaders soon advanced views that clashed with those of the Wittenberg
theologian. The major figure in the creation of the Reformed, or Calvinist,
tradition was the French humanist scholar John Calvin (1509–1564). Unlike Luther, Calvin was decidedly antiapocalyptic (John's Apocalypse was
the only biblical book he did not comment on), but he did agree with
Luther that Antichrist was a danger and that Christians needed to keep
before their eyes the indubitable fact that Antichrist was none other than
the pope of Rome. Although Calvin did not deny the Roman church the
name of church, he felt that it was only a church of corruption: "Daniel
and Paul foretold that Antichrist would sit in the temple of God. With us,
it is the Roman pontiff we make the leader and standard-bearer of that
wicked and abominable kingdom."[48] Like Luther, Calvin was a firm believer in a collective Antichrist: "The name Antichrist does not designate a

single individual, but a single kingdom which extends throughout many generations."[49] This kingdom was manifest in the "foul abomination of the papists" but also involved the depredations of Muhammad and his followers. Despite the fairly restricted attention Calvin gave to Antichrist, the Final Enemy was to play a large part in the Reformed tradition, especially among the English Puritans to be considered later in this chapter.[50]

ANABAPTIST APOCALYPTICISM

It was in the other main tradition of the Reformation, among the varied groups who are often referred to as belonging to the "Radical" Reformation,[51] that the image of Antichrist fully invaded the reform movement itself. From an early date, many of these reformers became convinced that not only the pope but also Luther and his followers belonged to the camp of the Final Enemy. The first major chapter in the Radical Reformation, represented by the teaching of Thomas Müntzer (c. 1489–1525) and the Peasants' Revolt (1524–26), makes this clear.[52]

Müntzer was a well-educated young priest who became a reform pastor at Zwickau in 1520. His program for both religious and social reform soon became more radical than Luther's, insisting on the priority of the inner experience of the Holy Spirit, the necessity for a vernacular liturgy, and the reorganization of society. Müntzer also came to believe in anabaptism, that is, the view that infant baptism could not be valid and only a conscious conversion experience leading to adult baptism counted for membership in the community of the saved. This was to become a distinguishing mark of many groups of radical reformers.[53]

After various moves from one pastoral charge to another, Müntzer, by now a fierce opponent of Luther, allied himself with the movement of German peasants seeking greater religious and economic freedom from princely control. By 1525 this protest issued in open revolt, one that was certainly abetted if not initiated by Müntzer's inflammatory preaching.[54] Both Müntzer and Luther may be called apocalypticists, but of very different stamps. Luther used his belief in the proximity of the end to counsel religious opposition to the pope while insisting on patient subservience to political authority; Müntzer was convinced that active opposition to the whole of Antichrist's forces was the duty of the Christian. Like Luther, his teaching emphasized Antichrist's presence in the world: "It is already the time of Antichrist as is manifestly clear in Matthew 24. The Lord makes it known that when the Gospel of the Kingdom is preached in the whole world, then the Abomination of Desolation is to be seen."[55]

Müntzer's view of Antichrist was more inclusive than Luther's. He insisted that the pope was not the final Antichrist but only his herald (*praeco*).[56] The whole religious and social hierarchy of the late medieval world was all part of Antichrist for the fiery prophet, a position from which Luther the social conservative recoiled with horror. The Wittenberger denounced the Peasants' Revolt, encouraging the princes to slaughter the revolutionaries with a fervor equal to that with which Müntzer had urged the overthrow and destruction of the entire *Obrigkeit,* or establishment of sixteenth-century society. The establishment won, and tens of thousands of peasants were slaughtered. Müntzer was captured and executed. Had his ideas triumphed, the slaughter might have been even greater.[57]

The Peasants' Revolt was only partly a religious movement. In the heated atmosphere of the debates over Christianity in the third and fourth decades of the sixteenth century, however, many views about the meaning of the gospel, and virtually any political movement that allied itself with Christian teaching to bolster its cause, seemed to think that it possessed a divine mandate to crush the opposition, which was to be thought of as a part of Antichrist's body. The increasing centripetal movement of the Antichrist legend that identified only groups and institutions within Christianity with the Final Enemy, grew at an exponential rate that eventually would lead to a kind of implosion. But this is to get ahead of our story.

Other radical reformers were not discouraged by the defeat of the Peasants' Revolt and Müntzer's fate. Many of them, unlike Müntzer, were convinced pacifists, among the only peaceable folk of the sixteenth century. They shared the apocalyptic worldview that saw the end as imminent, but they were convinced that in these last times their main task was to wait for Jesus' Second Coming to destroy the pervasive force of Antichrist, not to undertake the task themselves. A good example is found in Melchior Hoffman (c. 1495–1543). Hoffman began his preaching career in 1523 and sided with Luther against the peasants in 1525. However, his study of biblical apocalyptic texts led him by 1529 to create his own group of reformers, the Melchiorites. In his preaching in the Netherlands and Strassburg, he announced the coming of the end for 1533. The last ten years of his life were spent in prison in Strassburg, which he had predicted would be the site of the New Jerusalem.

Like many apocalypticists, Hoffman's view of history was presented through a commentary on John's Apocalypse published in Strassburg in 1530.[58] Hoffman envisaged three divisions in contemporary Christianity:

first, the Roman church under the papal Antichrist; second, their Lutheran and Zwinglian accomplices; and third, the true spiritual Christians, like himself and his followers. Hoffman was convinced he was writing in the midst of the final seven years of history. In medieval fashion, the first three and a half were devoted to the preaching of the two witnesses (Hoffman apparently thought of himself as Elijah), while the impending three and a half would see Antichrist's persecution against the "Spiritual Temple" of Hoffman and the other faithful.

Like most early Anabaptists, Hoffman did not advocate violence, believing that Christ himself would soon come to vindicate the sufferings of the just. Indeed, most radicals saw the use of violence and persecution, along with the apostasy of the clergy and the perversion of the sacraments of baptism and the Lord's Supper, as the identifying marks of Antichrist.[59] Pilgram Marpeck, in his treatise *The Expose of the Babylonian Whore and Antichrist,* expressed their position well when he averred: "Among the ancient Christians from the time of the Apostles until the Emperor Constantine, physical force and the use of the sword among the Christians were unknown, nor was it allowed them by command of their Master. . . . But when the pope, at that time a servant in the Church, claiming to act with the mind of Christ, was married to that Leviathan, the secular power, at that moment the Antichrist was made and born, as has now been revealed."[60]

While Hoffman languished in prison, Anabaptists inspired by his teaching flocked to the north German city of Münster in 1533 and 1534. Catholic Münster had been undergoing an increasingly radical movement toward reformation since 1531 under the leadership of the priest Bernard Rothmann. In February 1534, Jan Mathijs, a Dutch Melchiorite, gained control of the city government and forced the Lutherans and Catholics who disagreed with him to leave, a move that showed how easily some followers of Hoffman found the transition from pacifism to persecution.[61] The bishop overlord of Münster blockaded the city, and a savage conflict began. Once again, apocalyptic eschatology demonstrated that it was capable of turning into revolutionary ideology. Mathijs soon was killed in battle. His accomplice, John Beukels, or John of Leiden as he was called, took over. Both men were apocalyptic fanatics, but John was even more dangerous than Mathijs. He declared himself ruler of the world and added polygamy to the community of goods and other radical practices that had been instituted in the new messianic city. The radical Münsterites were doers, not theorists, but it is clear that they, like Thomas Müntzer, identified

all the forces opposed to them—clerical and lay, Catholic and Protestant—
with Antichrist.

In December 1534, Bernard Rothmann, in a treatise entitled *A Trust-worthy Report on the Vengeance and Punishment of the Babylonian Abomination,* called on all the proponents of adult baptism to come to the rescue of the besieged city: "Therefore, beloved brothers, prepare yourselves for the struggle, not only with the humble weapons of the apostles for suffering [2 Cor. 10:4], but also with the glorious armor of David for vengeance to exterminate with God's help all the powers of Babylon and godless existence."[62] Münster finally fell to a combined Protestant and Catholic army in June 1535. John of Leiden and the surviving leaders were tortured to death in January 1536, and their bodies were hung in iron cages from the cathedral spire.

The debacle at Münster gave Anabaptism an even worse reputation than it had previously enjoyed. The continued life of the movement was largely due to the work of Menno Simons (1496–1561), who returned believers in adult baptism to their original pacifist tradition (hence the term Mennonites for most present-day descendants of Reformation Anabaptism). Simons was a Dutch priest who renounced Catholicism in 1536 and received baptism from Obbe Philips, who had assumed the leadership of the peaceful wing of the Melchiorites after the fall of Münster. Simons preached widely throughout Holland, northern Germany, and the Baltic region. His view of Antichrist was a broad collective one that embraced all Christian groups except his own. His longest work, the *Reply to Gellius Faber* (1554), outlined six signs to enable the believer to distinguish the Church of Christ from the Church of Antichrist.[63]

This generic conception of Antichrist is found in a number of other radical reformers, especially in the "spiritualist" wing of the movement, that is, those who emphasized the priority of the inward Spirit over all religious externals, including Scripture, sacrament, and community. Sebastian Franck (1499–1542), for example, in his *Letter to John Campanus* (1531), says that Antichrist entered the Church immediately on the death of the apostles so that there has been no true Church on earth since then. For him it was only the so-called heretics who were members of the Church; the Fathers, like Ambrose and Augustine, "all were the apostles of Antichrist and are that still."[64] The sacraments, and even Scripture itself insofar as it is literally interpreted (a fundamental principle for Luther), are all part of Antichrist's deception. Franck concludes:

In brief, all that we have learned since childhood from the papists, we must all of a sudden unlearn again. Again, the same for what we have received from Luther and Zwingli—all must be abandoned and altered. For one will sooner make a good Christian out of a Turk than out of a bad Christian or a learned divine![65]

For Franck the history of Christianity is really the history of anti-Christianity—a startling reversal of traditional beliefs![66] As the term *Antichrist* came to be more and more used by one Christian group against another (and with Franck becoming coextensive with almost the whole of orthodox Christianity), we can agree with Reformation scholar Gottfried Seebass that "the concept loses any clear content and gradually comes to be used as a purely polemical generic term."[67]

ANTICHRIST VIEWS OF CONTINENTAL PROTESTANTS

Among the mainline reformers on the Continent, Antichrist kept his papal specificity during the century after Luther's death. This was especially the case with the Lutherans. From the confessional perspective, it was significant that the Formula and Book of Concord (1577 and 1580, respectively), which set the standard for Lutheran orthodoxy against the Catholic Council of Trent and divergent reform positions, included the denunciation of the pope as Antichrist, first set forth in the Confession of the Schmalcaldic League of 1537. Subsequent Lutheran theology continued to repeat this article of faith, though with less and less originality. One of the more entertaining aspects of pope-as-Antichrist history concerned the revising of the calendar by Pope Gregory XIII in 1582. Though almost all scholars recognized the chronological superiority of the Gregorian over the outmoded Julian calendar, many Protestants, especially Lutheran publicists, saw in it incontrovertible evidence of the ancient notion that Antichrist would change the times and the seasons.[68] The new calendar was not adopted in England until 1752.

Lutheran use of Antichrist between 1550 and 1660 shows little originality, with one exception, the revival of millenarian views that looked forward to the coming reign of Christ and the saints on earth after the defeat of the papal Antichrist. Tentatively present in Philip Nicolai's *History of the Kingdom of Christ* (1598), it was emphasized more strongly by Johann Andreae in his utopian *Christianopolis* (1620). The Reformed theologian John Henry Alsted was also a millenarian. His *Diatribe* of 1627 (translated into English in 1643 under the title *The Beloved City*) predicted the destruction of the papacy by 1694, an event that he believed would be followed by a literal thousand-year reign of Christ and the saints (including the converted Jews) on earth. In his words: "Therefore if the Jews should but see the wonderful overthrow of *Antichrist,* without doubt it would afford them a great occasion of their Conversion. Upon this ground, the overthrow of Antichrist shall immediately go before, not the *last judgement,* but the *happinesse of the Church* which shall happen in this life."[69]

The similarity of this view to various medieval accounts of a post-Antichrist millennium is striking, though the importance Alsted gave to the conversion of the Jews (also to be echoed among the English millenarians) was distinctive.

Antichrist in England

The Antichrist legend played a large role in the English Reformation from its beginnings.[70] One of the earliest English reformers, William Tyndale (c. 1494–1536), the Bible translator, held a general spiritual view of Antichrist, one that included the papacy, but only as part of the growing force of evil throughout history.[71] But Luther's identification of the papacy as *the* Antichrist soon came to the fore. In 1536, for example, Thomas Cranmer, the episcopal leader of the reformed party, preached a sermon at St. Paul's Cross on the papal Antichrist.[72] The discussion in Elizabethan England soon became so intense that Bishop Jewel (1522–1571) could note, "There is none, neither old nor young, neither learned nor unlearned, but he hath heard of Antichrist."[73]

The major spokesman of the early English Protestant view of the papal Antichrist was John Bale (1495–1563), a Carmelite friar turned reformer, publicist, and later bishop.[74] His lengthy work, *The Image of Both Churches* (1548), contained a commentary on the Apocalypse based in part on Joachim of Fiore's recapitulative interpretation of the text. Its basic message concerned the confrontation between the Church of Christ represented by the Heavenly Woman of Apocalypse 12 and the Church of Antichrist figured in the Whore of Babylon from Apocalypse 17. As Bale observed in the preface, "Herein is the true christian church, which is the meek spouse of the Lamb without spot, in her right-fashioned colours described. So is the proud church of hypocrites, the rose-coloured whore, the paramour of Antichrist. . . ."[75] Bale's view of Antichrist was a double one, involving both the papacy and the Turk as enemies of true Christianity. However, Bale also accepted the ancient emphasis on the universality of Antichrist. This emphasis was being revived by some of the radical reformers, like Sebastian Franck, who admitted there is "but one general antichrist for all, which hath reigned in the church in a manner since the ascension of Christ."[76]

After Henry VIII's break with the papacy, there was little to hinder attacks on the bishop of Rome, but it was not until the reign of his son Edward VI (1547–53) that real Protestantism took root in England. Edward's reform adopted a strong Calvinist cast, one that sowed the seeds for the later division between the established state Church of England, a conservative episcopal body under the control of the crown, and the more radical reformers who sought to purify (hence "Puritans") the English church from the remaining vestiges of the papal Antichrist.

English identification of the papacy with Antichrist was strengthened by the historical interlude of Catholic reaction in the reign of Mary Tudor (1553–58), under whom a savage repression of the reformed party took place. The accession of Elizabeth, who reigned from 1558 to 1603, saw the triumph of a middle position in the intense religious debates, one that became more officially Protestant after Elizabeth's excommunication in 1570 and especially after the defeat of the Spanish Armada in 1588, which was seen throughout Europe as a major blow to Catholic attempts to regain preponderance of power. During Elizabeth's reign, the Protestant view of the papal Antichrist became a fixture in English Protestant identity. A number of significant writings furthered this process, among them John Foxe's popular *Acts and Monuments of Matters Happening in the Church,* which appeared in English in 1563,[77] and some important commentaries on the Apocalypse.[78]

Under Elizabeth, leaders of the English church, such as John Jewel and Edwin Sandys, became fervent proponents of English Protestant abhorrence of the papal Antichrist. Elizabethan rhetoric gave new life to what by the 1570s was standard invective, as when Edwin Sandys proclaimed:

> We have forsaken him that hath forsaken God, and whom God hath forsaken; we have left that man of sin, that rose-colored harlot with whom the kings of the earth have commited fornication, that triple-crowned beast, that double-sworded tyrant, that thief and murderer, who hath robbed so

many souls of salvation, and sucked so much innocent blood of Christian martyrs, that adversary unto Christ, that pretensed vicar, who hath displaced the person, not only taking upon himself Christ's room and office, but also boasting himself as if he were a god, and being content of his parasites so to be called.[79]

In the late sixteenth and the seventeenth centuries English fascination with the figure of Antichrist, closely connected with efforts to unwrap the meaning of the Apocalypse, built to a crescendo. English national identity as the only Protestant nation-state, fostered by providential signs such as the defeat of the Spanish Armada, encouraged a hope for final deliverance that revived millenarianism. As on the Continent, speculation about the coming millennium was closely connected with expectations of the defeat of Antichrist, often involved with calculations of the 1260 days (that is, years) of Daniel and the Apocalypse. But exactly who was this Antichrist whose defeat would usher in the triumph of the saints? The success of the Reformation in Britain meant to most that the pope was clearly of Antichrist's party. Henry Smith in his *Sermons* (1631) put the standard English Reformation view in a nutshell when he said, "He who can swear that the Pope is Antichrist and that flesh is good of Fridays is a Protestant."[80] But the growing power of radical forms of Protestantism not satisfied with the Elizabethan religious settlement led many to think that Antichrist was *more* than just the papacy.[81]

SEPARATIST AND PURITAN VIEWS OF ANTICHRIST

During the last quarter of the sixteenth century, Separatists such as Robert Browne, Robert Harrison, "Martin Marprelate" (an anonymous author of antiepiscopal tracts in the late 1580s), and Henry Barrow contended that the English church remained a part of Babylon and its bishops themselves were therefore antichrists.[82] As early as 1567, an unlicensed minister named Patterson, during his investigation for heresy, denounced Edmund Grindal, the bishop of London, in the following terms:

B[ishop]: Well, Sir, did you well, think you, to charge me in your sermons, and to send me word that I am an antichrist, and a traitor to my God and my prince, and an heretic?

P[atterson]: I think I did not ill, so long as you show yourself to be such a one: but put away the cause, and I will cease from saying so.

B: Why, wherein can you prove me a traitor and an antichrist?

P: In that you use things accursed and abominable, whereby you yourself are made abominable before God also.[83]

Henry Barrow, arrested in 1587, during his trial denounced the archbishop of Canterbury to the lord chancellor in even more daring terms: "He is a monster, a miserable compound, I know not what to make [call] him: he is neither ecclesiastical nor civil, even that second beast spoken of in the Revelation."[84] While some of the early Separatists, like Patterson, may have maintained hope that the bishops would lay aside their Romish (anti-Christian) practices, the more radical publicists, like Browne, Harrison, and Barrow, denounced the office of episcopacy itself and advocated complete separation from the establishment to await the Second Coming of Christ. In his *True and Short Declaration* of 1584, Robert Browne warned Puritan ministers who received ordination from bishops that they bore the mark of the Beast. The Separatists had little effect. Robert Browne recanted, Harrison fled to the Netherlands, and Barrow was executed for sedition in 1593.

More important were the Puritans. They believed the Church of England had not gone far enough in its reform and therefore, in its present state, was to be identified with "Laodicea the lukewarm" (Apoc. 3:14–19), but they also saw it as their duty to struggle to complete England's Reformation. In the seventeenth century this party produced several major apocalyptic thinkers—and a notable revolution, the English Civil War.

Thomas Brightman (1562–1607) was a Bedfordshire parson, a Puritan admirer of Calvinism who kept his sympathies private, permitting his massive commentary on the Apocalypse to be published only after his death (first in Latin on the Continent in 1609, and only in the 1640s in England). This *Revelation of the Apocalyps* defended the Protestant view of the papal Antichrist, furthered the cause of ongoing reform in the lukewarm English church, helped forge the notion of England as an elect apocalyptic nation, and announced the millennium that would dawn before the end of the seventeenth century.[85]

In dealing with the seven vials of Apocalypse 16 and the succeeding chapters, Brightman commented on current events and used apocalyptic imagery to predict the future triumph of the Puritan cause. The vials were the divine judgments on the papal Antichrist, beginning with Elizabeth I's dismissal of the Romish clergy about 1560. Four of these had been accomplished by about 1600; three were still to come. Brightman's complex calculations of the various prophetic numbers for Antichrist's reign (1260,

1290, and 1335 day-years) allowed him to predict the three final vials as: (1) a destruction of the city of Rome by Reformed armies about 1650; (2) the conversion of many of the Jews; and (3) the final annihilation of the pope, the Western Antichrist, and the Turk, or Eastern Antichrist, which he believed was to come about the year 1695.[86] But the Puritan parson did not stop there. Aware that he was going against long-standing tradition, he felt compelled to follow the Apocalypse's teaching on a literal millennium. This thousand-year period had actually begun about 1300 when resistance to the papal Antichrist became evident, but it was to come into its own about 1700 and would last until the end of the world in 2300 C.E. It would be marked by the spiritual return of Christ to reign in his saints:

> For this is the Kingdom of Christ, when he ruleth in the midst of any people. And this is indeed the most true Empire and kingdom of any nation, when it is subjected to Christ's Empire alone, and when it is governed by his conduct and command alone. Now at length we may perceive, what kinde of kingdom of a thousand years lasting that is, whereof we arte a part. . . .[87]

The return to millenarianism found in Brightman's work was controversial,[88] but it was furthered by the second great Puritan commentator on the Apocalypse, Joseph Mede (1586–1638), a Cambridge don and teacher of John Milton. Mede's *Apocalyptic Key* was published in Latin in 1627 and translated into English in 1643. From the point of view of method, Mede's commentary was arguably the most original of the century,[89] but his conclusions were not more radical than those of Brightman.

Both Brightman and Mede represented the Puritan belief that the Reformation in England had not gone far enough; elements of Antichrist still appeared in the church of Laodicea. But they continued to give the English church a special providential role in the dawning millennium, and therefore they inspired their followers to continue the work of reform. In predicting an imminent final battle against the forces of Antichrist, these retiring scholars encouraged the fervent hopes of more militant Puritans in the 1640s.[90]

It would be a large task to survey the full extent of Puritan literature of the period 1640 to 1660 in which the bishops and other elements of the established church were attacked as signs of the presence of Antichrist. Fortunately, considerable recent literature has already been devoted to this investigation.[91] What is especially significant during this time was the movement from the critique of elements of English church life, especially high liturgical practices, as anti-Christian, to a more radical position in which the whole established church was as much Antichrist as Rome and therefore needed to be destroyed "root and branch." There were, of course, almost as many variations on this theme as there were pundits who expressed it. The increasing variety of targets against which Antichrist rhetoric was employed during these decades marks this as another "Golden Age" of Antichrist. Rhetorical overextension would enhance the traditional vagueness implied in the Antichrist accusation and lead eventually to a reaction against its use when Charles II reestablished the monarchy in 1660.[92]

In 1640 opposition to Charles I's high church religious policies led to the Long Parliament's "Root and Branch" Bill calling for the abolition of the entire episcopacy. But the more radical Puritan desire to return to a pure, "scriptural" Christianity had been born earlier. As early as 1628, Alexander Leighton, in his work *Sions Plea Against the Prelacy,* followed Martin Marprelate in constructing a syllogistic argument against church hierarchy:

> These governors are justly called antichristian who are assistant to the pope in his universal government.
> But the bishops, archbishops, chancellors, etc., are assistant to the pope in his universal government.
> Therefore bishops, archbishops, chancellors, etc., are justly called antichristian.[93]

Leighton suffered death under Archbishop Laud for his sedition, but by 1640 his views were those of a powerful party. Numerous divines preached such a position before the Long Parliament,[94] and Puritan publicists like John Milton enshrined it in their pamphlets.[95]

After the outbreak of the Civil War in 1642, views equating church hierarchy with the apocalyptic Beast became a part of the ideology of the Parliamentarian armies. A Royalist divine named Edward Symmons described an interview he had with some captured Parliamentarian soldiers on Easter of 1644, who told him that they fought against Antichrist and popery, because "'tis prophesied in the *Revelation*, that the Whore of Babylon shall be destroyed with fire and sword, and what do you know, but this is the time of her ruin, and that we are the men that must help pull her down?" When Symmons remonstrated that the Whore dwells in Rome and not in England, they replied: "All the true godly divines in England were of their opinion, that Antichrist was here in England, as well as at Rome, and that the bishops were Antichrist, and all that did endeavour to support them."[96]

In the midst of Civil War, with Charles I and the bishops on one side and Parliament and its presbyters on the other, it became easy for some to widen the scope of Antichrist even further, that is, to include in it "all that did endeavour to support them [the bishops]." The antiestablishment use of Antichrist rhetoric among the left-wing groups of the English Civil War rivals that found at the time of the Peasants' Revolt or at Münster in the previous century. Such views were evident among most of the radical groups of the Civil War period, such as the "Fifth Monarchy Men."

The First Civil War (1642–46) between king and Parliament was brought to a close by Charles's surrender to the Scots and the subsequent negotiations between him and the victors. Tensions between the radicals in the army and the moderates in Parliament were exacerbated by the king's negotiations with the Scots; the Scots then invaded England in his support in 1648 in the brief Second Civil War. A group of radicals in the army were already becoming known as the Fifth Monarchy Men because of their millenarian view that victory over the king had marked the beginning of the Fifth Monarchy predicted in Daniel 2, during which time Christ would return to rule on earth together with the saints. They were among the radicals who supported the "Rump Parliament" that condemned Charles I to death in January of 1649.[97] To those who denounced this act as regicide, the Fifth Monarchist William Aspinwall responded by demonstrating that Charles Stuart was actually the Little Horn and the Beast and that "'the saints' act of slaying the Beast and taking away his dominion was no rash nor seditious act, but an act of sound judgment, approved of God."[98]

The Fifth Monarchists at first supported Oliver Cromwell, who later dismissed the Rump Parliament and took over the government as lord protector of the Commonwealth of England, Scotland, and Ireland in 1653. John Spittlehouse, for instance, published a tract in that year calling on Cromwell to carry the fight against Antichrist into the land of the Canaanites, that is, onto the Continent and as far as Rome. In the same year, John Rogers predicted that Rome would fall by 1660 and the full Fifth Monarchy would be evident by 1666.[99] But as Cromwell's actions began to make it clear that he was not furthering the advance of the millennium, the Fifth Monarchists soon discovered that he too was Antichrist, and they rose up against him in an unsucessful rebellion in 1657.[100]

Mixed in with the Fifth Monarchists in the left wing of English Protestantism at the time were assorted Levellers, Diggers, Seekers, Ranters, and Quakers. Many of these groups began from a position identifying all religious (and often even civil) leadership as belonging to Antichrist; some went on to hold the conviction that Antichrist was actually the power of evil in every human heart. (Very generic external use of Antichrist language often has led to a universal interiorization.)[101]

The explosion of Antichrist rhetoric in the Civil War, however, soon exhausted itself. Indeed, the English Civil War was arguably the last major political event, in western Europe at least, in which Antichrist beliefs played a significant role. After the Restoration, forces both internal and external to the legend led to a decline in the general cultural impact of Antichrist's political clout. From the viewpoint of logic, the greater the extension of a term, the less its content, so that if everyone is Antichrist, the effectiveness of the name as a term of effective reproach diminishes. A universal vehicle of abuse can rapidly become nothing more than an occasion for humor. Even in the early decades of the seventeenth century, Ben Jonson had lampooned the Puritan habit of spotting an Antichrist under every bush,[102] and in 1664 Henry More, in his treatise *A Modest Inquiry into the Mystery of Iniquity,* had to apologize for investigating Antichrist because the "rude and ignorant vulgar . . . have so fouled these words by their unmannerly mouthing of them without all aim, that they have made them now unfit to pass the lips of any civil person."[103] Such an excuse would have been unthinkable to Brightman, Mede, or Milton a generation earlier. Thus, a kind of conceptual implosion was largely responsible for the fact that after 1660, in the words of historian Christopher Hill, "Antichrist disappeared into the nonconformist underworld, ultimately into the world of cranks."[104]

Factors external to the legend were also at work in this process. The restoration of king and episcopacy in 1660 made it politically dangerous to continue radical Puritan rhetoric, and even the standard English Reformation identification of the pope as Antichrist was increasingly suspect among the learned. The questioning of this identification by high church Anglicans of the 1620s and 1630s, enhanced by the attacks of the Jesuits (to be considered shortly below), spread to many (though not all) circles in the English church. Finally, a general exhaustion with religious conflicts evident throughout Europe in the latter seventeenth century and the growing Enlightenment critique of the more legendary and superstitious aspects of Christianity were part of a world in which Antichrist as a living fear began to play a noticeably smaller, though still not insignificant, role.

Catholics Respond to the Protestant Challenge

The challenge of the Reformation and its many variations on the pope as Antichrist had serious effects on the Antichrist beliefs of those who remained loyal to Rome in the sixteenth and seventeenth centuries. First, and most obvious, it made any assertion that an individual pope might be the Final Antichrist or even his predecessor exceedingly problematic for good Catholics.[105] In the Middle Ages even canonized saints had identified a particular evil pope as Antichrist. But although this view differed from Protestant belief in the papacy as Antichrist, it was too close to the Protestant position to allow most Catholics to continue to uphold it hereafter.

Catholic preaching and teaching on Antichrist down to the latter half of the seventeenth century was partly a repetition of patterns inherited from earlier eras and partly a reaction to the Protestant challenge. Some of this reaction was the typical urge to tar opponents with the same brush, that is, to prove that Luther was Antichrist or at least his immediate predecessor.[106] More interesting was the learned reaction spearheaded by the Jesuits toward the end of the sixteenth century, which sought to demonstrate by critical study of the New Testament and the Fathers that the papacy could not be Antichrist because the Last Enemy was a future figure without ties to current events. This "scientific" view undercut large elements of the medieval legendary accretions to Antichrist by returning to a rather strict Augustinian teaching on the Final Enemy. The sharp contrast that developed between the Protestant view and these Catholic attitudes testifies to the truth of historian Hans Preuss's remark: "In the final analysis there is not so much the opposition of two different pictures of Antichrist, but of two different principles of religious understanding."[107]

The Catholic resurgence in the face of Protestant challenges, doctrinally formulated in the Council of Trent (1545–63), was led by the new Jesuit order founded by Ignatius of Loyola and approved by Pope Paul III in 1540. The Jesuits were the best-organized, highest-educated, and most militant of the forces that formed the post-Tridentine response to Protestantism. From the intellectual point of view, the key figure in the Jesuit counterattack was the theologian and controversialist Robert Bellarmine (1542–1621), who taught at Louvain and Rome and was later made a cardinal. Bellarmine's learning and polemical skill, especially in his massive *Disputations Concerning the Controversies of the Christian Faith Against the Heretics of This Time,* published between 1586 and 1593, made him an adversary the Protestants could not disregard. The great controversialist combatted the Protestant view of Antichrist just as fervently as he attacked their mistaken attitudes toward grace, justification, and the sacraments, as we can see from the third book of the *Third Controversy* dealing with the papacy and its claims. This book, entitled "On the Antichrist, Who Has Nothing in Common with the Roman Pontiff," contained twenty-four chapters.[108] Basing himself on a literal reading of the scriptural texts referring to the Last Enemy, Bellarmine presented a sober version of the standard medieval account, emphasizing that Antichrist was still to come because the six scriptural signs associated with him had not yet appeared (chaps. 3–9). He concluded with a lengthy rebuttal of Protestant claims that the papacy is Antichrist (chaps. 18–24). The Jesuit insisted that Antichrist could not be identified with a present institution like the papacy but rather must be seen as a single individual who will conclude world history.[109] His position can be described as a return to a strict anti-apocalyptic Augustinianism after more than a millennium of legendary accretion to the figure of Antichrist. This is evident, for example, in his consideration of the number 666 in chapter 9. After surveying many traditional interpretations, and perhaps mischievously noting that Luther's name can be read as 666 in Latin, Greek, and Hebrew, he concluded, "The truest opinion is of those who confess their ignorance and say that the name of Antichrist is still unknown."[110]

The other great early Jesuit theologian, the Spaniard Francis Suarez (1548–1617), took a similar line.[111] Suarez admitted that "everything about Antichrist is very obscure (*perobscura*) and uncertain on many issues," and therefore he would present only what was clearly taught in Scripture and the ancient Fathers. His intent was the same as Bellarmine's—to refute the Protestant identification of the papacy with Antichrist. In arguing his case, Suarez was even more committed than the cardinal to a sober view of a purely future Antichrist, a view essentially in line with that of Augustine and Aquinas (though lacking Augustine's insistence that each Christian is obligated to search out the Antichrist within). Of course, Bellarmine and Suarez had been colored to some extent by the long centuries of medieval growth of the Antichrist legend, but in reading them one senses a hesitancy—almost an embarrassment—concerning much of the earlier tradition.

In the decades between 1590 and 1630 this line of attack against Protestant apocalypticism was furthered by a number of Jesuit commentators on the Apocalypse, who sought to undermine the Protestant view that the last book of the Bible predicts the papal Antichrist. Not all of these writers adopted the same hermeneutical stance, but many represent an early form of historical-critical approach to the biblical text in their seeking above all to discover what the human author had intended in light of the circumstances in which he was writing.[112] Even those commentators, like Blaise Viegas and Benedict Pereyra, who adhered to a more medieval, spiritual mode of exegesis still expended considerable effort to deny the Protestant interpretation centered on the Antichrist-papacy identification.[113] The commentary of the Portuguese Jesuit Francis Ribeira (written c. 1580, but not published until 1591, the year of his death) was among the first that can be said to have some scientific value in the modern critical sense.[114] Ribeira's work was strongly "literalist" in comparison with both his Catholic and Protestant predecessors, at least in the sense that he appealed to ancient patristic authorities to argue that the original intention of the author of the Apocalypse was to describe events that still lay in the future. For him the Apocalypse was not a blueprint of the history of the Church, as so many medieval exegetes had claimed; nor was it a clear prophecy of how the papal Antichrist came to power, as the Protestants held. No wonder the Protestant Apocalypse commentators, like Brightman, Pareus, and Mede, felt challenged by what was, after all, a good Protestant principle of exegesis: return to the letter of the biblical text.

Ribeira's work was continued by Louis Alcazar, whose interpretation first appeared in 1614. Alcazar denounced Joachite exegesis ("He who will may hold the Abbot Joachim to be a prophet of God, but not I," he said) and took a different tack than Ribeira in working out a historical reading of the Apocalypse. He argued that the events predicted in the first nineteen chapters of the Apocalypse had already been fulfilled in the early history of the Church down to the time of Constantine, while the last chapters pertained only to events to come at the end.[115] Ribeira and Alcazar were taken to task by the Puritan exegetes who felt compelled to devote hundreds of pages to refuting the Jesuit rebuttal of standard Protestant arguments for the papal Antichrist. Yet their incipient historical-critical approach to the Apocalypse also had a positive influence on some Protestant thinkers like Hugo Grotius, who wrote a literal *Commentary on Some Places in the New Testament Which Treat of Antichrist* in 1641.

In the long run, the Jesuits made an important contribution to the decline of Antichrist in the latter seventeenth century.

A similar concern for a more "scientific" (at least in the sense of historically informed) account of Antichrist led to the creation of what even today ranks as one of the major sources of information on the Last Enemy, Thomas Malvenda's *On Antichrist*.[116] A Spanish Dominican, Malvenda (1566–1628) spent much of his life in Rome, where his large folio volume representing twelve years of work "day and night" first appeared. Malvenda's tome mirrors the ambiguity in which the Catholic Antichrist found himself in the early seventeenth century: Catholics were still convinced that he existed, but they were increasingly uneasy about identifying him with any present or imminent person or movement. While Malvenda believed in a good deal more of the nonscriptural detail of the legend than did Suarez,[117] the fact that he too placed everything relating to Antichrist safely in the distant future indicates that this most detailed of all Antichrist volumes found its greatest import in helping to lessen the sense of the Final Enemy's reality among Catholics after 1600. In trying to shoot down the Protestant Antichrist, the learned Dominican inflicted a serious wound on the traditional Catholic Final Enemy as well.

A Dominican contemporary of Malvenda wrote one of the last original Catholic treatises on the Son of Perdition. Thomas Campanella (1568–1639), like Joachim of Fiore, was a Calabrian, and like Joachim he was controversial, both in his own day and afterward. He is best known for his utopian fantasy, *The City of the Sun* (1623), but in the same year he wrote a Latin treatise, *On Antichrist*.[118] Although it was without historical influence, Campanella's work testifies to the seriousness of the Counter-Reformation attack on the Protestant view of Antichrist.[119] His consideration of Antichrist was based on the late medieval distinction between Antichrist and anti-Christianity (*antichristianismus*). Campanella was more apocalyptic than Malvenda in the sense that he saw Luther as the "last precursor of the Great and Most Savage Antichrist," and he was convinced that this Great Antichrist was soon to appear.[120] The Final Antichrist would be a single historical individual who would recapitulate (note the Irenaean theme) all evil in his three-and-a-half-year reign. But Campanella was really more interested in the history of anti-Christianity than in Antichrist. For him Islam was the most formidable opponent of true Christianity throughout history, despite the evil contributions made by Luther, Calvin, and the other reformers as well as by Aristotelianism and

Machiavellianism. Campanella found the denial of free will by Muhammad, Luther, and Calvin a major root of the growing weight of the *antichristianismus* that would soon produce the Final Enemy.[121] Antichrist was, above all, a determinist.

Despite the thousands of pages written about Antichrist by Catholic polemicists between about 1520 and 1660 C.E., the century and a half of the most savage stages of Catholic-Protestant debate, one gets the sense that only a rearguard action was being fought. Protestants took Antichrist seriously during these years, as we have seen in looking at Luther and his successors. Catholics, by contrast, apparently wished they could have left him alone.

CHAPTER NINE

ANTICHRIST
IN DECLINE

(1660–1900)

Those who earnestly search for every mention of Antichrist during the period from 1660 to 1900 C.E., especially in English literature, can easily find a host of references. They may therefore be inclined to think that my brief treatment of the Great Deceiver during this time demonstrates his continuing ability to mislead the unwary. Perhaps. But from the viewpoint of almost two millennia of the legend's evolution, little new appeared in the accounts of the Final Enemy during this period, even when the events with which they were associated, such as the American and French Revolutions, were momentous for Western history. It is also significant that major historical changes did not produce new developments in the legend, as we have seen in earlier eras, with one exception to be treated below, that of Russia. While a number of important thinkers continued to speculate about Antichrist, in many ways the Last Enemy rapidly became the hobby of cranks after 1660.

The Catholic Antichrist

Catholic interest in Antichrist faded toward the end of the seventeenth century. A good illustration of this can be found in one of the few Catholic works of the period devoted to the Final Enemy, the Capuchin Denis of Luxemburg's treatise, *The Life of Antichrist,* first published in 1682.[1] This lengthy work in fifty chapters adopts a folksy and moralizing tone that seems often childish in comparison either with the evident fear found in medieval treatises or the desire for scientific completeness found in Thomas Malvenda. This is especially the case when the friar breaks off into one of his many pious exclamations.[2] His overt moralizing is evident, for example, in the description of Antichrist's conception, where he observes that this unholy manner of coming into the world should prompt Christians to honor the sanctity of marriage and to take proper care of their children's education.[3] The German Franciscan was strongly anti-Jewish. In the mouth of Antichrist's messengers he places thirteen articles of faith, actually Moses Maimonides's thirteen affirmations of Jewish belief (chap. 27), and the books the messengers use include the Talmud, which is savagely attacked in chapter 29. Although the Antichrist legend, from its origins, had contained an anti-Jewish element, this feature was often muted in late medieval and Reformation debates. Its return in Denis' often puerile book is a disturbing witness to continuing fear and distrust of Jews in traditional Christian circles.

The Life of Antichrist makes a few interesting concessions to eighteenth-century modernity, as when Antichrist sends out "postmen and couriers" to notify the world of the death of the two witnesses (chap. 45), or in the account of Antichrist's attempted ascension, which is accompanied by elaborate staging and a large orchestra, making the event almost grand opera (chap. 47). But Reformation scholar Hans Preuss is correct when he judges, "The book is written throughout in the tone of an old woman telling ghost stories to children at twilight."[4]

Antichrist rhetoric, to be sure, still found a place in Catholic reaction to major religious and political events of the modern era. The pressure of Enlightenment philosophical views and the politics of powerful Catholic monarchs anxious to maintain control over religion within their realms led to increasing opposition to the Jesuit order in the second half of the eighteenth century, culminating in Pope Clement XIV's suppression of the Jesuits in 1773. Some supporters of the order, both the uneducated and the cultivated, interpreted this papal surrender to outside pressure as an apocalyptic sign. Thus, Bernardina Renzi, a peasant prophetess, saw the anti-Jesuit campaign as the beginning of Antichrist's persecution of the Church, predicting that the Jesuits would soon arise under the protection of a great Christian emperor (the order actually was restored in 1814). In 1780 the ex-Jesuit Carlo Borgo issued a work entitled the Catholic Memorial (Memoria cattolica) (condemned and burned by the Roman authorities), in which he attacked Pope Clement as a new Antichrist and referred to a cabal of Enlightenment *philosophes,* Masons, and Jansenists who constituted Antichrist's army.[5] This form of conservative apocalypticism, with its frequent though generic references to Antichrist and his abettors, was used by traditionalist Catholic opponents to the French Revolution in the last decade of the eighteenth century and was often repeated during the nineteenth century. Perhaps the most noted adherent of this view was the pious priest Don Bosco, founder of the Salesian order, who communicated a series of visions featuring a Last Emperor (the "Warrior from the North") and an Angelic Pope (the "Venerable Old Man of Lazio") to Pius IX and the Austrian emperor Franz Joseph in the early 1870s.[6] There were also some philo-revolutionary Catholic apocalypticists, such as the French priest Hyacinthe-Marie Remuzat, whose *Letter of a Canon . . . on the Proximity of the End of the World* (published in French in 1786 and translated into Italian and Spanish) predicted world renewal for 1850 after the coming of Antichrist and the conversion of the Jews.[7] But appeals to old language, both among Catholic conservatives and liberals, were quite unoriginal, manifesting an exhaustion of creativity in the ability of the Catholic Antichrist to develop new mythic potential.

Before turning to Protestant uses of the legend after 1660, it is important to consider the one area in Christendom where Antichrist beliefs were both powerful and creative in the late seventeenth century and after—Russia in the movement known as the "Old Believers," or *raskolniki* (schismatics).[8]

Antichrist in Russia

Belief in Moscow as the "Third Rome" was strong in seventeenth-century Russia. The Russian Orthodox Church considered itself to be the guarantor of true Christian orthodoxy after the collapse of the First Rome to heresy and the Second Rome (Constantinople) to the Turk. The Russian Orthodox believed that the church-state system enshrined in Muscovy was the last representative of the Fourth Empire of Daniel 2, which was also the "Restraining Force" of 2 Thessalonians 2, empowered to prevent the appearance of the Man of Sin. Along with this ideology of the Third Rome appears evidence for growing apocalyptic fervor associated with the preaching of the mysterious hermit Kapiton.[9] But what if the Third Rome itself were to be taken over by the Final Enemy? Previous chapters in the history of Antichrist had already explored variations on this theme, but none of them seems to have equaled the force with which a peculiarly Russian view of Antichrist convulsed the vast reaches of the growing Russian empire and made itself endemic in Slavic religious history. During the eighteenth and nineteenth centuries, while comfortable English nonconformists feared the imminent persecution of an Antichrist who never arrived, Russian *raskolniki* suffered torture and death at the hands of an imperial church-state they identified with Antichrist or else often committed mass suicide (usually by fire) when faced with the alternative of submission. Rarely have Antichrist beliefs had more tragic consequences.

It was under Tsar Alexis I (1645–76) that the troubles began when the patriarch Nikon initiated a reform of traditional Russian liturgy in 1653 to bring it into conformity with Greek practices. Issues such as the sign of the cross being made with three fingers instead of two became rallying points for life-and-death decisions. If this seems strange to us it is because we have lost appreciation for the power of liturgical symbols, but in Eastern Orthodoxy true belief is inseparable from correct worship.[10] It is also clear that the protest that grew into the movement of Old Believers was a broad one that tapped into many feelings of discontent in Russia. As Slavic scholar Robert Crummey puts it, "Antichrist was the symbol of all that was new and oppressive in Muscovite society."[11] Thus, while Nikon's reforms met their original opposition largely within the ecclesiastical establishment, by the time of the synod of 1666–67 all those who opposed the reforms, both clergy and laity, were denounced as heretical enemies of the state church.[12] But who was really the heretic, especially when Antichrist, the ultimate deceiver, had been foretold as the one who would overturn true Christian worship for false practices?

The first leader of the opposition to Patriarch Nikon was the archpriest Avvakum, who tried to keep the struggle on a spiritual level, insisting that it was the "Spirit of Antichrist" that was alive in the decision of both patriarch and tsar to allow true worship to be perverted. Others soon became convinced that the Final Enemy himself, not just his spirit, was now present. An example of the more direct apocalyptic interpretation of the dispute can be found in a picture of Tsar Alexis and Patriarch Nikon as the two Beasts of chapter 13 of the Apocalypse in a contemporary manuscript. Among those who took up such views were the monks of the powerful monastery of Solovetskii in the White Sea, who refused to accept the liturgical reforms and eventually were slaughtered in 1676 after a ten-year siege of the monastery. How much of the opposition of the Solovetskii monks sprang from their love for an untainted liturgy and how much from the desire to maintain their independence against the tsar's growing power is difficult to determine.

Avvakum and his followers were executed in 1682, and in 1685 an imperial *ukase,* or law, ordered the suppression of all those who opposed the liturgical reforms. From this decade on we can speak of a real schism (*raskol*), one in which perhaps a fifth of the population shared the apocalyptic views of those who came to be known as the Old Believers. Like most sectarian protests, however, the movement was never a unified one.

As Michael Cherniavsky, a scholar of Russian history, has pointed out, the schismatics were confronted with difficult decisions about the nature of the Antichrist who opposed them. Three options were possible. They could assert that the Antichrist was actually present in the tsar and that the end was imminent, an option that many took but that was open to disconfirmation as time passed. They could, like Avvakum, see the spirit of Antichrist alive in the world and manifested in the apostasy of tsar and patriarch, a position that allowed for greater flexibility. Many of the Old Believers, however, adopted a third view that fused the first two by "the positing of an Antichrist who, though corporeal, was a body corporate—that is, the person of Antichrist was the Russian imperial dynasty." According to this view, "each successive Russian ruler . . . was the physical Antichrist while he ruled."[13] This option bears some analogy to the classic Protestant belief that the papacy itself was Antichrist but differs from it in giving the individual tsar greater symbolic weight as the actual embodiment of the ongoing presence of the Man of Sin.

The Old Believers' apocalyptic fears were solidified by the career of Peter I (the Great), who ruled from 1689 to 1725 and whose personal life and policy of westernization fit Antichrist's job description perfectly.[14] Peter's personal cruelty, his domination of the Russian church, the new titles he adopted, and the taxes and census he enjoined all helped mark him out as Antichrist and allowed elements of his person and career to color later Russian views of Antichrist. Even some who apparently did not belong to Old Believer groups came to be convinced that Peter was Antichrist. These included the Moscow scribe Grigorii Talitskii and Vasilii Levin, who had been a soldier in Peter's army but who fled to a monastery and in 1721 began preaching publicly against Peter as Antichrist; both men were executed. Also executed was one Akinfii Syseov, who was arrested in 1733 and under torture admitted that Peter I was the first Beast of Apocalypse 13 and that the seven heads of the Beast were the tsars from Ivan the Terrible through Peter II.[15] Peter also appeared in apocalyptic illustrations, for example, in a picture of the traditional scene of Antichrist's rebuilding of the Jerusalem temple with the assistance of demons, which is obviously based on the tsar's construction of his new capital at St. Petersburg (Fig. 29). Like former great persecutors from Nero through Frederick II, Peter not only exemplified Antichrist but also helped add to his legend, perhaps the last example of this dynamic in the history of Antichrist.

The subsequent story of the Old Believers' attitudes toward the Russian imperial Antichrist is bound up with the involved history of sects and groups little known in the West. Through various cycles of repression and toleration, the schismatics maintained their refusal to compromise with the rule of Antichrist, even when they achieved success in the mercantile world. Though the Vyg community studied by Robert Crummey had agreed to pray for the emperor (a sign of the more moderate Old Believers), when investigating one of their communities in Moscow in 1820 the imperial police were surprised to discover a portrait of the reigning Tsar Alexander I as Antichrist with horns, tail, and the fateful 666 inscribed on his forehead.[16]

Pietists and Colonists on Antichrist

Meanwhile, in Protestant Europe and America the Beast was also not dead, but he was well on the way to becoming a bit of a bore—a kind of aging relative about whom little new could be said. In continental Protestantism the movement known as Pietism, begun by Philip Jacob Spener (1635–1705), challenged Lutheran orthodoxy at the end of the seventeenth century. Spener and other Pietists, such as Gottfried Arnold, adopted a somewhat more flexible view of Antichrist than most Lutherans, though they continued to find Antichrist "concentrated" in the papacy.[17] Among the most scholarly of the Pietists was John Albert Bengel (1687–1752), whose *Exposition of the Revelation of St. John* (1740) and *Gnomon of the New Testament* (1742) provided a philologically learned but increasingly outmoded reading of the Apocalypse. Bengel saw the last book of the Bible as a linear prophecy of the whole of church history, which could be calculated with mathematical precision.[18] He identified the first Beast of Apocalypse 13 with the papacy as an institution, but he also expected a final personal Antichrist, a supremely evil pope whose coming he put safely at 1836 C.E.[19]

ЮН ВОЗГЛАВИПИТА СОБЕРОГАЛИИТ КАМЕНЕНТ УРАМИТ

FIGURE 29
Peter the Great as Antichrist
building St. Petersburg.
Russian Illuminated
Apocalypse (c. 1725).
Reproduced from Michael
Cherniavsky, "The Old
Believers and the New
Religion," *Slavic Review*
25(1966), plate 8, with
the permission of the
American Association
for the Advancement of
Slavic Studies.

The story of Antichrist in Protestant England and America after 1660 shows somewhat more vitality. Millenarianism (the belief in the reign of Christ and the saints on earth before the end) remained powerful in the English-speaking world even after the cessation of the radical hopes so evident during the English Civil War,[20] but Antichrist and the millennium are different, though often related, components of the ancient apocalyptic traditions. Millenarian thinking experienced considerable development, especially as it began to be associated with the fervent New World optimism of American Protestants, but Antichrist, for all that he took on an occasional new guise, was mostly a repetitive template (usually antipapal) of apocalyptic invective. As Thomas More Brown in his survey of antipapal rhetoric in colonial America observes, "The slow retreat from the grand confidence of the Reformers that the destruction of Antichrist could be expected in the near future gave to the language a tiredness, a formal, a stereotyped quality that turned from a description of reality into a metaphor."[21]

Old habits die hard, even in minds of remarkable originality. Isaac Newton (1642–1727), that paradigm of Enlightenment thought, was also a millenarian with a fondness (one might say almost obsession) for showing how scriptural prophecy revealed the course of history.[22] Following in the tradition of Mede and More,[23] Newton saw Antichrist, unsurprisingly, as the Church of Rome.[24] The majority of Enlightenment thinkers, of course, had little patience with Antichrist and apocalyptic calculations, which were mostly confined to commentators on the Apocalypse and popular prophets.[25] As noted in this book's introduction, Bishop Thomas Newton in his *Dissertations on the Prophecies,* an exhaustive three-volume defense of the veracity of biblical prophecy against the Deists of his day, felt compelled to note Voltaire's remark that "Sir Isaac Newton wrote his comment upon the Revelation to console mankind for the great superiority that he had over them in other respects." Although Newton was not the only Enlightenment sage to dabble in apocalyptic speculation,[26] Voltaire's remark gives us a good sense of how most eighteenth-century *philosophes* viewed such throwbacks.

ANTICHRIST IN THE NEW WORLD

Optimistic millenarianism was quite lively in the English-speaking New World in the eighteenth century. For its origins, we must step back a bit. The New England colony was founded in 1620 but did not begin to flourish until the influx in the 1630s of Puritans of the more radical sort, at least some of whom shared the apocalyptic expectations we have considered already.[27] They did not wish to separate themselves from the established church (at least not yet), but they did believe it needed to be purged of Romish practices and reformed along a congregational model. This first generation of American millenarians, which included figures like John Cotton, Richard Mather, and Thomas Hooker, preached sermons and published tracts on the Apocalypse like the Puritans who stayed on the other side of the Atlantic, arguing that not only Rome but also Canterbury had shown itself to be deeply infected with Antichrist.[28] Many of the radical Puritans were imminent premillennialists who looked forward to the arrival of God's kingdom on earth immediately after the return of Jesus.

The most interesting apocalyptic thinker in early America, however, was Roger Williams (1603–1683), a separatist and anabaptist whose views brought him into conflict with the congregationalist Puritans of the Massachusetts Bay Colony. In American history Williams is remembered as the founder of Rhode Island and a pioneer of religious toleration and rights for native Americans, but it is often forgotten that he arrived at these forward-looking views on the basis of a deeply apocalyptic theology of history.[29] From his reading of the Apocalypse, Williams was convinced that the 1260 days that the Heavenly Woman wanders in the wilderness fleeing from the Dragon (Apoc. 12:6) signified that there can be no true *established* church in the present. Since the beginning of the reign of the Antichrist in medieval Christianity, true religion had consisted of the witness of individual holy Christians symbolized in Apocalypse 11: "The Sufferings of Gods Witnesses since the Apostacie, have . . . been only right against the *darke* part, the Inventions, Abominations and Usurpations of Anti-christ, according to Rev. 11."[30] Any attempt to create a Christian state, even the very concept of Christendom, would partake of Antichrist, and the real Christian must avoid all contact with such a state and its claims, awaiting Christ's establishment of the true Church in the imminent millennium.[31] It is easy to see how Williams came into conflict with the theocratic society the Puritans were trying to establish in New England. As Thomas More Brown puts it, "Williams' contention that New England, eager to combat conspiracy [that is, the papal Antichrist], had erected a grotesque parody of the European Antichrist must have bewildered other Puritans."[32]

The generation of New England Puritans who came after the English Civil War and Restoration under Charles II displayed similar concerns. Samuel Sewall (1652–1730), for example, wrote a commentary on the Apocalypse (1697) that expressed a continued millenarian hope centered on the New World. The most important figure was Cotton Mather (1663–1728), heir to a powerful tradition of New England divines.[33] Mather and, after him, Jonathan Edwards (1703–1758) were the greatest intellectual figures of colonial New England. Both gave considerable attention to Antichrist in their theological writings, but in the long run it is difficult to say that they did more than repeat the main lines of the standard Puritan view.[34] In the large unpublished scriptural commentary he called *Biblia Americana,* Mather reflected his New World setting as he strove to understand the place of the imperial ambitions of the Catholic powers of Spain and France (Antichrist's allies) in the apocalyptic scenario. Above all, Mather was convinced that Antichrist's destruction was imminent and that the millennium was right around the corner.

Edwards was the greater thinker, but on Antichrist his views did not differ appreciably from Mather's. His many apocalyptic writings studied the same basic symbols that had fascinated Protestants for over two centuries—the 1260 days, the two witnesses, the beasts, the seven vials, and the millennium. At an early stage of his career, Edwards used a standard Protestant linear historical reading indicating that the papal Beast would not be finally destroyed until 1866. Later, under the influence of the hopes aroused by the religious revival known as the Great Awakening in the 1740s, he became convinced that the end was nearer. The fifth vial of the seven predicted in Apocalypse 16 had been the Reformation attack on the papacy, and the sixth he saw as present in his own day with the defeats of the French and Spanish that would end the flow of gold into Antichrist's coffers. Against those who believed that the millennium would not occur before a terrible persecution signified by the Beast's slaying of the witnesses, in his *An Humble Attempt* of 1747 Edwards argued that the slaying of the witnesses was in the past: "There are, as I apprehend, good reasons to hope, that that work of God's Spirit will begin in a little time, which, in the progress of it, will overthrow the kingdom of Antichrist. . . ."[35] Edwards, however, was more cautious than Mather, believing (like Robert Bellarmine) that neither the number nor the time of Antichrist could be determined with exactitude. Although his view of Antichrist was not notably original, Edwards was significant in projecting a powerful American-centered millenarianism that was to be adopted in various ways by his Protestant successors over the next century and more.[36]

Millenarians like Edwards and his generation found grist for their apocalyptic mills in the colonial struggles between Catholic and Protestant powers, especially in the French and Indian Wars that troubled the northern colonies between 1755 and 1763. James Cogswell, for example, encouraged Connecticut soldiers in 1757 with these words: "Fight for Liberty against Slavery. Endeavour to stand the Guardians of the Religion and Liberties of *America*; to oppose Antichrist, and prevent the barbarous Butchering of your fellow Countrymen."[37] What is most interesting about an exhortation of this sort is how easily it could be turned against the Protestant power of England in the struggle for freedom the colonies undertook less than twenty years later. Placing opposition to Antichrist within the rhetorical strategy of the conflict between liberty and tyranny was, of course, nothing new. But where was Antichrist's tyranny to be found? The idea that the late eighteenth-century papacy formed a real political threat to the English colonies was becoming increasingly far-fetched. Hence, the transfer of apocalyptic rhetoric to the actual threat found in England's attempt to rein in the refractory colonists was new but not really surprising, especially in light of Puritan denunciations of the government of Charles I more than a century before. Colonial historians have taken different positions on how important apocalyptic language actually was in the era of the Revolution.[38] From the perspective of the history of Antichrist, to denounce a political opponent as the Final Enemy was scarcely original.

Among the early groups fomenting opposition to England in the 1770s were the Sons of Liberty. An address given to this group in February 1776 and subsequently printed under the pseudonym "Pro-Patria" reviled the authors of the infamous Stamp Act, the Earl of Bute and Lord Grenville, as the two Beasts of Apocalypse 13:

> Here, my beloved brethren, he [Grenville] brings forth the Stamp Act, that mark of slavery, the perfection and sum total of all his wickedness; he ordained that none amongst us shall buy or sell a piece of land, except his mark be put upon the deed . . . : I beseech you then to beware as good christians and lovers of your country, lest by touching any paper with this impression, you receive the mark of the beast, and become infamous in your country throughout all generations.[39]

A number of New England divines, largely Congregationalists, Presbyterians, and Baptists, used similar language in sermons and treatises. A key incident that allowed the colonists to begin to see the English government as a part of Antichrist's establishment was the passage of the Quebec Act in 1774, which not only recognized the Catholic Church but also extended the boundaries of Canada at the expense of the thirteen colonies. Samuel Sherwood, for example, was convinced that such actions stemmed from the secret activity of Rome, the Whore of Babylon, and he identified the image of the Beast (Apoc. 13:14) with "the corrupt system of tyranny and oppression, that has of late been fabricated and adopted by the ministry and parliament of Great-Britain."[40] According to American historian Ruth Bloch, "In the context of the colonists' developing arguments about the constitutional limits of legitimate authority, the image of Antichrist as a tyrant took on a force it had not possessed since the days of revolutionary Puritanism."[41]

Painting England as part of Antichrist's array, however, was unusual and soon faded after the success of the American Revolution, when serious exegetes got back to their interminable and repetitive labors on scriptural prophecy. An equally momentous revolution beginning in France in 1789 soon provided greater opportunity for apocalyptic speculation, both in England and America.

Antichrist and the French Revolution

The French Revolution sparked one of the most important outpourings of political apocalypticism in modern times.[42] Given the association of Napoleon and his successors with this new chapter in European history, the relation between the French Revolution and apocalyptic speculation did not end in 1815 with the defeat of the Corsican adventurer but lasted into the 1870s when the last of his descendants left the scene.

The apocalyptic mentality has always found historical change ripe material for the application of biblical prophecy. The French Revolution enjoyed distinct advantages when it came to apocalyptic interpretation. Foremost among these from the Protestant perspective was France's position as the chief Catholic power (and therefore accomplice of Antichrist), as well as the fortuitous circumstances that allowed some Protestant interpreters of the Apocalypse to be seen as real prophets of the revolution.

As early as 1639, the Puritan Thomas Goodwin had claimed that the earthquake predicted to destroy a tenth part of the city in Apocalypse 11:13 signified a coming revolution in France. Christopher Love, a radical Puritan executed by Cromwell, was said to have authored a book of "strange and wonderful predictions" (printed six times in the United States between 1791 and 1798) announcing the destruction of the papal Antichrist for 1790 and the dawning of the millennium for 1805.[43] Even more startling was the lucky guess of the Huguenot scholar Pierre Jurieu, who first published his *The Accomplishment of Prophecies or the Coming Deliverence of the Church* in Holland in 1687 (it went through twenty-two French editions and twenty-six in English). Jurieu, an exile from the persecution of Louis XIV, also believed that the earthquake predicted in Apocalypse 11:13 referred to France, interpreting it as a humbling of the kingdom through revolution that would lead to a break with the papacy and the destruction of the Catholic religious orders. His calculations led him to predict that the earthquake would happen in 1785, adding, "If I should be mistaken by nine or ten years I do not think any could justly treat me as a false prophet and accuse me of rashness."[44] As it turned out, he was right on.

Robert Fleming, a Scots Presbyterian, friend of Jurieu, and later adviser to William of Orange, published his *Apocalyptical Key: An Extraordinary Discourse on the Rise and Fall of the Papacy* in 1701. Fleming interpreted the seven vials of Apocalypse 16 as God's judgment on the popish Antichrist. The fourth vial, poured out upon the sun so that it could scorch the people (Apoc. 16:8–9), referred to Louis XIV, the "Sun King," and his wars. The fifth vial, which was to be poured out over the throne of the Beast (Apoc. 16:10), would begin with the fall of the French monarchy in 1794 (another remarkable guess) and would culminate in a fatal blow given to the papal Antichrist in 1848 (when a rebellion against Pius IX actually took place!).[45] Other publicists followed these leads. An anonymous *Dissertation on the 13th and 14th Verses of the 11th Chapter of the Revelation* published in London in 1747 also identified France with the doomed tenth part of the city and distinguished between the ecclesiastical Antichrist who is the pope and the secular Antichrist, Louis King of France, noting that the Latin *LVDOVICVS* conveniently adds up to 666.[46]

The rapid course of the French Revolution, which began in 1789, outlawed the monarchy in 1792, and executed Louis XVI in 1793, gave these predictions a cachet rarely enjoyed by earlier prophets. No wonder that they were often reprinted and frequently cited in the midst of feverish hopes that the destruction of Antichrist was nigh and the millennium therefore just around the corner. The events of the time fit in perfectly with the revived postmillennial optimism of those biblical interpreters who believed Jesus would return only after an earthly millennium.[47] A number of thinkers in both England and America immediately climbed the pulpit and/or put pen to paper to show the consonance between the prophecies and the course of events in France.[48] What is interesting is that these pious nonconformists were so often untroubled by the opposition to religion found among the revolutionaries. It was enough for most of them, at least in the beginning, that the French monarchy and the Catholic Church were under attack.[49] All took a positive view of the events in France, seeing them as confirmation that Antichrist was breathing his last.

A more negative reading of the apocalyptic significance of events, however, began to emerge after 1798. This passage from francophilic to francophobic interpretation of the revolution was triggered in part by a new willingness on the part of the apocalypticists to recognize the antireligious ideology of the radical Jacobins. Also a new claimant emerged for the title of Antichrist—Napoleon. An example of the former tendency can be found in Samuel Horseley, bishop and savant, who edited Isaac Newton. Horseley believed that the Western aspect of Antichrist present in irreligious France would eventually be combined with the Eastern Antichrist found in Turkey in the person of a final individual Antichrist who was closer to medieval models than those found in most Protestant apocalypticists. In 1806 he allowed that Napoleon was his predecessor but refused to identify the Corsican with the Final Enemy.[50] George Stanley Faber, who produced a series of apocalyptic works between 1799 and 1853, held views that were a variant of Horseley's—a triple Antichrist consisting of the papacy, the Muslim "imposture" (still both active in the world), and the final Antichrist found in the collective threat of the anarchism and atheism of revolutionary France. Faber expected an alliance of these three dread forces throughout his life, even into the 1850s when the career of Louis Napoleon revived his fears.[51]

Napoleon Bonaparte, the Corsican adventurer, first made his name in the Italian campaign of 1796–97 and then in the Egyptian expedition of 1798–99. At the same time, the success of the Second Coalition of monarchies united against France had brought the future of the revolution into question. By the end of 1799 Napoleon established himself as First Consul, really dictator, of France and "saved" the revolution, or at least his version of it. In 1804 he became emperor of the French. The fifteen-year struggle between Napoleon and the rest of Europe, unlike the wars between Frederick II and the papacy or the wars of religion in the sixteenth and seventeenth centuries, provide little evidence of apocalyptic motivation or heavy use of apocalyptic rhetoric on the part of its leaders and ideologues. Antichrist and related symbols had moved to the fringes of religio-political discourse, but he could still be found there, as evidence both from England and the United States indicates.

For example, Hester Thrale Piozzi, Samuel Johnson's friend, collected contemporary English witnesses to popular apocalyptic expectations in a diary she kept between 1776 and 1809 called the *Thralliana*. Always opposed to the French Revolution, she was happy to cite increasing evidence of its Antichrist-like character, culminating in Napoleon whose name she believed meant "the Destroyer" in Corsican, and who she asserted "does come forwards followed by a Cloud of Locusts from ye bottomless Pit" (see Apoc. 9:1–11). She even noted that some women in Wales told her that Napoleon's titles added up to 666.[52]

In North America also a reaction against the French Revolution began to associate it with Antichrist. This is found as early as 1795 in a sermon of Harvard divinity professor David Tappan, and it became more common after 1798. In that year Jeremy Belknap, another Harvard worthy, observed, "The French power is not less antichristian for the revolution."[53] This swing of opinion also included reactions against Napoleon, though the Corsican was never the immediate threat in America that he was in England. Napoleon fell in 1815, and paradoxically the papal Antichrist was among those who reaped the spoils at the Congress of Vienna. In the rapidly industrializing world of nineteenth-century Europe and the United States, what role was there, if any, for ancient fears of Antichrist?

Antichrist in the Nineteenth-Century World

Despite a number of contributions, the role of apocalyptic thought in the nineteenth century, in both Catholic and Protestant areas, stands in need of further investigation. A number of works of the past decades have shown how widespread millenarianism remained on both sides of the Atlantic among some forms of Protestantism, even giving rise to new religions in the case of the Millerites (future Seventh-Day Adventists) and the Mormons.[54] The historian of American religion Ernest R. Sandeen has claimed, "America in the early nineteenth century was drunk on the millennium."[55] (One may wonder how much sobering up has taken place subsequently.) The optimism encouraged by the expanding new country gave millenarianism, both in traditional religious forms and in new, more secular ones, considerable power. Millenarian views, however, were also popular among British nonconformists who frequently preached on both sides of the Atlantic. All of these figures depended on the traditional Protestant apocalyptic scenario, which helps explain why insofar as Antichrist continued to play a role for them, it was mostly an unoriginal one.[56]

In the first half of the nineteenth century the traditional Protestant reliance on a historicist reading of the Apocalypse (the book as reflecting the course of history partly past and partly to come) was challenged by the rise of a futurist interpretation, which held that none of the events predicted in Apocalypse 4 and the following chapters had yet occurred. But the historicists continued to be strong with such figures as Edward Irving (1792–1834) and Henry Drummond (1786–1860).[57] Drummond identified Antichrist with the spirit of apostasy, advancing a theory of developing

Antichrists. Rome was surely one form of the Final Enemy, but a second was to be found in the established Protestant churches, especially in England and Scotland, which had fallen away from apostolic purity. In his *Dialogues on Prophecy* (1828–29), he specified a triple Antichrist—papal, Protestant, and a coming third form, a "monster of infidel apostasy," which would arise from the former two.

Later in the century the historicist mentality targeted one more figure as the personal Antichrist, none other than Napoleon III (1808–1873), the nephew of the great general. The younger Napoleon, a devious politician rather than a world conqueror, seems to us a much less likely candidate for the Final Enemy than his uncle, but the apocalyptic fears that had clustered around the name of Napoleon from early in the century seemed to be fulfilled in his rise to power and underlined by his assumption of the imperial title in 1852. An example can be found in G. S. Farber's *The Revival of the French Emperorship*.[58] Farber claimed to have foreseen the revival of the French imperial office, which he identified with the seventh head of the Beast, as early as 1818. Slain in the person of the first Napoleon, it had now been brought back to life by Napoleon III. (In both cases the head and the Beast to which it is attached emerge out of "the figurative Oceanic Abyss of Revolutionary Violence," that is, the revolutions of 1789 and 1848.) The year 1864 would witness the final struggle between the forces of good and evil, which Farber predicted would begin in Europe but end in Palestine.[59]

Napoleon III's career was also closely studied by American millenarians. A Protestant interdenominational journal called the *Prophetic Times,* published between 1863 and 1881, is among the best examples of American millenarianism at this time. Mainly the work of the Lutheran pastor Joseph A. Seiss, the journal featured many articles on the emperor and his impending revelation as Antichrist. Michael Baxter, an English missionary preacher active in Canada and the United States, published a treatise in Philadelphia in 1866 entitled *Louis Napoleon: The Destined Monarch of the World and Personal Antichrist.* Even as the French emperor's plight grew worse and his political moves more ineffective, firm believers were convinced that this was merely a ploy of the Final Deceiver. On the eve of his downfall, a writer in the *Prophetic Times* of 1869 asserted, "He has acted for years with that consummate prudence which superficial men have mistaken for imbecility."[60] Given judgments of this sort, one is allowed to think that it was the imbecility of the historicist millenarians that contributed the most to the decline of literal interpretations of Antichrist over two centuries.

Millenarianism in the United States in the first half of the nineteenth century was marked by what historian of American religion Nathan O. Hatch has described as a democratic and rationalistic bent, one in which the ideal of civil and religious liberty and an insistence on the study of "the facts of the Bible" set the tone.[61] This helps explain why many of the new millenarian movements of the time, such as the Millerites and Mormons, developed a strand of thought present at the time of the American Revolution, in which any form of tyranny, but especially religious tyranny, partakes of Antichrist. Alexander Campbell (1788–1866), the founder of the Disciples of Christ, was a representative of this in his claim that "Catholic and Protestant Popery are plodding and plotting for supremacy."[62] Despite the importance of these movements in American religious history, they did not make any significant new contribution to wider Antichrist traditions.

After the Civil War in the United States, futurist millenarianism began to dominate and did much to dampen the ardor of those who tried to identify particular present rulers or institutions with the Antichrist. The rise of futurism is associated with John Nelson Darby (1800–1882) and the Plymouth Brethren. Darby was the originator of "dispensationalism," the theory that Christ would end the present era, or dispensation, of history by an imminent secret rapture of the faithful to heaven (see 1 Thess. 4:16). This belief is still a powerful factor in contemporary Protestant Fundamentalism.[63] Such eschatological positions did not, of course, put an end to all presentist uses of the Antichrist legend, and repetitive predictions of futurist views of Antichrist continued to be advanced. We will look at some examples during the past hundred years in the final chapter. What remains here is to return to the question of why Antichrist declined in creativity and effectiveness during the years between 1660 and 1900.

Why Antichrist Waned

A fully adequate answer to the question of why Antichrist waned remains elusive, but some of the factors at work have already been mentioned. Certainly, the Enlightenment critique of Christianity had greater effects on its legendary elements than on its central doctrines. Believers more easily let go of Antichrist than of Christ, of their convictions about the eternity of hell than of their hopes for some kind of reward for the just.[64] Many other impulses were at work—some already noted, others hinted at, doubtless others neglected. In closing this chapter, I suggest that the central theme of this book, Antichrist's symbolizing of ultimate human evil, allows us to see significant factors in the decline that might be easily overlooked.

The conception of absolute human evil that gave birth to Antichrist took many forms in the centuries prior to 1500. Although some foundational New Testament texts, especially the Little Apocalypse and the Johannine Epistles, pointed to multiple internal threats—*pseudochristoi, antichristoi polloi*—the pull toward a single Final Enemy emphasized in 2 Thessalonians 2 and in early interpretations of the symbols of the Apocalypse made it easy to view Antichrist as a figure external to Christianity, first as a pagan persecutor, then as a Jewish pseudo-Messiah, later as a heretical "outsider," for example, a Muslim. But the Antichrist legend never excluded the "insider" dimension, both in individual and collective senses. Many thought that the ultimate Antichrist would arise from within the Church as a supremely deceptive teacher; others emphasized the collective weight of error and hypocrisy as the essential meaning of Antichrist. Augustine and his followers contended that Antichrist was omnipresent as the internal spirit of denial of Jesus that could be found in the heart of any Christian. During the later Middle Ages, the interior aspect of Antichrist not only became dominant but was also clericalized in the sense that the hypocrisy of priests and friars, culminating in the person of a false pope, was seen as the most likely mode of Antichrist's appearance. As long as these diverse external and internal symbolizations continued to interact in a mutual, if scarcely logical, process of enrichment, as they did for much of the Middle Ages, the Antichrist legend experienced growth and change as an integral part of the Christian *mythos*. This rich interaction began to break down after 1500 when Antichrist was divided.

I would not argue that merely Protestants calling the papacy Antichrist and Catholics finding Antichrist among the reformers marked the change. Rather, the insistence that only one form of Antichrist belief could be correct hinted at the underlying problem. A rich and varied symbol of human evil that could be used in a variety of ways lost effectiveness when it was reduced to a few simple models subject to endless repetition. The symbolic flattening of Antichrist is evident as much in the repetitions of antipapal invective found in the reformers as it is in the sober futurist view found in the Jesuit controversialists or in the vague language of Catholic traditionalists.

Alongside this evisceration of symbolic content is the phenomenon of ecclesiastical "implosion." The increasing centripetal motion of Antichrist, by which he penetrates more and more deeply into the fabric of the institutional church, was evident in the late Middle Ages, and accelerated in the sixteenth and seventeenth centuries. In the classic Reformation view it took the form of a clear division between good and evil, between papal Antichrist and true reformed Christianity. But the more radical reformers noted that even the Reformed churches continued to show evidence of what they regarded as Antichrist and his practices, and so ecclesial identification with Antichrist spread easily and rapidly to any— and eventually to every—form of church governance. Since Antichrist was no longer chiefly a person, but rather a force of deception and tyranny, any ecclesio-political entity that seemed deceptive or tyrannical could eventually be identified with Antichrist. Finally, the increasing vagueness of the term reached the point where universal invective overwhelmed effective application.

Finally, we can note a rather curious atrophy of the element of personal appropriation of the symbolism of evil found in Antichrist. Origen, Augustine, and others had used Antichrist, at least in part, as a call for each believer to test his or her heart according to the spirit of Christ. The polemic use of Antichrist rhetoric in the era of the divided Antichrist left little room for this personal application. Some of the radical reformers of the sixteenth and seventeenth centuries continued an interest in the personal dimension of the Antichrist tradition, but they used it in ways that— like the rest of their theology—were unacceptable to the major opposed forms of Christian belief.

Perhaps these last two elements can be seen as related. Antichrist as a form of vague rhetoric to be used against any opponent helped weaken the content of a term that was already being undercut by the neglect of its more personal applications. When the Enlightenment view of human nature began to suggest that maybe humanity was not really vitiated by original sin, that poor education and not bad will was the source of evil, it also challenged the validity of belief in such a thing as *ultimate* human evil. Antichrist's reality became increasingly problematic as Enlightenment ideas spread, but Christianity itself had prepared the way for this collapse. Because of this, most eighteenth- and nineteenth-century views of Antichrist seem empty repetitions of once-vibrant symbols.

CHAPTER TEN

ANTICHRIST OUR CONTEMPORARY

I n the final century of the second millennium Antichrist has become increasingly problematic. The decline of the Final Enemy sketched in the previous chapter was as much a decline of creativity in the growth of the legend as it was a reduction in the number of those who gave Antichrist an important role in their faith (though we have no statistics for how many Christians believed in a literal Antichrist then or now). Still, witnesses to continuing conviction in Antichrist as an imminent, at times even as a present, figure during the past century are not lacking. These witnesses to the legend's persistence tend to come from a limited, if powerful, segment of conservative Protestant Christians, usually called Fundamentalists. Christians of other persuasions in recent decades have more often than not simply forgotten Antichrist.

There is another side to Antichrist during the past hundred years, however—what I will call the literary or fictional Antichrist. If earlier centuries had delighted in illustrating what Antichrist was to look like (a phenomenon curiously absent in the twentieth century), our own era has been more interested in producing fictional accounts of the Final Enemy. Pondering the implications of the literary Antichrist will also help raise the issue that will close this chapter and the book—what meaning the legend about the ultimate human evildoer can have today.

The Roman Catholic View

The Roman Catholic Church has used Antichrist very little in the twentieth century. Theological views, as reflected in encyclopedias and dictionaries, tend to be sober historical accounts that often either caution against treating belief in Antichrist as a doctrine[1] or at times even admit that the idea of Antichrist has lost its effectiveness.[2] Some Catholic theologians, such as Karl Rahner, continue to admit the validity of both collective and individual interpretations,[3] but most modern Catholic theologians do not even mention the Final Enemy.

On the popular level, literal belief in Antichrist has not been totally absent from modern Catholicism. There is an apocalyptic dimension to some modern Marian apparitions.[4] The apparition at La Salette in 1846 involved hints about Antichrist from the beginning, but these did not become explicit until the publication of the so-called *Secret of La Salette* in 1879 by Melanie Calvat (1831–1904), one of the original visionaries. This millenarian text underwent considerable editing and expansion over succeeding decades. Probably as a reaction to the suspicion of the hierarchy toward such private revelations, the later versions included the prophecy that "Rome would lose the faith and become the seat of Antichrist." In the 1930s some of the suspect "Melanists" (as Melanie Calvat's followers were called) went even further, discovering that the papal title "Vicarius Filii Dei" (Vicar of the Son of God) added up to 666.[5] This revival of medieval fears that Antichrist had taken over the papacy (usually because of what were perceived as Rome's doctrinal errors) continues on in the lunatic fringe of Catholicism. For example, the *New York Times* of November 12, 1982, reported on a Mexican sect based on a series of Marian visions and led by a renegade priest, Father Nabor Cardenas. (The group was located at a site called New Jerusalem 180 miles northwest of Mexico City.) One of the visionaries, a peasant girl called Mama Maria de Jesus, supposedly speaking in the voice of the Archangel Gabriel, declared, "The Pope is a fraud. Pope Paul VI [who died in 1978] is imprisoned in the basement of the Vatican so that Antichrist can enter. The Antichrist is already here. He is 29 years old and comes from Guadalajara and soon he will be called to Rome."[6]

Belief in a literal Antichrist of a traditional Catholic sort, without directly identifying the papacy with the Final Enemy, can also be found in more respectable Catholic circles. Three examples will suffice to show how little originality is to be found in these reprisals of the past.

Father Gerard Culleton (1902–1950), a priest of the diocese of Monterey in California, became fascinated with prophecies of the endtime in the 1930s. At his death he left a manuscript entitled *The Reign of Antichrist,* which is a collection of some 170 prophecies of Antichrist from Scripture and the Catholic tradition.[7] More fascinating is the modern revival of the French-Joachite apocalyptic tradition involving a Last

Emperor and Angel Pope who will combat a false Antipope before the coming of the Final Antichrist. An example can be found in the work of a former French army officer, Yves Dupont, entitled *Catholic Prophecy: The Coming Chastisement* (1970). Dupont's collection of prophetic texts and commentary preaches a right-wing Catholic apocalypticism that sees in Vatican II and the subsequent liturgical changes introduced into the Mass a sign of the imminence of the end.[8] A more complete recent survey of Antichrist beliefs from a conservative Catholic perspective can be found in Vincent P. Miceli, *The Antichrist* (1981). Miceli does not denounce Vatican II, as Dupont does, and he rejects any attempts to date the end of the world, in good Augustinian fashion. His main concern is to denounce any attempts to create a "détente" between the Catholic Church and contemporary culture as evidence of Antichrist's increasing activity.[9]

The Tenacious Influence of the Dispensationalists

Antichrist beliefs among mainline Protestants in the past century have been equally muted, even with regard to the standard Reformation identification of the Man of Sin with the papacy, though the accusation has not been totally rejected, especially in the sectarian atmosphere of Northern Ireland. After Vatican II, traditional Lutheran and Reformed claims that the pope was Antichrist have been either forgotten or explicitly rejected. Even the Evangelical Fundamentalists, for whom Antichrist is certainly alive and well, have been uncomfortable with a papal Antichrist, partly because they have found so many better candidates.

Most contemporary literal belief in the Antichrist is to be found among Protestants who adhere to the dispensationalist apocalypticism created among English sectarians in the 1830s. From the perspective of the history of Christian apocalypticism, what is most intriguing about the dispensationalist view is its strict adherence to a futurist interpretation of biblical prophecy. (Contemporary American Fundamentalists would probably be surprised to know that it was actually Jesuit exegetes of the late sixteenth century who pioneered such futurist explanations of prophecy.) Rigorous futurism is more important than another often-cited difference between the dispensationalists and previous Protestant apocalypticists, namely, their adherence to a premillennialist view in which Christ's return is to initiate the thousand-year earthly kingdom, rather than the postmillennialism of such noted early American apocalyptic thinkers as Jonathan Edwards.[10]

This form of Protestant apocalypticism was imported into the United States from England through the preaching of John Nelson Darby and others, as we have seen in the previous chapter. In the troubled decades after the Civil War it experienced considerable growth among conservative Protestants who felt threatened by the spread of a liberal Christianity willing to give up belief in the literal inerrancy of the Bible and seeking to establish a dialogue between Christianity and modernity. Not all of the antiliberal Evangelicals were premillennialists, of course, but belief in a coming rapture (Christ's bodily rescue of the faithful by way of a collective, physical ascent to heaven) before the final events was a strong component in the Evangelical movement, as witnessed, for instance, in the career of Dwight L. Moody (1837–1899), the famous Evangelical preacher and founder of the Moody Bible Institute (1886).

The American followers of revived premillennial dispensationalism were futurist rather than historicist, perhaps because they learned from the errors of historicist interpreters, such as William Miller, who had predicted the Second Coming for 1844. They also felt increasingly estranged from the mainline Protestant denominations and therefore found it difficult to conceive how God would have made these bodies objects of his prophetic message. In the long history of Christian apocalypticism, few traditions have been as successful in conveying the sense that the end is imminent while generally resisting the temptation to set a definite date. The other factor that has given premillennialist dispensationalism a power not unlike that of Franciscan Spiritualism in earlier times has been the surprising congruity between crucial elements of their apocalyptic program (especially the revival of a Jewish state) and the actual course of events in the twentieth century.

Dispensationalism is founded upon one of the more unlikely premises in the history of Christian apocalypticism, that is, the conviction that after predicting ancient history quite fully for many centuries, biblical prophecy took a holiday for almost two thousand years (the dispensation of the Gentiles) between the fall of the Second Temple of Jerusalem in 70 C.E. and the restoration of a Jewish state in 1948. By separating the history of Israel from the history of the "true Church" (not to be confused with classical Christian denominations), the dispensationalists were able to affirm a "postponement theory" by means of which all the prophecies left unfulfilled when the Jews rejected Jesus and lost Jerusalem and its temple had to wait for completion until the return of the Jews to Palestine.[11] Only then could the precise apocalyptic clock whose hands had been stopped for almost two millennia begin ticking again.

Three imminent events frame the apocalypticism that forms the basis for modern Fundamentalist expectations of the end—the rapture, the tribulation, and the millennium. All three are based on literalist readings of the Bible, though the first represents a relatively new emphasis in the history of Christian apocalypticism. Basing themselves primarily upon Paul's statement in 1 Thessalonians 4:16–17 that the faithful who are still alive will be caught up with the dead saints to meet Christ before the end, the dispensationalists created a powerful new hope that true believers would not have to face the final and most severe persecution of Antichrist but would be able to wait things out in heaven while the rest of humanity was tormented and destroyed.[12] (Traditional apocalypticism for over two millennia had insisted that only real suffering could lead to glory, both here and hereafter. From this perspective, the optimistic premillenarian rapture appears to be both an innovation and perhaps a form of cheap grace.)

More traditional is the dispensationalist view of the tribulation itself, that is, the final seven years of history when the Antichrist will gain power and first Israel and then the whole world (though not the raptured church) will be subjected to persecution and terror. This is usually based on a synthetic reading of biblical prophecies, both from the Old Testament (especially Dan. and Ezek. 38–39), and from the New, particularly the Synoptic Little Apocalypse and John's Apocalypse. While the interpretation of details has fluctuated considerably, there is a broad agreement among premillennialists about the general scenario. Finally, in the tradition of Protestant dissidents from the early seventeenth century on, the premillenarian dispensationalists believe in a literal millennium, that is, a thousand-year reign of Christ and the saints on earth after Antichrist's defeat.

In the twentieth century, largely since World War I, premillennialism has become a powerful part of the American religious scene. This has been due both to the evolution of American Fundamentalism and to historical events, especially those connected with the state of Israel. In his pioneering work, *The Roots of Fundamentalism,* the historian of American religion Ernest R. Sandeen argued for the necessity of distinguishing between a broad Fundamentalist *movement* and the Fundamentalist *controversy* focusing on the literal interpretation of the Bible and culminating in the famous Scopes trial of 1925 over the teaching of evolution in schools. For Sandeen, "It is millenarianism which gave life and shape to the Fundamentalist movement."[13]

After trying to work within the denominations in the latter nineteenth century, especially the more conservative branches of the Baptist and Presbyterian communions, the Fundamentalist movement, strengthened by the flourishing Bible institutes and increasingly allied with revivalist preaching, began to take a more independent route in the early decades of the present century. In 1919 the Philadelphia World's Conference on Christian Fundamentals and the foundation of the World's Christian Fundamentals Association (WCFA) marked the birth of Fundamentalism in the narrower sense. Historian Timothy Weber rightly reminds us that "not everyone who called himself a fundamentalist believed in the premillennial coming of Christ and that not every premillennialist took an active part in the fundamentalist controversy."[14] Still, millenarianism, especially of the pretribulational variety, was crucial to the evolution of American Fundamentalism and remains central to it to this day.

The growing strength of premillenarianism in the twentieth century has been aided by a series of events that seemed to confirm that the great parenthesis of the dispensation of the Gentiles was about to end and the biblical prophecies about Israel and the endtime were soon to be fulfilled. Premillennial expectations were fairly well set, at least in general fashion, by the early twentieth century and were widely diffused by useful handbooks like the *Scofield Reference Bible,* first published in 1909.[15] All they lacked was some connection with political realities. This began to change with World War I and the Balfour Declaration of 1917, which encouraged Zionist hopes for the establishment of a Jewish state.

The upheaval and destruction of the First World War formed sufficient argument for some premillennialist preachers, such as F. C. Jennings, to see the conflict as the immediate antecedent to the rapture and the rise of the World Dictator, that is, the Antichrist, who alone could bring (false) terrestrial peace. Most, however, were content to see the great struggle as a sign of the coming realignment of powers that would precede the final events.[16]

From the start, dispensationalist apocalypticism had been obsessed with the place of the Jews in the endtime (in this it was the heir to a long tradition in English Protestant apocalyptic thought).[17] Apocalyptic traditions, based on a different logic from standard views of history, have always been more attentive to events that fit their picture of divine meaning rather than those that secular history might consider more important. Hence, for the premillennialists the most significant event connected with World War I was not the epic struggle that cost millions of lives or the collapse of the Russian Empire and the Bolshevik Revolution, but rather the 1917 declaration by Lord Balfour, the British foreign secretary, that "His Majesty's Government view with favor the establishment in Palestine of a national home for the Jewish people." It would take another three decades before the Jewish state became a reality in 1948, but the Balfour Declaration paved the way and gave the premillennialist program an impetus similar to that given the Spiritual Franciscans by John XXII when he declared apostolic poverty a heresy—that is, a clear case of prophecy fulfilled. In the words of one of the most important recent premillennialist spokesmen: "The most significant prophetic event in the twentieth century has been the restoration of the people of Israel to their land."[18] Not even the advent of the atomic bomb, which threatened a world destruction that seemed to match the dire threats of the biblical texts, had quite the same impact.

Several historical developments between 1917 and 1948 also provided grist for the mill of premillennial hopes and fears. The formation of the League of Nations revived speculation about the rebirth of Rome as a ten-nation democracy. Arno C. Gaebelein (1861–1945), one of the foremost premillennialists of the time, pointed out that the league contained too many countries to fit the prophecy, but I. M. Haldeman declared that the league was "preparing the way for the final and desperate revival of Rome under the form of ten confederate nations, with its last kaiser, that dark and woeful figure, the man of sin, the son of perdition, the Antichrist."[19]

A promising candidate for Antichrist as the leader of a revived Roman Empire appeared in the figure of Benito Mussolini, the Fascist dictator who gained control of Italy in 1924. In 1927 Oswald J. Smith published a book entitled *Is the Antichrist at Hand?—What of Mussolini?* which predicted the coming of the end between 1928 and 1933. Mussolini's attempts to restore Roman glory led Smith to conclude that "Mussolini may not be the Emperor himself, but if he is not, he is certainly a remarkable foreshadowing of the one whom the Bible predicts will reign."[20] Louis Bauman of the Bible Institute of Los Angeles also hailed the Italian dictator as Antichrist, but most premillennialists sided with James M. Gray of the Moody Bible Institute, who saw in him only another forerunner.[21]

The far greater threat to world peace represented by the rise to power of Adolf Hitler in Germany held fewer apocalyptic overtones for the American premillennialists, because the German dictator made no claims for reviving the Roman Empire. Germany's role, as the premillennialists saw it, was to combine with Russia as the invading Gog and Magog of the endtime—an event that seemed to be made quite likely for a brief time by the unexpected announcement of the nonaggression pact between Hitler and Stalin in August 1939. At a Prophetic Conference meeting in New York in November of that year, the aged Arno C. Gaebelein spoke for many when he announced, "For all we know, this may be the last prophetic conference which will be held, for 'our gathering together unto him' cannot be far away."[22] The onset of World War II swallowed up all these false hopes. Hitler may have been rhetorically denounced by some as Antichrist, especially during the war, but not by the literal believers in biblical prophecy. The fact that evil dictators like Hitler and Stalin, who in former ages might have inspired whole new chapters in the story of the Final Enemy, have added nothing to Antichrist traditions is another sign of the current weak status of the legend's literal interpretation. The shrinking of the literal view of the legend to one simple and endlessly repeated scenario has meant that it has become less and less a reflection of the real evil figures of current history, however much it continues to allow an interpretation of the events that fit its predetermined view of what is significant.

The Late Great Prophets of Armageddon

Premillennial views connected with Christian Fundamentalism experienced a rebirth after World War II as a result of the foundation of the state of Israel, but other events of the past fifty years have also been seen as signs of the approaching tribulation. Among these were the explosion of the atomic bomb, the growth of the European Common Market and European Community (EC), Russian interest in the Middle East, and several less obvious signs. Fundamentalists have shown remarkable ingenuity in adapting their message to current historical fears, especially since the 1960s. Through a number of best-selling books and especially through the use of televangelism, the premillennial message has achieved a wider diffusion in the past decades than it enjoyed at any time since its birth a century and a half ago. To this extent at least, a literal Antichrist still exists for millions of Americans and other Fundamentalists around the world. A look at two of the best-known recent premillenarian authors can provide some insight into this latest form of the ancient legend of Antichrist.

Both Hal Lindsey and John F. Walvoord are connected with Dallas Theological Seminary, which Timothy Weber describes as the Vatican of American premillennialism.[23] Lindsey was educated at Dallas and served as a campus minister at UCLA in the 1960s. In 1970 he published an apocalyptic volume with the catchy title *The Late Great Planet Earth*. It proved to be *the* best-selling book of the 1970s and is still in print, claiming total sales of over 25 million copies. (*Late Great Planet* was also made into a movie in the late 1970s, starring assorted atomic bombs and the voice of Orson Welles.) Even if only a fraction of the book's readers actually believe its message, *Late Great Planet Earth* proves that millions are still willing to entertain the idea of a literal, imminent Antichrist.[24]

Lindsey's picture of Antichrist contains nothing beyond what we have already seen in the standard premillennial scenario. The beginning of the Jewish state in 1948 and Jewish conquest of the whole of Jerusalem in 1967 are viewed as signs that we are living in the last generation. (Lindsey is typical both in denying exact knowledge of the time of the end and in originally estimating that the scenario was to begin *by* 1988.)[25] The activity of the European Common Market is taken as an indication that by about 1980 Rome will be revived in a ten-nation United States of Europe (see chap. 8 of Lindsey's book, "Rome on the Revival Road") to provide the power base for the coming dictator, or Antichrist (who is described in chap. 9, "The Future Fuehrer"). This Gentile dictator is supposed to sign a peace treaty with Israel that will allow for the rebuilding of the temple. He will be revealed as Antichrist when he is miraculously healed of a serious head wound; he will then enthrone himself as God in the rebuilt temple. Associated with him will be a Jewish False Prophet (see Apoc. 13:11–18) who will compel everyone to worship the dictator. Those who do not, especially the 144,000 recently converted Jews (see Apoc. 7:9–14), will suffer severe persecution. The account of Antichrist's wars before the final battle at Armageddon is standard fare too (see especially chaps. 12–13).[26]

John F. Walvoord served as the president of Dallas Theological Seminary from 1952 to 1986 and later as its chancellor. He has written many works on biblical prophecy, the most important being *Armageddon, Oil and the Middle East Crisis,* first issued in 1974 but revised in light of the latest news from the Middle East in 1990. (The book claims to have sold a million copies in two months during the recent Gulf War.) Walvoord's presentation, more theological in tone than Lindsey's, differs only in details. Less Europe-centered than Lindsey, he predicts a ten-nation Mediterranean confederacy whose leader will force Israel to make peace with the Arabs. This will mark the end of the time of the Gentiles and the beginning of the final seven years of history.[27] With the true Christians removed by the rapture, the Mediterranean leader, or Antichrist, will ally himself with a "Super-Church" consisting of the Catholic, Protestant, and Orthodox believers (an alliance Walvoord finds predicted in the Harlot riding on the Beast in Apocalypse 17). During the first three and a half years of his reign, divine intervention will destroy the Russian invasion of Israel predicted in Ezekiel 38–39 (which Walvoord thinks will actually be conducted by cavalry as predicted because of disarmament and scarcity of oil). Antichrist will declare himself world ruler and "God" in the rebuilt temple at Jerusalem and will then crush all opposition in a fearsome persecution. Eventually, there will be a worldwide revolt against him and the assembled millions will gather at Armageddon. Christ will descend on the Mount of Olives, accompanied by "huge hailstones, each weighing a hundred pounds." Then Antichrist will be cast into hell, both Jews and Gentiles will be judged, and the millennium will begin.[28]

Hal Lindsey and John Walvoord offer not the most detailed of the recent premillennial accounts of Antichrist,[29] but they do provide a good general picture of Fundamentalist apocalypticism. Both represent a premillenarianism that has made considerable impact on the general public, partly no doubt out of mere curiosity but also, in the case of many, out of apocalypticism's ability to provide meaning in a time of historical uncertainty.[30] Both have been coy about predicting exact dates and names, leaving the details of the prophetic scenario open-ended enough to survive a good deal of factual discomfiture. Not all premillennialists have been as wise. Some have assigned exact dates for Antichrist's manifestation and even tried to identify him with at times surprising contemporary figures.[31]

Edgar C. Whisenant, a retired NASA engineer, published his brief work, *On Borrowed Time,* in 1988, listing eighty-eight reasons why the rapture would take place on the Jewish Feast of Rosh Hashanah (Sept. 11–13, 1988).[32] According to this fairly incoherent pamphlet, Antichrist, a Syrian Jew, was scheduled to sign a peace treaty with Israel ten days later, on Yom Kippur, 1988, the Feast of the Atonement. Whisenant's account of the seven years of Antichrist's reign involved a confusing prophecy of World War III scheduled for 1988 and World War IV for May 1992.[33] His mixture of biblical endtime prophecies (he counts 886 of these) and mathematical and astrological proofs did not endear him to the more cautious premillennialists.

One of the astrological proofs that Whisenant cited came from the newspaper astrologer Jeane Dixon. In her *My Life and Prophecies* Dixon recounted a vision she had at 7:00 A.M. on February 5, 1962, indicating that Antichrist had been born somewhere in the Middle East, possibly a direct descendant of Pharaoh Ikhnaton and Queen Nefertiti. Dixon went on to predict that Antichrist's power would continue to grow until 1999 when he would reveal his new religion.[34] Dixon's mixing of astrology and apocalypticism, while novel in the twentieth century, had many medieval predecessors. Her identification of 1999 as the date for the real fun to begin promises this prophecy's possibility for revival in the near future.

The list of contemporary figures who have been identified as Antichrist is partly predictable and partly puzzling. Considerable apocalyptic logic lay behind the identification by Noah Hutchins (of the Southwest Radio Church) of Pope John Paul II as Antichrist in April 1984, especially after the pope's miraculous recovery from his "fatal" wound (though it was not a wound to the head as in Apoc. 13:3).[35] Similarly, it should come as no surprise that right-wing American Fundamentalists would see an Antichrist in the deceptive offers of Mikhail Gorbachev on arms reduction and peace, especially since the Russian leader had that suspicious red mark on his head![36] More surprising is the tentative identification of Henry Kissinger as the Antichrist by David Webber and Noah Hutchings in the 1984 edition of their *Countdown to Antichrist*.[37] (Kissinger, of course, has a suspicious accent as well as a reputation for deviousness.) But what about Ronald Reagan, someone who even by his enemies has not been considered a triumph of deviousness (unless this be thought of as the ultimate deception, as in the case of Napoleon III). But Ronald Wilson Reagan's three names each have six letters (666), and James Brady, one of his "heads," was shot in the head and miraculously recovered. Antichrist identifications have been made on the basis of much less evidence.[38] Equally surprising a candidate is the televangelist Pat Robertson, who himself had once announced (in 1980) that the Antichrist was about twenty-seven years of age. Constance Cumbey in a self-published book entitled *A Planned Deception* (1985) argued that Robertson's interest in the Middle East and effective television style were indications that he might be the Final Enemy. Robertson threatened to sue, and Cumbey dropped the charge.[39] For a few months in 1990 a fearful public, if not apocalyptic tracts, even pondered whether Saddam Hussein might not be the Antichrist.

We should also note in closing this section that Antichrist continues to be found in forms of contemporary American premillenarianism that do not agree that the rapture will take place *before* the tribulation. Post-tribulationalism, that is, the teaching that Christians must live through the time of Antichrist to prove their faithfulness, has experienced a minor revival since the Second World War.[40] Jim McKeever's 1978 book, *Christians Will Go Through the Tribulation: And How to Prepare for It,* is an interesting combination of survivalism and literal apocalypticism.[41] Convinced that believers will have to live through the terrors of the tribulation, including nuclear war and Antichrist's ban on Christian buying and selling (see Apoc. 13:17), McKeever counsels a survivalist strategy of building bomb shelters, stockpiling food, preparing alternate energy sources, and military training to protect one's food supply for the coming dark days of Antichrist's rule before the rapture.

Perhaps the strangest recent contribution to contemporary literal views of Antichrist has been the so-called 666 System. Mary Stewert Relfe, whom Timothy Weber describes as a midtribulationist, that is, one who believes that the rapture will not precede the tribulation but come at some point during it, provides an example.[42] Since the supermarket and department store are far more real to most Americans than the Middle East, Relfe ties the advent of Antichrist to pocketbook issues more than political ones—the insidious growth of the 666 System. Her 1981 book, *When Your Money Fails,* witnesses to a fear that has spread in Fundamentalist circles since the 1970s.[43] The prediction in Apocalypse 13 that Antichrist will mark his followers and that those without this mark will be forbidden to buy and sell casts fear into the hearts of the stoutest Christian consumers. Relfe's book finds that the 666 System is already well advanced in computer programs, credit cards, production programs, and especially in the electronic bar codes that appear on so many products. Quite soon Antichrist (whom she identified as Anwar Sadat in 1981) will have a 666 code imprinted on the foreheads of his followers and will issue a universal credit card that will be necessary for all transactions (for one version of this see Fig. 30). Relfe advises true Christians to pay off their debts, get rid of their credit cards, turn their assets into gold or silver, and hang on until the rapture.[44] Fears of the 666 System can also be found among mainstream pretribulational Fundamentalists.

In light of these views, it is difficult not to think that the once dread Antichrist has been reduced to a child's plaything. Even those literalists who avoid easy identifications and things like the 666 System in the long run provide nothing more than a cardboard figure of a fanatical persecutor and evil deceiver. Since most Fundamentalists believe that they will be

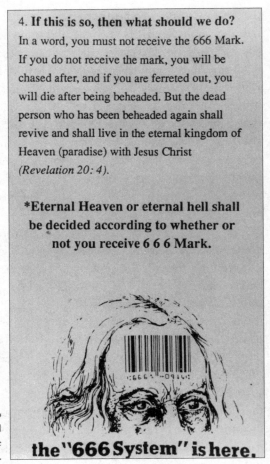

4. If this is so, then what should we do?
In a word, you must not receive the 666 Mark.
If you do not receive the mark, you will be
chased after, and if you are ferreted out, you
will die after being beheaded. But the dead
person who has been beheaded again shall
revive and shall live in the eternal kingdom of
Heaven (paradise) with Jesus Christ
(Revelation 20: 4).

***Eternal Heaven or eternal hell shall
be decided according to whether or
not you receive 6 6 6 Mark.**

the "666 System" is here.

FIGURE 30
The "666 System" is here. Reproduced
from a broadsheet published by the
Mission for the Coming Days (1992).

raptured away before Antichrist's persecution begins, it may even seem
paradoxical that they display so much interest in so banal a persecutor.

The Literary Antichrist

If the modern literal Antichrist seems extrinsic, repetitive, at times even
ludicrous, another form of the Antichrist legend in the past century—the
literary, or fictional, Antichrist—has shown more creativity. Antichrist has
not been used extensively in modern literature, but where he appears he is
often an intriguing and original figure. What is most significant about
Antichrist's appearance in literature has been the attempt to probe the mo-

tivation (and at times even the psychology) behind ultimate human evil—with regard to both Antichrist himself and his followers. It is probably no accident that novels and novellas, where motivation and character development are so important, display the most interesting Antichrists. Some of these fictional accounts were written by believers as contemporary ways of presenting a message that they were convinced was also theologically true; others were produced by writers who found in Antichrist a useful fictional tool for revealing something about the human condition. The most complex examples come from Russia and England, two countries where literal uses of Antichrist remained strong after the Enlightenment.[45]

In recent decades there has been a growth of studies concerning the relation between apocalypticism and Western literature, ranging from Frank Kermode's penetrating *The Sense of an Ending*[46] to a host of more detailed though sometimes pedestrian investigations of how the apocalyptic scenario has influenced aspects of modern fiction.[47] This new chapter in the study of apocalypticism is a witness to its ongoing importance, despite the many debates among the critics about what constitutes literary apocalypticism. In what follows I will not try to evaluate these disagreements but only to survey what some literary works of the past century have contributed to the legend of Antichrist.

RUSSIAN WRITERS AND ANTICHRIST

As I noted in the previous chapter, the Antichrist legend has probably been more powerful in Russia than in any other Christian land in the past three centuries. Even though the Old Believers remained a sectarian minority in Russian Orthodoxy, their profoundly felt convictions about the pervasiveness of Antichrist in the world had a powerful effect. The apocalyptic mentality is present in many aspects of Russian culture, not least in its literature.[48]

In the absence of detailed studies of apocalyptic traditions in nineteenth-century Russia, it is difficult to know just how widespread fears of the end actually were. The evidence of literature, both fictional and philosophical, suggests a definite apocalyptic mentality not only among the masses but also within the intelligentsia.[49] The great novelist Fyodor Dostoevsky (1821–1881) spoke of the imminence of Antichrist, especially in his *Diary of a Writer,* written in the 1870s.[50] Dostoevsky also used elements from the Christian apocalyptic scenario, as well as John's Apocalypse in particular, in his novels. David M. Bethea argues that *The Idiot,* written in 1867–69 during Dostoevsky's exile in western Europe, is best understood as an "apocalyptic fiction" in which the figure of Rogozhin, if not an Antichrist, is at least "antichrist-like."[51] Similarly, in *The Brothers Karamazov,* published in 1880, the influence of the Apocalypse and its imagery is evident throughout the famous section of book 4 entitled "The Grand Inquisitor." The Inquisitor himself is ultimately too ambiguous and tragic a figure to be identified directly with Antichrist. While he seems to perform the work that predecessors of Antichrist usually do (especially clerical ones), he does so from a different motivation—not ultimate malice but a tragic sense of deceiving humanity "in the name of Him in whose ideal the old man had so fervently believed all his life." (The Grand Inquisitor *knows* he is deceiving himself as much as he is deceiving others, whereas Antichrist deceives only others in his adherence to the "ultimate truth" of evil.) As a meditation on the mystery of freedom and evil, the parable of the Grand Inquisitor testifies to the modern literary concern with the mystery of evil that at times has also used the Antichrist legend as its focus.

Literary treatment of the Antichrist legend found one of its most important witnesses in the work of the Russian philosopher Vladimir Solovyev (1853–1900), a friend of Dostoevsky and mentor to many younger Russian intellectuals.[52] Solovyev is an important thinker insufficiently known in western Europe and America. The Swiss theologian Hans Urs von Balthasar has praised him, somewhat extravagantly, as "perhaps second only to Thomas Aquinas as the greatest artist of order and organization in the history of thought."[53] Deeply attached to Russia and its messianic role in history, he was also conversant with many aspects of German idealist philosophy. Solovyev is well known for his distinctively Russian devotion to the figure of Divine Sophia. As an ecumenist who sought to combine into one great "all-unity" the divergent religious, cultural, and philosophical tendencies of the day,[54] he was strongly opposed to the Slavophile movement of many of his contemporaries. During the 1880s he expended much effort on quixotic attempts to unite Roman Catholicism and Orthodoxy, appealing both to Tsar Alexander III and to Pope Leo XIII. In the last year of his life he tried to summarize "the vital aspects of Christian truth insofar as it connected with the question of evil" in his *Three Conversations: War, Progress, and the End of History, Including a Short Story of the Antichrist,* which was published in 1900 shortly before his death.[55]

Solovyev's fascinating work, which he described as "apologetic and polemic," is presented under the entertaining guise of three conversations that take place in a villa somewhere near Monte Carlo. The issue is theodicy, but theodicy of a typically modern sort in an era still dominated by belief in progress: "Is *evil* only a natural defect, an imperfection disappearing of itself with the growth of good, or is it a real *power*, possessing our world by means of temptations, so that for fighting it successfully assistance must be found in another sphere of being?"[56] The Russian philosopher's conservative defense of evil as a real power is presented through the interchange among five characters: the General, who represents a traditional Christian position; the Prince, a pacifist Tolstoyan; the Politician, a modern man who believes in progress; the Lady, who represents the voice of common sense; and finally Mr. Z, who is an alter ego for Solovyev himself.

The key to the whole and therefore to Solovyev's view of the nature of evil comes in the third discussion devoted to the "End of History."[57] Here Mr. Z, the presenter of the discussion, insists that progress itself is a symptom of the end and that this end must involve Antichrist.[58] If, as Solovyev believed, evil really exists as "a clearly acknowledged act of saying No to love" (in von Balthasar's words), then he became convinced by the end of his life that the evolutionary progress toward the greater good that he had believed in at an earlier stage was a delusion: "'The ways of history do not lead directly upwards to the Kingdom of God'; they pass by way of the final unveiling of the Antichrist, who conceals himself under the last mask to be stripped away, the mask of what is good and what is Christian."[59] Solovyev and C. G. Jung (though from radically different perspectives) were perhaps the last major Western thinkers who were convinced that real consideration of the problem of evil necessarily involves Antichrist.

Antichrist, as Mr. Z informs his listeners, is not just infidelity and the denial of Christianity but "a religious imposture, when the name of Christ will be arrogated by such forces in mankind which are in practice and in their very essence alien, and even inimical, to Christ and His Spirit."[60] He refuses to identify Antichrist with any present perversion of Christianity but instead turns attention back to the essential issue of evil itself. For Solovyev, the crux of the nature of evil lies in death and resurrection. Evil is a power and not merely a temporary defect because, ultimately, humans die. Hence, "Our remedy is one: actual resurrection. . . . If death is more powerful than mortal life, resurrection to eternal life is even more powerful than both of them."[61] Mr. Z insists that he who *commands* the good without *performing* the good (that is, the good of resurrection) is really a deceiver, none other than the devil, the "god of this world."[62]

The issue of deception of the good introduces Mr. Z's reading of "A Short Story of the Antichrist," which purports to be an unfinished manuscript left to him by the monk Pansophius (that is, All-Knower). The introduction of the story suggests a subtle but significant development in Solovyev's argument about the nature of evil. Only a human being, not the devil, can possess the ability to both command and perform or refuse to perform the good. There is no understanding of the real meaning of evil, then, apart from Antichrist.

Polish writer Czeslaw Milosz aptly characterizes "A Short Story of the Antichrist" as science fiction in the broad sense of narrative where "that which is predicted is told as something that has already occurred."[63] Mr. Z's retelling of the Antichrist story recounts the history of the next two centuries. The twentieth century begins with the triumph of "Pan-Mongolism," an alliance of Japan and China that leads to the defeat of Russia and Asian dominance over Europe. In the twenty-first century the United States of Europe reasserts itself at a time when religion has largely failed and been replaced by a vague "spiritualism." Enter the Antichrist, who is "among the few believing spiritualists." A man of remarkable talents—"many called him a superman" (an obvious reference to the philosopher Friedrich Nietzsche)—he is described as believing in "good, God and Messiah," but always from the perspective of his own "immense self-love." Constantly measuring himself against Christ (again the implied criticism of Nietzsche comes to the fore), he sees himself as the final savior, the true benefactor of the humanity that Christ hoped to reform but could not.[64] His task is to unite what Christ has divided—good and evil, progress and resurrection—into a higher unity.[65] Finally, as he waits for a divine sign that will enable him to effect his work of saving humanity, Antichrist confronts what for him is the ultimate temptation—to turn to Christ, risen from the dead, to ask him what to do at this crucial moment. Refusing to believe in the resurrection and unwilling to bow before Christ, the Antichrist throws himself from a precipice in a suicide attempt, only to be borne up by the devil, who adopts him as his son and surrenders to him all his power.[66]

The rest of the Antichrist story is an entertaining reprisal of traditional elements of the legend for the purposes of Solovyev's attack on Tolstoy, Nietzsche, and all belief in a religion of humanity that lacks a sense of sin and suffering.[67] At the conclusion, the Lady, puzzled by the strange tale, asks Mr. Z what it all means. "I cannot understand," she continues, "why your Antichrist hates God so much while in essence he is really kind and not wicked at all." Mr. Z responds,

> No. Not "in essence." That is just the point. That is the whole matter. I will withdraw the words I said before that "you cannot explain Antichrist only by proverbs." In point of fact, he is completely explained by a single and extremely simple proverb: "All is not gold that glitters." Of sham glitter he indeed has more than enough; but of essential force—nothing.[68]

This account, with its reminiscences of Dostoevsky's Grand Inquisitor (though with a very different moral), holds a special place in the literature about Antichrist. Perhaps for the first time, an author has tried to take us within the Final Enemy's mind by presenting his inner motivation. However we judge Solovyev's handling of the legend, by framing it within an investigation of the nature of evil and in probing both the psychological and theological meanings of total malice, the Russian philosopher made one of the few creative advances in the legend during the last three centuries.

Vladimir Solovyev had a deep influence on the Russian symbolist novelist Andrei Bely (1880–1934), who was present at the first reading of the *Three Conversations*. Bely's novel *Petersburg,* first published in 1916 and in a corrected edition in 1922, is considered by many to be one of the masterpieces of twentieth-century fiction.[69] David Bethea suggests that "*Petersburg* can be read as Bely's *long* tale about the Antichrist and that the entire question about authorship and narrative hierarchy (Pansophius—Mr. Z—Solovyev) that is raised rather superficially in *Three Conversations* can be seen as a central issue in Bely's novel."[70] Unlike Solovyev, Bely does not appeal directly to the details of the Antichrist legend, and no single Antichrist figure appears. However, we can agree with Bethea that this rich and difficult novel is filled with a sense of apocalyptic foreboding and that the spirit of Antichrist is refracted in a number of its characters.

The action takes place during a few days in the autumn of 1905 in St. Petersburg (the city itself, with its buildings, monuments, and climate, is the chief protagonist of the story). Any summary, however long, would fail to do justice to the elusive, spiraling, "musical" way in which Bely, like James Joyce, builds his imaginal world. The main narrative concerns a high government official, Apollon Apollonovich Ableukhov,[71] the very symbol of the stifling old order, and his estranged son, Nikolay Apollonovich, who has become involved with terrorists and has received a

bomb hidden in a sardine tin with which he is to destroy his father. Nikolay gets the bomb from the low-life terrorist Alexander Ivanovich Dudkin, a kind of Nietzschean figure, who is being manipulated by the evil
provocateur, Nikolai Stepanych Lippanchenko. Each of these figures can
be considered as different manifestations of the spirit of Antichrist, but the
central Antichrist of *Petersburg* is a more supernatural figure, none other
than Peter the Great in the person of the great Bronze Horseman, the
statue of the tsar that dominates the city.[72]

The Bronze Horseman's most dramatic intervention occurs in the
section of chapter 6 entitled "The Guest." Dudkin, in the last stages of al-
coholism, has been reading the Apocalypse and experiencing hallucina-
tions. Finally, the Bronze Horseman himself comes to visit Dudkin in a
scene of phantasmagoric horror:

> Someone made of metal was moving up toward the landing. Now many
> tons were falling with an earth-shattering din. The steps were splintering,
> and now the landing at the door flew away with a crash.
>
> And there was a sudden cracking as the door flew off its hinges.
> And the wan semidarkness out there billowed in smoking, bright green
> clouds. . . . In the middle of the threshold, from walls which emitted vit-
> riol-hued spaces, stood an immense body, glowing phosphorescent, its
> crowned, patinated head inclined and heavy patinated arm stretched forth.
>
> The Bronze Horsman stood there . . .
> The Bronze Horseman said to him:
> "Greetings, my son!"

In a scene reminiscent of Solovyev's portrayal of the encounter between
Antichrist and the Devil, the Bronze Horseman adopts Dudkin and pours
his spirit into him.

> The Metallic Guest sat before him, glowing red hot in the moonlight,
> singeing, crimson red. Now he turned white hot, and flowed over Alexan-
> der Ivanovich, who was kneeling before him, in a stream that could reduce
> all to ashes. He poured into his veins in metals.[73]

Filled with the essence of Antichrist, Dudkin brutally murders Lippanchenko.

Peter the Great as Antichrist also appears in the trilogy of historical
novels published under the title *Christ and Antichrist* by Dmitri Merezhkovsky (1865–1941). Merezhkovsky was a major figure in the religious
renaissance of Russia around the turn of the century, though his view that

Christianity and paganism were opposed halves of a coming higher religion that would unify all opposites was scarcely orthodox.[74] His trilogy was designed as a Nietzschean critique of historical Christianity and the opposition it had set up between flesh and spirit. The first volume, *The Death of the Gods: Julian the Apostate,* appeared in 1895; the second, *The Birth of the Gods: Leonardo da Vinci,* in 1901. The final volume, *Antichrist: Peter and Alexis,* of 1905 tells the story of Peter the Great and his son Alexis from the perspective of the Old Believers. Merezhkovsky's identification of political autocracy with Antichrist subsequently led him to strongly oppose the Bolshevik regime both before and after his exile from Russia in 1919.

OTHER LITERARY ANTICHRISTS

The most important non-Russian Antichrist novels of the twentieth century have been written in England.[75] A number of English Antichrist fictions appeared shortly before the First World War,[76] witnessing to the same forebodings about the course of the twentieth century evident among the Russians. The most arresting was *Lord of the World,* published in 1907 by Monsignor Robert Hugh Benson, an Anglican convert to Roman Catholicism and noted preacher and writer. Benson's novel, much like Solovyev's "Short Story," is part science fiction and part polemical tract from a conservative Christian stance concerning the menacing trends of the day that he saw as preparing the way for Antichrist.[77] Like Solovyev, Benson set the major action of his tale in the twenty-first century.

Benson's novel is still readable, however openly it bears its polemics on its sleeve. The major enemy is what today is often called secular humanism. Humanity is God, and Benson's Antichrist, a world ruler named Julian Felsenburgh, as the perfect representation of the "divine man," is its culmination. (Unlike Solovyev, Benson does not try to take us inside Antichrist himself; we see him only from the viewpoint of others.) Catholicism, with its insistence on the reality of the supernatural world, "was treason to the very idea of man."[78] By casting his polemical attack on modernity in novelistic guise, Benson keeps us guessing as to whether he truly held views that were as anachronistic as they seem—for example, that democracy was suited to Antichrist while royalty belonged to true Christianity. Despite its fictional form, Benson's picture of Antichrist can be judged the most serious Catholic presentation of the Final Enemy in the twentieth century. The English monsignor obviously felt Antichrist was a growing threat in the world and that only the strictest of divisions between Rome and the modern humanistic world could preserve the faith. He would not have welcomed the Second Vatican Council.

The best of the modern English novelistic treatments of the Antichrist legend (also by a conservative Christian, this time an Anglican) is better known than Monsignor Benson's work, but it has not always been recognized as a contemporary rendition of the Antichrist. The novel is *All Hallows' Eve,* written by Charles Williams and published in 1945. T. S. Eliot, in his introduction to the novel, paid tribute to Williams's ability to communicate "a para-normal experience with which the author is familiar, for introducing us into a real world in which he is at home."[79] Like his friend C. S. Lewis, Williams was fascinated with the problem of evil, "not with the Evil of conventional morality and the ordinary manifestations by which we recognize it" (again to cite Eliot) "but with the essence of Evil."[80] The evil magician, Father Simon or Clerk Simon, of *All Hallows' Eve* is none other than Simon Magus *redivivus*—and a Simon Magus who is certainly an Antichrist, though perhaps not the Final Antichrist since he fails in his attempt to gain control of the world.[81]

The story takes place both in the everyday world of London and in the strange half-world of the "City," London's shadow-self, where the recently dead Lester Furnival and her friend Evelyn wait until called to heaven or hell. Richard Furnival, Lester's husband, and his friend Jonathan, a painter, come into contact with Clerk Simon through Jonathan's fiancée, Betty, and her mother, Lady Wallingford, who is under the magician's domination. Simon is a Jewish magician who has won a large following through his cures and his preaching of love and peace. He has alter egos in Russia and China (actually magical projections of himself), through whom he intends to achieve world domination. Simon's desire for absolute power achieved by means of deceptive preaching, his measuring of himself against the other Jewish "magician" (Jesus), his use of divine and quasi-divine language about himself, and a number of other hints show how skillfully Williams has worked elements of the Antichrist legend into his story.[82]

In order to gain final mastery, Simon needs to establish a permanent link with the spirit world by murdering Betty and preserving her dead body so that her spirit will be in his power. (Williams's idiosyncratic ideas about the relation of soul and body and his fascination with magical techniques play a large role in the story.) In the second part of the book, Simon is foiled in this endeavor primarily by the power of the dead Lester Furnival, who has become the kind of archetypal platonic reality often found in

Williams's books. Tempted to increasingly risky magical procedures, the Antichrist-magician oversteps the bounds. He fails to kill Betty and Lady Wallingford, which allows the two evil projections of himself to return to wreak vengeance. At this point, Williams invokes another key motif of the Antichrist legend, the parodic reference to Christ's ascension, as he describes Simon's descent into hell:

> An opaque cloud gathered. It had been so when that other Jew ascended; such a cloud had risen from the opening of the new dimensions into which he had physically passed, and the eyes of the disciples had not pierced it. But that Jew had gone up into the law and according to the law. Now the law was filling the breach in the law. . . . The shapes began to advance and it also. The Clerk stood rigid, at his feet the body of his mistress; across the floor those other Clerks came.
>
> . . . He began to bid them stop, but as he did so he found himself stiffen into an even more fixed rigidity. . . . He unexpectedly thought, "This is death," and knew himself weaken at the thought.
>
> He managed to pronounce a word of command. They stopped, but then also he too stopped. He obeyed himself. . . . He hated them, and since they held his hate they hated him. The hate seemed to swell in a nightmare bubble within the rose which was forming round them, cloud in cloud, overlying like petals. . . . He looked down; he saw below him the depth of the rose. A sudden blast of rain fell on him and drove him deeper, and so those others. . . .[83]

Many readers, like myself, have found Williams's strange supernatural story eerily compelling. As portrayals of the conflict between essential good and evil, Williams's novels occupy a special place in modern English literature. It is significant to note that in *All Hallows' Eve,* arguably the most profound of his fictional works, Williams chose a transmutation of the Antichrist legend for his vehicle.

The works of Benson and Williams by no means exhaust the twentieth-century treatment of Antichrist in novelistic form, either in Britain or in America. Unfortunately, other offerings mostly witness to the banal decline of the Son of Perdition. In the past two decades, for instance, a number of Antichrist novels have been published in the United States, most, as might be expected, written by premillennial Fundamentalists and meant to put this message into entertaining form.[84] Other recent apocalyptic novels, such as *Good Omens,* by Neil Gaiman and Terry Pratchett, which features an eleven-year-old Antichrist who eventually refuses to take on his fated career, are comic inversions of Fundamentalist views.[85] The major new development in the fictional career of Antichrist has come in the form of movie versions of the ancient legend.

ANTICHRIST AT THE MOVIES

Antichrist at the movies has not exactly been an unqualified success, either artistically or at the box office. The Final Enemy seems to have little of the appeal of Count Dracula, Frankenstein's monster, or the Wolfman and their successors. He has, however, given rise to one memorable horror movie, Roman Polanski's *Rosemary's Baby* (1968), which represents an original twist on centuries of speculation about Antichrist's mother. Less convincing, even ridiculous at times, was the "Omen trilogy" produced by Twentieth Century–Fox: *The Omen* (1976), *Damien* (1978), and *The Final Conflict* (1981).[86]

Rosemary's Baby includes little direct reference to the traditional Antichrist legend, but it is a stylish rendition of the fear of radical evil lurking beneath the surface of polite modern society. (Monsignor Benson might have appreciated the movie, except for the brief scenes of nudity.) Despite centuries of theological argument against the possibility of Satan fathering a human son, popular conviction that demons can impregnate humans forms the film's presupposition. There is no overt reference to the tradition that such a child is destined to be the Antichrist, but who else could he be? *Rosemary's Baby,* however, focuses on the unwitting mother who gradually becomes aware that all the nice, helpful people around her—neighbors, doctor, and even her husband—are agents of the devil whose main purpose is to guarantee a successful completion to her frightening pregnancy. Mia Farrow, as Antichrist's troubled mother, conveys a disturbing picture of how an ordinary person could pass from opposition to radical evil to eventual complicity, largely because there seems to be no other choice available. As arresting as the movie is, it seems to have much more to do with an ironic commentary on the psychological pressures of pregnancy and a new twist on films involving demonism than with the Antichrist.

Explicit reference to the Antichrist pervades the "Omen trilogy." From the perspective of Antichrist aficionados, intrigued by the possibility of a screen presentation either of the traditional legend or a modern adaptation of the theme of ultimate human evil (as Charles Williams tried), the trilogy must be judged another demonstration of the banality of Hollywood's view of evil.[87] The first part, *The Omen,* is by far the best, possibly because it dealt with the theme of Antichrist's birth and also because it employs well-known actors, especially Gregory Peck as the human surrogate father of the Final Enemy. Suggestive locations and a sense of foreboding—at times even of terror—give this presentation of Antichrist's coming into the world some power, though the details are largely based on cinematic ideas of what constitutes a good horror film rather than what might have any relation to the story of Antichrist.

The Omen was successful enough to spawn two sequels: *Damien,* which sees the Antichrist through childhood and adolescence; and *The Final Conflict,* in which he achieves world domination and is finally defeated by what can only be described as the least successful screen rendition of the Second Coming ever attempted. If *The Omen* has its redeeming moments, it is difficult to discover any in the two last parts of the trilogy. Still, it is sobering to reflect that millions today probably know more about Antichrist from this trilogy than from the Bible or from the popular traditions that played a part in the development of the legend. These films present an Antichrist that is far less horrific than recent monsters of human evil like the Jason of the *Halloween* series or the slasher Freddy of the *Nightmare on Elm Street* movies.[88] In movieland, at least, Antichrist is no longer the acme of human evil.

The Contemporary Meaning of Antichrist

Despite the belief in a literal Antichrist held by millions of Fundamentalist Christians, and notwithstanding the ways in which Antichrist has appeared in novels and movies of this century, it is clear that the ancient legend no longer enjoys the power it did in former centuries. To accuse someone of being "an Antichrist"—rhetoric used, for example, against Saddam Hussein of Iraq in 1990—is really to add little to other epithets of obloquy that help marshall opposition to evil. Outside the Fundamentalist camp, most believing Christians seem puzzled, even slightly embarrassed, by Antichrist, especially given the legend's use in fostering hatred and oppression of groups, such as Jews and Muslims, seen as collective manifestations of Antichrist's power. We may conclude by asking, "Is Antichrist irrelevant?"

JUNG AND THE SHADOW SIDE

Besides Vladimir Solovyev, at least one other important thinker of the past century has seen Antichrist as essential for the true understanding of evil. Carl Gustav Jung (1875–1961), in his 1951 work *Aion: Researches into the Phenomenology of the Self,* claimed that "Christian tradition from the outset . . . is filled with intimations of a kind of enantiodromian reversal of dominants. I mean by this the dilemma of Christ and Antichrist."[89] Jung presents his case not as a theologian but as a psychologist whose main concern was to study the inner assimilation of symbols during the "Christian aeon." His reflections form perhaps the most original twentieth-century investigation of the Antichrist legend.

Jung's depth psychology entails a different view of evil from traditional Christian theories identifying evil with a privation of good (*privatio boni*), that is, not just an absence but a lack of the good that *should* be present. For the Swiss psychologist, evil is the shadow side of good, forming an inseparable whole with it in the constitution of the archetypal forces present in the self, or the total personality. As he put it, "Good and evil, being coexistent halves of a moral judgment, do not derive from one another but are always there together."[90] He believed that during the Christian aeon, Christ had functioned psychologically as the exemplification of the archetype of the self. "There can be no doubt," Jung asserted, "that the original Christian conception of the *imago Dei* [image of God] embodied in Christ meant an all-embracing totality that even includes the animal side of man."[91] Early on, however, Christianity split off the "shadow of the self," that is, the dark half of the human totality, into the figure of Antichrist. Thus, "In the empirical self, light and shadow form a paradoxical unity. In the Christian concept, on the other hand, the archetype is hopelessly split into two irreconcilable halves, leading ultimately to a metaphysical dualism—the final separation of the kingdom of heaven from the fiery world of the damned."[92]

For Jung this means that "Antichrist is not just a prophetic prediction" but "an inexorable psychological law." The split between Christ and Antichrist, at least insofar as the two figures are considered as psychological archetypes, was bound to have unfortunate repercussions in the history of Christianity. Total neglect of Antichrist, or denial of the reality he symbolizes, is psychologically unwise. If Antichrist is not integrated in the world of the psyche, he will project himself outward into culture through the process of "enantiodromia," or emergence of an unconscious opposite, which Jung saw beginning with the Renaissance and culminating in the modern world with its anti-Christian spirit that fulfills early Christian expectations of the end (that is, *its* own end).[93] For Jung, the totalitarian ideologies of the twentieth century, such as Nazism, were the external projections of the pyschological denial of the Antichrist within: "Our blight is ideologies—they are the long-expected Antichrist!"[94] It is only the reintegration of the two sides of the self symbolized in Christ and Antichrist that can allow for psychological wholeness.

This is not the place to survey the many uses of Jung's ideas in contemporary culture. Some authors have appropriated Jung's understanding of evil from a Christian perspective;[95] others have applied Jungian perspectives to the investigation of Antichrist in Western culture. Thomas J. Altizer, for example, in his study of William Blake entitled *The New Apocalypse,* sees the English poet as announcing a distinctive apocalypticism in which Antichrist is nothing else but "the final kenotic [self-emptying] manifestation of Christ," a manifestation Altizer insists is to be greeted not with the traditional horror but with joy! The goal of this *coincidentia oppositorum,* or coincidence of opposites, is a positivity beyond current divisions between good and evil: "An apocalyptic and dialectical coincidence that unites Christ and Antichrist can be nothing less than a total process of cosmic regeneration, a process that in reversing the opposites of fallen history makes possible their final reintegration."[96]

Jung's original analysis of the meaning of Antichrist does not seem to me a plausible reading of the legend. He asserts what Christ and Antichrist *must* have meant, not what they *did* mean insofar as this is recoverable to the historian on the basis of the evidence of texts and monuments relating to the Final Enemy (though Jung shows considerable knowledge of them). All Christian understandings of Antichrist have been founded on the sense of absolute and final opposition between the Jesus who said of himself, "I am the Truth" (John 14:6), and the human manifestation of the lie in Antichrist. Jung would claim that this has been due to a failure to recognize the higher psychological law of the coincidence of opposites, but those who are not convinced by his model can still beg to differ. Opposition, not coincidence, is the meaning of the tradition, as Solovyev and others recognized. Jung has at least provided a new view of the inner meaning of the figure of Antichrist, however much his position conflicts with almost two millennia of tradition. Alternative recent Christian interpretations are virtually nonexistent.

A HINT OF AN EXPLANATION

The question of the possible relevance of Antichrist is a different question from that of the continuing importance of speculations about the end. Nevertheless, I believe in trying to understand what meaning the

Antichrist legend may have today we must begin by asking how important speculations about the end continue to be. Some form of apocalypticism, however transformed and reinterpreted, seems inseparable from Christianity. This is because belief in Jesus as Redeemer always implies conviction that God acts in history, at least in some way, and because the expectation of Jesus' return has been integral to this faith since the time of the apostles. Views of the final events can be revised and reinterpreted, but they cannot be avoided. Given the pivotal role that Christianity has played in shaping Western society, apocalyptic eschatology has often been at work even when it is not easily recognized, as in the various forms of contemporary secular apocalypticism, that is, the adoption of apocalyptic modes of thought in recent scientific and quasi-scientific projections of the future.

Many of the pessimistic accounts of what looms ahead for the planet issuing from our think tanks and planning centers are really forms of secularized apocalyptic rhetoric. This is not to say that these projections are inaccurate; it is merely to recognize the structure of their argument. An example can be found in Robert L. Heilbroner's *An Inquiry into the Human Prospect,* first published in 1974.[97] There is a remarkable formal similarity between this widely read scientific projection of coming doom and contemporary apocalyptic prophecy as we find it in Hal Lindsey. In both authors intense pessimism about the future is expressed in the form of attractively packaged arguments based on the most secure "evidence," biblical prophecies for Lindsey and generalized scientific extrapolations about the possible consequences of current ecological trends for Heilbroner. Like all good apocalypticists, both authors mingle optimism and pessimism in their projections. Lindsey's message promises the coming rapture for true Christians; Heilbroner, in more secular fashion, believes in the possibility of a "post industrial" society that many would feel is just as much an act of faith as is the rapture.

The persistence of apocalypticism in the secular vein rests, in large part, on one of the fundamental characteristics of humanity: the necessity of living in expectation. We are defined by our hopes and therefore also by hope's opposite, fear of future evil. The great world religions have dealt with human hopes and fears in a number of ways, sometimes arguing that they are mere illusions, other times linking them to recurring cosmic cycles of various kinds, or, as in the case of the apocalyptic mentality born among Jews of the Second Temple period, incorporating present hope and fear into a view of universal history finally vindicated in a cataclysmic divine judgment. Some Christians still accept all the elements of this scenario in a literal way; most do not. But even those who are no longer literal apocalypticists, as long as they are Christians, need to consider the possible meaning of apocalypticism today.

The easiest way to deal with apocalyptic beliefs and the symbols that express them is to reinterpret them in a purely private and immanent way. This strategy has been adopted by some of the most powerful theological figures of the twentieth century, such as the German biblical scholar Rudolf Bultmann in his 1955 Gifford Lectures published as *History and Eschatology.*[98] Bultmann recognized that the apocalyptic mentality was crucial to the origins of the Christian view of history, but he chose to see apocalypticism as a part of early Christianity's mythological worldview that needed to be demythologized, arguing that the real meaning of history is to be found totally within, in each individual's confrontation with his or her own story as mediated by the preaching of the message of salvation. External history for Bultmann, even the history of the believing community, in the long run counts for little. This position, though influential in the middle decades of the twentieth century, seems too privatized to have much effect on contemporary discussion.

A more effective option seeks to find in the symbolic worldview of apocalyptic eschatology not just a mythology to be discarded but a symbolism to be pondered, as Paul Ricoeur has suggested. Such a strategy can also allow a greater role to the external history of Church and society as contrasted with the internal historicity of each believer, though not necessarily for a literal reading of the "signs of the times" as practiced so often in the history of apocalyptic traditions. Separating naive apocalyptic timetables from the powerful symbols in which apocalypticism has expressed its sense of the universal meaning of history is not always an easy task, but it is at least an option. These apocalyptic symbols can never be merely private—they are always ineluctably both communal and personal. To privatize them completely, as Bultmann did, is to cut them free of history in the full human sense and to remove an essential part of their reality and power to inspire.

Apocalyptic symbols are capable of retaining an archaic power to reveal meaning even when the precise beliefs they originally expressed have long become outmoded. The great images of John's Apocalypse, such as the Woman and the Dragon in chapter 12, the Beasts of chapters 13 and 17, the Angels with the Seven Vials, and the like, are not necessarily less compelling manifestations of the confrontation between good and evil in human history because we no longer give them the same historical referents that early Christians did. They can still be used in gripping fashion to reveal the struggle at the heart of current conflicts, as illustrated, for example, in the Nicaraguan priest-poet Ernesto Cardenal's poem "Apocalypse," which fuses the biblical images with symbols of contemporary death and destruction.[99] In its function as the communal memory of any society, history involves more mythologizing and remythologizing than it does demythologizing.

Reappropriating apocalyptic symbols independently of their original literal understandings but in line with their fundamental power to reveal meaning is a delicate and controversial procedure, especially because the symbols were designed more to *portray* good and evil than to *decide* what is really good and bad. An important part of the revelatory power of these symbols, however, is rooted in how they relate to the role of human choice and commitment in both personal and communal ways. Apocalyptic symbols are not merely images to be pondered; they are also stimuli to action. Even the earliest apocalypses combined a literal sense of a divinely predetermined plan for history with an insistence on the necessity for choice within history. This is the essential root of what I have elsewhere called apocalyptic spirituality.[100] Traditional apocalyptic eschatology frequently expressed this choice in highly moralistic and exclusivistic terms—the easy division between the sheep and the goats, Christ's faithful and the adherents of Antichrist. However much we may recognize this often smug division as a powerful motive for perseverance by repressed minorities during times of persecution, it still strikes us today with a false note, for we know how often and how easily repressed minorities have become persecuting majorities. Nevertheless, the apocalyptic stress on the need to take a stand in history—to choose and not drift, and to choose in a public way—is deeper and richer than merely locating human evil externally in some other group. As we have seen, a strong tradition in the history of Antichrist speculation has insisted that Antichrist is within as well as without, multiple as well as individual. This recognition may provide at least one clue to the question raised above: "Is Antichrist irrelevant?"

The polyvalence of the figure of Antichrist has been with us for almost two millennia. A good part of the explanation of the legend's recent loss of creativity, as I have argued, springs from the narrowing and even loss of this rich, if confusing, mythic complexity during the past few centuries. To revivify the once-dread figure of the Son of Perdition is not the work of any single thinker—theologian, historian, even poet or novelist—but of the Christian community at large and its understanding of the nature of evil as we approach the end of the second millennium.

From its origins, the Antichrist legend has had a collective dimension—the *pseudochristoi* of the Synoptic Apocalypse and the *antichristoi* of the Johannine Letters. While it has been easy for many Christians over the centuries to identify these multiple opponents of Christ in a purely external fashion with some easily identifiable group of opponents—heretics, Jews, or others—their original character was that of the enemy *within* the community of believers. Furthermore, from the early centuries, through the writings of such thinkers as Origen, Augustine, Gregory the Great, and others, the image of Antichrist has often been personally internalized by insisting, as Augustine put it, that "everyone must question his own conscience whether he be such." It is this recognition of the Antichrist within, both within Christianity and in each Christian, that needs renewed emphasis today.

The nature of Antichrist's malice as the image of absolute human evil has varied over the centuries, as we have seen. Still, it is clear that the dominant view of ultimate evil has not been one of cruel tyranny so much as one of deception, the masquerading of the lie that perverts the good that saves. Each age has had to contend with its own forms of deception. These deceptions have done more than anything else to shape the development of the Antichrist legend.

I would suggest, in closing, that contemporary forms of deception, especially deception on a worldwide scale never possible before, might spur our meditation on the meaning of the legend of Antichrist as the image of essential human evil. The dominance of appearance over substance may not have been invented in the electronic era, but some contemporary social critics remind us that deceit has reached a new level of sophistication as we approach the beginning of the third millennium.[101] Even the recent Fundamentalist interpretations of Antichrist have emphasized how their literal Final Enemy will be a master of deception, both in himself and in his ability to project an artificial image of his intentions to the world through the latest means of communication. The most impressive modern literary renderings of the legend, especially those of Vladimir Solovyev and Charles Williams, have explored the same issue with remarkable insight.

It would, of course, be a mistake to think of the contemporary forms of deception and their relation to the Antichrist legend in a purely extrinsic way as an evil that is only outside us. Evil is both within and without. If we are all part of a culture in which forms of deceit, both overt and covert, are present in many ways, we can admit that the most dangerous form of deceit is self-deceit, our ability to convince ourselves that we are doing what is best and for the best reasons, even when this is not the case—and somehow, however obscurely, we *know* it not to be the case. This is just another way of putting Augustine's ancient message: "There you have the Antichrist—everyone that denies Christ by his works."

It may no longer be possible for most of us to believe in the legendary figure of a coming individual who will sum up all human evil at the end of time. But at the end of this millennium we can still reflect on deception both within and without each of us and in our world at large as the most insidious malice—that which is most contrary to what Christians believe was and still is the meaning of Christ. But for now, *Satisne fatigavimus nos cum Antichristo isto maledicto?* ("Have we not worn ourselves out with that accursed Antichrist?").[102]

Preface

1. In a *Time*/CNN poll of 1,000 adult Americans conducted on April 28–29, 1993, by Yankelevich Partners Inc., 20 percent answered yes to the question "Will the second coming of Jesus Christ occur sometime around the year 2000?" In addition, 49 percent answered no and 31 percent were not sure.

2. Scheltco à Geveren, *Of the ende of this worlde, and second commynge of Christ* (London: Andrew Maunsell, 1578), fol. 12v. The Talmudic traditions used here can be found in the Babylonian Talmud, e.g., Tractate Sanhedrin 97ab and Tractate 'Abodah Zarah 9a.

3. The literature on Antichrist is extensive, but there is only one general survey, and this was written almost four centuries ago. The Spanish Dominican Thomas Malvenda (1566–1628) published his massive *De Antichristo libri undecim* in Rome in 1604. Malvenda will be treated more fully in chap. 8, but his rich account of patristic and medieval sources has been used by later investigators down to the present. At the end of the last century, Wilhelm Bousset issued his noted *Der Antichrist in der Überlieferung des Judentums, des Neuen Testament und der alten Kirche: Ein Beitrag zur Auslegung der Apokalypse* (Göttingen: Vandenhoeck & Ruprecht, 1895), which was rapidly translated into English by A. H. Keane under the title *The Antichrist Legend: A Chapter in Christian and Jewish Folklore* (London: Hutchinson, 1896). Bousset was most interested in the origins of the Antichrist, which he argued were fundamentally a projection into the endtime of the chaos monster of the primordial cosmogonic myth of the ancient Near East. Bousset made a real contribution in uncovering this important dimension of Antichrist's story and in showing through his massive learning how much the ancient mythic paradigms were present in later materials down through the High Middle Ages, but his neglect of other factors in the evolution of the legend, as well as his postulation of secret oral tradition as the essential factor in the evolution of Antichrist, led to unwarranted conclusions about the antiquity of a full-fledged Antichrist figure in Second Temple Judaism. Many of the same presuppositions are to be found in the other major early twentieth-century account of the beginnings of Antichrist, that of R. H. Charles, as summarized, for instance, in his *A Critical and Exegetical Commentary on the Revelation of St. John,* International Critical Commentary, vol. 2 (Edinburgh: T & T Clark, 1920), pp. 76–87. Most recently, this position on the origins of Antichrist has been questioned by Gregory C. Jenks, *The Origins and Development of the Antichrist Myth* (Berlin and New York: Walter

de Gruyter, 1991), who correctly argues that Antichrist must be seen as a distinctively Christian development. Jenks's book, however, takes too narrow a view of the meaning of the Antichrist legend (not myth) and therefore misconstrues important moments in the early history.

Introduction

1. As quoted in Frank E. Manuel, ed., *The Religion of Isaac Newton* (Oxford: Oxford Univ. Press, 1974), p. 109.

2. As quoted in James West Davidson, *The Logic of Millennial Thought* (New Haven and London: Yale Univ. Press, 1977), p. 266.

3. Recent literature on the devil is extensive and varied. Contrast, for example, Jeffrey Burton Russell's tetralogy on the history of the devil, which argues the importance of a "real" devil, with such works as Henry Ansgar Kelly's *The Devil, Demonology, and Witchcraft* (Garden City, NY: Doubleday, 1968), which defends the opposite position. Russell's four-volume study includes *The Devil: Perceptions of Evil from Antiquity to Primitive Christianity* (Ithaca, NY: Cornell Univ. Press, 1977); *Satan: The Early Christian Tradition* (Ithaca, NY: Cornell Univ. Press, 1981); *Lucifer: The Devil in the Middle Ages* (Ithaca, NY: Cornell Univ. Press, 1984); and *Mephistopheles: The Devil in the Modern World* (Ithaca, NY: Cornell Univ. Press, 1986).

4. A minority view within Christian apocalyptic traditions has seen Antichrist as the devil incarnate, as we shall see below.

5. In this, I agree with the recent work of Jenks, *Origins,* which says "the Antichrist myth developed as a result of the convergence of older traditions under the influence of specific historical and sociological circumstances within the early Christian church" (p. 25; cf. pp. xvi, 13, 161, 361–62). I disagree with him, as will become evident in chap. 2, about where this convergence first becomes evident.

6. See the discussion in chap. 3, pp. 76–77

7. Paul Ricoeur, *The Symbolism of Evil* (New York: Harper & Row, 1967), p. 348.

Chapter One

1. Some indication of the outpouring of literature on the origins of apocalyptic eschatology may be seen from the bibliography in David Hellholm, ed., *Apocalypticism in the Mediterranean World and the Near East,* 2nd ed. (Tübingen: Mohr, 1989). For overviews, see John J. Collins, *The Apocalyptic Imagination: An Introduction to the Jewish Matrix of Christianity* (New York: Crossroad, 1984); M. E. Stone, "Apocalyptic Literature," in *Jewish Writings of the Second Temple Period: Compendium Rerum Iudaicarum ad Novum Testamentum, sect. 2,* ed. M. E. Stone (Assen and Philadelphia: Van Gorcum and Fortress, 1984), pp. 383–441; and Ithamar Gruenwald, "Jewish Apocalypticism to the Rabbinic Period," in *Encyclopedia of Religion,* vol. 1, ed. Mircea Eliade et al. (New York: Macmillan, 1987), pp. 336–42.

2. For what follows see also my two previous summaries of the nature of early apocalypticism, "Early Apocalypticism: The Ongoing Debate," in *The Apocalypse in English Renaissance Thought and Literature,* ed. C. A. Patrides and Joseph Wittreich (Ithaca, NY: Cornell Univ. Press, 1984), pp. 2–39; and "Introduction: John's Apocalypse and the Apocalyptic Mentality," in *The Apocalypse in the Middle Ages,* ed. Richard K. Emmerson and Bernard McGinn (Ithaca, NY: Cornell Univ. Press, 1992), pp. 3–19.

3. For a brief history of Second Temple Judaism from the time of the scribe Ezra (c. 400 B.C.E.), see Michael Stone, *Scriptures, Sects, and Visions: A Profile of Judaism from Ezra to the Jewish Revolts* (Philadelphia: Fortress, 1980).

4. John J. Collins, ed., *Apocalypse: The Morphology of a Genre. Semeia 14 (1979)* (Missoula, MT: Scholars Press, 1979), p. 9.

5. For a study of apocalyptic literature that stresses the centrality of the revelation of heavenly secrets, see Christopher Rowland, *The Open Heaven: A Study of Apocalyptic in Judaism and Early Christianity* (New York: Crossroad, 1982). On the apocalyptic ascensions, see Martha Himmelfarb, *Ascent to Heaven in Jewish and Christian Apocalypses* (New York: Oxford Univ. Press, 1993). For the tours of hell, which seem to begin about the turn of the era, see Martha Himmelfarb, *Tours of Hell: An Apocalyptic Form in Jewish and Christian Literature* (Philadelphia: Univ. of Pennsylvania Press, 1983).

6. The motif of ascension into heaven, with or without the body, is one of the dominant religious forms of the Hellenistic world and late antiquity. For two introductions to the broad context, see Alan F. Segal, "Heavenly Ascent in Hellenistic Judaism, Early Christianity and Their Environment," in *Aufstieg und Niedergang der Römischen Welt: Principiat,* vol. 23, no. 2, ed. Wolfgang Haase (Berlin: De Gruyter, 1980), pp. 1333–93; and Ioan Petru Culianu, *Psychanodia I. A Survey of the Evidence Concerning the Ascent of the Soul and Its Relevance* (Leiden: E. J. Brill, 1983).

7. Due to displacement when incorporated into the later compilation, the Apocalypse of Weeks is now found in 1 Enoch 91:12–17 and 93:1–10. The ten weeks are divided into three sections: three weeks of primordial history (Adam to Enoch, Enoch to Noah, Noah to Abraham); four middle weeks centering on the building of Solomon's temple in week five (the author places his own time in the evil seventh week); and three final messianic weeks consisting of (a) judgment on the wicked, (b) the restoration of Israel, and (c) the establishment of a new heaven and "weeks without number forever" (91:17). This text, as well as the other Jewish apocalypses, are now available in *The Old Testament Pseudepigrapha,* vol. 1, *Apocalyptic Literature and Testaments,* ed. James H. Charlesworth (Garden City, NY: Doubleday, 1983). On the importance of this and other apocalyptic timetables, see Jacob Licht, "Time and Eschatology in Apocalyptic Literature and in Qumran," *Journal of Jewish Studies* 16 (1965): 177–82.

8. In the interest of consistency, all quotations from the Old Testament, unless otherwise noted, will be taken from *The Jerusalem Bible* (Garden City, NY: Doubleday, 1966). The Christian, and esp. the Roman Catholic version, of the Old Testament is broader than the recognized books of Judaism, the Hebrew Bible (*tanakh*).

9. See John J. Collins, "Apocalyptic Eschatology as the Transcendence of Death," *Catholic Biblical Quarterly* 36 (1974): 21–43.

10. For a survey of the messianic expectations of the Jewish apocalypses, see D. S. Russell, *The Method and Message of Jewish Apocalyptic* (Philadelphia: Westminster, 1964), chaps. 11–12.

11. In the modern study of religion, *messianism* has taken on a broader meaning of any expectation of a coming better state of society, often being used synonymously with *utopianism* and *millenarianism*. I will use the term in the restricted sense found in early Jewish and Christian documents.

12. For some earlier reflections on apocalyptic spirituality, see Bernard McGinn, "Introduction," in *Apocalyptic Spirituality,* Classics of Western Spirituality (New York: Paulist Press, 1979), pp. 7–16.

13. For some reflections on the variety of political functions of apocalyptic rhetoric in the Middle Ages, see B. McGinn, "Introduction," in *Visions of the End: Apocalyptic*

Traditions in the Middle Ages, Columbia Records of Civilization Series (New York: Columbia Univ. Press, 1979), pp. 28–36.

14. See Mircea Eliade, *Cosmos and History: The Myth of the Eternal Return* (New York: Harper Torchbooks, 1959), chap. 4.

15. See Hermann Gunkel, *Schöpfung und Chaos in Urzeit und Endzeit* (Göttingen: Vandenhoeck & Ruprecht, 1895).

16. See, e.g., Adela Yarbro Collins, *The Combat Myth in the Book of Revelation* (Missoula, MT: Scholars Press, 1976); John J. Collins, *The Apocalyptic Vision of the Book of Daniel* (Missoula, MT: Scholars Press, 1977); John M. Court, *Myth and History in the Book of Revelation* (Atlanta: John Knox, 1979), and more recently, John Day, *God's Conflict with the Dragon and the Sea* (Cambridge: Cambridge Univ. Press, 1985).

17. See, e.g., Adela Yarbro Collins, *Apocalypse* (Wilmington, DE: Glazier, 1979), pp. x–xi.

18. According to Paul Ricoeur in *The Symbolism of Evil* (New York: Harper & Row, 1967), p. 5, myth is "a traditional narration which relates to events that happened at the beginning of time and which has the purpose of providing grounds for the ritual actions of men of today and, in a general manner, establishing all the forms of action and thought by which man understands himself in his world." For a survey of the understanding of myth in history of religions, see Kees W. Bolle, "Myth: An Overview," in *Encyclopedia of Religion,* vol. 10, pp. 261–73. I have also found the following helpful: Mircea Eliade, *Myth and Reality* (New York: Harper & Row, 1963); William Blake Tyrrell, *Amazons: A Study in Athenian Mythmaking* (Baltimore: Johns Hopkins Univ. Press, 1984); and, more directly related to the apocalyptic use of myths, Neil Forsyth, *The Old Enemy: Satan and the Combat Myth* (Princeton, NJ: Princeton Univ. Press, 1987).

19. Tyrrell, *Amazons,* p. xiv.

20. See Paul Ricoeur, "Myth and History," in *Encyclopedia of Religion,* vol. 10, pp. 273–82.

21. Ibid., p. 277.

22. Ibid., p. 281.

23. See Michael Fishbane, "'The Holy One Sits and Roars': Mythopoesis and the Midrashic Imagination," *Journal of Jewish Thought and Philosophy* 1(1991): 1–21.

24. For a survey and modern presentation of the differences, see William Bascom, "The Forms of Folklore: Prose Narratives," *Journal of American Folklore* 70 (1965): 3–20.

25. See Ricoeur, "Myth and History," p. 278, for a review of their contribution.

26. This is evident in the most recent account of the early stages of Antichrist, Jenks's *Origins.* Jenks never says what he means by myth and never discusses its relation to legend.

27. On the distinction between myth, legend, and folktale, see Bascom, "The Forms of Folklore"; and Forsyth, *Old Enemy,* pp. 3–18.

28. On the basic similarity of the mythic pattern underlying Dan. 7–12, see Collins, *Apocalyptic Vision of the Book of Daniel,* chap. 4, esp. pp. 109–10.

29. This distinction, one of Goethe's less valuable contributions to Western culture, has been defended by Ricoeur in *Symbolism of Evil,* e.g., p. 16. If allegory is conceived of as only an attempt to translate the power of a symbolic narrative into a logical explanation that obviates the need for any opaque veil, then it is clearly different from the symbolic discourse of myth. The problem is that much of the history of allegorical theory and practice resists such simple reduction, especially the polymorphous modes of composition that appear in many great allegorical poems.

30. There is no general survey of apocalyptic symbolism. One of the earliest investigators of the symbolic dimensions of the apocalypses, despite his antipathy to apocalypticism, was D. H. Lawrence in *Apocalypse* (New York: Viking, 1960), first published in 1931. Another classic study of the symbolism of John's Apocalypse is Austin Farrer's *A Rebirth of Images: The Making of St. John's Apocalypse* (London: A & C Black, 1949). There are also valuable comments in J. Collins, *Apocalyptic Imagination.* In the following comments I will make use of two earlier programmatic pieces: "Symbols of the Apocalypse in Medieval Culture," in *The Bible and Its Traditions,* ed. Michael Patrick O'Connor and David Noel Freedman, *Michigan Quarterly Review* 22, no. 3 (1983): 265–83; and "Joachim the Symbolist," which forms chap. 3 in my book *The Calabrian Abbot: Joachim of Fiore in the History of Christian Thought* (New York: Macmillan, 1985), pp. 101–22.

31. For broad definitions of *dualism,* see R. M. McInerny, "Dualism," in *The New Catholic Encyclopedia,* vol. 4 (New York: McGraw-Hill, 1965), p. 1075; and Ugo Bianchi, "Dualism," *Encyclopedia of Religion,* vol. 4, p. 506. For dualism in apocalyptic literature, see John G. Gammie, "Spatial and Ethical Dualism in Jewish Wisdom and Apocalyptic Literature," *Journal of Biblical Literature* 93 (1974): 356–85.

32. Gammie, "Spatial and Ethical Dualism," pp. 357 and 371, downplays the importance of temporal dualism. Others, such as Walter Schmithals, *The Apocalyptic Movement: Introduction and Interpretation* (Nashville: Abingdon, 1975), pp. 20–28, tend to exaggerate it.

33. For comments, see Gammie, "Spatial and Ethical Dualism," pp. 366–72; and C. Rowland, *Open Heaven,* pp. 78–135.

34. For an introduction, see J. Bruce Lond and Alfred Ribi, "Demons," in *Encyclopedia of Religion,* vol. 4, pp. 282–92. For Christian teaching on demons, see esp. the multi-author article "Démon" in the *Dictionnaire de spiritualité,* vol. 3 (Paris: Beauchesne, 1937–): cols. 141–238.

35. Some other examples of this perspective can be found in Gen. 32 where Jacob wrestles with God, and in Exod. 4:24 where Yahweh threatens to kill Moses.

36. Here I am using the translation of John L. McKenzie, *Second Isaiah,* Anchor Bible (New York: Doubleday Anchor, 1968), who has a useful discussion of this text on pp. 77–78.

37. For a translation, see James B. Pritchard, ed., *Ancient Near Eastern Texts in Relation to the Old Testament,* 3d ed. (Princeton, NJ: Princeton Univ. Press, 1969), pp. 60–72.

38. See Forsyth, *Old Enemy,* pp. 39–40, 44–48, and 136; for the possible cosmogonic implications, see John Day, *God's Conflict,* pp. 7–18.

39. For brief treatments, see Forsyth, *Old Enemy,* pp. 94–96; and Day, *God's Conflict,* pp. 97–101.

40. See Forsyth, *Old Enemy,* pp. 103–04 and 145; and Day, *God's Conflict,* pp. 91–93. See also the comment on this text in McKenzie, *Second Isaiah,* pp. 123 and 126.

41. See Forsyth, *Old Enemy,* pp. 119–23.

42. The text is available in a translation by E. Isaac in Charlesworth, *Old Testament Pseudepigrapha,* vol. 1, pp. 13–29. For discussions, see J. Collins, *Apocalyptic Imagination,* pp. 36–46; and *Jewish Writings of the Second Temple Period,* pp. 90–93 and 395–406.

43. See G. W. E. Nickelsburg, "Apocalyptic and Myth in I Enoch 6–11," *Journal of Biblical Literature* 96 (1977): 383–405.

44. See Forsyth, *Old Enemy,* pp. 135–39.

45. According to the commentary of Walther Zimmerli, *Ezekiel 2: A Commentary on the Book of Ezekiel, Chapters 25–48,* Hermeneia Series (Philadelphia: Fortress, 1983), pp. 281–324, the original oracle is contained in 38:1–9 and 39:1–5 and 17–20.

46. According to Zimmerli, *Ezekiel 2,* p. 304: "A first step is taken on the way to apocalyptic, the aim of which is to set up a sequential order of future events."

47. For one thing, it is clear that Gog acts only as Yahweh's agent: There is no independent source of evil (see, e.g., 38:3–4 and 16). Gog is twice spoken of as prince of Magog (38:2 and 39:6). Although this term does not stem from the original oracle, it too had a role in later apocalypticism.

48. The "abomination of desolation," or "desolating sacrilege" is also mentioned in 1 Macc. 6:7 and in Dan. 9:27 and 11:31 (and cf. Dan. 8:11). It was to become one of the most potent symbolic denominations of Antichrist.

49. The four accounts of the career of Antiochus found in Dan. 7–12 (such repetitions are characteristic of apocalyptic texts) follow a structurally similar pattern involving (a) a symbolic review of the history prior to Antiochus (see 7:1–7 and 17; 7:19 and 23–24; 8:1–8 and 20–22; and 11:2–20); (b) an account of the tyrant's career (see 7:8 and 11; 7:21–22 and 24–25; 8:9–12 and 23–25; and 11:21–45); (c) his destruction through God's action (7:9–12; 7:21–22 and 26; 8:25; and 11:45–12:1 and 7); and finally (d) the eschatological reward of the just (7:13–14 and 18; 7:22 and 27; and 12:1–3). This analysis depends on that of John J. Collins, *Apocalyptic Vision of the Book of Daniel,* pp. 132–33. For an exhaustive treatment, see John J. Collins, *Daniel,* Hermeneia Series (Minneapolis: Fortress, 1993).

50. The literature on the "son of man" figure, both in Daniel and in later Jewish and Christian literature, is immense. Current scholarship finds the mythic origin of the "son of man" in the figure of Baal as "rider on the clouds" in Canaanite myth. See Collins, *Apocalyptic Vision,* pp. 99–101; and Day, *God's Conflict,* pp. 157–67.

51. The belief that the angelic powers have a bodily form or appearance was widespread in Second Temple Judaism. In the Book of Jubilees to be considered below, the "angels of presence and angels of sanctification" are created circumcised so that they can engage in temple worship (Jubilees 15:27).

52. On Belial, see Peter von der Osten-Sacken, *Gott und Belial* (Göttingen: Vandenhoeck & Ruprecht, 1969). Among older works, there is an extensive treatment in Beda Rigaux, *L'Antéchrist et l'opposition au royaume messianique dans l'ancien et le Nouveau Testament* (Paris: Gabalda, 1932), chap. 7. See also Jenks, *Origins,* pp. 131–32.

53. On dating and context, see G. W. E. Nickelsburg, "The Bible Rewritten and Expanded," in *Jewish Writings of the Second Temple Period,* pp. 97–104; and O. S. Wintermute, "Jubilees," in *Old Testament Pseudepigrapha,* vol. 2, pp. 35–51.

54. See, e.g., Jubilees 10:8–9, 17:15–18:13, 48:2–19, and so on. According to N. Forsyth, *Old Enemy,* pp. 182–91, the importance of Jubilees for the Satan myth is in its combining of the figure of Satan-Mastema (see esp. 10:11) with the story of the fallen Watchers. On Mastema, see Jenks, *Origins,* pp. 132–34.

55. Belial appears in eleven of the twelve testaments, e.g., Testament of Levi 3:3, 18:12, and 19:1; Testament of Judah 25:3; Testament of Issachar 6:1 and 7:7; Testament of Zebulon 9:8; Testament of Dan 1:7, 4:7 and 5:1 and 10–11; Testament of Asher 1:8–9 and 3:2; Testament of Joseph 7:4; and Testament of Benjamin 3:3–5. On the controversies surrounding the Testaments, see John J. Collins, "Testaments," in *Jewish Writings of the Second Temple Period,* pp. 331–44.

56. This survey is by no means meant to include all the appearances of Belial in texts of late Second Temple Judaism. One indication of his popularity is a brief appearance in *Sibylline Oracles* 2.167, a Jewish text probably emanating from Asia Minor about the turn of the era.

57. The literature—and disputes—about Qumran are immense, forming a separate subdiscipline within studies of early Judaism. Two pioneering works that retain

importance are J. T. Milik, *Ten Years of Discovery in the Wilderness of Judaea* (London: SCM, 1959); and F. M. Cross, Jr., *The Ancient Library of Qumran and Modern Biblical Studies,* rev. ed. (Garden City, NY: Doubleday, 1961). For a recent survey, see Devorah Dimant, "Qumran Sectarian Literature," in *Jewish Writings of the Second Temple Period,* pp. 483–550.

58. On Qumran's apocalyptic beliefs, see John J. Collins, "Patterns of Eschatology at Qumran," in *Traditions in Transformation,* ed. B. Halpern and J. D. Levenson (Winona Lake, IN: Winston, 1981), pp. 351–75. For a useful survey and translation of texts relating to apocalyptic adversaries at Qumran, see Jenks, *Origins,* pp. 135–52.

59. In the Community Rule (1QS) 3:19 we read, "And He created man for dominion over the earth; and He set to him two spirits to conduct himself according to them until the time of His visitation. They are the Spirit of Truth and the Spirit of Perversity." See the translation (used here) and discussion in D. Dimant, "Qumran Sectarian Literature," p. 533. Many have seen Persian influence in this doctrine of the two spirits; see, e.g., P. J. Kobelski, *Melchizedek and Melchiresaʼ* (Washington, DC: Catholic University of America, 1981), chap. 6.

60. For a summary of texts on the two Messiahs, see J. Collins, "Patterns of Eschatology," pp. 353–59. Priestly and royal Messiahs also appear in the Testaments of the Twelve Patriarchs, e.g., Testament of Levi 18:2–12 and Testament of Judah 24, and elsewhere in late Second Temple Judaism.

61. For a translation and commentary, see Kobelski, *Melchizedek and Melchiresaʼ,* pp. 3–23.

62. See Collins, "Patterns of Eschatology at Qumran," pp. 364–65 and 374.

63. See the second Hymn found in 1QH 3 and translated in G. Vermes, *The Dead Sea Scrolls in English,* 2nd ed. (Harmondsworth: Penguin, 1982), pp. 158–60 (Vermes translates *Belial* as "Satan"). For a discussion, see Collins, "Patterns of Eschatology at Qumran," pp. 370–72.

64. See, for example, the fragment known as 4Q Testimonia (4Q 175) dating from before 100 B.C.E., discussed in F. L. Cross, *Ancient Library of Qumran,* pp. 112–13; and the strange physiognomies of uncertain date from cave four (4Q 186 and 4Q Mess ar) discussed in J.-M. Rosenstiehl, "Le portrait de l'Antichrist," *Pseudépigraphes de l'Ancien Testament et manuscrits de la mer morte,* ed. Marc Philenko et al., vol. 1 (Paris: Presses universitaires de France, 1967), pp. 45–60.

65. On this text, see David Flusser, "The Hubris of the Antichrist in a Fragment from Qumran," *Immanuel* 10 (1980): 31–37. Joseph A. Fitzmyer gives a different interpretation in "The Contribution of Qumran Aramaic to the Study of the New Testament," *New Testament Studies* 20 (1974): 391–94; and D. Jenks, *Origins,* pp. 180–82, notes that even if Flusser's reading is correct, the text witnesses to a final tyrant and not an explicit Antichrist.

66. For a translation and study, see M. A. Knibb, "Martyrdom and Ascension of Isaiah," in *Old Testament Pseudepigrapha,* vol. 2, pp. 143–76. See also G. W. E. Nickelsburg, "Stories of Biblical and Early Post-Biblical Times," in *Jewish Writings of the Early Second Temple Period,* pp. 52–56.

67. David Flusser, "The Apocryphal Book of *Ascensio Isaiae* and the Dead Sea Sect," *Israel Exploration Journal* 3 (1953): 30–47, argues for its origin among the Qumran community. This has been doubted by Knibb, "Martyrdom and Ascension of Isaiah," pp. 152–53; and Nickelsburg, "Stories of Biblical and Early Post-Biblical Times," pp. 55–56.

68. When the text was first published in the nineteenth century, it was incorrectly identified as the Assumption of Moses. The most recent translation is by J. Priest,

"Testament of Moses," in *Old Testament Pseudepigrapha,* vol. 1, pp. 919–34. For comments, see J. J. Collins, "The Testament of Moses," in *Jewish Writings of the Second Temple Period,* pp. 344–49. See also Jenks, *Origins,* pp. 182–83, who concludes that the text seems to refer to an Endtyrant.

69. Chap. 9 concerns a "man of the tribe of Levi whose name is Taxo," whose voluntary death along with that of his seven sons is designed to compel God's intervention to effect apocalyptic vindication. The meaning of this unusual messianic (?) figure has been much debated. Chap. 10 is one of the most powerful descriptions of final judgment in apocalyptic literature.

70. There is considerable dispute about the proper relation of the possibly second-century B.C.E. chaps. 7–8 and chaps. 5–6, which clearly reflect the time of Herod. This makes it difficult to determine exactly where the enigmatic figure of Taxo (chap. 9) originally fit in.

71. See, for example, the Psalms of Solomon (first century B.C.E.), which demonstrate both a profound messianic hope and a willingness to locate recent crises, such as the Roman general Pompey's capture of Jerusalem in 63 B.C.E., within an apocalyptic framework. In Psalm 17 (see *Old Testament Pseudepigrapha,* vol. 2, pp. 665–69), the coming Messiah, the son of David, will be given divine power "to destroy the unrighteous rulers, to purge Jerusalem from gentiles who trample her to destruction; in wisdom and in righteousness to drive out the sinners from the inheritance; . . . to shatter all their substance with an iron rod; to destroy the unlawful nations with the word of his mouth" (vv. 22–24). Victor Maag in his "The Antichrist as Symbol of Evil," in *Evil* (Evanston, IL: Northwestern Univ. Press, 1967), pp. 66–70, notes that the latter part of this combination of Ps. 2:9 and Isa. 11:4 to describe the power of the messiah against his foes reappears in the description of the destruction of Antichrist in 2 Thess. 2:8. Also, the famous late first-century C.E. Jewish apocalypse known as 4 Ezra contains a cryptic reference to the reign of "one whom the inhabitants of the earth do not anticipate" (5:6a), which has been seen as a reference to the Final Tyrant (see Jenks, *Origins,* pp. 281–82).

72. On the role of the false prophet (based on Deut. 13:2–6 and 18:18–22) in developing conceptions of apocalyptic opposition, see Wayne A. Meeks, *The Prophet-King: Moses Traditions and the Johannine Christology* (Leiden: Brill, 1967), pp. 47–61; and Jenks, *Origins,* pp. 17–18, 169–72, 174, and 363.

73. For some remarks on this, see Dimant, "Qumran Sectarian Literature," pp. 533–38.

Chapter Two

1. Jaroslav Pelikan, *Jesus Through the Centuries: His Place in the History of Culture* (New York: Harper & Row, 1985).

2. See, for example, Burton Mack, "The Kingdom Sayings in Mark," *Forum* 3 (1987): 3–47.

3. See, e.g., Norman Perrin, *Rediscovering the Teaching of Jesus* (New York: Harper & Row, 1967); and Ernst Käsemann, "The Beginnings of Christian Theology," in *Apocalypticism,* ed. Robert W. Funk (New York: Herder & Herder, 1969), pp. 17–46.

4. See, most recently, E. P. Sanders, *Jesus and Judaism* (Philadelphia: Fortress, 1985), especially the "Conclusion" (pp. 319–40), which argues that Jesus is a representative of "Jewish restoration eschatology." Sanders also contains a review of key modern interpretations of Jesus on pp. 23–58.

5. See the critical remarks on this criterion of "double dissimilarity," as it is often termed, in Sanders, *Jesus and Judaism,* pp. 16–18.

6. For a helpful survey of this much-discussed issue, see Adela Yarbro Collins, "The Origin of the Designation of Jesus as 'Son of Man'," *Harvard Theological Review* 80 (1987): 391–407.

7. See John J. Collins, "The Son of Man in First Century Judaism," *New Testament Studies* 38(1992): 448–66.

8. Rudolf Bultmann, *The History of the Synoptic Tradition* (New York: Harper & Row, 1968), pp. 151–52.

9. Norman Perrin, *Rediscovering the Teaching of Jesus,* pp. 154–206; Philipp Vielhauer, *Aufsätze zum Neuen Testament* (Munich: Kaiser, 1965).

10. A. Y. Collins, "The Origin of the Designation," summarizes thus: "The conclusion seems warranted then that the ultimate origin of the designation of Jesus as 'Son of Man' is in the teaching of Jesus himself. Jesus closely associated, but probably did not identify, himself with that heavenly being. The proximate origin of the designation is thus in the reflection of some of Jesus' followers upon his death who were convinced of his vindication." See also Sanders, *Jesus and Judaism,* pp. 142–46; and M. Eugene Boring, *Sayings of the Risen Jesus: Christian Prophecy in the Synoptic Tradition* (Cambridge: Cambridge Univ. Press, 1982).

11. Käsemann, "The Beginnings of Christian Theology," p. 40.

12. Gerhard Ebeling, "The Ground of Christian Theology: On Ernst Käsemann's Essay, 'The Beginnings of Christian Theology'," in *Apocalypticism* (see note 3), p. 56.

13. For a brief introduction to the standard critical views on the "two source" theory of the Synoptics, i.e., Q and Mark, see Norman Perrin and Dennis Duling, *The New Testament: An Introduction,* 2nd ed. (New York: Harcourt Brace Jovanovich, 1982), pp. 68–69.

14. This is not a universally held position. One recent commentary argues for the priority of Matthew and would place all the Synoptics before 70 c.e. See C. S. Mann, *Mark,* Anchor Bible 27 (Garden City, NY: Doubleday, 1986), pp. 47–71.

15. See Adela Yarbro Collins, "The 'Son of Man' Tradition and the Book of Revelation," in *The Messiah: The First Princeton Symposium on Judaism and Christian Origins,* ed. James H. Charlesworth (Minneapolis: Fortress, 1992), pp. 536–86.

16. Oscar Cullmann, *Christ and Time,* 3rd ed. (London: SCM, 1962), pp. xxv–xxvi, 84, 139–43, 145, and 199.

17. This is where I differ from the recent account of the beginnings of the Antichrist legend of Gregory C. Jenks, *Origins.* Though I agree with Jenks in finding a true Antichrist only in Christian documents (e.g., pp. xvi, 13, 25, and 361–62), I disagree with his contention that it is not present until late in the first century c.e.

18. Lars Hartman, *Prophecy Interpreted: The Formation of Some Jewish Apocalyptic Texts and of the Eschatological Discourse Mark 13 Par.* (Lund: Gleerup, 1966). Among other treatments, see Beda Rigaux, *L'Antéchrist et l'Opposition au Royaume Messianique dans l'Ancien et le Nouveau Testament* (Paris: Gabalda, 1932), pp. 205–49; and Josef Ernst, *Die eschatologischen Gegenspieler in den Schriften des Neuen Testaments* (Regensburg: Pustet, 1967), pp. 3–23.

19. Hartman, *Prophecy Interpreted,* pp. 147–59. The Lukan version, while having much in common with Mark, has sufficient differences to indicate that it represents a separate tradition in the evolution of the underlying apocalyptic scriptural meditation (see

Hartman, *Prophecy Interpreted,* pp. 226–35). I use Hartman's literal translation here with a few minor variations.

20. Jenks, *Origins,* pp. 200–7, denies this, claiming that "it shows that ideas later to be found in the Antichrist myth [sic] were latent in the tradition, but not yet developed" (p. 206).

21. See Hartman, *Prophecy Interpreted,* pp. 159–62, for a detailed study of the relation to Daniel and a listing of commentators who note the implied claim to divinity.

22. This is clear in Luke 21:20 where the abomination is replaced by "When you see Jerusalem surrounded by armies, you must realize that she will soon be laid desolate."

23. See the remarks in Hartman, *Prophecy Interpreted,* p. 162; and B. Rigaux, "Bdelygma tēs erēmōseōs Mc 13,14; Mt 24,15," *Biblica* 40(1959): 675–83.

24. See Irenaeus, *Against Heresies* 5.25.1–2 and 5.30.2. This identification became standard in Christian exegesis, e.g., Jerome, *Commentary on Matthew* 4.24.15.

25. This identification was aided, at least in the Markan version, by a personalizing of the language used. Although *to bdelugma tēs erēmōseōs* is neuter in Greek, the qualifying participle "standing" is masculine (*hestēkota*). See Ernst, *Die eschatologischen Gegenspieler,* pp. 8 and 11–12.

26. For a presentation of the case for authenticity, see, e.g., W. G. Kümmel, *Introduction to the New Testament,* rev. ed. (Nashville: Abingdon, 1990), pp. 262–69; and F. W. Beare, "Thessalonians, Second Letter to the," in *The Interpreter's Dictionary of the Bible,* vol. 4 (New York and Nashville: Abingdon, 1962), pp. 625–29. For arguments against authenticity, see, e.g., W. Marxsen, *Introduction to the New Testament* (Philadelphia: Fortress, 1968), pp. 37–44; and N. Perrin and D. Duling, *The New Testament: An Introduction,* pp. 208–9. New Testament scholars of the "critical" approach show a clear preponderance against the authenticity of the letter. Among older commentaries on Thessalonians presupposing unity of authorship, the most extensive is B. Rigaux, *Saint Paul: Les Épitres aux Thessaloniens* (Paris: Gabalda, 1956).

27. Hartman, *Prophecy Interpreted,* chap. 6. From the viewpoint of conceptions of Antichrist, one argument in favor of a dating before 70 C.E. is the absence of any reference to Nero as Antichrist. For a list of verbal parallels between Mark 13 and 1 and 2 Thessalonians, see Ernst, *Die eschatologischen Gegenspieler,* p. 23, who also has an excellent discussion of the text and a history of its exegesis on pp. 24–79.

28. Here the Apostle insists on the apocalyptic doctrine (see Dan. 12:2) of the resurrection of the body (1 Thess. 4:14–17).

29. These include the eschatological trumpet and motif of clouds in 1 Thess. 4:16 (see Matt. 24:31) and the labor pains of 1 Thess. 5:3 (see Matt. 24:8). It should also be noted that the frequent Pauline term *parousia* for the Lord's return (e.g., 1 Thess. 2:19, 3:13, 4:15, 5:23; 2 Thess. 2:1, 2:8; 1 Cor. 15:23) occurs in the Synoptics only in the Little Apocalypse (Matt. 24:3, 27, 37, and 39).

30. Helpful here are Hartman, *Prophecy Interpreted,* pp. 195–205; and Rigaux, *Les Épitres aux Thessaloniens,* pp. 644–80. For the translation given here, I am using *The New English Bible* (Oxford-Cambridge: Oxford Univ. Press, 1961) with some adaptations.

31. For vv. 3b–4a I have preferred to use my own translation of the Greek: *hoti ean mē elthē hē apostasia prōton kai apokaluphthē ho anthrōpos tēs anomias, ho huios tēs apōleias, ho antikeimenos. . . .* (Some mss. read *ho anthrōpos tēs hamartias.*) A full discussion of these terms can be found in Rigaux, *Les Épitres aux Thessaloniens,* pp. 654–59. The use of *anomia* (sin, lawlessness) in terms of an apocalyptic contrast also appears in 2 Cor. 6:14–15: "Do not harness yourselves in an uneven team with unbelievers. Virtue (*dikaio-*

sune) is no companion for crime (*anomia*). Light and darkness have nothing in common. Christ is not the ally of Beliar. . . ."

32. For a history of the exegesis, see Rigaux, *Les Épitres aux Thessaloniens,* pp. 259–66 and 274–80. Among modern exegetes who hold the latter view, see Cullmann, *Christ and Time,* pp. 164–67.

33. See Hartman, *Prophecy Interpreted,* pp. 204–5.

34. Paul Ricoeur, *Symbolism of Evil,* p. 238.

35. It is important to point out here that the Adamic myth never functions alone in the history of Christian ideas of evil. Chapter 5 of Ricoeur's *Symbolism of Evil* (pp. 306–46) is dedicated to a study of the dynamics of the interaction between the Adamic myth and the other three myths: the theogonic myth, the tragic myth, and the orphic myth. Insightful as this section is, I believe that it too could be enriched by attention to the Antichrist legend.

36. Hartman himself is of the opinion that it goes back to Jesus (*Prophecy Interpreted,* pp. 245–48), though he admits that the question cannot be proven but depends on "the image the scholar has of Jesus and His work" (p. 247).

37. The Jewish Revolt that ended in the destruction of Jerusalem had begun during Nero's reign, however, so some accounts of Nero's apocalyptic doings accuse him of responsibility for the temple's fate (e.g., Sibylline Oracles 4:125–29 and 5:150–51).

38. For a history of Nero's rule, see Michael Grant, *Nero* (New York: American Heritage Press, 1970). Grant discusses the legends concerning his return on pp. 250–51.

39. The word for Antichrist in Armenian, *nerhn,* appears to be a transliteration for the Greek *Neron.* See W. Bousset, *The Antichrist Legend* (London: Hutchinson, 1896), p. 253. On the twelfth-century Armenian Antichrist saga, see chap. 5, m. 6.

40. For a brief account of Nero's persecution of the Christians in 64 C.E., in which, according to tradition, Peter and Paul were martyred, see Robert M. Grant, *Augustus to Constantine* (New York: Harper & Row, 1970), pp. 78–79.

41. The main ancient sources here are Tacitus, *Histories* 2.8, and Suetonius, *Life of Nero* 57. Suetonius, *Life* 40 also mentions that during his life Nero had been promised world rule with Jerusalem as his capital.

42. For an interesting study, see David Flusser, "The Four Empires in the Fourth Sibyl and in the Book of Daniel," *Israel Oriental Studies* 2(1972): 148–75.

43. The role of the Nero legends in the development of Antichrist was already discussed by early students of apocalyptic eschatology, such as H. Gunkel, W. Bousset, and R. H. Charles. The most complete recent treatments, superseding these early accounts, are those of John J. Collins, *The Sibylline Oracles of Egyptian Judaism* (Missoula, MT: Scholars Press, 1974), pp. 80–87; and Adela Yarbro Collins, *The Combat Myth in the Book of Revelation* (Missoula, MT: Scholars Press, 1976), pp. 174–90.

44. The Sibylline Oracles are a different genre of revelatory literature, but their view of history demonstrates a large degree of overlap with apocalyptic eschatology. The Jewish Sibyllines were produced from the mid–second century B.C.E. until the seventh century C.E. (many of the older ones in Egypt), and the form was widely imitated by Christians from the beginning of the second century. For an introduction and translation of the ancient Sibylline texts, see J. J. Collins, "Sibylline Oracles," in *Old Testament Pseudepigrapha,* vol. 1, pp. 317–472. On a more general level, see B. McGinn, "*Teste David cum Sibylla:* The Significance of the Sibylline Tradition in the Middle Ages," in *Women of the Medieval World,* ed. Julius Kirshner and Suzanne F. Wemple (Oxford: Blackwell, 1985), pp. 7–35.

45. Sibylline Oracle 4:137–39 (J. Collins, p. 387). See also 4:119–24. This form of adaptation of the returning Nero legend is similar to that found in Sibylline Oracle 8:65–72 and 139–59, probably Jewish and dating c. 175 C.E. (though possibly containing earlier materials).

46. Sibylline Oracle 5:106–10 (J. Collins, p. 395):

> But when he attains a formidable height and unseemly daring,
> he will also come, wishing to destroy the city of the blessed ones,
> and then a certain king sent from God against him
> will destroy all the great kings and noble men.
> Thus there will be judgment on men by the imperishable one.

47. Sibylline Oracle 5:220–24 (J. Collins, p. 398). In these obscure verses Nero, though evil himself, appears as an instrument of God's vengeance—a position different from that of Antichrist. However, the reference to cutting off the roots of the heads of three kings recalls the action of the "little horn" in uprooting three other horns in Dan. 7:8. Later versions of the Antichrist story understood these three uprooted horns as the three kingdoms (often Egyptians, Libyans, and Cushites) defeated by the "king of the North" (refering to the little horn, i.e., Antiochus IV) described in Dan. 11:43. Something of the origins of this conflation may be evident here. On this theme, see Bousset, *The Antichrist,* pp. 158–60.

48. To be sure, the two personalities are not directly juxtaposed here, as in vv. 105–10, but it seems difficult to deny some apocalyptic relationship. On the basis of these texts of Sibylline Oracles 4 and 5, it seems difficult to disagree with Adela Yarbro Collins, who argues that there are two forms of the Jewish use of the Nero legends: one in Book 4 (and also Book 8), which takes it over as anti-Roman propaganda; the other in Book 5 in which "Nero is mythicized and given the role of an eschatological adversary" (*Combat Myth,* p. 181).

49. One problematic text from 5:367 has been taken to hint at his death when it says *hēs charin ōletō t'autos, helei tautēn parachrēma.* But A. Collins, *Combat Myth,* pp. 180–81, argues that the verb *ōleto* here would be better translated by "ruined" or "undone" than by "perished," so that the line should read "He [Nero] will immediately seize that one [i.e., Rome] because of whom he himself was undone."

50. The identification of Beliar with Nero depends on the interpretation of this unusual word, which can be taken to mean either "from the Sebasti" (i.e., the line of Augustus) or "from Sebaste" (a city in Samaria). For reasons favoring the former, see J. Collins, *Sibylline Oracles of Egyptian Judaism,* pp. 86–87; and "Sibylline Oracles," p. 360.

51. There was to be much debate in centuries to come over whether or not Antichrist had the power to raise the dead, on which see Bousset, *Antichrist Legend,* pp. 177–79. This appears to be the earliest mention of the theme.

52. Translation from J. Collins, "Sibylline Oracles," p. 363. This text, though it represents "the highest degree of mythicization of Nero in the Jewish portions of the Sibylline books" (A. Collins, *Combat Myth,* p. 182), lacks both a clear contrast with a coming messiah and any reference to Nero as having died and been brought back to life.

53. M. A. Knibb, "Martyrdom and Ascension of Isaiah: A New Translation and Introduction," in *Old Testament Pseudepigrapha,* vol. 2, pp. 143–76, suggests a date toward the end of the first century (see p. 149). Given the early Jewish-Christian character of the text, we may well think of it as prior to the more sophisticated use of the Nero materials in the Johannine Apocalypse (dated c. 95).

54. According to the Julian calendar, this would comprise 1,335 days, which is the same number as that found in Dan. 12:12. John's Apocalypse will also make use of Daniel to determine the duration of Antichrist's reign but will cite the alternate 1,260 days (see Apoc. 11:3 and 12:6, depending on Dan. 7:25).

55. For some remarks on the history of this tradition, see Bousset, *Antichrist Legend,* pp. 138–42.

56. The major classic commentaries of the early historical-critical approach to the Apocalypse still remain useful. These are Wilhelm Bousset, *Die Offenbarung Johannis,* 2nd ed. (Göttingen: Vandenhoeck & Ruprecht, 1906); and R. H. Charles, *A Critical and Exegetical Commentary on the Revelation of St. John,* The International Critical Commentary, 2 vols. (Edinburgh: T & T Clark, 1920). Among more recent commentaries, note Adela Yarbro Collins, *Crisis and Catharsis: The Power of the Apocalypse* (Philadelphia: Westminster, 1984); and Elisabeth Schüssler Fiorenza, *The Book of Revelation: Justice and Judgment* (Philadelphia: Fortress, 1985). For treatments of the Antichrist in the Apocalypse, see B. Rigaux, *L'Antéchrist,* pp. 318–83; and J. Ernst, *Die eschatologischen Gegenspieler,* chap. 3.

57. For a defense of the early dating among contemporary scholars, see Christopher Rowland, *The Open Heaven,* pp. 403–13.

58. The differences in theology and in language between the Apocalypse and the Gospel and Epistles ascribed to John, "the Beloved Disciple," are such that almost no modern scholar thinks they could have been the product of the same pen.

59. On the genre of the Apocalypse, see John J. Collins, "Pseudonymity, Historical Reviews and the Genre of the Revelation of John," *Catholic Biblical Quarterly* 39 (1977): 329–43.

60. For a study, see A. Collins, *Combat Myth,* especially chaps. 2 and 3.

61. Satan, of course, still plays his part. In 13:4 he is worshiped along with the Beast, while in 16:13–14 the Dragon, the Beast, and the False Prophet cooperate in summoning the kings to the final battle. After the Beast's defeat in chapter 19, Satan again takes a role, first as bound for a thousand years (20:1–2), and then as released to summon Gog and Magog for one last attempt to overthrow the "camp of the saints" (20:7–10). This relatively restricted role of Satan in relation to Antichrist in the scenario of the final events of this aeon has been noted above. On the role of the Beast, see also John M. Court, *Myth and History in the Book of Revelation* (Atlanta: John Knox, 1979), pp. 122–53.

62. For a comparison of the descriptions of the Beast in chaps. 13 and 17, see A. Collins, *Combat Myth,* p. 171. The exact meaning of the seven heads has been a major puzzle in the interpretation of the Apocalypse. A helpful discussion in A. Collins, *Crisis and Catharsis,* pp. 58–64, outlines four basic positions: (1) the seven heads include all Roman emperors up to the author's time and he is writing under the sixth head; (2) the seven heads include all the emperors chronologically; however, the author is not writing under the sixth head but either using an earlier source or antedating his work; (3) the seven heads represent only selected emperors; and (4) the heads are purely symbolic. Bousset and Charles held to position (2), but Collins and many recent exegetes argue for various forms of (3). The question need not detain us here.

63. This is recognized by commentators both new and old, e.g., Bousset, *Die Offenbarung,* pp. 360–62, 407–8; Charles, *Revelation,* vol. 2, pp. 67–73; A. Collins, *Combat Myth,* pp. 174–90; and Court, *Myth and History,* pp. 127–37.

64. In 17:8 the Beast arises from the *abyssos,* while in 13:1 he emerges from the sea (*thalassa*). The reference to the sea doubtless comes from the Danielic source of chap. 13,

but we may take it as equivalent to *abyssos,* the LXX translation for the Hebrew *sheol,* the abode of the dead (e.g., Ps. 70 [that is, 71]:20).

65. As A. Collins points out in *Combat Myth,* p. 186, there are a number of other symbolic contrasts between the Lamb and the Beast dependent on the central double-resurrection theme, e.g.: (1) the Beast has ten crowns (13:1) and Christ has many crowns (19:12); and (2) the Beast has blasphemous titles written on it (13:1, 17:3) while Christ has a secret name written on him (19:12).

66. Irenaeus, *Against Heresies* 5.30.3 gives a number of possibilities that will be studied below.

67. In Sibylline Oracles 1:324–30 (a Christian interpolation of c. 150 C.E.) the name of Jesus (*Iesous*) is shown to be equivalent to 888. Irenaeus (*Against Heresies* 1.15.2) tells us that the Gnostic Marcosians also added up Jesus' name in similar manner (my thanks to Robert Grant for this reference).

68. Thus, nun=50, resh=200, waw=6, nun=50, qoph=100, samech=60, resh=200, totalling 666. A. Collins (*Combat Myth,* pp. 174–75) points out that a Latinized Hebrew form, *nrw qsr,* would explain the variant 616. See also Michael Oberweis, "Die Bedeutung der neutestamentliche 'Rätselzahlen' 666 (Apk 13.18) und 153 (Joh 21.11)," *Zeitschrift für Neutestamentliche Wissenschaft* 77(1986): 226–41.

69. Bousset, *Die Offenbarung,* pp. 324–30, argued this view. It has been taken up in different ways by many recent scholars, e.g., A. Collins, *Combat Myth,* pp. 166–70; and J. Court, *Myth and History,* pp. 99–104.

70. Later Christian exegesis most often identified them with Enoch and Elijah. See Bousset, *Antichrist Legend,* pp. 203–11, who thinks they were more likely Elijah and Moses in the intention of John, as does Charles, *Revelation,* vol. 1, pp. 280–84.

71. A. Collins, *Combat Myth,* p. 170, summarizes: "His [i.e., John's] contribution was to combine the contemporary tradition about an eschatological adversary expected to appear in Jerusalem with the myth about the chaos beast from the abyss, possibly inspired by the form that myth took in Daniel 7."

72. Gilles Quispel, *The Secret Book of Revelation* (New York: McGraw-Hill, 1979), pp. 76–80, makes the interesting suggestion that the Woman of chap. 12 is to be seen as the Holy Spirit whose Child is the Christ, the agent of "our God" (12:10) whose angels win victory over Satan. Thus chap. 12 would contain a symbolic presentation of the Trinity, and chaps. 12–13 its evil parody.

73. This is found both in 1 Enoch 60:7–10, a text from the early first century B.C.E., and in 4 Ezra 6:49–52 from the late first century C.E. In 2 Baruch 29:1–8 (early second century C.E.) the faithful in the messianic kingdom feed on Leviathan and Behemoth.

74. This suggestion occurs among ancient commentators and has been defended by modern ones as well, e.g., Charles, *Revelation,* vol. 1, pp. 357–59.

75. Bousset, *Antichrist Legend,* pp. 183–85, argued that the second Beast was a remnant of the older "nonpolitical" version of the Antichrist, but this seems forced.

76. The most recent major study is Raymond E. Brown, *The Epistles of John,* Anchor Bible (Garden City, NY: Doubleday, 1982). I will use Brown's translation here. On Antichrist in the Johannine Letters, see also J. Ernst, *Die eschatologischen Gegenspieler,* pp. 168–77.

77. For a summary of Brown's thesis about the context and dating, see *Epistles,* pp. 69–71 and 100–103.

78. Though both the Hebrew Bible and other New Testament texts speak of the "last days" or "last times," the term "last hour" occurs only in 1 John. The Little Apocalypse had used the phrase "that hour" (see Mark 13:11 and Matt. 24:44 and 25:13) to de-

scribe the apocalyptic time, and the "hour" of Jesus was an important theme in John's Gospel. For a discussion, see Brown, *Epistles,* pp. 330–32.

79. For a study of the term and its meaning, see Brown, *Epistles,* pp. 332–37.

80. The most influential interpretation of Early Christian history in this vein remains Martin Werner, *The Formation of Christian Dogma* (Boston: Beacon, 1965). The German original appeared in 1941.

Chapter Three

1. Relatively little literature from the period c. 100–175 c.e. survives, and we would not expect much about Antichrist in the apologetic works directed to pagans. It is true that Antichrist is not mentioned in a number of important nonapologetic Christian documents of the time, such as Clement's First Letter (last decade of first century c.e.), Ignatius's Epistles (c. 110), and, more surprisingly, in the partially apocalyptic Shepherd of Hermas, probably composed between the late first century and c. 140 c.e. In Vision 4 Hermas encounters a great beast like Leviathan who is "a type of the great persecution to come" (Vis. 4.2.5), but this beast does not seem to have any direct relation to Antichrist.

2. The *Didache,* only discovered in the late nineteenth century, consists of three parts: (1) chaps. 1–6, a moral treatise on the "two ways" very similar to the ethical materials from Qumran; (2) chaps. 7–15, the earliest "church order," that is, description of Christian liturgy and offices; and (3) chap. 16, a brief apocalypse with obvious connections with the Little Apocalypse. All scholars agree that it comes from Syria, but two datings have been proposed: either late first century (c. 70–100 c.e.), or the first half of the second century. Recent scholarship seems to prefer the earlier dating.

3. See Phil. 7:1. There is some doubt about the dating of this letter. I am following the theory that sees it as a conflation of two original letters, with chaps. 1–12 written long after chap. 13.

4. Justin's *Dialogue with Trypho,* probably written c. 150 c.e., takes as a central theme the disputes between Jews and Christians over the coming of the messiah, with Justin arguing from the Scriptures for the necessity of two comings (*parousiai*), one in humility, the other in majesty. Chap. 32 concerns the proper interpretation of the "time, times and half a time" of Dan. 7:25 for the coming of the one who will speak blasphemies against God. Chap. 51 has a reference to "false prophets" reminiscent of Mark 13:22, while chap. 110 echoes the language of 2 Thess. in defending the view that Christ will return only after the coming of the "man of apostasy."

5. For an introduction, see Adela Yarbro Collins, "The Early Christian Apocalypses," in *Apocalypse: Morphology of a Genre,* ed. John J. Collins (Missoula, MT: Scholars Press, 1979), pp. 61–121. Many of these Christian apocalypses produced between the first and the sixth century are accounts of otherworldly journeys without much interest in apocalyptic eschatology. This accounts for the fact that only eight of twenty-four have significant materials on Antichrist.

6. See A. Collins, "Early Christian Apocalypses," pp. 72–73, for a discussion and citation of the ancient authorities on Bar-Kochba's persecution.

7. The best edition is to be found in the *Sources chrétiennes* series (SC hereafter). Book 5, which contains the account of Antichrist, was edited and commented upon by A. Rousseau, L. Doutreleau, and C. Mercier in two volumes, SC 152–53 (Paris: Les Éditions du Cerf, 1969). My translations are from this edition.

8. Recapitulation in the sense of summarizing, consummating, and leading back to origins was a notion that Irenaeus developed from Paul (see Rom. 13:9, Eph. 1:10). A

good description is found in *Against Heresies* 3.16.6: "Thus there is one God the Father, as we have demonstrated, and one Christ Jesus our Lord who came in fulfillment of God's comprehensive design and recapitulates all things in himself. Man is in all respects the handiwork of God; thus he [Christ] recapitulates man in himself. . . ." See, e.g., 3.18.1–7, 3.21.10, 3.22.3, 5.20.2–21, and so on.

9. The bishop advances conjectural numerological equivalents to 666 in 5.30.3–*Euanthos, Lateinos* (i.e., pertaining to the Roman Empire), and *Teitan* (giant). More interesting is the discussion in 5.28.2 and 5.29.2 of 666 as "a recapitulation of the whole apostasy which has been done during six thousand years" (i.e., the course of world history).

10. While Irenaeus uses the term *antichristos,* he makes no reference to the Johannine Epistles, which is probably another sign that the term was well known in many Christian circles.

11. Among the most interesting of these exegeses are those of John 5:43 (the logion about the "other" who will be accepted by the Jews) and Luke 17:2, the parable of the widow and the unjust judge (see 5.25.4). Irenaeus is the first witness for the application of these texts to Antichrist.

12. A broad range of Old Testament texts indicating something suspicious or evil about the tribe of Dan was to be used in later apocalyptic traditions to prove that Antichrist must originate from this source, e.g., Gen. 49:17, Lev. 24:10–11, Deut. 33:22, 1 Kings 12:29, Judges 18:11–31, as well as Jer. 8:16–17. These suspicions seem to be reflected in the Jewish *Testament of the Twelve Patriarchs* (second century B.C.E.), specifically in the Testament of Dan 5:1–12. On Dan as the tribe of Antichrist, see Bousset, *Antichrist Legend,* pp. 171–74.

13. The final stage in Irenaeus's account of the last events is the triumphant return of Christ to effect judgment on the evil and to reward the just. Briefly adumbrated in *Against Heresies* 5.30.4, this vital part of Irenaeus's eschatology is expounded at length in 5.31–36.

14. The best edition and study of this work is in the SC 14, *Hippolyte: Commentaire sur Daniel,* ed. M. Lefevre (Paris: Éditions du Cerf, 1947). The translations that follow are my own.

15. The treatise on Antichrist was last edited by G. N. Bonwetsch, *Hippolytus Werke,* Band 1 (Leipzig: J. C. Hinrich, 1897). There is a translation in *The Ante-Nicene Fathers,* ed. Alexander Roberts and James Donaldson, reprint of 1866–72 ed., vol. 5 (Grand Rapids, MI: Eerdmans, 1981), pp. 204–19, which will be used here unless otherwise noted.

16. Little has been written on Hippolytus's eschatological teaching. Among older works, see Adhémer d'Alès, *Le théologie de saint Hippolyte* (Paris: Beauchesne, 1906), pp. 179–206; and, more recently, David G. Dunbar, "Hippolytus of Rome and the Eschatological Exegesis of the Early Church," *Westminster Theological Journal* 45(1983): 322–39; and William C. Weinrich, "Antichrist in the Early Church," *Concordia Theological Quarterly* 49(1985): 135–47. See also David G. Dunbar's Ph.D. dissertation, *The Eschatology of Hippolytus of Rome* (Drew University, 1979).

17. Hippolytus, *Com. on Dan.* 4.18–19 (ed. Lefevre, pp. 296–300), refers to two contemporary apocalyptic movements led by bishops, while Eusebius, *Church History* 6.7, refers to the calculations of one Jude who argued on the basis of Daniel's seventy weeks (Dan. 9) that Antichrist would come in the tenth year of Severus's reign (202–3 C.E.).

18. Hippolytus, *Com. on Dan.* 4.23–24 (ed. Lefevre, pp. 306–10). Throughout the commentary, Hippolytus insists that the end is not near, e.g., 4.5–6 and 16–17. On this delay of the *parousia,* see David G. Dunbar, "The Delay of the Parousia in Hippolytus," *Vigiliae Christianae* 37(1983): 313–27.

19. For a survey, see Richard Landes, "Lest the Millennium Be Fulfilled: Apoca-lyptic Expectations and the Pattern of Western Chronography 100–800 C.E.," in *The Use and Abuse of Eschatology in the Middle Ages,* ed. Werner Verbeke, Daniel Verhelst, and Andries Welkenhuysen (Leuven, Belg.: Leuven Univ. Press, 1988), pp. 137–211. Hippoly-tus's dating of Christ's Incarnation, which Landes calls AM I, is discussed on pp. 144–49 and 161–65. It was challenged in the fourth century by the new dating (AM II) advanced by Eusebius and later by Jerome, which had Christ begin his public ministry in AM 5228.

20. On recapitulation, see *Antichrist* 26 and *Com. on Dan.* 4.11.

21. Hippolytus, *Antichrist* 6 (ed. Bonwetsch, pp. 7–8).

22. Hippolytus is the first to state explicitly that Antichrist will rebuild the Jerusalem temple; see also *Com. on Dan.* 4.49.

23. *Antichrist* 27 (ed. Bonwetsch, p. 19.4–5). In the wake of the French Revolution and the beginning of modern democracies, a number of commentators hailed Hippoly-tus's prescience here, such as John Henry Newman in an Advent sermon of 1835 later published as Tract 83, *Tracts for the Times* (London: Rivington, 1840), pp. 22–27.

24. Emphasized by Jenks, *Origins,* pp. 108–12.

25. On this final week of years (based on Irenaeus, *Against Heresies* 5.25.4), see *Com. on Dan.* 4.58.

26. Hippolytus is the first to make an explicit identification of the two witnesses with Enoch and Elijah in *Antichrist* 43.

27. *Antichrist* 49 (ed. Bonwetsch, p. 31.20–22, my trans.). This is different from Irenaeus (5.28.1), for whom the second Beast is nothing more than the "armor-bearer" of the first Beast who is Antichrist.

28. *bdelugma erēmōseōs* is the reading of the LXX; *bdelugma aphainismou* is found in the translation of Theodotion. See Dunbar, "Hippolytus of Rome," p. 333.

29. *Com. on Dan.* 4.54 (ed. Lefevre, p. 372.8–10).

30. See Robert E. Lerner, "Refreshment of the Saints: The Time After Antichrist as a Station for Earthly Progress in Medieval Thought," *Traditio* 32(1976): 97–144.

31. As noted by Dunbar, "Hippolytus of Rome," pp. 336–37. Lerner, "Refresh-ment of the Saints," pp. 101–3, incorrectly claims that Jerome began this tradition.

32. Tertullian, *Resurrection of the Flesh* 24 (J.-P. Migne, ed., *Patrologia Latina* [hereafter PL] [Paris: Migne, 1844–64] 2:829).

33. E.g., *Resurrection of the Flesh* 24–25; *Against Marcion* 3.8 and 5.16; *Prescription Against Heresies* 4 and 33; and *On Fasting* 11.

34. Dunbar, "Hippolytus of Rome," p. 339.

35. Hippolytus, *Antichrist* 25 (ed. Bonwetsch, 18.4–6, my trans.). See also *Anti-christ* 53 and 57; *Com. on Dan.* 4.49–50; and Irenaeus, *Against Heresies* 5.26.1.

36. See, e.g., Origen, *On First Principles* 2.11.

37. *Origen: Contra Celsum* 6.45, translated with an introduction and notes by Henry Chadwick (Cambridge: Cambridge Univ. Press, 1980), p. 362. It is possible that Origen's polemical argument directed to a pagan intellectual about the possibility of completely just and unjust men may reflect Glaucon's speech in Plato's Republic 2 (360E–361A).

38. Origen, *Commentary on John* 2.56, ed. Cecile Blanc in *Origene: Commentaire sur Saint Jean* (Paris: Éditions du Cerf, 1966. SC 120), p. 240 (my trans.).

39. Origen, *Commentary on Matthew* nn. 29–47 (J.-P. Migne, ed., *Patrologia Graeca* [hereafter PG] [Paris: Migne, 1857–66] 13:1639–70, surviving only in Latin. Especially im-portant for the understanding of Antichrist are cc. 1641B, 1643AB, 1644D–45C, 1660AD, 1662A, 1664AD, 1666B, 1667A, and 1669D–70C.

40. On the double Antichrist tradition, see Bousset, *Antichrist Legend,* pp. 79–86.

41. See especially Josef Martin, "Commodianus," *Traditio* 13(1957): 1–71; and M. Sordi, "Commodianus, *Carmen apol.* 892ss: *rex ab oriente,*" *Augustinianum* 22(1982): 203–10. For an introduction to the theology of Commodian, see Jean Daniélou, *Origins of Latin Christianity* (Philadelphia: Westminster, 1977), pp. 99–123 and 273–88.

42. See the edition of J. Martin, *Commodiana Carmina* (Turnhout, Belg.: Brepols, 1960. *Corpus Christianorum* [hereafter CC] 128), pp. 33–34. The picture of the *Nero redivivus* is not unlike what we have seen in Sibylline Oracles 5, especially in its stress on Nero as coming from Rome to Jerusalem (see above p. 47); but it has a clearer idea of his resurrection and it adds many of the details we have seen in Irenaeus and especially Hippolytus. On Commodian, see also Jenks, *Origins,* pp. 103–6.

43. *Commodiani Carmina* (ed. Martin, pp. 106–7). I prefer the reading "rex ab oriente" to "rex ad orientem" in line 892.

44. E.g., M. Sordi, "Dionigi d'Alessandria, Commodiano ed alcuni problemi della storia del III sec.," *Rendiconti della Pontificia Accademia Archeologica* 35(1962–63): 123–46, makes an argument for a third-century referent, but it is scarcely secure.

45. For an introduction to Lactantius, as well as a translation of Book 7 of the *Divine Institutes,* see B. McGinn, *Apocalyptic Spirituality* (New York: Paulist Press, 1979), pp. 17–80.

46. Lactantius, *Epitome of the Divine Institutes* 73 (ed. S. Brandt in *Corpus Scriptorum Ecclesiasticorum Latinorum* [hereafter CSEL] 19, pp. 760–61).

47. The Hermetic treatises were composed in Greek, probably in the second and third centuries c.e. The *Asclepius,* which contains an apocalypse in chaps. 24–26, survives in a Latin version. For a general introduction to this literature, see Garth Fowden, *The Egyptian Hermes: A Historical Approach to the Late Pagan Mind* (Cambridge: Cambridge Univ. Press, 1987).

48. On the Oracle of Hystaspes, see J. R. Hinnels, "The Zoroastrian Doctrine of Salvation in the Roman World: A Study of the Oracle of Hystaspes," in *Man and His Salvation: Studies in Honor of S.G.F. Brandon* (Manchester: Manchester Univ. Press, 1973), pp. 125–48.

49. The tradition of a single coming prophet, usually identified with Elijah (see Mal. 3:23), is found in a number of early Christian apocalyptic texts, e.g., Sibylline Oracles 2.187–95; Commodian, "Song of Two Peoples," vv. 833–34. On one versus two prophets, see Bousset, *Antichrist Legend,* pp. 203–11.

50. In his description of this evil ruler it is possible that Lactantius had access to Jewish traditions about the false messiah because there are suggestive analogies, if not exact parallels, with Jewish themes stretching back to late Second Temple Judaism. For example, when the just flee into the desert (as in the Martyrdom of Isaiah), not the mountains (as in the Little Apocalypse), "the Unholy One will hear of this and enflamed with rage will come up with a great army" (7.17). Then God will send "the Great King, who will rescue them and free them."

51. Belief that Antichrist will be the devil himself or else conceived by the devil is found in a number of fourth-century Latin sources, e.g., Firmicus Maternus, *The Error of Profane Religions* 22 (PL 12:1030, written c. 345); Ambrosiaster, *Commentary on 2 Thessalonians* 2 (PL 17:482D), who says, ". . . just as the Son of God born and made man demonstrated his divinity by signs and wonders, so too Satan will appear in a man to show himself as God by means of the wonders of the Lie." Perhaps the most unusual example of this belief is found in the Christian apocalypse known as the *Questions of Bartholomew* (Greek original possibly third century). In chap. 4 of this work Bartholomew interrogates

the bound demon Beliar-Satan about the secrets of the cosmos and history. The Latin version of this (of uncertain date) uses both *diabolus* and *antichristus* to describe this bound figure (see U. Moricca, "Un nuovo testo dell'Evangelo di Bartolomeo," *Revue Biblique* 30[1921], pp. 501–3).

52. Sulpicius Severus, *Dialogues* 1.41 (ed. C. Halm, CSEL 1, p. 197): "When we asked him about the end of the world, he told us that Nero and the Antichrist were to come first. Nero will rule the western region after subduing the ten kings. He will conduct a persecution to compel worship of pagan idols. Antichrist will first seize the eastern empire and will have Jerusalem as the seat and capital of his kingdom. He will rebuild the city and the temple. His persecution will be to compel denial that Christ is God, rather setting himself up as the Anointed One. He will order all circumcised according to the Law. Then Nero himself will be destroyed by the Antichrist so that the whole world and all nations may be drawn under his power until that wicked one is destroyed by the coming of Christ. There is no doubt that Antichrist, conceived by an evil spirit, has already been born. He is now a child and will take over the empire when he comes of age. We heard all this from him seven years ago. Ponder how close these fearful events are!" I have used my translation from *Visions of the End*, p. 52. On Sulpicius's apocalyptic views, see Jos Vaesen, "Sulpice Severe et la fin du temps," in *Use and Abuse of Eschatology in the Middle Ages*, pp. 49–71.

53. In this account I will largely follow what I have already written on this issue in "Portraying the Antichrist in the Middle Ages," in *Use and Abuse of Eschatology in the Middle Ages*, esp. pp. 3–13.

54. See Richard Foerster, *Scriptores Physiognomici Graeci et Latini*, 2 vols. (Leipzig: Teubner, 1893), for a collection of texts.

55. Chap. 5 deals with a persecuting "king of foreign race" from the West. This has been seen as a reference to Maximinus Thrax (235–238 C.E.), but the identification is not certain. Chap. 7 discusses a number of unusual birth prodigies as signs of the end.

56. The translation is that of James Cooper and Arthur J. McLean, *The Testament of the Lord* (Edinburgh: Clark, 1902), pp. 57–58. For a discussion of the text, see A. Y. Collins, "Early Christian Apocalypses," pp. 77–78. Pliny mentions two pupils in the left eye as a sign of the evil eye in his *Natural History* 7.18, but I have not been able to find specific references to the other marks in the physiognomical literature.

57. See O. S. Wintermute in *Old Testament Pseudepigrapha*, vol. 1, pp. 721–53. There is an excellent discussion in David Frankfurter, *Elijah in Upper Egypt: The Apocalypse of Elijah and Early Egyptian Christianity* (Minneapolis: Fortress, 1993), esp. chap. 5, "The Lawless One and the Fate of the Saints" (pp. 103–40). I will use Frankfurter's translation here (pp. 299–328). See also Jenks, *Origins*, pp. 33–34.

58. The text was ed. K. von Tischendorff, *Apocalypses Apocryphae* (Leipzig: Mendelssohn, 1866), pp. 70–94. For some comments, see A. Y. Collins, "Early Christian Apocalypses," pp. 76–77.

59. Using the translation of James Tabor in McGinn, *Visions of the End*, p. 55. Another Greek text, the *Apocalypse of Ezra* (of uncertain date), contains a description of Antichrist's appearance that is almost identical with Pseudo-John. See the introduction and translation by M. E. Stone, *Old Testament Pseudepigrapha*, vol. 1, pp. 561–79.

60. Later examples of Antichrist physiognomies, such as those in the Byzantine Pseudo-Daniel Apocalypse (ninth century) and in the medieval Irish tradition, will be treated in the next chapter.

61. See Ernst von Dobschütz, *Christusbilder: Untersuchungen zur christlichen Legende* (Leipzig: Teubner, 1899).

62. I have left out such important Latin authors as Hilary of Poitiers and Ambrose, both of whom showed interest in the Final Enemy. On Ambrose's teaching, see the handy summary in F. Homes Dudden, *The Life and Times of St. Ambrose,* vol. 2 (Oxford: Clarendon Press, 1935), p. 664.

63. The *Catechetical Lectures* are found in PG 33:331–1180. I will use the translation of William Telfer in *Cyril of Jerusalem and Nemesius of Emesa,* Library of Christian Classics, vol. 4 (Philadelphia: Westminster, 1955), pp. 147–67 for Lecture 15.

64. The story of Simon Magus, based on Acts 8:9–25, took on considerable importance in Christian literature from the second century. The popular story of his flight before amazed multitudes in Rome and his fall due to the prayers of Peter first appears in the apocryphal *Acts of Peter* 32 (c. 190 C.E.). The picture of Simon as one who claimed to be God and Christ has obvious similarities with Antichrist, which seem to have led to his being viewed as an "antichrist," at least in the immanent sense understood by Origen (see *Commentary on Matthew* 24 in PG 13:1643A and 1659D). The legend of his attempted flight seems to have influenced subsequent accounts of Antichrist's ascension (to be studied below), not the other way round, as Bousset claimed in *Antichrist Legend,* pp. 147–51. For an introduction to the figure of Simon, see G. N. L. Hall, "Simon Magus," *Encyclopedia of Religion and Ethics,* ed. James Hastings, vol. 11 (New York: Scribners, 1921), pp. 514–25.

65. Not all believed that Antichrist would be enthroned in the physical temple in Jerusalem. John Chrysostom, for example, argued that the temple meant is the Church; see *Homily 3 on 2 Thess.* (PG 62:482). Hilary of Poitiers shows the contemporary uncertainty by advancing both views (cf. PL 9:1054A and PL 10:616C).

66. The homily is edited in PG 10:901–52 and in G. Bonwetsch and H. Achelis, *Hippolytus Werke 1* (Leipzig: J. C. Hinrichs, 1897), pp. 287–309. References to monks (c. 912A) and praise of virginity (944C) point to a date not earlier than the mid–fourth century. Hippolytus's treatise is used extensively, constituting about a fifth of the whole. Bousset's argument that Pseudo-Hippolytus depends on Pseudo-Ephrem and not vice versa (*Antichrist Legend,* pp. 41–42) I find questionable. H. Achelis, *Hippolytenstudien, Texte und Untersuchungen,* Neue Folge I.4 (Leipzig: J. C. Hinrichs, 1897), p. 79, claimed that the text was at the earliest ninth century in date, but because the Pseudo-Hippolytus lacks the double manifestation of Antichrist, as well as other motifs characteristic of Byzantine apocalyptic literature c. 600 C.E. and after, I see no strong reason for such a late dating.

67. On the identification of Antichrist with the devil, see cc. 913A, 924B, 941C, and esp. 923D–25A: "Because the Savior of the world, wishing to save the human race, was born from the immaculate virgin Mary, in the form (*schēma*) of flesh treading down the Enemy by the power of his divinity, in the same way the devil will come forth upon the earth from an impure woman, deceptively born from a virgin. . . . Even if the devil can take on flesh, it is only by way of appearance."

68. In the East, for instance, John Chrysostom clearly denies that Satan is the Antichrist; see *Homily 3 in 2 Thess.* (PG 62:482).

69. Pseudo-Hippolytus, *On the Consummation* 23 (c. 925C).

70. Some elements in the text are innovative, e.g., 666 is interpreted as *arnoumai,* that is, "I deny"—the slogan his followers are to address to all Christian beliefs (see c. 933A). This seems to be based on 1 John 2:22 where the Antichrist is anyone who denies (*ho arnoumenos*) Jesus is the Christ.

71. *On the Consummation* 29 (c. 933AB): "Before all he shows himself taken up into heaven with trumpets and sounds and the great shout of those proclaiming with un-

speakable hymns." Bousset has plausibly argued that this witnesses to the conflation of the legend of Simon Magus with that of Antichrist (*Antichrist Legend,* pp. 146–47).

72. Jerome's views on Antichrist are to be found mostly in his exegesis, especially in his *Commentary on Daniel,* which he published after much delay in 407. The work was a polemical one, designed in large part to counter a lost work of the pagan Porphyry who had discerned the truth about Daniel—that it was not a sixth-century prophecy of things to come but was written in the second century by a contemporary of Antiochus Epiphanes. The *Commentary on Daniel* is edited by F. Glorie in *Sancti Hieronymi Presbyteri Opera. Pars I. Opera Exgetica 5* (Turnhout, Belg.: Brepols, 1964. CC 75A). For an introduction, see J. N. D. Kelley, *Jerome* (New York: Harper & Row, 1975), pp. 298–301. Also important is Letter 121 to Algasius, which summarizes Antichrist's career, citing a standard range of texts (2 Thess. 2, Matt. 24, Apoc. 17, John 5:43, Isaiah, and Daniel).

73. *Commentary on Daniel* 7:8 (ed. Glorie, pp. 843–44).

74. Letter 121.11 (ed. I. Hilberg, CSEL 66.2), p. 53.

75. Ep. 121.11 (ed. Hilberg, p. 55); and *Comm. on Dan.* 11.24 (ed. Glorie, p. 917).

76. *Comm. on Dan.* 11:39 (ed. Glorie, p. 928).

77. *Comm. on Dan.* 11:45 (ed. Glorie, pp. 933–34). See also *Comm. on Isa.* 8:25 (CC 73, p. 327). It should be noted that this is not yet explicitly an attempt to parody Christ's Ascension. It is only when the theme of Antichrist's flight (found in the Pseudo-Hippolytus) is combined with the Mount of Olives location that this important element in the legend, which will bulk large in later chapters, is born.

78. *Comm. on Matt.* (CC 77, p. 233). See *Comm. on Dan.* 12:12 (ed. Glorie, p. 944). On this aspect of Jerome's thought, see R. E. Lerner, "The Refreshment of the Saints," pp. 102–3.

79. For an overview of the importance of the two, especially in the history of the interpretation of the Apocalypse, see Paula Fredriksen, "Tyconius and Augustine on the Apocalypse," in *The Apocalypse in the Middle Ages,* ed. Richard K. Emmerson and Bernard McGinn (Ithaca, NY: Cornell Univ. Press, 1992), pp. 30–37. "Bible belt" is Fredriksen's expression (p. 21).

80. The standard edition of F. C. Burkitt (1894) has been reprinted with a translation by William S. Babcock, *Tyconius: The Book of Rules* (Atlanta: Scholars Press, 1989). All references will be to this text and translation. For a recent interpretation, see Pamela Bright, *The Book of Rules of Tyconius: Its Inner Purpose and Logic* (Notre Dame, IN: Univ. of Notre Dame, 1988).

81. See Kenneth B. Steinhausen, *The Apocalypse Commentary of Tyconius: A History of Its Reception and Influence* (New York and Frankfurt: Peter Lang, 1987).

82. Babcock, *Tyconius,* pp. 111–15.

83. Ibid., pp. 121–25.

84. E.g., the conclusion of Rule 3 (Babcock, *Tyconius,* p. 54) presupposes this. For a general study of Tyconius's view of Antichrist, see Horst Dieter Rauh, *Das Bild des Antichrist im Mittelalter: Von Tyconius zum Deutschen Symbolismus* (Münster: Aschendorff, 1973), pp. 102–21. A number of scholars (e.g., Rauh, pp. 105, 110) have thought that Tyconius considered the final Antichrist to be imminent, but Paula Fredriksen has shown that, in keeping with the real thrust of his thought, Tyconius maintained an antiapocalyptic agnosticism about the time of the end, one which was to be echoed by Augustine. See her article, "Tyconius and the End of the World," *Revue des études augustiniennes* 28(1982): 59–75.

85. There is a large literature on this. For recent surveys, see B. McGinn, *Calabrian Abbot,* pp. 62–67, 82–85; and P. Fredriksen, "Tyconius and Augustine," pp. 29–35.

86. The key texts are *Homily* 3.4–10 and *Homily* 7.2 (PL 34:1999–2003 and 2030). I make use here of the translation of John Burnaby in *Augustine: Later Works,* Library of Christian Classics (Philadelphia: Westminster Press, 1955), pp. 280–83, 312.

87. This is not to say that interest was lacking in the East in the fifth century. For example, Theodoret of Cyrus (393–466 C.E.), the last of the great Antiochene exegetes, has an interesting section on Antichrist in his *Compendium of All the Heresies* 5.23 (PG 83:525–32).

88. See *Quodvultdeus: Livre des promesses,* ed. René Brau, vol. 2 (Paris: Éditions du Cerf, 1964. SC 101–2), pp. 632–34.

89. Victorinus, *Commentary on the Apocalypse* (ed. I. Haussleiter in CSEL 49, pp. 123–27). A similar identification is found in the continuations of the *Liber Genealogus* of the fifth century. See R. Landes, "Lest the Millennium Be Fulfilled," p. 162. The Vandal Huneric who persecuted the Catholics in Africa c. 480 was also identified with the Beast by Victor Vitensis in his *History of the Persecution of the African Province* 3.21.

90. The *Paschale Campanum* was edited by T. Mommsen in *Monumenta Germaniae Historica* (hereafter MGH), *Auctores Antiquissimi* vol. 9, pp. 745–50. Corrections to this and a detailed study by Fabio Troncarelli, "Il consolato dell'Antichristo," *Studi Medievali,* 3e Serie, 30(1989): 567–92, show that the text probably comes from Vivarium and reflects the interests of Cassiodorus and his followers in apocalypticism.

91. The point is also emphasized by Jenks, e.g., *Origins,* p. 361: "The Antichrist myth was a specific form of theodicy with a marked Christocentric character."

Chapter Four

1. A number of studies of early medieval uses of Antichrist exist. Among older works, W. Bousset's *Antichrist Legend* retains considerable value. Horst Dieter Rauh's *Das Bild des Antichrist im Mittelalter: Von Tyconius zum Deutschen Symbolismus,* Beiträge zur Geschichte der Philosophie und Theologie des Mittelalters, Neue Folge, Band 9 (Münster: Aschendorff, 1973) concentrates on the twelfth-century German uses, but pp. 138–64 deal with the earlier period. The most useful work is Richard Kenneth Emmerson, *Antichrist in the Middle Ages: A Study of Medieval Apocalypticism, Art, and Literature* (Seattle: Univ. of Washington Press, 1981). For a list of 188 mostly pseudonymous apocalyptic texts, many from the medieval period, see Klaus Berger, *Die griechische Daniel-Diegese: Eine altkirchliche Apokalypse* (Leiden: Brill, 1976).

2. This dual aspect is well brought out by Emmerson, *Antichrist in the Middle Ages,* pp. 74–76.

3. This tradition was particularly strong among the commentators on the Apocalypse, on which see Wilhelm Kamlah, *Apokalypse und Geschichtstheologie: Die mittelalterliche Auslegung der Apokalypse vor Joachim von Fiore,* Historische Studien Heft 235 (Berlin: Ebering, 1935); and E. Ann Matter, "The Apocalypse in Early Medieval Exegesis," in *Apocalypse in the Middle Ages,* pp. 38–50.

4. For recent studies on the continued presence of true apocalypticism in the early Middle Ages, see Richard Landes, "Lest the Millennium Be Fulfilled: Apocalyptic Expectations and the Pattern of Western Chronography 100–800 C.E.," in *Use and Abuse of Eschatology in the Middle Ages,* pp. 137–211; and Johannes Fried, "L'attesa della fine dei tempi alla svolta del millennio," in *L'attesa della fine dei tempi nel Medioevo,* ed. Ovidio Capitani and Jürgen Miethke (Bologna: il Mulino, 1990), pp. 37–86.

5. Byzantine apocalypticism, surprisingly little investigated, has been enriched in recent years by a number of studies, notably those of Paul J. Alexander, such as "The

Diffusion of Byzantine Apocalypses in the Medieval West and the Beginnings of Joachimism," *Prophecy and Millenarianism: Essays in Honour of Marjorie Reeves,* ed. Ann Williams (Essex: Longford, 1980), pp. 53–106; and his posthumous *The Byzantine Apocalyptic Tradition,* ed. Dorothy deF. Abrahamse (Berkeley: Univ. of California Press, 1985).

6. Primasius's *Commentary on the Apocalypse,* written about 550 C.E., is dependent on Tyconius. He interpreted the wounded and restored head of the first Beast (Apoc. 13:3 and 12) as Antichrist's parody of Christ's Resurrection, and the second Beast's fire miracle (Apoc. 13:13) as a false Pentecost (see PL 68:879A and 882BD). These are two of the elements in what later was to become a noted threefold contrast between Christ and Antichrist. Cassiodorus, in his *Exposition on the Psalms* (CC 97–98), interpreted a number of Psalm texts as applying typologically to Antichrist and his times.

7. For Gregory on the Antichrist, see H. Savon, "Grégoire le Grand et l'Antéchrist," in *Grégoire le Grand* (Paris: CNRS, 1990), pp. 389–405.

8. Gregory the Great, *Dialogues* 3.38 (PL 77:316C). Numerous other texts witness to the same conviction, e.g., *Homily on Ezekiel* 2.6; and, among the pope's letters, those in *Register* 3.39, 10.15, and 11.37. For a translation of some of these texts, see McGinn, *Visions of the End,* pp. 62–65.

9. On Gregory's spirituality, see Carole Straw, *Gregory the Great: Perfection in Imperfection* (Berkeley: Univ. of California Press, 1988). Straw notes the extensive literature on Gregory's view of the end on p. 1, n. 2. On this, see esp. Raoul Manselli, *La "Lectura super Apocalypsim" di Pietro di Giovanni Olivi: Ricerche sull'Escatologismo Medioevale* (Rome: Istituto Storico Italiano per il Medio Evo, 1955), pp. 5–16; and Jacques Fontaine, "L'expérience spirituelle chez Grégoire le Grand," *Revue d'histoire de la spiritualité* 52 (1976): 141–54.

10. This view had contemporary applications. In 597 C.E., in the controversy over the title "universal priest" (*universalis pontifex*) that the patriarch of Constantinople had recently adopted, Gregory wrote to the Emperor Maurice condemning such pride as a sign of Antichrist's work. See *Register* 7.30, translated in McGinn, *Visions of the End,* p. 64; and Savon, "L'Antéchrist," pp. 398–400.

11. *Moralia* 25.15.34 (PL 76:343B). (I will cite the *Moralia,* as the work is called in Latin, from the readily available text found in PL 75–76, though there are more recent editions in SC and CC.) On the body of Antichrist, see especially *Moralia* 34.4.8 (722AC). For an overview of this lengthy work, see Susan E. Schreiner, "'Where Shall Wisdom Be Found?': Gregory's Interpretation of Job," *American Benedictine Review* 39(1988): 321–42.

12. Interiority is a central concept in Gregory, as shown by Paul Aubin, "Interiorité et extériorité dans le Moralia in Job de Saint Grégoire le Grand," *Recherches sciences religieuses* 62(1974): 117–66.

13. *Moralia* 33.29.56 (PL 76:709–10).

14. *Moralia* 14.21.25 (PL 75:1052–53). See Savon, "L'Antéchrist," pp. 390–96, who notes that Gregory seems to be drawn to this view by his desire to express the complete opposition between Christ whose humanity was assumed by the Word (*assumptus homo* Christology) and the devil who also assumes a human nature in Antichrist.

15. For a treatment of the Biblical types of Antichrist, see Emmerson, *Antichrist in the Middle Ages,* pp. 24–32.

16. Gregory lays such emphasis on these signs that it is clear he considered them as actual miracles. See, e.g., *Moralia* 32.15.24–25 and 33.27.48 (PL 76:650–51 and 703–4). These signs and trials will be of such strength that they cannot be overcome without divine aid (*Moralia* 34.8.17–9.20). The primary way in which the faithful will resist will be through preaching—"The higher that Behemoth lifts himself up against God's elect

through miracles, the more powerfully the saints will bind themselves to the task of preaching against him" (*Moralia* 34.9.20; PL 76:728A). Gregory's emphasis on Antichrist's miracles appears to have influenced the later traditions, both Latin and vernacular, that insisted on the reality of the Final Enemy's miraculous powers.

17. *Moralia* 34.3.7 (PL 76:721–22).

18. See *Moralia* 32.15.27 (PL 76:652B).

19. See *Homily on the Gospels* 2.34.9 (PL 76:1251B).

20. *Moralia* 32.16.23 (PL 76:653D). This interconnection of all evildoers is especially to the fore in *Moralia* 29.7.14–8.18 (PL 76:484–87). On Gregory's collective view of Antichrist, see Savon, "L'Antéchrist," pp. 396–98.

21. *Moralia* 29.7.14 (PL 76:653D).

22. The quoted phrase comes from *Moralia* 29.7.17 (PL 76:486C). For reflections on how preachers attack Antichrist every day, see *Moralia* 15.58.69 (PL 75:1117).

23. The most detailed studies of early medieval views on Antichrist are to be found in the investigations of the sources for the tenth-century treatise of Adso of Montier-en-Der to be treated below. The best of these is Daniel Verhelst, "Le préhistoire des conceptions d'Adson concernant l'Antichrist," *Recherches de théologie ancienne et médiévale* 40(1973): 52–103. See also Robert Konrad, *De ortu et tempore Antichristi: Antichristvorstellung und Geschichtsbild des Abtes Adso von Montier-en-Der* (Kallmunz: Michael Lassleben, 1964), especially chaps. 2 and 3; and Maurizio Rangheri, "La 'Epistola ad Gerbergam reginam de ortu et tempore Antichristi' di Adsone di Montier-en-Der e le sue fonti," *Studi Medievali,* 3e serie 14(1973): 677–732.

24. Among these conveyors of traditional teaching, the most important are Isidore of Seville (d. 636), the Venerable Bede (d. 735), and the Carolingian exegetes, Rabanus Maurus (d. 856) and Haymo of Auxerre (d. c. 865). Sometimes we even find a purely spiritual interpretation of Antichrist, as, for instance, in the ninth-century Irish thinker, John Scottus Eriugena, in his *Periphyseon* 5 (PL 122:1009B).

25. Among such writers we can number Agobard, bishop of Lyons 816–40. In his polemical work *Jewish Superstitions,* he claims that Jewish denial of Christ makes all Jews "antichrists," and he advises Emperor Louis the Pious to commission someone "to collect everything which the Church's teachers have understood, explained or signified concerning Antichrist in the sacred Scriptures," because his deception is drawing near (PL 104:94BC and 100C).

26. These texts can be found in McGinn, *Visions of the End,* pp. 67–68. Their connection with themes from the Antichrist legend has been studied by Berthold Rubin, *Das Zeitalter Justinians,* vol. 1 (Berlin: Walter de Gruyter, 1960), pp. 204, 441–54.

27. One other source has been thought to represent a possible tie between Justinian and Antichrist. A sixth- or seventh-century Roman chronicle known as the *Fasti Vindobonenses,* closely tied to the circle of Cassiodorus, under the year 523 records both the death of Boethius and Symmachus and the accession of Justinian—none of which actually took place in that year. F. Troncarelli ("Il Consolato dell'Anticristo," pp. 587–89) notes that if Boethius and Symmachus in their opposition to the Arian Theodoric might be considered as the "two witnesses" of Apocalypse 11, then Justinian could be seen as the Antichrist himself, born in 493 (see chap. 2, n. 232) and now revealed in his thirtieth year.

28. Gregory of Tours, *History of the Franks* 10.25.

29. *Passion of Leodegar* 1.15 in *MGH. script. rer. Meroving.* 5:296.

30. For a study of some of these passages, see R. Konrad, *De ortu et tempore Antichristi,* chap. 3.

31. E.g., Sibylline Oracle 2:187–95 (Jewish and Christian possibly from Phrygia, second century C.E.). It is interesting that this Sibylline mention is followed in ll.196–213 by an account of world conflagration just as we find in the "Muspilli." See also Justin, *Dialogue with Trypho* 49; and Lactantius, *Divine Institutes* 7.17.

32. E.g., Apocalypse of Elijah 4:13 and 5:32; and Gospel of Nicodemus 25.

33. I am using the translation by Kenneth Northcott found in McGinn, *Visions of the End,* p. 81. The term *Muspilli* appears to mean "end of the world."

34. I will use Henry A. Sanders, *Beati in Apocalypsim Libri Duodecim,* originally published in 1930 in Rome and reprinted in 1975 by Edilan in Madrid. For material on the Antichrist, see esp. pp. 495–509. For the role of this text in medieval art, still fundamental is Wilhelm Neuss, *Die Apokalypse des hl. Johannes in der altspanischen und altchristlichen Biblelillustrationen,* vol. 1 (Münster: Aschendorff, 1931), pp. 73–80.

35. Beatus, *Commentary on the Apocalypse* 4 (ed. Sanders, p. 368). On this passage, see R. Landes, "Lest the Millennium Be Fulfilled," pp. 193–94.

36. On Beatus's apocalypticism, see John Williams, "Purpose and Imagery in the Apocalypse Commentary of Beatus of Liébana," in *The Apocalypse in the Middle Ages,* pp. 217–33.

37. Beatus, *Letter to Elipandus* 2.6 and 16 (PL 96:981, 987–88, 1028).

38. *Letter of the Bishops of Spain to the Bishops of Gaul* 5, ed. Ioannes Gil, in *Corpus Scriptorum Muzarabicorum* (Madrid: Instituto "Antonio de Nebrija," 1973), p. 92.

39. The illustrated apocalypses and related manuscripts of the Middle Ages (174 in all) have recently been surveyed in "Census and Bibliography of Medieval Manuscripts Containing Apocalypse Illustrations, ca. 800–1500" by Richard Kenneth Emmerson and Suzanne Lewis appearing in *Traditio* 40(1984): 337–79; 41(1985): 367–409; 42 (1986): 443–72. The Beatus Apocalypses are nos. 8–32.

40. The ninth-century Byzantine chronicler, Theophanes, claimed that Sophronius, the patriarch of Jerusalem at the time of its fall, cited Daniel on the Abomination of Desolation as the Muslims set up the al-Aksa mosque on the temple mount, but this may well be the historian's reconstruction. See Walter E. Kaegi, "Initial Byzantine Reactions to the Arab Conquest," *Church History* 38(1969): 139–49.

41. Among older works, see Paul Alphandéry, "Mahomet-Antichrist dans le Moyen Age," *Mélanges Hartwig Derenbourg* (Paris: Leroux, 1909), pp. 261–77. In what follows I have been helped by the unpublished paper of John Tolan, "*Spes nostra Christus est:* Christian Views of Islam in Eighth- and Ninth-Century Spain." My thanks are due to him.

42. Eulogius, *Memorial of the Saints* II.1.2 (PL 115:766).

43. *Memorial* I.6 (PL 115:744). For another contemporary reference to Muhammad as a "predecessor of Antichrist," see John of Seville, Letter VI.9 (PL 121:460).

44. This is developed in the second part of *Illuminated Instructions (Indiculus luminosus),* chaps. 21–35 (PL 121:535–66).

45. Paulus Alvarus, *Illuminated Instructions* 21 and 25–33 (PL 121:535A, 539C–52D).

46. *Illuminated Instructions* 21 and 34–35 (PL 121:535AC, 553A–56A). On Alvarus's method of exegesis in these identifications, see Henri de Lubac, *Éxègese médiévale,* vol. 2, no. 1 (Paris: Aubier, 1959–63), pp. 547–48.

47. *Illuminated Instructions* 21 (PL 121:536BD). This tally is based on a calculation of the apocalyptic three and a half times as equaling 245 years, because the Hebrews identify one "time" with 70 years (cf. Ps. 90:10). With some mistaken arithmetic, Alvarus figures the year 854 C.E., in which he is writing, as the year 229 of Arab domination. The use

of the apocalyptic three and a half would seem to indicate that he expects the end when the sixteen years elapse.

48. *Illuminated Instructions* 31 (PL 121:535D–36A).

49. On Odo's apocalypticism, see R. Manselli, *La "Lectura super Apocalypsim,"* pp. 32–36.

50. Odo of Cluny, *Life of St. Gerald of Aurillac,* Preface and 2.10 (PL 133:641A, 676C).

51. See, e.g., *Occupation* 7.116–24 and 579–84; and *Collations* 2.38.

52. See especially Gerhard Podskalsky, *Byzantinische Reichseschatologie: Die Periodisierung der Weltgeschichte in den vier Grossreichen (Daniel 2 und 7) und dem tausendjährigen Friedensreich (Apok. 20)* (Munich: Fink, 1972).

53. See McGinn, *Visions of the End,* pp. 32–36.

54. Among older works on this theme, see Franz Kampers, *Kaiserprophetieen und Kaisersagen im Mittelalter* (Munich: Luneberg, 1895). For an introduction to the Byzantine role, consult Paul J. Alexander, "Byzantium and the Migration of Literary Works and Motifs: The Legend of the Last Roman Emperor," *Mediaevalia et Humanistica* n.s.2 (1971): 47–82. For the later period, there is much material in Marjorie E. Reeves, *The Influence of Prophecy in the Later Middle Ages: A Study of Joachimism* (Oxford: Clarendon Press, 1969), pt. 3.

55. One of these versions was edited by Ernst Sackur, *Sibyllinische Texte und Forschungen* (Halle: Niemeyer, 1898), pp. 177–87. Sackur also included a lengthy study. The section on the Last Emperor is translated in McGinn, *Visions of the End,* pp. 49–50.

56. David Flusser, "An Early Jewish-Christian Document in the Tiburtine Sibyl," *Paganisme, Judaisme, Christianisme: Mélanges offerts à Marcel Simon* (Paris: Boccard, 1978), pp. 153–83, argues for a late first-century date for the core of this Sibylline work. My reasons for doubting this have been spelled out in "The Sibylline Tradition in the Middle Ages," *Women in the Middle Ages: Essays in Honor of John H. Mundy* (Oxford: Blackwell, 1985), pp. 27–28.

57. Paul J. Alexander, *The Oracle of Baalbek: The Tiburtine Sibyl in Greek Dress* (Washington, DC: Dumbarton Oaks, 1967).

58. For a summary, see *Oracle of Baalbek,* pp. 136–43, and the chart on p. 66, which is also reproduced in McGinn, *Visions of the End,* p. 295.

59. Notably, the fact that the Last Emperor's career is usually tied to overcoming the Ismaelites, that is, the Arabs, and therefore makes more sense in a seventh-century setting. There are also signs that the Pseudo-Methodius account was known to the eleventh-century redactors of the *Tiburtine Sibyl.* Even Alexander, who at one time thought that the Last Emperor account in the *Tiburtine Sibyl* might date from the fourth century, eventually gave up this view; see Alexander, *Byzantine Apocalyptic Tradition,* p. 163, n. 44.

60. Among the distinctive characteristics of the account of the Last Emperor found in the surviving Latin versions of the *Sibylla Tiburtina* are (1) the physical description and name, (2) his victory over Gog and Magog, (3) the length of his reign, and (4) the description of the imperial regalia. These differences led Sackur, *Sibyllinische Texte,* pp. 167–69; R. Konrad, *De ortu et tempore Antichristi,* pp. 43–52; and M. Rangheri, "La 'Epistola ad Gerbergam de ortu et tempore Antichristi," pp. 708–10, to argue that the *Tiburtine Sibyl's* account is not dependent on the Pseudo-Methodius but was found in the fourth-century original.

61. This text, which survives in a Latin version, was first edited and studied by C. P. Caspari, *Briefe, Abhandlungen und Predigten* (Christiana, Sweden: n.p., 1890). There

is a better edition by Daniel Verhelst, "Scarpsum de dictis sancti Efrem prope fine mundi," *Pascua Mediaevalia: Studies voor Prof. Dr. J.M. de Smet* (Leuven: Univ. Press, 1983), pp. 518–28. The most recent critical study is found in Alexander, *Byzantine Apocalyptic Tradition,* pp. 136–47, who argues for a Syriac origin in the late sixth or early seventh century. For a partial translation, see McGinn, *Visions of the End,* pp. 60–61. There are also Greek and Syriac materials about the end ascribed to Ephrem (see Berger, *Daniel-Diegese,* pp. xv–xvi), but I will concentrate on the surviving Latin text.

62. A critical edition of the Syriac, Greek, and Latin versions of this work is currently being prepared for the *Corpus Christianorum* Series under the editorship of G. J. Reinink and D. Verhelst. Marc Laureys and Daniel Verhelst survey 196 Latin mss. of four different recensions in "Pseudo-Methodius, *Revelationes:* Textgeschichte und kritische Edition, Ein Leuven-Groninger Forschungsprojekt," in *Use and Abuse of Eschatology in the Middle Ages,* pp. 112–36. There is no complete edition of the Syriac text, but there is a translation of the version found in one ms. in Alexander, *Byzantine Apocalyptic Tradition,* pp. 36–51. The Greek texts have been edited by Anastasios Lalos in two volumes: *Die Apokalypse des Ps.-Methodios,* Beiträge zur klassischen Philologie 83 (Meisenheim am Glan: Anton Hain, 1976); and *Die dritte und vierte Redaktion des Ps.-Methodios,* Beiträge zur klassischen Philologie 94 (Meisenheim: Hain, 1978). I will use the Latin text of the first redaction as edited in Sackur's *Sibyllinische Forschungen,* pp. 59–96, part of which I have translated in McGinn, *Visions of the End,* pp. 73–76.

63. Pseudo-Ephrem was not the first writer to use 1 Cor. 15:24 in relation to the end of the Roman Empire. It is also found in Ambrose, *Exposition on the Gospel of Luke* X.10–14 (ed. Adriaen in CC 14, pp. 348–49).

64. Ed. Verhelst, pp. 525 l.75–526 l.79. The races referred to, the "gentes bellicae," are described in terms commonly used of the Huns in the fifth- and sixth-century versions of the Alexander Legend, on which see McGinn, *Visions of the End,* pp. 56–59. The Pseudo-Ephrem does not, however, identify them with Gog and Magog, as other apocalyptic texts do.

65. Earlier scholarship often argued for a date in the 650s or 660s, but G. J. Reinink in his article "Pseudo-Methodius und die Legende vom Römische Endkaiser," in *Use and Abuse of Eschatology,* pp. 82–111, makes a cogent argument for the later date (see esp. p. 85, n. 15).

66. There is a considerable literature devoted to Pseudo-Methodius. Among older contributions, we should note the article of Michael Kmosko, "Das Rätsel des Pseudomethodius," *Byzantion* 6(1931): 273–96. Paul J. Alexander wrote much on the text. Especially important are his "Byzantium and the Migration of Literary Works and Motifs: The Legend of the Last Roman Emperor," and the materials contained in *The Byzantine Apocalyptic Tradition.* Most recently G. J. Reinink has published a series of important papers devoted to it.

67. This account of world history shows dependence on the sixth-century Syriac work known as *The Cave of Treasures.* See Alexander, *Byzantine Apocalyptic Tradition,* p. 26; and especially G. J. Reinink, "Der Verfassername 'Modios' der syrischen Schatzhöhle und die Apokalypse des Pseudo-Methodios," *Oriens Christianus* 67(1983): 46–64.

68. Josephus, *Jewish War* 7:7,4; and *Antiquities* 1:6,1.

69. Andrew Runni Anderson, *Alexander's Gate, Gog and Magog, and the Enclosed Nations* (Cambridge: Mediaeval Academy, 1932), p. 8. This is still the best study of this tradition.

70. Earlier Christian interpreters, possibly Commodian, and certainly Ambrose in the fourth century and Quodvultdeus in the fifth, had already identified the invading Goths with Gog and Magog. See Anderson, *Alexander's Gate,* pp. 9–12.

71. In the Pseudo-Methodian version, which depends on the "Syriac Legend of Alexander" of c. 630 C.E., Philip, king of Macedon, marries Chuseth, daughter of the king of Cush (i.e., Ethiopia) to produce Alexander. Alexander died without issue, but the Methodian text has Chuseth marry one of Alexander's generals, Byzas, the founder of Byzantium, and treats their issue as descendants of the great conqueror. Their daughter, Byzantia, weds Armalaos (i.e., Romulus), king of the Romans. The purpose of this convoluted genealogical fiction is to show that the Byzantine Last Emperor will be the heir of both Alexander and the imperial line of Ethiopia, which, as we will see, made claims to this special eschatological status.

72. The most important earlier texts are the metrical homily ascribed to the Syrian church leader Jacob of Sarugh (d. 521), which has both Gog and Magog and subsequently the Antichrist issuing through Alexander's Gate (see the translation of E. A. Wallis Budge reprinted in McGinn, *Visions of the End,* pp. 57–59), and the Syriac Alexander Legend mentioned above. On these two (whose chronological relationship is not easily determined), see the discussion in Anderson, *Alexander's Gate,* pp. 20–27. The apocalyptic aspects of the career of Alexander (who is known as Dulcarnain) also are found in the sacred book of Islam, the Qur'an, in Sura 18.85 ff.

73. Alexander trans., pp. 44–46 (Sackur ed., pp. 80–86).

74. Alexander trans., pp. 47–48 (Sackur ed., pp. 86–89). See Reinink, "Pseudo-Methodius und die Legende," pp. 104–5.

75. Alexander trans., p. 48 (Sackur ed., p. 89). For the Greek text of this important passage, see Lalos, *Die Apokalypse,* pp. 122–23.

76. Alexander trans., p. 49 (Sackur ed., p. 91).

77. Alexander trans., p. 50 (Sackur ed., pp. 92–93).

78. Alexander trans., p. 50 (Sackur ed., pp. 93–94; Lalos ed., pp. 132–35). The central role ascribed to the Cross and Golgotha as history reaches its climax is an element that Methodius took over from the *Cave of Treasures.*

79. Alexander has studied the history of these biblical passages, both in the Pseudo-Methodius and in texts influenced by it, especially in *Byzantine Apocalyptic Tradition,* pp. 22–23, 164–70.

80. See Alexander, *Byzantine Apocalyptic Tradition,* pp. 174–84; and Alexander, "The Medieval Legend of the Last Roman Emperor and Its Messianic Origin," *Journal of the Warburg and Courtauld Institutes* 41(1978): 1–15.

81. See the discussion in G. J. Reinink, "Die syrischen Würzeln der mittelalterlichen Legende vom römischen Endkaiser," *Non Nova, sed Nove. Mélanges de civilisation médiévale dediés à Willem Noomen,* ed. M. Gosman and J. van Os (Groningen: n.p., 1984), pp. 195–209, who refutes Alexander point by point.

82. Alexander, *Byzantine Apocalyptic Tradition,* pt. 2, sect. 3, *The Legend of the Antichrist,* esp. pp. 217–22.

83. On the importance of this, see Alexander, *Byzantine Apocalyptic Tradition,* pp. 197–200.

84. For the text, see Alexander, *Oracle of Baalbek,* pp. 19–21 (trans. pp. 28–29), as well as the discussion pp. 111–17. The Eastern emperor Olibos may represent one Antichrist, while the "king who has a changed shape" would be the final Antichrist, who is reminiscent of the Antichrist who changes his signs in the Apocalypse of Elijah 3:17–18.

A curious detail, unique to the Oracle of Baalbek, has the Antichrist reigning for thirty years (ed. Alexander, p. 21, l.192). This may well be a mistake or scribal error for "after thirty years," that is, the standard distinction between the concealed and manifest stages of Antichrist's career.

85. The structure of the two accounts looks like this:

PSEUDO-METHODIUS	PSEUDO-EPHREM
I. Arab Invasions	[lacking]
II. Last Emperor Appears	[lacking]
1. Warlike Races of North	1. parallel
3. First Manifestation of Antichrist	2. End of Roman Empire
2. Last Emperor Surrenders Empire	3. First Appearance of Antichrist
4. Second Manifestation of Antichrist	4. parallel
[5. and 6. are lacking in Syriac]	5.–6.
7. Second Coming and End of Antichrist	7. parallel

It is noteworthy that the Syriac text translated by Alexander lacks all reference to the two witnesses (6.), but this is inserted into the Greek and Latin versions (see Lalos ed., pp. 138–40; Sackur ed., pp. 95–96). All versions of the Pseudo-Methodius omit mention of the forty-two months of Antichrist's reign (5.).

86. Antichrist's origin in Galilee is given a scriptural foundation. In most cases, the Final Enemy is said to be born in Babylon, but according to Methodius, "He will be conceived in Chorazin and will be born in Saidan [Bethsaida] and rule in Capernaum . . . And because of this Our Lord pronounced the *Woes* over the three of them (see Matt. 11:20–24) . . ." (Alexander trans., p. 50; cf. Sackur ed., p. 93).

87. The original Latin translation of the fourth century was reworked around 1000 C.E. by someone living in North Italy during the time of the Ottonian emperors. This version (I.) introduces a long *vaticinium ex eventu* listing rulers of Italy. It closes with a negative portrait of Otto III (d. 1002) whose reign is prophesied to last not more than five years. This text was recast c. 1030 (version II.) with another list of monarchs to bring it up to date. This is the text edited by Ernst Sackur in *Sibyllinische Texte und Forschungen,* pp. 177–87. A third form (III.) of c. 1090 added more material to create an anti-imperial prophecy often called the *Cumaean Sibyl.* Finally, about 1100, the Ottonian version was again reworked, incorporating some elements from the *Cumaean Sibyl* but also reflecting other traditions, in a text (version IV.) that appears to have been produced in south Germany or Austria.

88. Sackur ed., p. 185 (trans. McGinn, *Visions of the End,* p. 49).

89. See the translation in McGinn, *Visions of the End,* p. 50.

90. Examples are found in Arabic, Armenian, Greek, Hebrew, Coptic, Persian, Slavonic, and Syriac.

91. For a survey of the Pseudo-Daniel literature, see Albert-Marie Denis, *Introduction aux Pseudépigraphes grecs d'Ancien Testament* (Leiden: Brill, 1970), pp. 309–14. Berger, *Daniel-Diegese,* pp. xiii–xiv, lists sixteen different Pseudo-Daniel texts in various languages. The account in Alexander, *Byzantine Apocalyptic Literature,* pp. 61–95, is full, but deals with only three texts.

92. In 1976 Klaus Berger edited the text with a German translation and an extensive commentary in *Die griechische Daniel-Diegese.* In 1983, G. T. Zervos provided an English translation with introduction and comment, "Apocalypse of Daniel," *Old Testament Pseudepigrapha,* vol. 1, pp. 755–70. Zervos's text division (different from Berger's) and his

translation will be used here. Several other "Danielic" texts have interesting Antichrist sections, including the Slavonic Daniel (based on a Greek original of c. 829 C.E.) and the *Life of Andrew Salos,* a tenth-century work based in part on the *Apocalypse of Daniel.* See Lennart Ryden, "The Andreas Salos Apocalypse: Greek Text, Translation and Commentary," *Dumbarton Oaks Papers* 28(1974): 197–261.

93. *Apocalypse of Daniel* 3:12 even reads "This is his name: that which begins with the letter *K* of the alphabet." A name beginning with *C* (Greek *K*) also characterizes the Last Emperor of the *Tiburtine Sibyl.*

94. See Berger, "Exkurs V: Der Antichrist nach Dn.-D., die Aberkiosinschrift und der Ursprung des Fischsymbols im frühen Christentum," in *Daniel-Diegese,* pp. 104–15, esp. p. 110.

95. See the edition and translation in J. B. Lightfoot, *The Apostolic Fathers,* vol. 1, pt. 2 (London and New York: Macmillan, 1889), pp. 496–97.

96. For a structuralist interpretation of biblical water and fishing symbolism, see Edmund Leach, "Fishing for Men on the Edge of the Wilderness," in *The Literary Guide to the Bible,* ed. Robert Alter and Frank Kermode (Cambridge, MA: Belknap Press, 1987), pp. 579–99.

97. Berger, "Exkurs V," in *Daniel-Diegese,* also points out the traditional association of the monster from the sea in the background to Antichrist (e.g., Dan. 7:3, Apoc. 13:1, and Leviathan as in Syriac Baruch 29). The account of Antichrist's birth is followed by a description of his monstrous appearance showing some affinities with the Pseudo-John Apocalypse and Greek Ezra Apocalypse discussed in the last chapter, but with unique elements (see *Apocalypse of Daniel* 9:16–27).

98. Three witnesses appear in Pseudo-Hippolytus, *On the Consummation of the World* 21, which some have taken as an argument for the late dating of the work, but this theme is also found in the sixth-century *Commentary on the Apocalypse* of Andrew of Caesarea, discussing Apoc. 10:10 and 11:3 (PG 106:310–11). Therefore, it is also possible to see the Pseudo-Hippolytus as the source for the three witnesses motif that appears both here and in other late Byzantine apocalypses, such as the Andrew Salos Apocalypse, the Greek Pseudo-Methodius, and the Vision of Daniel II. See the chart in Berger, *Daniel-Diegese,* at p. 148; and Bousset, *Antichrist Legend,* pp. 208–9.

99. The modern form of the legend was popularized by Jules Michelet in the second volume of his *History of France* first published in 1833. See esp. Jules Roy, *L'an mil: Formation de la légende de l'an mil; état de la France de l'an 950 à 1050* (Paris: Hachette, 1885); and Emile Gebhardt, "L'État d'âme d'un moine de l'an mil," *Revue des deux mondes,* ser. 9, 107(1891): 600–628.

100. In his *Apologetic Work* Abbo writes: "When I was a young man I heard a sermon about the end of the world preached before the people in the cathedral of Paris. According to this, as soon as the number of a thousand years was completed, the Antichrist would come and the Last Judgment would follow in a brief time. I opposed this sermon with what force I could from passages in the Gospels, the Apocalypse and the Book of Daniel" (PL 139:471, as translated in McGinn, *Visions of the End,* p. 89).

101. E.g., Ferdinand Lot, "Le myth des terreurs de l'an mille," *Mercure de France* 301(1947): 639–55; and Pierre Riché, "Der Mythos von den Schrecken des Jahres 2000," in *Die Schrecken des Jahres 1000,* ed. H. Cavanna (Stuttgart: Klett, 1977), pp. 10–19.

102. E.g., Henri Focillon, *The Year 1000* (New York: Harper & Row, 1969), chap. 1; and recently Johannes Fried, "L'Attesa della fine dei tempi alla svolta del millennio," who delimits the period of fears as 979–1033 C.E.

103. Given Ireland's isolation due to the Viking invasions beginning c. 800 C.E., it is difficult not to think that these Eastern materials arrived much earlier, but the channels of communication and dating are shrouded in mystery.

104. See Martin McNamara, *The Apocrypha in the Irish Church* (Dublin: Institute for Advanced Studies, 1975); and D. N. Dumville, "Biblical Apocrypha and the Early Irish: A Preliminary Investigation," *Proceedings of the Royal Irish Academy,* vol. 73, sect. C, no. 8 (1973): 299–338.

105. See Bernhard Bischoff, "Vom Ende der Welt und vom Antichrist (I); Fragment einer Jenseitsvision (II) (Zehntes Jahrhundert)," in *Anecdota Novissima: Texte des vierten bis sechzehnten Jahrhunderts* (Stuttgart: Anton Hiersemann, 1984), pp. 80–84. The ms. is today in the Municipal Library in Avranches, ms. 108, and the text, partially destroyed, is found on fols. 111v–15r.

106. Bischoff, "Vom Ende der Welt," p. 82.

107. For background on the phoenix legend, see Sister Mary Francis McDonald, "Phoenix Redivivus," *The Phoenix* 14(1960): 187–206.

108. See Douglas Hyde, "Mediaeval Account of Antichrist," in *Mediaeval Studies in Memory of Gertrude Schoepperle Loomis* (New York: Columbia Univ. Press, 1927), pp. 391–98. The text uses many particulars from the standard Western account, as found in Adso and his successors. A more recent translation can be found in *Irish Biblical Apocrypha,* ed. Maire Herbert and Martin McNamara (Edinburgh: T & T Clark, 1989), pp. 149–50.

109. This history of this text has been studied by William W. Heist, *The Fifteen Signs Before Doomsday* (East Lansing: Michigan State Press, 1952); see pp. 93–95 for the connection with the Antichrist legend. The ultimate source is in the seven signs of the end found in the possibly fifth-century *Apocalypse of Thomas.* This pattern was reworked into fifteen signs in Ireland, the earliest witness being the tenth-century *Saltair na Rann* (see the summary in Heist, pp. 193–203). Heist lists 120 later versions of this popular account in his Appendix A.

110. R. Glaber, *History of His Times* 4.6 (PL 142:681D–82A), as translated in McGinn, *Visions of the End,* p. 90. In the *History* 4.4 Glaber also says that some saw the great famine of 1033 as announcing the end of mankind. See also the *History* 2.6 and 12.

111. The author, like Abbo, is antiapocalyptic, doubtless an adherent of the standard Augustinian suspicion of expectations of the end in his argument that Gog and Magog are to be seen as heretics. For an edition of this text, see R. B. C. Huygens, "Un témoin de la crainte de l'an 1000: la lettre sur les Hongrois," *Latomus* 15(1956): 225–39, esp. pp. 231–33.

112. Gerbert of Aurillac, *Acts of the Council of Reims* in MGH *Scriptores,* vol. 3, p. 672. See also p. 676, which says that the split between Rome and various churches in East and West is the "falling away" (*discessio*) announced by Paul in 2 Thess. 2:3, implying that the Antichrist is near. Defenders of Rome took the Pope's opponents to task and in turn accused them of being "antichrists" (pp. 686–87).

113. See Fried, "L'Attesa della fine," pp. 38–39, for a discussion.

114. See Walter L. Wakefield and Austin P. Evans, *Heresies of the High Middle Ages* (New York: Columbia Univ. Press, 1969), p. 74.

115. The earlier (c. 950) Anglo-Saxon homilies of the Blickling and Vercelli collections, though much concerned with eschatology in general, have very little on Antichrist. See Milton McC. Gatch, "Eschatology in the Anonymous Old English Homilies," *Traditio* 2(1965): 117–65.

116. For a brief overview, see Emmerson, *Antichrist in the Middle Ages,* pp. 150–55. For more detail, the standard work is Milton McC. Gatch, *Preaching and Theology in Anglo-Saxon England: Ælfric and Wulfstan* (Toronto: Univ. of Toronto Press, 1977). On Wulfstan's use of Adso, see Gatch, pp. 105–16.

117. The edition is *Adso Dervensis: De Ortu et Tempore Antichristi necnon et Tractatus qui ab eo Dependunt,* ed. D. Verhelst (Turnhout, Belg.: Brepols, 1976. CC 45). I have translated the text with introduction and notes in *Apocalyptic Spirituality,* pp. 81–96, which is the translation that will be used here.

118. See Richard Kenneth Emmerson, "Antichrist as Anti-Saint: The Significance of Abbot Adso's *Libellus de Antichristo,*" *American Benedictine Review* 30(1979): 175–90, developing ideas advanced by André Jolles, *Einfache Formen* (Darmstadt: Wissenschaftliche Buchgesellschaft, 1958), pp. 51–55.

119. Emmerson, "Antichrist as Anti-Saint," p. 177.

120. On the sources of Adso, see the studies of Konrad, *De Ortu et Tempore Antichristi*; Rangheri, "La *De Ortu et Tempore Antichristi* e le sue fonti"; and Verhelst, "La préhistoire des conceptions d'Adson concernant l'Antichrist." Verhelst, p. 101, and Rangheri, pp. 711–12, doubt that Adso knew the Ephrem or Methodius texts; but I would agree with Konrad, pp. 33, 37–42, 49, and 52, as well as Paul J. Alexander, "Byzantium and the Migration of Literary Works and Motifs," pp. 53 and 61, that he did. While it is possible that this Eastern structure reached the monk through lost sources, it is more likely, given the presence in the West of these materials, that he adapted them to his own purposes. A comparison of the two illustrates this:

ADSO	PSEUDO-EPHREM
I. Name of Antichrist and a Discussion of His Types	[lacking]
[1. lacking]	
	1. Warlike Races
	2. End of Empire
3. First Manifestation of Antichrist	3. First Manifestation (parallels)
—conception	(Matt.11:21)
—birth and early years (Matt. 11:21)	
—preaching and miracles	
5. Persecution of Christians for Three and a Half Years	[parallels with 5 below]
2. Last Emperor and End of Roman Empire	[parallels with Methodius]
4. Second Manifestation of Antichrist	4. Second Manifestation
	5. Three-and-a-Half-Year Persecution
6. The Two Witnesses	6. The Two Witnesses
7. Death of Antichrist and Time of Refreshment	7. Death of Antichrist and Second
[Second Coming lacking]	Coming

121. The opening of the second account (Verhelst ed., p. 126, ll.124–26) is especially forced, given how much has already been said: "Immediately, according to the saying of Paul the Apostle cited above, they say that Antichrist will be at hand. And then will be revealed the man of sin, namely, the Antichrist."

122. See Verhelst ed., p. 28, ll.157–60, and Bede, *Explanation of Times* 69 (PL 90:574A).

123. The miracles are: (1) fire coming down from heaven (Apoc. 13:13), (2) trees suddenly blossoming and withering, (3) the sea becoming stormy and suddenly calm,

(4) the elements changing, (5) diversions of bodies of water, (6) disturbing the air, and (7) raising the dead. The last, as we have seen, was often denied to Antichrist; but Haymo, one of Adso's primary sources, allowed it in his *Commentary on 2 Thessalonians* (PL 117:782A).

124. See Alcuin, *The Faith of the Holy Trinity* 3.19 (PL 101:51C); and Haymo, *Exposition on the Apocalypse* (PL 117:1073AB).

125. Adso's account of the Last Emperor is closer to Pseudo-Methodius than to the *Tiburtine Sibyl,* but there are still important differences between the two, especially the location (the Mount of Olives rather than Golgatha), the description of the imperial regalia, and the lack of any attention to the Holy Cross.

126. Verhelst ed., p. 36, ll.117–24 (McGinn trans., p. 93).

127. The confusion, which goes back at least to Gregory the Great, as we have seen, is also to be found in both Bede and Haymo.

128. See the discussion above, p. 75.

129. See Lerner, "The Refreshment of the Saints," pp. 106–8, on Haymo and Adso.

130. The later versions are edited and studied in Verhelst, pp. 30–166. They include:

1. the early eleventh-century version known as "Cuiusdam sapientis" (23 mss.)
2. a shorter form of this done in twelfth-century France (3 mss.)
3. the "Alcuin version," supposedly written by the Carolingian monk Alcuin and addressed to Charlemagne, but actually produced in late eleventh-century France (19 mss.)
4. a twelfth-century French version inserting passages from the *Tiburtine Sibyl* (4 mss.)
5. a version ascribed to "Albuinus" (eleventh century—56 mss.)
6. a late eleventh-century version based on this and ascribed to Rabanus Maurus (8 mss.)
7. a twelfth-century version from England ascribed to Anselm of Canterbury (24 mss.)
8. a version composed by Lambert of St. Omer about 1120 and ascribed to Methodius (14 mss.).

131. On the Old English version, see Richard K. Emmerson, "From *Libellus* to *Sermo*: The Old English Version of Adso's *Libellus de Antichristo,*" *Journal of English and Germanic Philology* 82(1983): 1–10.

132. Two dissertations have been devoted to the study of medieval Antichrist iconography: Jessie Poesch, *Antichrist Imagery in Anglo-French Apocalypse Manuscripts* (Ph.D. dissertation, University of Pennsylvania, 1966. Available through University Microfilms International, Ann Arbor, MI); and Gosbert Schüssler, *Studien zur ikonographie des Antichrist* (Inaugural-Dissertation, Ruprecht-Karl-Universität zu Heidelberg, 1975).

133. See Dale Kinney, "The Apocalypse in Early Christian Monumental Decoration," in *Apocalypse in the Middle Ages,* pp. 200–16.

134. See Peter Klein, "The Apocalypse in Medieval Art: An Introduction," in *Apocalypse in the Middle Ages,* pp. 175–77.

135. In my previous study in this area, "Portraying Antichrist in the Middle Ages," in *Use and Abuse of Eschatology,* pp. 13–15, I did not give sufficient attention to this part of the tradition.

136. See André Grabar and Carl Nordenfalk, *Early Medieval Painting* (Paris: Skira, 1957), pp. 144–45, on the relation of the Carolingian Utrecht Psalter to earlier prototypes.

137. See Jean Hubert, Jean Porcher, and W. F. Volbach, *Europe of the Invasions* (New York: Brazillier, 1969), illus. 205 (p. 196); and the discussion in Emmerson, *Antichrist in the Middle Ages,* pp. 119–20.

138. See Ahuva Belkin, "The Antichrist Legend in the Utrecht Psalter," *Rivista di storia e letteratura religiosa* 23(1987): 279–88.

139. Augustine and Cassiodorus read Ps. 13 as referring to the Jews. Ps. 52, whose relationship to Ps. 13 centers on the common text "the fool has said in his heart there is no God," is interpreted by Augustine as applying to the Jews and other evil persons. Cassiodorus refers it to all sinners but also notes that it treats the Last Judgment. See his *Commentary* (CC 97, pp. 478 and 481).

140. The name, under the form *Teitan,* is present both in the Beatus "Tables" and in many other Western sources, e.g., Bede, *Explanation of the Apocalypse* (PL 93:172B). These giant figures are also related to the illustrations of Abaddon, the angel of the abyss, in Apoc. 9. For discussions of the Antichrist images in the Beatus mss., see Poesch, *Antichrist Imagery,* pp. 77–116; and Schüssler, *Studien,* pp. 59–86.

141. A twelfth-century Beatus ms. from Lisbon has a possible third form of human Antichrist pictured under the opening of the sixth seal (Apoc. 6:12–14) as a mounted warrior shooting at a female figure representing the church. This too conforms to the tyrant image. See Carl-Otto Nordstrom, "Text and Myth in Some Beatus Miniatures," *Cahiers archéologiques* 25(1976): 10–12.

142. Bamberg Apocalypse, fol. 49v, showing the victory over the Beast and his prophet and their binding (Apoc. 19:19–20), and fol. 51r showing the binding and loosing of Satan (Apoc. 20:1–10) have the same figure accompanying the respective monsters—a naked human with dark skin and wild black hair. This latter can be seen as Satan incarnate, that is, Antichrist. See Ernst Harnischfeger, *Die Bamberger Apokalypse* (Stuttgart: Urachhaus, 1981), plates 45 and 46, and pp. 188–90 for a discussion. The same figure appears chained in hell in the Last Judgment scene on fol. 53r.

143. See Jessie Poesch, "The Beasts from Job and the *Liber Floridus* Manuscripts," *Journal of the Warburg and Courtauld Institutes* 33(1970): 41–51. Cf. Schüssler, *Studien,* pp. 87–99.

144. The Talmud is the standard collection of Jewish law and tradition consisting of the Mishnah and the Gemara. The two main forms, the Babylonian Talmud and the Palestinian Talmud, were formed between the second and the sixth centuries c.e.

145. Among older presentations, I have used Israel Levi, "L'Apocalypse de Zorobabel et le roi de perse siroes," *Revue des études Juives* 68(1914): 129–60. More recent accounts include Raphael Patai, *The Messiah Texts* (Detroit: Wayne State Univ. Press, 1979), pp. 157–64; and David Berger, "Three Typological Themes in Early Jewish Messianism: Messiah Son of Joseph, Rabbinic Calculations, and the Figure of Armillus," *AJS Review* 10 (1985): 141–64.

146. Patai, *Messiah Texts,* pp. 157–64, translates eight major accounts, which I will number as follows: (1) Midrash 'Aseret haSh'vatim; (2) T'fillat R. Shim'on ben Yohai; (3) Midrash waYosha'; (4) Nistarot R. Shim'on ben Yohai; (5) Sefer Zerubbabel; (6) Yemen ms. from Cambridge University Library, no. 890, Add. 3381; (7) Ma'ase Daniel; and (8) Doenmeh notebook.

147. Gershom Scholem, *The Messianic Idea in Judaism and Other Essays on Jewish Spirituality* (New York: Schocken, 1971), p. 18.

148. Joseph Heinemann, "The Messiah of Ephraim and the Premature Exodus of the Tribe of Ephraim," *Harvard Theological Review* 68(1975): 1–16.

149. Berger, "Three Typological Themes," pp. 143–48.

150. Patai, *Messiah Texts,* p. 156. The targums are Aramaic translations and often commentaries on biblical texts.

151. The descriptions given in 2, 3, 4, 5, and 7 have considerable similarity, while 6 represents a completely different tradition. There are individual parallels with a number of the Christian descriptions, but no consistent matches.

152. Patai, *Messiah Texts,* pp. 157–58.

153. The Syriac text (Alexander trans., p. 42) has "Armalaos," while the Latin (Sackur ed., p. 76) expands this to "Romyllus, qui et Armaleus." The same is found in the Greek (ed. Lalos, p. 86).

154. Berger, "Three Typological Themes," pp. 155–65.

155. This is the account in 3 (Patai, *Messiah Texts,* p. 160). In 4 and 5, the Messiah ben David slays Armillus with his breath, just as Christ slays the Man of Perdition in 2 Thess. 2:8.

156. Account 6 in Patai, p. 162, speaks of Antichrist's miracles, such as raising the dead; but in account 7 (p. 163) the children of Israel recognize his falsity because of his inability to perform three miraculous signs.

157. For a survey of Islamic eschatology, see William C. Chittick, "Eschatology," in *Islamic Spirituality: Foundations,* World Spirituality, vol. 19, ed. Seyyed Hossein Nasr (New York: Crossroad, 1987), pp. 378–409. For an account of more properly apocalyptic elements, see Arthur Jeffrey, "The Descent of Jesus in Muhammadan Eschatology," in *The Joy of Study.* Papers presented to Honor Frederick Clifton Grant, ed. Sherman F. Johnson (New York: Macmillan, 1951), pp. 107–26.

158. Literature on the Dajjāl is relatively sparse. For a brief survey, see A. Abel, "Al-DADJDJAL," in *The Encyclopedia of Islam,* vol. 2 (Leiden: Brill, 1965), pp. 76–77. I wish to thank Jeffrey Kaplan whose unpublished paper "The Dajjāl Legend" has also been helpful.

159. David J. Halperin, "The Ibn Sayyad Traditions and the Legend of Al-Dajjāl," *Journal of the American Oriental Society* 96(1976): 213–25.

160. Halperin, "The Ibn Sayyad Traditions," p. 220: "Umar said, 'O Apostle of God, give me leave to strike his neck!' The Apostle of God said, 'Leave him alone. If it is he whom you fear, you will not be able to kill him.'"

161. I am using the translation of J. Kaplan, "The Dajjāl Legend," from the *hadith* collection known as the *Sahih Al-Muslim.*

162. One *hadith* from the Al-Muslim collection, translated by Kaplan, "The Dajjāl Legend," says: "Anas b. Malik reported that Allah's Messenger (may peace be upon him) said: 'The Dajjāl would be followed by seventy thousand Jews of Isfahan wearing Persian shawls.'" Nevertheless, the Dajjāl legend never developed the excessive anti-Jewish sentiments of many elements of the Christian Antichrist legends.

163. Halperin, "The Ibn Sayyad Traditions," pp. 221–23.

164. For an argument in this direction, see Stephen Wasserstrom's unpublished paper, "The Moving Finger Writes: Mughira ibn Sa'id and the Interplay of Past and Future in the Institutionalization of the Dajjāl Myth."

165. As translated in John Alden Williams, *Themes of Islamic Civilization* (Berkeley: Univ. of California Press, 1971), p. 30. The notion that the Dajjāl will have three letters—*KFR,* for *kafir,* or unbeliever—written on his forehead parallels a number of Christian physiognomies, especially those of the Pseudo-John and Pseudo-Daniel Apocalypses.

166. Halperin, "The Ibn Sayyad Traditions," p. 223. In the Tamim al-Dari traditions the Dajjāl is guarded by a hairy Beast who also appears with him when he is

released. This might reflect the two Beasts of Apocalypse 13, given the witness's Christian background.

167. E.g., see the text of the great fourteenth-century Islamic historian Ibn Khaldun translated in Williams, *Themes,* p. 217: "He will be called the Mahdi, and shortly after this, the Dajjāl will emerge. After that, Jesus will come down and slay the Dajjāl. According to another version, Jesus will descend with the Mahdi and assist him to kill the Dajjāl and then will let the Mahdi lead him in ritual prayer." In Sunni traditions it is always Jesus who slays the Dajjāl; in Shi'i accounts it is often the Mahdi.

168. *Kanz al-'Ummal* VII, No. 2939, as translated in Jeffrey, "The Descent of Jesus," p. 110.

169. These were brought to my attention by Cornell H. Fleischer and are studied in his forthcoming paper, "The Lawgiver as Messiah: The Making of the Imperial Image in the Reign of Suleyman."

Chapter Five

1. There is a large literature on this period, though few general works. I shall again make use of my own *Visions of the End,* as well as Richard K. Emmerson's valuable *Antichrist in the Middle Ages.* Among older works we have the survey of Ernst Wadstein, *Die eschatologische Ideengruppe: Antichrist—Weltsabbat—Weltende und Weltgerichte in den Hauptmomenten ihrer christlichmittelalterlichen Gesamtentwicklung* (Leipzig: Reisland, 1896). For the twelfth century, see also Horst Dieter Rauh, *Das Bild des Antichrist im Mittelalter*; and for the later Middle Ages a work that retains value is Hans Preuss, *Die Vorstellungen vom Antichrist im späteren Mittelalter, bei Luther und in der konfessionellen Polemik* (Leipzig: Hinrich, 1906).

2. Ralph of Flavigny's account occurs in the midst of his *Commentary on Leviticus* in which he gives a typological application of Lev. 24:10–13 to Antichrist (the passage relates to a man of mixed Egyptian-Israelite blood whom Moses commanded to be stoned for blasphemy). This minitreatise can be found in the *Maxima Bibliotheca Veterum Patrum* (Lyon: n.p., 1677), vol. 17, pp. 217–21 (the passages cited are on p. 218).

3. For an attempt to describe some characteristics of reformist apocalypticism, see Kathryn Kerby-Fulton, *Reformist Apocalypticism and 'Piers Plowman'* (Cambridge: Cambridge Univ. Press, 1990).

4. For some suggestions regarding the relation of the Great Reform movement and apocalypticism, see McGinn, *Visions of the End,* sect. 12.

5. See Robert E. Lerner, "Refreshment of the Saints: The Time After Antichrist as a Station for Earthly Progress in Medieval Thought," *Traditio* 32(1976): 97–144; and "The Black Death and Western European Eschatological Mentalities," *American Historical Review* 86(1981): 533–52.

6. In concentrating on Western views of Antichrist, much interesting material from Eastern Christianity must be left out. This includes both texts that were restricted to the East, such as the twelfth-century Armenian *Sermon on Antichrist* (for the text and a Latin translation, see Giuseppe Frasson, *Pseudo Epiphanii Sermo de Antichristo* [Venice: S. Lazzaro, 1976]), and materials that originated in the East and were later made available in Latin. Among these was the *Prophecy of the Erythraean Sibyl,* a twelfth-century Byzantine work that became popular in Latin from the mid–thirteenth century on. For an introduction to and partial translation of this sibylline, see McGinn, *Visions of the End,* pp. 122–25.

7. The *Ordinary Gloss,* which was produced by theological scholars in northern France in the first half of the twelfth century, provided a compilation of passages from

the Fathers and early medieval exegetes "glossing," i.e., explaining each verse in the Bible. The version of the *Gloss* found in PL 113 under the name of Walafrid Strabo is defective, containing only the marginal and not the interlinear parts. More complete versions (though sometimes with later additions) are found in the early printings of Nicholas of Lyra's *Postilla universalis* and in the *editio princeps, Biblia Latina cum glossa Ordinaria* (Strassburg: Adolph Rusch, 1480/81), now available in reprint with modern editorial comments by Karlfried Froehlich and Margaret T. Gibson (Turnhout, Belg.: Brepols, 1992).

8. Emmerson, *Antichrist in the Middle Ages,* p. 37.

9. Berengaudus's *Exposition on the Seven Visions of the Book of the Apocalypse* is found in PL 17:843–1058; Richard's *On John's Apocalypse* is in PL 196:683–888.

10. Peter Lombard's *Commentary on 2 Thessalonians* is in PL 192:315–22.

11. The most extensive treatment of Honorius on Antichrist is to be found in Rauh, *Das Bild des Antichrist,* pp. 235–68.

12. See esp. *Elucidarium* 3.10 (PL 172:1163A–64A).

13. *Mirror of the Church,* "St. Michael" (PL 172:1011AC). The connection between hypocrisy and Antichrist is an ancient one, but it received new emphasis in the twelfth century. For some remarks (without notice of Honorius), see F. Amroy, "Whited Sepulchres: The Semantic History of Hypocrisy to the High Middle Ages," *Recherches de théologie ancienne et médiévale* 55(1986): 5–39.

14. Honorius, *Gem of the Soul* 3.134 (PL 172:679AC). See also 726AB.

15. The text is found in PL 172:347–496. For an introduction, see E. Ann Matter, *The Voice of the Beloved: The Song of Songs in Western Medieval Christianity* (Philadelphia: Univ. of Pennsylvania Press, 1990), pp. 58–76.

16. *Exposition* (351C–53C).

17. *Exposition* (351D and 471A–72D); cf. *Gem of the Soul* 3.134 (c. 679C).

18. See *Exposition* (472C–73A). On these illustrations, see Schüssler, *Studien zur Ikonographie des Antichrist,* pp. 100–09.

19. See Hugo Rahner, *Greek Myths and Christian Mysteries* (London: Burns & Oates, 1963), pp. 223–77 (pp. 272–75 on Honorius).

20. For a facsimile and study, see Rosalie Green et al., *Herrad of Hohenbourg: Hortus Deliciarum,* 2 vols. (London-Leiden: Brill, 1979).

21. For studies, see Jessie Poesch, *Antichrist Imagery in Anglo-French Apocalypse Manuscripts,* pp. 177–83; Schüssler, *Studien,* pp. 132–48; and Gérard Cames, *Allégories et symboles dans L'Hortus deliciarum* (Leiden: Brill, 1971), pp. 111–15. Poesch, pp. 209, 316, suggests that these pictures are based on earlier cycles, but there is no proof for this.

22. See, e.g., Horst Dieter Rauh, "Eschatologie und Geschichte im 12. Jahrhundert: Antichrist-Typologie als Medium der Gegenwartskritik,"in *Use and Abuse of Eschatology in the Middle Ages,* pp. 333–58; see esp. pp. 340, 344, 356–58.

23. See Gregory's *Register* 8.5 (the letter was written in 1080). Other uses of Antichrist language occur in *Register* 1.11, 1.15, 4.1, 4.2, 4.24, and *Collected Letters* 42 and 46.

24. Cardinal Beno, *Decree Against Hildebrand* 3.4 (*MGH. Libelli de Lite* 2:383). On these and other texts from the Investiture controversy, see Rauh, *Das Bild des Antichrist,* pp. 171–73.

25. Guibert of Nogent, *Deeds of God Through the Franks* 4 (tran. McGinn, *Visions of the End,* p. 92).

26. See McGinn, *Visions of the End,* pp. 88–89, for a discussion.

27. For a translation of part of this poem and comments, see McGinn, *Visions of the End,* pp. 97–98. For remarks on the importance of this shift, see McGinn, "Symbols of

the Apocalypse in Medieval Culture," *The Bible and Its Traditions,* ed. Michael Patrick O'Connor and David Noel Freedman (*Michigan Quarterly Review* 22, no. 3(1983): 265–83.

28. Rupert of Deutz, *Commentary on the Apocalypse* 8.13 (PL 166:1066BD, and so on). For a general study of Rupert, see John Van Engen, *Rupert of Deutz* (Berkeley: Univ. of California Press, 1983). On Rupert's teaching on Antichrist, the most complete survey is in Rauh, *Das Bild des Antichrist,* pp. 178–235, esp. on the seven kingdoms (pp. 206–17).

29. *Commentary on the Apocalypse* 9.16 (PL 169:1124B–25C).

30. On Gerhoh, see McGinn, *Visions of the End,* pp. 96–100 and 103–7. For studies of Gerhoh's apocalypticism and view of Antichrist, see Erich Meuthen, *Kirche und Heilsgeschichte bei Gerhoh von Reichersberg* (Leiden: Brill, 1959); Rauh, *Das Bild des Antichrist,* pp. 416–74; and Karl F. Morrison, "The Exercise of Thoughtful Minds: The Apocalypse in Some German Historical Writings," in *Apocalypse in the Middle Ages,* pp. 352–73.

31. This use of the four watches of the night as a way to present history's structure appears as early as Hilary of Poitiers, *Comm. on Matt.* (PL 9:1001D–02A).

32. Gerhoh, *The Fourth Watch* 11 (trans. McGinn, *Visions of the End,* p. 104.)

33. Gerhoh, *The Investigation of the Antichrist* 1.19 (cf. McGinn, *Visions of the End,* pp. 99–100).

34. E.g., Rauh, *Das Bild des Antichrist,* pp. 448–53; and R. Manselli, *La "Lectura super Apocalypsim" di Pietro di Giovanni Olivi,* pp. 63–64.

35. Gerhoh, *The Praise of Faith* in *Opera Inedita,* vol. 1, ed. D. Van Den Eynde and A. Rijmersdael (Rome: Spicilegium Pontificii Athenaei Antoniani, 1955–56), p. 197.

36. Gerhoh, *The Fourth Watch* 19 (trans. McGinn, *Visions of the End,* p. 106).

37. Gerhoh, *The Fourth Watch* 11 (trans. McGinn, *Visions of the End,* p. 105).

38. Evidence for this view has been seen in Gerhoh's claim that all the biblical prophecies about Antichrist have been fulfilled, "even if such a Beast which the crowd call the Antichrist to come has not arrived" (see *The Investigation of Antichrist,* "Preface" in *MGH. Libelli de Lite* 3:308). But this passage can also be interpreted in terms of a typological fulfillment that still awaits its historical complement.

39. E.g., see *The Fourth Watch* 18–19; and *Investigation of Antichrist* 1.66–67. Cf. Rauh, *Das Bild des Antichrist,* pp. 471–72.

40. The recent historical event referred to was the descent of Barbarossa on Rome in the summer of 1167, which ended in ignominious withdrawal after an outbreak of malaria in his army. The text from *Fourth Watch* is translated in McGinn, *Visions of the End,* pp. 106–7.

41. For a discussion of such passages, see Rauh, *Das Bild des Antichrist,* pp. 425–27, 430, 437–40, 456, 467–74.

42. Gerhoh, *Commentary on Psalm 64,* chap. 67 (*MGH. Libelli de Lite* 3:468).

43. Gerhoh, *Investigation of Antichrist* 1.44 (*MGH. Libelli de Lite* 3:352).

44. See Lerner, "The Refreshment of the Saints," pp. 113–15, on Gerhoh's place in the evolution of a post-Antichrist millenarianism.

45. There is, of course, no distinct Angel Pope figure in Gerhoh, but his place in the evolution of this new element in the apocalyptic scenario is important to note. See Bernhard Töpfer, *Das kommende Reich des Friedens* (Berlin: Akademie Verlag, 1964), pp. 30–32; and B. McGinn, "Angel Pope and Papal Antichrist," *Church History* 47(1978): 155–58.

46. For Anselm's view of Antichrist, see Rauh, *Das Bild des Antichrist,* pp. 270–302.

47. Bernard found the four eras symbolized in the four temptations of Ps. 90:5–6 (see his *Sermons on the Song of Songs* 33.7 and *Sermons on Psalm 90* 6.7). In one place (his *Sententia on the Four Temptations*) he ties the schema to the first four horsemen of the

Apocalypse. On Bernard's eschatological thought, see B. McGinn, "St. Bernard and Eschatology," *Bernard of Clairvaux: Studies Presented to Dom Jean Leclercq* (Washington, DC: Cistercian Publications, 1973), pp. 161–85.

48. E.g., Letters 124–26, 336, and 338.

49. Letter 56. See the translation and discussion in McGinn, "St. Bernard and Eschatology," pp. 169–70.

50. These are discussed in McGinn, "St. Bernard and Eschatology," pp. 170–72, 182–84.

51. For a translation of this letter, see McGinn, *Visions of the End*, pp. 113–14.

52. Eberwin, Letter 432 (under Bernard) in PL 182:676–80. On Eberwin, see Guntram G. Bischoff, "Early Premonstratensian Eschatology: The Apocalyptic Myth," in *The Spirituality of Western Christendom*, ed. E. Rozanne Elder (Kalamazoo, MI: Cistercian Publications, 1976), pp. 41–71.

53. The poem is no. 16 in Karl Strecker's edition, *Moralisch-Satirische Gedichte Walters von Chatillon* (Heidelberg: Carl Winter, 1929), pp. 139–47. Walter also denounces Barabarossa's Antipopes as antichrists in no. 15 in Strecker (pp. 137–38), and there is mention of Antichrist in several other poems. For an introduction to Walter, see F. J. E. Raby, *A History of Secular Latin Poetry in the Middle Ages*, vol. 2 (Oxford: Clarendon Press, 1957), pp. 190–204.

54. Since the translation cannot approach the flavor of Walter's effortless mastery of the medieval poetic form known as the "Goliardic stanza" (Vagantenstrophe), I also supply the Latin from Strecker:

> 10. Pape! que iam mora me tenet nasciturum?
> Fatum, quid me detines seculo venturum?
> Pande fores, quod si me tenes exiturum,
> in deo Beelzebub transgrediar murum (cf. Ps. 17:30).

55. Among the other twelfth-century Antichrist poems, the most interesting is the "Rime on the Last Days" ascribed to Peter the Deacon but actually written at Monte Cassino, probably in the 1130s during the schism of Anacletus II (there is a partial edition in PL 173:1143–44). It addresses contemporary issues of clerical simony and an evil, erroneous pope.

56. On Hildegard's apocalypticism in general, see K. Kerby-Fulton, *Reformist Apocalypticism and 'Piers Plowman,'* chap. 2. For her views on Antichrist in particular, see Rauh, *Das Bild des Antichrist*, pp. 478–527. In addition, I have profited from consulting the unpublished paper of Neal R. Clemens, "The Image of Woman and the Rape of Ecclesia in Hildegard of Bingen's *Scivias*," for which I thank the author.

57. On the connection of the *tempus muliebre* with Henry IV, see Letter 48 (PL 197:248D–49C) and the *Book of Divine Works* 3.10 (PL 197:1005BC and 1017AC).

58. On the images of women in Hildegard, see esp. Barbara Newman, *Sister of Wisdom: St. Hildegard's Theology of the Feminine* (Berkeley: Univ. of California Press, 1987).

59. Hildegard, *Scivias* 3.11 (trans. McGinn, *Visions of the End*, p. 101).

60. Ibid. (trans. McGinn, *Visions of the End*, p. 102). On Hildegard's view of the time after Antichrist, see Lerner, "The Refreshment of the Saints," pp. 112–13.

61. Hildegard, *Scivias*, Book 3, Vision 11.25–40 (PL 197:714–22). There is a full translation in *Hildegard of Bingen: Scivias*, trans. Mother Columba Hart and Jane Bishop (New York: Paulist Press, 1990), pp. 497–508.

62. Hildegard, *Book of Divine Works* 3.10 (PL 197:997–1038).

63. On this, see K. Kerby-Fulton, *Reformist Apocalypticism,* pp. 34–45. The theme also appears in some of Hildegard's letters, such as Letter 48 to the Clergy of Cologne (PL 197:243–53) and Letter 52 to Werner of Kircheim (PL 197:269–71).

64. On Hildegard's apocalyptic scenario, see Kerby-Fulton, *Reformist Apocalypticism,* pp. 47–50.

65. This ongoing struggle is evident in many texts, e.g., *Scivias* 1.2 on the Fall (PL 197:387–404) and the *Book of Divine Work,* 2.5.15–16 (PL 197:914–16). See N. Clemens, "The Image of Woman and the Rape of Ecclesia"; and B. Newman, *Sister of Wisdom,* pp. 238–49.

66. Hildegard, *Book of Divine Works* 3.10.30 (c.1030B). Cf. 3.10.37 (c.1036D).

67. See Clemens, "The Image of Woman and the Rape of Ecclesia," who notes that the Gregorian reformers often compared simony to rape; on which see Gerd Tellenbach, *Church, State and Christian Society at the Time of the Investiture Controversy* (New York: Harper & Row, 1970), pp. 131–32.

68. See *Scivias* 3.11.25 and the *Book of Divine Works* 3.10.28.

69. Along with Clemens, also consult Rauh, *Das Bild des Antichrist,* pp. 500–502, on the issue of Antichrist's unchastity.

70. *Book of Divine Works* 3.10.32 (PL 197:1032C).

71. *Book of Divine Works* 3.10.36 (c.1036A). See also 3.10.35 and *Scivias* 3.11.37–39.

72. Rauh, *Das Bild des Antichrist,* pp. 520–27, also stresses Hildegard's originality.

73. For an introduction to Gebeno, which includes a citation of the text where he mentions Joachim, see Kerby-Fulton, *Reformist Apocalypticism,* pp. 28–31.

74. Otto of Freising, *The Two Cities* 6.36 (see McGinn, *Visions of the End,* pp. 98–99).

75. The most original observations are found in *The Two Cities* 8.4, where Otto presents Antichrist as a false dialectician in the scholastic mode whose arguments against the faith as contrary to reason and to pleasure delude "those who philosophize regarding the causes of things." On Otto's view of Antichrist, see Rauh, *Das Bild des Antichrist,* pp. 302–65.

76. Klaus Aichele surveys forty-three examples in his *Das Antichristdrama des Mittelalters, der Reformation und Gegenreformation* (The Hague: Nijhoff, 1974); pp. 27–34 deal with the *Ludus.*

77. Gerhoh of Reichersberg condemned a drama about Antichrist in his *The Investigation of Antichrist* 1.5 (*MGH. Libelli de Lite* 3:315). Gerhoh would scarcely have applauded the Tegernsee play, but we cannot be sure this was the play he was referring to. For a study, see Rauh, *Das Bild des Antichrist,* pp. 365–415.

78. A full English version is available in John Wright, *The Play of Antichrist* (Toronto: Pontifical Institute of Mediaeval Studies, 1967), based on the edition of Karl Young, *Drama of the Medieval Church,* vol. 2 (Oxford: Oxford Univ. Press, 1962), pp. 371–87. Unless otherwise noted, though, I shall use the partial translation in McGinn, *Visions of the End,* pp. 119–21.

79. The monarchs are: (1) the Roman emperor, who after his abdication reverts to his role as king of Germany; (2) the king of France; (3) the king of Greece (i.e., Byzantine emperor); (4) the king of Babylon (i.e., ruler of the Muslims); and (5) the king of Jerusalem, at that time a Western Christian ruler.

80. McGinn, *Visions of the End,* pp. 119–20.

81. F. Amory, "Whited Sepulchres," pp. 33–37, notes that this is the earliest appearance of Hypocrisy as an actual personified character.

82. Using the rhyming translation of Wright, *The Play of Antichrist,* p. 89. The Latin text is:

> Sanguine patrie honor est retinendus,
> Virtute patrie est hostis expellendus.
> Ius dolo perditum est sanguine venale.
> Sic retinebimus decus imperiale.

83. Wright, *The Play of Antichrist,* p. 97.

84. There is an extensive literature on Joachim. For brevity, I cite here only my book, *The Calabrian Abbot: Joachim of Fiore in the History of Western Thought* (New York: Macmillan, 1985).

85. Robert E. Lerner in "Antichrists and Antichrist in Joachim of Fiore," *Speculum* 60(1985): 553–70, argued (pp. 558–59) that Joachim developed the new reading of the Apocalypse, which made possible his novel Antichrist views, partly out of reading Bede. This is possible, but by no means certain. See also Lerner, "The Refreshment of the Saints," pp. 115–20.

86. See McGinn, *Calabrian Abbot,* chap. 6.

87. The importance of these patterns was first discerned by Marjorie E. Reeves, whose many works on Joachim remain central to modern study of the Calabrian. See esp. *The Influence of Prophecy in the Later Middle Ages* (Oxford: Clarendon Press, 1969), pp. 19–27. A key text is found in the *Book of Concordance,* book 2, pt. 1, chaps. 2–12, translated by E. R. Daniel in McGinn, *Apocalyptic Spirituality,* pp. 120–34.

88. From the abbot's "Letter to All the Faithful" (trans. in McGinn, *Apocalyptic Spirituality,* p. 117). See McGinn, *Calabrian Abbot,* p. 191, for texts on the imminence of the end of this *status.*

89. The "Dragon Figure" appears as Tavola 14 in *Il libro delle figure dell'Abate Gioachino da Fiore,* ed. Leone Tondelli, Marjorie E. Reeves, and Beatrice Hirsch-Reich (Turin: SEI, 1953). I quote from the translation of the accompanying text found in McGinn, *Apocalyptic Spirituality,* pp. 135–41. Another important summary of the abbot's teaching on Antichrist is found in chap. 8 of the introduction to the *Exposition on the Apocalypse* (Venice, 1527. Reprint, Frankfurt: Minerva, 1964), fols. 10ra–11ra, where Antichrist is also characterized as "king, priest, and prophet" (fol. 10vb).

90. Joachim, "Preface," *Book of Concordance,* ed. E. Randolph Daniel, *Abbot Joachim of Fiore: Liber de Concordia Novi ac Veteris Testamenti,* vol. 78, pt. 8 (Philadelphia: Transactions of the American Philosophical Society, 1983), p. 13. This appears to be a slap at Adso. Joachim had no place for the imperial myths found in Adso and others. For him the German emperors were always agents of evil, though ones permitted by God for the good end of cleansing the Church.

91. The importance of the seven seals in Joachim's thought was first studied by Marjorie Reeves, "The Seven Seals in the Writings of Joachim of Fiore," *Recherches de théologie ancienne et médiévale* 22(1954): 211–31.

92. See McGinn, *Apocalyptic Spirituality,* p. 137. Joachim understood the seven-headed beasts of the Apocalypse, that is, the Dragon of Apoc. 12:3–4, the first Beast of Apoc. 13, and the Beast on which the Whore of Babylon rides in Apoc. 17:3–10, as various manifestations of the same force—the growth of the *corpus malorum* in the second *status.*

93. McGinn, *Apocalyptic Spirituality,* p. 136. There are a number of variations in the description of these persecutions in Joachim's writings. In the *Exposition,* fols. 10r–11r,

the kings are Herod, Nero, Constantius, Chosroes, one of the Kings of Babylon (which for Joachim means a persecuting German emperor), Saladin, and the Antichrist.

94. *Exposition,* fol. 133ra.

95. The caption on the "Dragon Figure" reads "Gog. He is the Final Antichrist" (*ultimus antichristus*). See Fig. 8.

96. Lerner, "Antichrists and Antichrist," pp. 559–60.

97. McGinn, *Calabrian Abbot,* p. 150. See chap. 5, esp. the chart on pp. 148–49, which lays out the structure of the *Exposition*.

98. Lerner, "Antichrists and Antichrist," pp. 560–65, gives a good account of the development and hesitations. Even as late as *Exposition,* fol. 215ra, Joachim wonders whether it is better to call Gog Antichrist or the "general of Antichrist's armies."

99. Lerner, "Antichrists and Antichrist," p. 566.

100. "Dragon Figure," in McGinn, *Apocalyptic Spirituality,* p. 138.

101. In *Exposition,* fol. 134rb, Joachim recounts his conversation with a man who had been held captive in Alexandria concerning a projected alliance between the two dread "sects," that of Islam and that of the Western heretics (*patareni*).

102. *Exposition,* fol. 168ra. See Lerner, "Antichrists and Antichrist," pp. 568–70, on the priestly and royal aspects of the seventh-head Antichrist.

103. In the famous account of Joachim's interview with Richard the Lionhearted, the abbot is said to have asserted this unambiguously. See Roger of Howden, in the Pseudo-Benedict of Peterborough, *Deeds of Henry II and Richard I* (Rolls Series 49.2, pp. 153–54): "The king said to him, 'Where is Antichrist born? Where will he reign?' Joachim responded . . . that it is believed that Antichrist himself is already born in the city of Rome and he will obtain the apostolic see there. . . . The king said to him, 'If Antichrist is born in Rome and will possess the apostolic see there, I know that he is the Clement who is now pope' [Clement III]. He said this because he hated that pope."

104. The abbot's role in the development of the Holy Pope of the last times who would withstand Antichrist is present in a number of texts, the best known being *Book of Concordance* 4.1.45 (ed. Daniel, p. 402). For a discussion, see McGinn, *Calabrian Abbot,* p. 112; and McGinn, "Angel Pope and Papal Antichrist," pp. 158–59. The pope would be aided in this task by the two new religious orders of "spiritual men" (*viri spirituales*), an important aspect of the abbot's apocalypticism that cannot be taken up here (see McGinn, *Calabrian Abbot,* pp. 112–13, 152–55).

105. See McGinn, *Calabrian Abbot,* chap. 4, esp. pp. 126–27.

Chapter Six

1. The most readily available edition is that published under the works of Albert the Great, *B. Alberti Magni . . . Opera Omnia,* vol. 34, ed. S. Borgnet (Paris: Vivés, 1895), pp. 241–45, for the materials on Antichrist. On Hugh, see Emmerson, *Antichrist,* pp. 77–79; and Lerner, "Refreshment of the Saints," pp. 122–23.

2. *Compendium* 7.9 (ed., pp. 242–43). Hugh cites the *Ordinary Gloss* on Apoc. 13:12 for the parody of Pentecost. He does not tie the false Ascension to Antichrist's destruction, as we have seen it in Hildegard.

3. Hugh's *Treatise on Christ's Victory against Antichrist* was written in 1319 and published at Nuremberg in 1471.

4. On Nicholas's interpretation of the Apocalypse, see Philip D. Krey, *Nicholas of Lyra: Apocalypse Commentary as Historiography* (Ph.D. diss., University of Chicago, 1990).

5. Nicholas of Lyra, *Postil on All Scripture,* vol. 6 (Basel, 1506–8), fol. 246v.

6. A *quaestio* that some attribute to Nicholas also denied that we can know the time of Antichrist's coming. See Franz Pelster, "Quodlibeta und Quaestiones des Nikolaus von Lyra, OFM (d. 1349)," in *Mélanges Joseph de Ghellinck* (Gembloux: J. Ducolot, 1951), Quodlibet 1, q. 15 (p. 954).

7. At least five French poems dealing with Antichrist survive from the period (two written in England). Henri d'Arci, a Templar, composed his *Antichrist,* a translation of Adso into Anglo-Norman, in the first half of the thirteenth century, while Geoffroi de Paris inserted an account based on Adso (whether written by Geoffroi himself or not is unclear) into his lengthy *Bible of the Seven Ages of the World* in the 1240s. Two other Adsonian poems are known; the more interesting is the *De l'avenement Antechrist (On Antichrist's Coming)* of one Berengier, a northern French cleric of the first half of the thirteenth century. From the fourteenth century (c. 1330) we also have the only French Antichrist play, *Judgment Day,* found in a single illustrated manuscript in Besançon. Although it does not contain an account of the Last Emperor (so central to the twelfth-century German play), in general it is close to the Adsonian view of the Final Enemy.

8. For an edition, see *Li Touroiemenz Antécrit von Huon de Méry: Ausgaben und Abhandlungen aus dem Gebiete der romanischen Philologie* LXXVI, ed. Georg Wimmer (Marburg: Elwert, 1888).

9. Emmerson, *Antichrist in the Middle Ages,* pp. 188–93. See also Barbara Nolan, *The Gothic Visionary Perspective* (Princeton: Princeton Univ. Press, 1977), pp. 129–33.

10. Emmerson, *Antichrist in the Middle Ages,* p. 192. According to Nolan (pp. 131–32): "In Huon's poem . . . the narrator is the hero of a romance as well as a wandering visionary, and he perceives his revelation of the apocalyptic conflict through the filter of political and personal history."

11. Four versions in parallel columns appear in *Cursor Mundi (The Cursor of the World): A Northumbrian Poem of the Fourteenth Century,* ed. Richard Morris (London: Early English Text Society [hereafter EETS] 66, 1877), pp. 1258–83 (lines 21,975–22,426).

12. On this text, one of the most interesting expansions of Adso, see above, p. 313, n. 130.

13. Among the smaller programs we may note the five scenes based on the *Tiburtine Sibyl* found in the Pamplona Bibles of the 1190s. These include: (1) Antichrist preaching, (2) the invasion of Gog and Magog, (3) Antichrist ordering Enoch and Elijah to be slain, (4) the great persecution, and (5) Antichrist slain by Michael. See François Bucher, *The Pamplona Bibles,* vol. 2 (New Haven: Yale Univ. Press, 1970), plates 555–59. Alexander of Bremen's *Exposition on the Apocalypse* of the 1240s was illustrated with a series of eighty to ninety pictures, including a portrayal of Antichrist in the illustration to Apoc. 20:7–10. See Max Huggler, "Der Bilderkreis in den Handschriften der Alexander-Apokalypse," *Antonianum* 9(1934): 148–49.

14. See Reiner Hausherr, "Sensus literalis und sensus spiritualis in der Bible moralisée," *Frühmittelalterliche Studien* 6(1972): 356–80.

15. See Robert Branner, *Manuscript Painting in Paris During the Reign of Saint Louis: A Study of Styles* (Berkeley: Univ. of California Press, 1977), esp. pp. 49–65. For a list of the mss. with Apocalypse illustrations, see Richard Kenneth Emmerson and Suzanne Lewis, "Census and Bibliography of Medieval Manuscripts Containing Apocalypse Illustrations, ca. 800–1500 (III)," *Traditio* 42(1986): 153–58. The Antichrist illustrations in the Moralized Bibles are discussed in Poesch, *Antichrist Imagery,* pp. 136–68; and Schüssler, *Studien,* pp. 157–222.

16. The Old Testament illustrations provide a good summary of the major types, including: (1) Job 40:10–28 (Leviathan); (2) Ps. 51:1–2 (Doeg the Idumenean); (3) Judg. 6:25 (Gideon's overthrowing Baal's altar); (4) Judg. 9 (Abimelech); (5) Judith 13 (Holofernes); (6) Isa. 27:1 (Leviathan); (7) 2 Macc. 6:18–21 (Eleazer's martyrdom as Antichrist's slaying of the witnesses); and (8) 2 Macc. 7 (the martyrdom of the seven brothers as Antichrist's persecution of the faithful). For a list of both Old Testament and New Testament passages containing Antichrist illustrations, see Schüssler, *Studien,* pp. 167–68.

17. Based on the classification of Schüssler, *Studien,* pp. 204–5, these include: (1) Antichrist teaching, (2) Antichrist enthroned, (3) Antichrist bribing, (4) Antichrist inflicting torture, (5) Antichrist's miracles, (6) worship of Antichrist, (7) episodes with Enoch and Elijah, (8) the death of Antichrist, and (9) Antichrist's damnation.

18. The "Census and Bibliography" of Emmerson and Lewis lists seventy-nine examples; see *Traditio* 41(1985): 38–117. For discussion, see Peter Klein, "The Apocalypse in Medieval Art: An Introduction," in *Apocalypse in the Middle Ages,* pp. 188–92; and esp. Suzanne Lewis, "Exegesis and Illustration in Thirteenth-Century English Apocalypses," in *Apocalypse in the Middle Ages,* pp. 259–75.

19. As Suzanne Lewis has shown, the commentary is of two kinds: (1) Latin (very rarely French) excerpts from the twelfth-century Berengaudus commentary (forty-eight mss.), or (2) a French prose gloss close to the Latin texts found in the "Moralized Bibles" (twenty-five mss.). A few mss. lack any commentary. According to Lewis, "In the Berengaudus cycles, illustrations and exegesis work together to promote a theological comprehension of the text, as the reader is invited to 'see' John's visions on several allegorical levels. In contrast, the Corpus-Lambeth cycle created for the French prose gloss transforms John's experiences into a series of moral lessons in pictorial *exempla* that take on the character of sermons" (art. cit., p. 265).

20. See Peter Klein, *Endzeiterwartung und Ritterideologie: Die englischen Bilderapokalypsen der Frühgotik und MS Douce 180* (Graz: Akademische Druck, 1983).

21. See Poesch, *Antichrist Imagery,* pp. 172–284, as well as her paper, "Revelation 11:7 and Revelation 13:1–10: Interrelated Antichrist Imagery in Some English Apocalypse Manuscripts," in *Art the Ape of Nature: Studies in Honor of H. W. Janson,* ed. M. Barash, L. F. Sandler (New York: Abrams, 1981), pp. 15–33. Cf. Schüssler, *Studien,* pp. 223–42; and George Henderson, "Studies in English Manuscript Illumination. Parts II and III: The English Apocalypse I and II," *Journal of the Warburg and Courtauld Institutes* 30(1967): 104–37 (esp. 105–11); and 31(1968): 103–47.

22. Three thirteenth-century examples are (1) Bodleian Library Ms. Auct. D.4.17, (2) Morgan Library Ms. M.524, and (3) Bibliothèque Nationale Ms. franc.403.

23. See Schüssler, *Studien,* pp. 243–46.

24. I see no evidence that this fresco had a topical significance in relation to the quarrels between John XXII and Lewis of Bavaria; see my discussion in "Portraying Antichrist," p. 21.

25. Innocent III, Reg. 4725 (PL 216:818AB). On this text, see Paul Alphandéry, "Mahomet-Antichrist dans le Moyen Age latin," *Mélanges Hartwig Derenbourg* (Paris: Leroux, 1909), pp. 263–65.

26. On this text, see McGinn, *Visions of the End,* pp. 153–54. The name Mexadeigan may well reflect Arabic influence.

27. Robert E. Lerner, *The Powers of Prophecy: The Cedar of Lebanon Vision from the Mongol Onslaught to the Dawn of the Enlightenment* (Berkeley: Univ. of California Press, 1983), pp. 16, 43–44, 57–59, 190–93.

28. Matthew Paris, *Chronica Majora,* vol. 6, *Additamenta,* ed. H. R. Luard, Rolls Series (London: Longman, 1882), p. 80. The Latin of these verses is:

> Cum fuerint anni transacti mille ducenti
> Et quinquaginta post partum Virginis almae,
> Tunc Antichristus nascetur daemone plenus.

29. For what follows, see the texts translated in McGinn, *Visions of the End,* pp. 155–57.

30. On Joachim as prophet of Antichrist in early testimonies, see Herbert Grundmann, "Anhang II. Joachim im Spiegel der zeitgenossischen Geschichtsschreibung bis 1250," *Deutches Dante-Jahrbuch* 14(1932): 247–50. Cf. M. W. Bloomfield and M. Reeves, "The Penetration of Joachism into Northern Europe," *Speculum* 29(1954): 772–93.

31. Amalric of Bene, the leader of the sect who died about 1207, does not appear to have been influenced by Joachim, but his followers William the Goldsmith and Master Godin were, as shown by Gary Dickson, "Joachism and the Amalricians," *Florensia* 1(1987): 35–45. For their views on Antichrist, see Caesarius of Heisterbach, *Dialogue of Miracles,* ed. Joseph Strange (Cologne: Heberle, 1851), dist. 5, cap. 22, pp. 305–7.

32. On these developments, see esp. Hans Martin Schaller, "Endzeit-Erwartung und Antichrist-Vorstellung in der Politik des 13. Jahrhunderts," *Festschrift für Hermann Heimpel* (Göttingen: Vandenhoeck & Ruprecht, 1972), pp. 923–47; McGinn, *Visions of the End,* sect. 20, pp. 168–79; and R. E. Lerner, "Frederick II, Alive, Aloft, and Allayed in Franciscan-Joachite Eschatology," in *Use and Abuse of Eschatology,* pp. 359–84.

33. From the papal letter "Convenerunt in unum," written in June of 1240. Gregory issued one more apocalyptic broadside, the letter "Vox in Rama," before his death in August 1241.

34. From the pamphlet "Iuxta vaticinium Isaie," ed. E. Winkelmann, *Acta imperii inedita,* vol. 2 (Innsbruck: Wagner, 1880), pp. 709–21 (the passages cited are on pp. 711 and 715).

35. For a translation, see McGinn, *Visions of the End,* pp. 175–76.

36. For the importance of this, see R. E. Lerner, "Frederick II," pp. 359–62.

37. In the absence of a critical edition of the versions found in twenty-seven mss., nothing is certain. I am following the research of Robert Moynihan, "The Development of the 'Pseudo-Joachim' Commentary 'Super Hieremiam': New Manuscript Evidence," *Melanges de l'école français de Rome: Moyen Age—Temps modernes* 98(1986): 109–42.

38. My italics. For this translation and its source in the early printed edition, see McGinn, *Visions of the End,* p. 177. For the text's teaching on the Antichrist, see the summary in Töpfer, *Das kommende Reich,* pp. 118–23.

39. See McGinn, *Visions of the End,* p. 171; and Reeves, *Prophecy in the Middle Ages,* p. 525.

40. For a discussion of the verse and numerous examples, see Reeves, *Prophecy in the Middle Ages,* pp. 49–53.

41. Thomas of Eccleston, *Treatise on the Entry of the Friars into England,* ed. in MGH. Scriptores, vol. 28, pp. 567–68. See Lerner, "Frederick II," pp. 370–71.

42. See Lerner, "Frederick II," pp. 372–74; and Töpfer, *Das kommende Reich,* pp. 131–35.

43. For an edition and study of this work, see Kathryn Kerby-Fulton and E. Randolph Daniel, "English Joachimism, 1300–1500: The Columbinus Prophecy," in *Il profetismo gioachimita tra Quatrocento e Cinquecento: Atti del III Congresso Internazionale di Studi Gioachimiti,* ed. Gian Luca Potestà (Genoa: Marietti, 1991), pp. 313–50.

44. This is the gist of the original core of the prophecy in the edition of Kerby-Fulton and Daniel (quotation from p. 334, lines 46–50). Two sections added later, probably in the 1290s, form a pro-Angevin political prophecy reflecting the fall of Acre in 1291 and political struggles in France and Italy. On these sections, see also Lerner, *Powers of Prophecy,* p. 40.

45. For a recent introduction, see Penn R. Szittya, *The Antifraternal Tradition in Medieval Literature* (Princeton: Princeton Univ. Press, 1986). See also K. Kerby-Fulton, *Reformist Apocalypticism,* pp. 135–43.

46. William's responses to the Cardinals who questioned him indicate that he did not think the end was near, but this might be an example of saying what was prudent in the circumstances. See E. Faral, "Les 'Responsiones' de Guillaume de Saint Amour," *Archives d'histoire doctrinal et littéraire du moyen âge* 18/19 (1950–51): 356–59.

47. On William's *Dangers of the Last Times,* see the good summary in Szittya, *The Antifraternal Tradition,* chap. 1, esp. pp. 54–61 on the friars as antichrists. William's *Treatise on Antichrist and His Ministers,* which appears to have been written c. 1265 after his condemnation, one of the longest accounts of the standard Adsonian view in the Middle Ages, continues the polemic against the friars and also attacks Joachim of Fiore. The work is edited under the name of Nicholas Oresme in E. Martène and U. Durand, *Veterum scriptorum et monumentorum . . . amplissima collectio,* vol. 9 (Paris: Montalent, 1733), cols. 1273–1446.

48. Bonaventure characterizes Aristotelian error with apocalyptic symbols—e.g., the Great Harlot Reason of Apoc. 17 (*Coll.* 2.7 and 19.18), the smoke from the abyss of Apoc. 9:1 (*Coll.* 6.5), and the number 666 (*Coll. on the Gifts of the Holy Spirit* 8.16).

49. Earlier work about Olivi's views on Antichrist include R. Manselli's *La "Lectura super Apocalypsim,"* pp. 219–35, and a series of later papers by the same author. On the Apocalypse commentary, see esp. David Burr, *Olivi's Peaceable Kingdom: A Reading of the Apocalypse Commentary* (Philadelphia: Univ. of Pennsylvania Press, 1993).

50. The terms have generally been understood to contrast a "Mystical Antichrist" against a "Great" or "Open Antichrist." But, as the study of Isaac Vazquez Janeiro indicates (see "Anticristo 'mixto,' Anticristo 'mistico': Varia fortuna de dos expresiones escatologicas medievales," *Antonianum* 63[1988]: 522–50), the later form *mistus* or *mixtus Antichristus,* popular from the fifteenth century, is not a corruption as R. Manselli argued but actually means "mixed" or "hypocritical" Antichrist, and this might be the sense of the original, since *misticus* (though apparently not *mysticus*) is used as an alternate form of *mistus.*

51. For this translation from the *Commentary on the Apocalypse,* see McGinn, *Visions of the End,* p. 211.

52. This ingenious view may be clearer in the following diagram:

PETER OLIVI'S VIEW OF ANTICHRIST:

Antichristus mysticus	Antichristus magnus
1. Beast from Sea	1. Beast from Sea
collectively: carnal laity	collectively: Islam
individually: revived Frederick	individually: Muslim ruler
2. Beast from Land	2. Beast from Land
collectively: wicked clergy	collectively: false prophets (i.e., heretics)
individually: pseudopope	individually: pseudopope

53. For this passage, see Marino Damiata, *Pietà e Storia nell'Arbor Vitae di Ubertino da Casale* (Florence: Edizioni 'Studi Francescani,' 1988), p. 285 n. 110.

54. There is, however, a foreshadowing in Gerhoh of Reichersberg's identification of the final form of Antichrist with the *Antichristus avarus,* on which see pp. 123–24.

55. For a survey of the development of the papal Antichrist, see McGinn, "Angel Pope and Papal Antichrist," esp. pp. 161–70, on this period.

56. Among the most important witnesses for this hope was Roger Bacon, writing 1267–72. See McGinn, *Visions of the End,* pp. 190–91.

57. There is a large literature on the *Vaticinia,* including older studies by H. Grundmann, M. Reeves, and more recent considerations of R. E. Lerner and M. Fleming. Translated excerpts appear in McGinn, *Visions of the End,* pp. 194–95 (the first set), and pp. 235–36 (for the second). I have discussed the *Vaticinia* in my article, "'Pastor Angelicus': Apocalyptic Myth and Political Hope in the Fourteenth Century," in *Santi e santità nel secolo XIV* (Assisi: Università degli Studi di Perugia, Centro di Studi Francescani, 1989), pp. 219–51. For a survey, see R. E. Lerner, "Recent Work on the Origins of the 'Genus Nequam' Prophecies," *Florensia* 7 (1993): 141–57.

58. Andreas Rehberg has argued that the surviving *Vaticinia* depend on a previous version, a "Cardinal's Prophecy" directed against the Orsini cardinals during the papal conclave of 1287. See his "Der 'Kardinalsorakel': Kommentar in der 'Colonna'—Handscrift Vat. lat. 3819 und die Entstehungsumstande der Papstvatizinien," *Florensia* 5(1991): 45–112.

59. See Ubertino of Casale, *The Tree of Life of the Crucified Jesus* V.8 (trans. in McGinn, *Visions of the End,* p. 214). On this text, see Mariano Damiata, *Pietà e Storia nell'Arbor Vitae,* esp. chap. 11.

60. A good introduction to medieval heresy can be found in Malcolm Lambert, *Medieval Heresy: Popular Movements from the Gregorian Reform to the Reformation,* 2nd ed. (Oxford: Blackwell, 1992). Chap. 11 deals with "Spiritual Franciscans and Heretical Joachimites." See also Gordon Leff, *Heresy in the Later Middle Ages: The Relation of Heterodoxy to Dissent c. 1250–c. 1450,* vol. 1, pt. 1, "Poverty and Prophecy"(New York: Barnes & Noble, 1967).

61. The most complete account, including much material on Fraticelli beliefs about Antichrist, is in R. Manselli, *Spirituali e Beghini in Provenza* (Rome: Istituto Storico Italiano per il Medio Evo, 1959).

62. See McGinn, *Visions of the End,* pp. 218–21. Gui goes on to note that they give different dates for the coming of the *magnus Antichristus*—1325, 1330, and 1335.

63. For a brief account, see Robert E. Lerner, "The Pope and the Doctor," *Yale Review* 78(1988–89): 62–79. See also Harold Lee, "*Scrutamini Scripturas*: Joachimist Themes and *Figurae* in the Early Religious Writings of Arnold of Villanova," *Journal of the Warburg and Courtauld Institutes* 37(1974): 33–56.

64. John of Paris, as he is also known, was an important follower of Thomas Aquinas. His *Antichrist and the End of the World* is known in nine mss. and one early printed edition found in the *Expositio magni prophete Joachim in librum beati Cirilli de magnis tribulationibus* (Venice: de Soardis, 1516), fols. 44r–51v. The best recent accounts are in Lerner, *Powers of Prophecy,* pp. 63–72 and 204–7; and in Manfred Gerwing, "Toleranz im Streit um den Antichrist: Bemerkungen zum Antichrist-Traktat des Johannes von Paris (d. 1306)," in *Universalität und Toleranz: Der Anspruch des christlichen Glaubens. Festschrift für Georg Bernhard Langemeyer,* ed. Nicolaus Klimek (Essen: n.p., 1989), pp. 49–68.

65. This was edited by Franz Pelster, "Die Quaestio Heinrichs von Harclay Über die zweite Ankunft Christi und die Erwartung des baldigen Weltendes zu Anfang des XIV Jahrhunderts," *Archivio Italiano per la Storia della Pietà* 1(1951): 53–81 (text).

66. See John of Paris (John Quidort), *Antichrist and the End of the World* (Venice ed.), fol. 46r.

67. Henry of Harclay, "Whether Astrologers or Any Calculators Can Prove Christ's Second Coming." The quotations are taken from the Pelster ed., pp. 76, 68, 71.

68. For defenses of this reading, see Szittya, *Antifraternal Tradition,* pp. 186–90; and Richard Kenneth Emmerson and Ronald B. Herzman, "The Apocalyptic Age of Hypocrisy: Faus Semblant and Amant in the *Roman de la Rose,*" *Speculum* 62(1987): 612–34, which is also available in the same authors' *The Apocalyptic Imagination in Medieval Literature* (Philadelphia: Univ. of Pennsylvania Press, 1992), chap. 3. On the moral dimension of the poem, see also John Fleming, *Reason and the Lover* (Princeton: Princeton Univ. Press, 1984).

69. Emmerson and Herzman, "The Apocalyptic Age of Hypocrisy," p. 632.

70. Jean may also be using some of the antifraternal poems of Rutebeuf, who wrote satirical attacks on the friars as forerunners of Antichrist in the time of William. See Szittya, *Antifraternal Tradition,* pp. 184–86.

71. *Romance of the Rose,* lines 14,740–52, using the translation of Charles Dahlberg, *Guillaume de Lorris and Jean de Meun: The Romance of the Rose* (Princeton: Princeton Univ. Press, 1971), p. 251.

72. Szittya in *Antifraternal Tradition* puts it well: "The deflowering of the Rose is a romance parody of the rape of the church, borrowing the military language and the narrative action from the tradition of the psychomachia. . . . The connection between the Lover's and the friars' assaults lies in the nature of the attackers: in a word, hypocrisy" (pp. 189–90).

73. For a translation, see McGinn, *Visions of the End,* pp. 217–18. A full translation of the *Laudi* can be found in *Jacopone da Todi: The Lauds,* trans. Serge and Elizabeth Hughes, Classics of Western Spirituality (New York: Paulist Press, 1982).

74. See Richard Kenneth Emmerson and Ronald B. Herzman, "Antichrist, Simon Magus, and Dante's 'Inferno' XIX," *Traditio* 36(1980): 373–98, esp. pp. 376 and 396; and chap. 4 in their *The Apocalyptic Imagination in Medieval Literature.* Recent authors who have done much to expose the apocalyptic dimensions of the *Comedy* include R. Manselli, R. E. Kaske, Charles Davis, Marjorie Reeves, and J. B. Friedman. Dante's reformist eschatology has been well described by Charles Davis, who says, "Dante's eschatology rests on twin premises: total authority for the Empire and total poverty for the Church" ("Poverty and Eschatology in the *Commedia,*" *Yearbook of Italian Studies* 8[1980]: 65).

75. This is the suggestion of John Block Friedman, "Antichrist and the Iconography of Dante's Geryon," *Journal of the Warburg and Courtauld Institutes* 35(1972): 108–22.

76. R. E. Kaske, "Dante's *Purgatorio* XXXII and XXXIII: A Survey of Christian History," *University of Toronto Quarterly* 43(1974): 193–214; cf. Charles T. Davis, "Poverty and Eschatology in the *Commedia,*" *Yearbook of Italian Studies* 4(1980): 59–86.

77. Few things in Dante have provoked as much controversy as this messianic prophecy that seems to refer to a Last Emperor figure. For one view, see R. E. Kaske, "Dante's 'DXV' and 'Veltro'," *Traditio* 17(1961): 185–254.

Chapter Seven

1. For an introduction to some of the apocalyptic themes of the time, see Eugenio Dupré Theseider, "L'Attesa escatologica durante il periodo avignonese," in *L'Attesa dell'età nuova nella spiritualità della fine del medioevo* (Todi: L'Accademia Tudertina, 1962), pp. 65–126.

2. For some lists of years announced as the time of Antichrist's coming, see Emmerson, *Antichrist in the Middle Ages,* pp. 54–56; Lerner, "Refreshment of the Saints,"

pp. 138–39; and Roberto Rusconi, *L'Attesa della fine: Crisi della società, profezia ed Apocalisse in Italia al tempo del grande scisma d'Occidente (1378–1417)* (Rome: Istituto Storico Italiano per il Medio Evo, 1979), pp. 137–38.

3. To cite just two examples, see the late fourteenth-century translation of the Pseudo-Methodius into Middle English sometimes ascribed to John Trevisa (d. 1412), entitled *The Bygynnyng of the World and the Ende of Worldes*, ed. A. J. Perry in EETS no. 167 (London: n.p., 1925); and the mid–fifteenth-century Italian translation of the "Cuiusdam sapientis" version of Adso edited and studied by Lucia Fontanella, "Un volgarizzamento quattrocentesco, d'ambiente ferrarese, della *Descriptio cuiusdam sapientis . . . de Antichristo*," *Atti della Accademia delle Scienze di Torino* 114(1980): 49–72.

4. Rusconi, *L'Attesa*, p. 136.

5. The evidence is assessed by Robert E. Lerner in "The Black Death and Western European Eschatological Mentalities," *American Historical Review* 86(1980): 533–52, where he treats of John of Rupescissa, who is discussed here, as well as other contemporary witnesses, such as the French prophet John of Bassigny and the English William of Blofield.

6. The fundamental book remains that of Jeanne Bignami-Odier, *Études sur Jean de Roquetaillade (Johannes de Rupescissa)* (Paris: Vrin, 1952). There are useful materials in English in Reeves, *Prophecy in the Middle Ages*, pp. 225–28, 321–24; and in Lerner, *Powers of Prophecy*, pp. 136–41; and Lerner, "The Black Death," pp. 541–45.

7. For a translation of some selections, see McGinn, *Visions of the End*, pp. 231–33.

8. For a survey of John's teaching on Antichrist, see Harold Lee, Marjorie Reeves, and Giulio Silano, *Western Mediterranean Prophecy: The School of Joachim of Fiore and the Fourteenth-Century "Breviloquium"* (Toronto: PIMS, 1989), pp. 76–80.

9. From the *Companion in Tribulation*, 5th Instruction (McGinn, *Visions of the End*, p. 231).

10. See Robert E. Lerner, "The Medieval Return to the Thousand-Year Sabbath," in *Apocalypse in the Middle Ages*, pp. 66–68.

11. E.g., Birgitta of Sweden, *Revelations* 6.67 and 89 (which may contain a critique of John of Rupescissa). See McGinn, *Visions of the End*, pp. 244–45. On Birgitta, see Rusconi, *L'Attesa*, pp. 116–18; and Kerby-Fulton, *Reformist Apocalypticism*, pp. 102–11.

12. This illustration is taken from a second set of *Vaticinia* relating to the papacy, probably composed by Fraticelli in Italy in the 1340s. Consisting of fifteen pictures highly critical of the popes from Nicholas III on, it ends with this fearful monster, a dragonlike figure representing the final papal Antichrist.

13. See McGinn, *Visions of the End*, pp. 237–38.

14. On the *Breviloquium*, see the edition and study of Lee, Reeves, and Silano referred to in n. 8 above. The text's view of Antichrist is much dependent on Olivi and John of Rupescissa, though its political perspective is anti-French.

15. For details on Peter, a member of the royal family of Aragon (hence given the title "the Infant"), see Lerner, *Powers of Prophecy*, pp. 141–52; and Lee, Reeves, and Solano, *Western Mediterranean Prophecy*, pp. 81–85.

16. Clement VII was jeered as Antichrist when he entered Naples in 1379, and Urban was identified with the Antichrist Beast of the second set of *Vaticinia* in several mss. See Rusconi, *L'Attesa*, pp. 54–55.

17. For a discussion and partial translation, see McGinn, *Visions of the End*, pp. 246–50. There is no modern edition of Telesphorus. A helpful account remains that of

E. Donckel, "Studien über die Prophezeiung des Fr. Telesphorus von Cosenza, O.F.M.," *Archivum Franciscanum Historicum* 33(1926): 29–104, 282–314. See also Rusconi, *L'Attesa,* pp. 171–84.

18. Rusconi, *L'Attesa,* p. 182.

19. See Etienne Delaruelle, "L'Antéchrist chez S. Vincent Ferrier, S. Bernadin de Sienne et autour Jeanne d'Arc," in *L'Attesa dell'età nuova,* pp. 62–63.

20. Translations from some of Vincent's texts on Antichrist can be found in McGinn, *Visions of the End,* pp. 256–58. See also Rusconi, *L'Attesa,* pp. 221–33; and E. Delaruelle, "L'Antéchrist chez S. Vincent Ferrier. . . ," pp. 40–46.

21. Rusconi, *L'Attesa,* pp. 220–22, distinguishes two periods in Vincent's Antichrist preaching: 1399–1409, concentrating on a more moral message; and 1409–19, which is more directly apocalyptic.

22. McGinn, *Visions of the End,* p. 257.

23. For instance, about 1412 an adherent of the Pisan Pope John XXIII put together the two earlier sets of papal *Vaticinia* with the second set coming first. This was apparently done to support John's case at the upcoming council, but to no avail. It did, however, hit upon the happy accident of identifying the papal Antichrist of the second set with the pope of the schism, and thus allowing the combined *Papal Prophecies* new life for several centuries to come. Furthermore, not all were happy with Constance's solution to the problem of the divided papacy. A vernacular text from Spain of c. 1420, possibly by the Franciscan Diego Moxena, claimed that Martin V was the *Antichristus mixtus* (apparently the earliest appearance of this term in Western apocalyptic expectations).

24. On Bernardino, see Rusconi, *L'Attesa,* pp. 236–57, and the same author's "Apocalittica ed escatologia nella predicazione di Bernardino da Siena," *Studi Medievali,* 3a Serie, 22(1981): 85–128.

25. See Rusconi, *L'Attesa,* pp. 251–55; and "Apocalittica ed escatologia," pp. 106–8.

26. A similar shift away from earlier preaching of an imminent Antichrist can be found in Bernardino's contemporary, Lawrence Giustiniani. See Giorgio Cracco, "Momenti escatologici nella formazione di Lorenzo Giustiniani," *L'Attesa dell'età nuova,* pp. 217–31.

27. The distinction I am using here is analogous to that suggested by Curtis Bostick in a paper given at the 1990 meeting of the Society for Sixteenth-Century History in St. Louis entitled "The Antichrist as Agent of Change in Early Modern Society" between "reformist" uses of Antichrist language and the "subversive" use found in the Lollards and Thomas Müntzer. I thank Mr. Bostick for allowing me to note his paper.

28. For Wycliffe on Antichrist, see Gordon Leff, *Heresy in the Later Middle Ages,* vol. 2 (New York: Barnes & Noble, 1967), pp. 516–46; and Szittya, *Antifraternal Tradition,* chap. 4.

29. Leff, *Heresy* 2:539.

30. The *De apostasia, Opus evangelicum,* and *De potestate papae* appear in *Wyclif's Latin Works* (London: Wycliffe Society, 1889, 1896, and 1907, respectively).

31. See John Wycliffe, *Opera minora* in *Wyclif's Latin Works* (London: Wycliffe Society, 1913), p. 375; and *Opus evangelicum* Book III (p. 102).

32. See Szittya, *Antifraternal Tradition,* pp. 167–72.

33. E.g., Wycliffe, *De apostasia,* pp. 65, 77–78. Cf. Szittya, pp. 161–67.

34. *Opus evangelicum,* Book III (p. 107). For other texts on the pope as Antichrist in this work, see, e.g., pp. 131–38 and esp. 181. See also *De potestate papae,* pp. 321–23.

35. *The Lanterne of Light* (London: Kegan Paul, 1917. EETS 151).

36. For accounts of the Hussites and Czech interest in Antichrist c. 1360–1450, see Leff, *Heresy* 2:606–707; and esp. Howard Kaminsky, *The Hussite Revolution* (Berkeley: Univ. of California Press, 1967). Milič's charming *Little Book About Antichrist* is available as part of Book III of Matthew of Janov's *Rules of the Old and the New Testament* in Vlastimil Kybal, ed., *Matěje z Janova. Regulae veteris et novi Testamenti* (Innsbruck: Wagner, 1911), pp. 368–81.

37. On Matthew, see Leff, *Heresy* 2:612–19; Kaminsky, *Hussite Revolution,* pp. 14–23; and also Kaminsky's "On the Sources of Matthew of Janov's Doctrine," *Czechoslovakia Past and Present,* vol. 2, ed. M. Rechcigl (The Hague: Mouton), pp. 1175–83.

38. On the role of the Schism as a sign of Antichrist, see Book III, d. 5, cap. 9 (ed. Kybal, pp. 32–35) and d. 6, cap. 6 (pp. 72–75).

39. *Regulae,* Book III, d. 4, cap. 3 (ed. Kybal, pp. 9–10).

40. *Regulae,* Book III, d. 9, cap. 9 (ed. Kybal, pp. 167–70).

41. Kaminsky, *Hussite Revolution,* p. 53.

42. See Leff, *Heresy* 2:662–76, for a good discussion of this work. On the teaching on Antichrist, see p. 669.

43. Kaminsky, *Hussite Revolution,* p. 55.

44. For an edition of this text, which makes considerable use of Matthew of Janov, see V. Kybal, "M. Matěj z Janova a M. Jakoubek ze Stříba," *Česky časopis historicky* 11(1905): 22–37. Jakoubek provides one of the most fulsome medieval definitions of Antichrist: "Antichrist is a false Christ or Christian, contrary to the truth and life and teaching of Christ in a fraudulent way, superabounding in the highest level of malice, covered with evil totally or in large part, *possessing the highest level in the Church and claiming the highest authority over every person, clerical and lay, from 'fullness of power'. . .*" (p. 29, my italics).

45. The text has been edited, translated, and studied by Howard Kaminsky, Dean Loy Bilderback, Imre Boba, and Patricia N. Rosenberg, *Master Nicholas of Dresden: The Old Color and the New,* N.S. 55, pt. 1 (Philadelphia: Transactions of the American Philosophical Society, 1965). For a brief description, see Kaminsky, *Hussite Revolution,* pp. 40–51.

46. On the illustrated versions of the text, see H. Kaminsky et al., *Master Nicholas,* pp. 34–36.

47. See Matthew Spinka, trans., *The Letters of John Hus* (Totowa, NJ: Rowman & Littlefield, 1972), especially Letters 33 and 34 to the Rector of the University of Prague. In the former letter Hus puts the case of all reformist opponents of a papal Antichrist with great clarity: "For by what means can the Antichrist extol himself more above all that is called God (2 Thess. 2:4)—that is, above Christ's deity and humanity—than to assert that God cannot give his Church other successors than the pope with the cardinals? If they had asserted that God cannot give the Church *worse* successors than the pope and the cardinals, they would have shown greater evidence for their statements. I suppose that God by their inventions occasionally reveals to us the Antichrist with his disciples" (p. 95). It may well be from this period that the curious work ascribed to Hus entitled *The Anatomy of Antichrist* comes. This is a moralizing allegorical description of the parts of Antichrist's body.

48. For this text, see McGinn, *Visions of the End,* p. 263. Several of Hus's letters from Constance contain important materials on Antichrist; see Spinka, *The Letters,* nos. 52, 86, and esp. 87 (pp. 188–91).

49. Manifesto of Bzí Hora (Sept. 17, 1419), in McGinn, *Visions of the End,* p. 264.

50. Reeves, *Prophecy in the Middle Ages,* p. 431. For Antichrist expectations at this time, see Eugenio Garin, "L'Attesa dell'età nuova e la 'renovatio'"; and Cesare Vasoli, "L'Attesa della nuova èra in ambienti e gruppi fiorentini del Quattrocento," both in *L'Attesa dell'età nuova,* pp. 11–35 and 370–432, respectively. See also André Chastel, "L'Antéchrist à la Renaissance," in *Cristianesimo e Ragion di Stato: L'Umanesimo e il demoniaco nell'Arte,* ed. Enrico Castelli (Rome: Fratelli Bocca, 1953), pp. 177–86.

51. On Savonarola, see esp. Donald Weinstein, *Savonarola and Florence: Prophecy and Patriotism in the Renaissance* (Princeton: Princeton Univ. Press, 1970).

52. E.g., Savonarola, *Prediche sopra Aggeo,* ed. Luigi Firpo (Rome: A. Belardetti, 1965), pp. 234–50. For the friar's expectations for the immediate future, see the translation of his *Compendium of Revelations* in McGinn, *Apocalyptic Spirituality,* pp. 195–208.

53. On the opposition to Savonarola, see Weinstein, *Savonarola and Florence,* chap. 7. For Ficino's attack on Savonarola as Antichrist, see McGinn, *Visions of the End,* pp. 282–83.

54. On Francesco of Montepulciano, see Weinstein, *Savonarola and Florence,* pp. 348–49; and Vasoli, "L'Attesa della nuova èra," pp. 405–08. On Francesco of Meleto there are studies in Weinstein, pp. 353–57, and Vasoli, pp. 411–31.

55. Typical of the time are fairly moderate scholastic summaries of traditional lore, such as the Dominican Michael Francis de Insulis's *Determination Concerning the Advent of Antichrist* published in Cologne in 1478. Another example can be found in the recently published "Sermon on Antichrist" from a fifteenth-century Trier manuscript; see Walter Simon, "Incerti Auctoris Sermo de Antichristo," *Via Augustini: Augustine in the Later Middle Ages, Renaissance, and Reformation,* ed. Heiko A. Oberman and Frank A. James III (Leiden: Brill, 1991), pp. 42–54.

56. Sigismund Brettle proved that this work could not be by Vincent in his *San Vicente Ferrer und sein literarischer Nachlass* (Münster: Aschendorff, 1924), pp. 157–64. See Lerner, "Refreshment of the Saints," p. 137.

57. Among these works, the most important is the edition and commentary on the Pseudo-Methodius by the Dominican Wolfgang Aytinger, first published in 1496. See McGinn, *Visions of the End,* pp. 274–76.

58. I will use the B-Text, as edited by A. V. C. Schmidt, *William Langland: The Vision of Piers Plowman, A Complete Edition of the B-Text* (New York: Dutton, 1978).

59. Morton W. Bloomfield, *Piers Plowman as a Fourteenth-Century Apocalypse* (New Brunswick: Rutgers Univ. Press, 1961), p. 43: "*Piers* attempted to analyze the ills of contemporary society and to redefine the ancient concept of Christian perfection, both desperately needed in the crisis of late medieval life."

60. For a sketch and interpretation, see Emmerson, *Antichrist in the Middle Ages,* pp. 193–203.

61. For Langland's antifraternalism, see Szittya, *Antifraternal Tradition,* chap. 7. As K. Kerby-Fulton puts it in her *Reformist Apocalypticism,* "Like so many reformers, Langland sees the state of the clergy as a barometer of apocalyptic pressure" (p. 17).

62. The role of Need in Langland's apocalyptic scenario has been studied by Robert Adams, "The Nature of Need in 'Piers Plowman' XX," *Traditio* 34(1978): 273–301.

63. Emmerson, *Antichrist in the Middle Ages,* pp. 198–99, notes how the reversed agricultural images both reflect on Antichrist's false miracles (making a tree bloom upside down) and comment on his reversal of truth.

64. The optimistic case was argued by R. W. Frank, "The Conclusion of *Piers Plowman,*" *Journal of English and Germanic Philology* 49(1950): 309–16; and was also de-

fended in Bloomfield's book. Recently, K. Kerby-Fulton's *Reformist Apocalypticism* has also decided in its favor (see esp. pp. 9–23, 164–200).

65. The pessimistic case is argued by Emmerson, Adams, and others.

66. Emmerson, *Antichrist in the Middle Ages,* pp. 194–95 and 200–1, contends that these represent the failure of all merely human attempts at reform within history.

67. See Aichele, *Das Antichristdrama,* #3–17 (pp. 34–50), for brief descriptions.

68. For the text, R. M. Lumiansky and David Mills, *The Chester Mystery Cycle,* EETS (New York: Oxford Univ. Press, 1974), pp. 408–38. This is the twenty-third play of the twenty-four that make up the Chester cycle. The earliest recorded performance for a cycle of plays dealing with salvation history on the Feast of Corpus Christi is in 1378. In the early sixteenth century the Chester plays were reorganized according to a three-day cycle performed during Pentecost week. It is difficult to give a more precise date to the drama within this time frame.

69. For the interlocking structure, see Richard Kenneth Emmerson, "'Nowe ys common this daye': Enoch and Elias, Antichrist, and the Structure of the Chester Cycle," in *HOMO MEMENTO FINIS: The Iconography of Just Judgment in Medieval Art and Drama* (Kalamazoo, MI: Medieval Institute Publications, 1985), pp. 89–120 (the phrase "sermon on eschatology" is Emmerson's). See also his account in *Antichrist in the Middle Ages,* pp. 180–87. Among older studies, see L. Lucken, *Antichrist and the Prophets of Antichrist in the Chester Cycle* (Washington, DC: Catholic Univ. Press, 1940).

70. See Emmerson, "'Nowe ys common this daye'," pp. 109–10, who notes the relation this scene bears to late medieval Antichrist illustrations.

71. Paris, Bibliothèque Nationale ms. neerl.3 (#136 in the Emmerson-Lewis Census). There is a full account with color plates in Frederick van der Meer, *Apocalypse: Visions from the Book of Revelation in Western Art* (London: Thames & Hudson, 1978), chap. 13. For some other examples of illustrated Apocalypses with Antichrist, see Emmerson, *Antichrist in the Middle Ages,* pp. 115–16.

72. For a facsimile of the text, see *Velislai Biblia Picta,* ed. Karel Stejskal (Prague: Orbis, 1970), 2 vols.

73. See Fritz Saxl, "A Spiritual Encyclopaedia of the Later Middle Ages," *Journal of the Warburg and Courtauld Institutes* 5(1942): 82–142; and Gertrude Bing, "The Apocalypse Blockbooks and Their Manuscript Models," *Journal of the Warburg and Courtauld Institutes* 5(1942): 143–58.

74. For some reflections on the role of blockbooks in the wider context of late medieval Apocalypse illustration, see Michael Camille, "Visionary Perception and Images of the Apocalypse in the Later Middle Ages," in *Apocalypse in the Middle Ages,* pp. 276–89.

75. See H. Th. Musper, *Der Antichrist und die Fünfzehn Zeichen,* 2 vols. (Munich: Prestel, 1971), a Nuremberg version; and K. Boveland, C. P. Burger, and R. Steffen, *Der Antichrist und die Fünfzehn Zeichen vor dem Jüngsten Gericht,* 2 vols. (Hamburg: Wittich, 1979), the earliest typographical version of c. 1480 from Strassburg.

76. The caesarean birth of Antichrist has recently been studied by Renate Blumenfeld-Kosinski, *Not of Woman Born: Representations of Caesarean Birth in Medieval and Renaissance Culture* (Ithaca, NY: Cornell Univ. Press, 1990), pp. 125–42. She identifies two versions, a "satanic" one in which devils assist as midwives and a more neutral "obstetrical" one.

77. André Chastel in his article "L'Apocalypse en 1500: La fresque de l'Antéchrist à la chapelle Saint-Brice d'Orvieto," *Bibliothèque d'Humanisme et Renaissance* 14(1952): 124–40, argued for a connection between the Antichrist fresco and Ficino's opposition to

Savonarola. This position was ably rebutted by Emmerson and Herzman in "Antichrist, Simon Magus and Dante's 'Inferno' XIX," pp. 373–78. More recently, Jonathan B. Reiss in "Republicanism and Tyranny in Signorelli's *Rule of Antichrist*," in *Art and Politics in Late Medieval and Early Renaissance Italy, 1250–1500* (Notre Dame: Univ. of Notre Dame, 1990), pp. 157–85, has tried to tie the fresco to Vincent Ferrer, Saint Antoninus, and Annius of Viterbo, but the connections are tenuous.

Chapter Eight

1. For Antichrist traditions from the sixteenth through nineteenth centuries, see esp. Hans Preuss, *Die Vorstellungen vom Antichrist im späteren Mittelalter, bei Luther und in der konfessionellen Polemik* (Leipzig: Hinrich, 1906); and Gottfried Seebass, "Antichrist IV: Reformations-und Neuzeit," *Theologisches Realenzyklopädie,* vol. 3, ed. G. Krause, G. Muller, et al. (Berlin: De Gruyter, 1978), pp. 28–43.

2. See Ernst Troeltsch, *Protestantism and Progress: A Historical Study of the Relation of Protestantism to the Modern World* (Boston: Beacon, 1958). On the debate, see Steven Ozment, *The Age of Reform 1250–1550* (New Haven: Yale Univ. Press, 1980), pp. 260–64.

3. Heiko A. Oberman, *Luther: Man Between God and the Devil* (New Haven: Yale Univ. Press, 1989), p. 79.

4. Among older accounts of Luther's teaching on Antichrist, Preuss, *Die Vorstellungen,* pt. 2, retains value, despite his overemphasis on Luther's originality and "modernity." Helpful among recent works is Scott H. Hendrix, *Luther and the Papacy: Stages in a Reformation Conflict* (Philadelphia: Westminster, 1981). See also Jane E. Strohl, *Luther's Eschatology: The Last Times and the Last Things* (Ph.D. diss., University of Chicago, 1989). For Luther's writings, I will make use of the standard Weimar edition, abbreviated as follows:

> *WA: D. Martin Luthers Werke: Kritische Gesamtausgabe, Abteilung Werke,* vols. 1– (Weimar, 1883–).
>
> *WABr: D. Martin Luthers Werke: Kritische Gesamtausgabe, Briefwechsel,* vols. 1–18 (Weimar, 1930–85).
>
> *WATr: D. Martin Luthers Werke: Kritische Gesamtausgabe, Tischreden,* vols. 1–6 (Weimar, 1912–21).
>
> *WADB: D. Martin Luthers Werke: Kritische Gesamtausgabe, Die Deutsche Bibel,* vols. 1–12 (Weimar, 1906–61).

5. Hendrix, *Luther and the Papacy,* p. 123.

6. In October 1988, when Pope John Paul II addressed a meeting of the European Parliament at Strassburg, the Rev. Ian Paisley, the well-known anti-Catholic Protestant leader from Northern Ireland, hoisted a banner denouncing the pope as Antichrist. It was snatched from his hands by a member of the Parliament, Otto von Hapsburg, lineal descendant of Charles V, who strove against Luther's original protest. Once again, history repeated itself as farce.

7. For Luther's early views, see Preuss, *Die Vorstellungen,* pp. 91–93.

8. *WATr* 3, 438.21–439.2, no. 3593. I have used the translation of Hendrix, *Luther,* pp. 160–61, who interprets the "twenty years prior to that day" as signifying the beginning of Luther's studies c. 1499. Kurt Aland, *Der Weg zur Reformation* (Munich: C. Kaiser, 1965), p. 71, thinks Luther is referring to 1517, i.e., twenty years prior to 1537.

9. *WABr* 1, 270.11–14. Cf. also a letter to George Spalatin of Dec. 21, 1518, found in *WABr* 1, 286.82–86.

10. *WABr* 1, 359.29–31.

11. See Hendrix, *Luther and the Papacy,* pp. 97–98.

12. Another letter to Spalatin, dated Feb. 24, 1520, in *WABr* 2, 48.20–49.2 (translation of Hendrix, p. 98).

13. Two of Luther's works of June 1520, *The Papacy at Rome* and his edition of Sylvester Prierias's *Epitome,* had already publicly claimed that the papacy was Antichrist.

14. *Address to the Christian Nobility* in *WA* 6, 416.12–16 (cf. 414.35–415.6). I have used the translation of Charles M. Jacobs found in *Three Treatises: Martin Luther* (Philadelphia: Fortress, 1970), p. 27. On this treatise, see Hendrix, *Luther and the Papacy,* pp. 104–7.

15. *The Babylonian Captivity of the Church* in *WA* 6, 537.24–25. I use the translation in Hendrix, *Luther and the Papacy,* p. 111.

16. *Against the Execrable Bull of Antichrist* in *WA* 6, 597–629; see esp. 604.19–38.

17. The *Passional of Christ and Antichrist* appears in *WA* 9, 677–715 with the pictures at the end. For Luther's role as inspirer, see Hendrix, *Luther and the Papacy,* pp. 124–25; and Preuss, *Die Vorstellungen,* pp. 140–41. There is a detailed study in Hartmann Grisar and Franz Heege, *Luthers Kampfbilder,* vol. 1 (Herder: Freiburg, 1921).

18. The characterization as illustrated morality play is taken from R. W. Scribner, *For the Sake of Simple Folk: Popular Propaganda for the German Reformation* (Cambridge: Cambridge Univ. Press, 1981), pp. 149–58 on the *Passional* (quotation on p. 155).

19. See the letters in *WABr* 2, 283.24–25 and 347.23–26.

20. E.g., Preuss, *Die Vorstellungen,* pp. 128, 142.

21. *WADB* 7, 404.

22. For the 1530 preface (also reprinted in 1545), see *WADB* 7, 407–21. For Luther on the Apocalypse, see Hans-Ulrich Mohr, *Luther und die Johannes-Apokalypse* (Tübingen: Mohr, 1982).

23. For more on Antichrist in Scripture, see Luther's preface to Daniel in *WADB* 11.2, 102.3–104.7.

24. For a survey of texts on this, see Preuss, *Die Vorstellungen,* pp. 157–64. However, Luther claimed that even good popes like Gregory depended too much on their own merits (e.g., *WA* 32, 347.20–37). A summary of his view on the value of the study of the history of the papal Antichrist can be found in the preface he wrote for the 1545 edition of Robert Barnes, *The Lives of the Popes,* to be found in *WA* 150, 3–5.

25. An interesting document in this connection is the preface Luther wrote in 1528 for an edition of a Wycliffite commentary on the Apocalypse. See *WA* 26, 123–24.

26. On Luther's apocalyptic mentality, see Oberman, *Luther,* chap. 2; and Robin Bruce Barnes, *Prophecy and Gnosis: Apocalypticism in the Wake of the Lutheran Reformation* (Stanford: Stanford Univ. Press, 1988), pp. 36–53.

27. For Luther's view of the Turk, see esp. the "Army Sermon Against the Turks" in *WA* 30.2, 149–97.

28. See the passages assembled in Preuss, *Die Vorstellungen,* pp. 172–75.

29. *Against the Roman Papacy: An Institution of the Devil* is found in *WA* 54, 195–299, while the *Depiction* is in 346–73 of the same volume. For a study, see Grisar and Heege, *Luthers Kampfbilder,* vol 4; (Freiburg: Herder, 1924); Hendrix, *Luther and the Papacy,* pp. 154–56; and esp. Scribner, *For the Sake of Simple Folk,* pp. 81–87.

30. *WA* 54, 215.22–25.

31. See Scribner, *For the Sake of Simple Folk,* pp. 82–84.

32. In a revealing comment given at table in the autumn of 1533 he made an important distinction between life and doctrine: "Life is as evil among us as among the papists, thus we do not argue about life but about doctrine. Whereas Wycliffe and Hus attacked the immoral life style of the papacy, I challenge primarily its doctrine" (*WATr* 1, 294.19–23, no. 624). This remark is not totally fair. Although medieval accusations that particular popes were Antichrist, such as those found among the Franciscan Spirituals, had been directed against individual popes and not the papal office as such, they had already begun to involve issues of false teaching as well as moral failure. For a discussion of this text, see Oberman, *Luther,* pp. 55–57, whose translation I am using here.

33. Barnes, *Prophecy and Gnosis,* p. 3. Barnes's claim that Lutherans were more apocalyptic than other Christian groups during the sixteenth and seventeenth centuries is difficult to prove without a lengthy comparative study.

34. Barnes's *Prophecy and Gnosis* is one of the few recent studies of continental Protestant apocalypticism in English. A number of works investigating English Protestant apocalypticism will be discussed below.

35. The Schmalcaldic Articles of belief, drawn up by Luther in 1537, contain the first creedal expression of what became the standard Lutheran belief in the papal Antichrist. The fourth article asserts that because the papacy has arrogated to itself what belongs only to Christ, "the pope is the very Antichrist, who has exalted himself above and opposed himself against Christ, because he will not permit Christians to be saved without his power." See *Concordia or Book of Concord: The Symbols of the Evangelical Lutheran Church* (St. Louis: Concordia, 1952), p. 141.

36. I quote this text from R. Emmerson, *Antichrist in the Middle Ages,* p. 8.

37. On Stifel, see Barnes, *Prophecy and Gnosis,* pp. 188–94. Stifel appears to have been the first to give Luther himself an apocalyptic role, identifying him with the angel of Apocalypse 14:6 (see Barnes, p. 54).

38. On Osiander's apocalypticism, see Preuss, *Die Vorstellungen,* pp. 205–06; Barnes, *Prophecy and Gnosis,* pp. 65, 116–17, and 128–30; and M. Reeves, *Prophecy in the Later Middle Ages,* pp. 453–54. His *Treatise on Antichrist* (1525) and his reworking of the Pseudo-Joachim papal prophecies under the title *A Wonderful Prophecy About the Papacy* (1527) have been edited by Hans-Ulrich Hofmann in *Andreas Osiander Gesamtausgabe,* vol. 2 (Gutersloh: Mohn, 1977), pp. 401–501. On the *Wonderful Prophecy,* see also Scribner, *For the Sake of Simple Folk,* pp. 142–47. There is a recent edition of Osiander's most important apocalyptic work, his *Conjectures on the Last Days and the End of the World* (1544), by Martin Hein in *Andreas Osiander Gesamtausgabe,* vol. 8 (Gutersloh: Mohn, 1990), pp. 150–271.

39. See Martin Stupperich, "Das Augsburger Interim als apokalyptisches Geschehnis nach den Konigsberger Schriften Andreas Osiander," *Archive for Reformation History* 64(1973): 225–45.

40. On the apocalyptic understanding of the Interims, see Barnes, *Prophecy and Gnosis,* pp. 64–66; on Amsdorf in particular, p. 83.

41. On this illustration, see Scribner, *For the Sake of Simple Folk,* pp. 175–77.

42. On this picture, see Grisar and Heege, *Luthers Kampfbilder,* vol. 4, pp. 68–70; and Scribner, *For the Sake of Simple Folk,* pp. 134–36. Note the appearance of the defecation motif both in the excrement at the top of the papal tiara and in the portrayal of the devil wearing the cardinal's hat in the lower right who excretes a papal bull.

43. For an account, see Preuss, *Die Vorstellungen,* pp. 183–202. Much of this literature is edited and discussed in the old work of Oskar Schade, *Satiren und Pasquille aus der Reformationszeit,* 2 vols. (Hannover: Rumpler, 1863).

44. Luther's "Table Talk" (see Preuss, *Die Vorstellungen,* pp. 188–89) contains a Latin song against Antichrist composed by his friend Urban Rhegius containing the verse:

> Si te ventris onus urget,
> Papae bulla nates purget,
> cum sit Antichristica.

Which might be translated:

> If you have an urge to shit,
> Use a papal bull where you sit,
> Since it belongs to Antichrist.

45. On Pamphilus Gegenbach, see Aichele, *Das Antichristdrama,* pp. 49–50, 56.

46. See Aichele, *Das Antichristdrama,* pp. 51–75, 82–93. Most of these were produced in the early decades of the Reformation, but the *Phasma* of Nicodemus Frischlin, which attacked both Anabaptists and Catholics, was not written until 1580.

47. Aichele, *Das Antichristdrama,* pp. 65–66.

48. *Institutes of the Christian Religion* IV.ii.12. For other references in the *Institutes,* see III.xx.42, IV.vii.24–25, and IV.ix.4. In addition, Calvin spoke of Antichrist in his commentaries on Dan. 11, 1 John, and esp. 2 Thess. 2. For a translation of the last, see *Calvin's New Testament Commentaries,* ed. David W. Torrance and Thomas F. Torrance, *The Epistles of Paul to the Romans and Thessalonians,* trans. R. Mackenzie (Grand Rapids, MI: Eerdmans, 1960), pp. 398–408.

49. *Commentary on 2 Thessalonians,* pp. 403–04. For Calvin's view of Antichrist, see Katharine R. Firth, *The Apocalyptic Tradition in Reformation Britain 1530–1645* (Oxford: Oxford Univ. Press, 1979), pp. 32–37.

50. Antichrist also had a role in Reformed dogmatics on the Continent. For example, see John Wollebius, *Compendium of Christian Theology,* a standard work first published in 1626, which discusses Antichrist in chap. 27 (2), in *Reformed Dogmatics,* ed. and trans. John W. Beardslee III (New York: Oxford Univ. Press, 1965), pp. 152–57.

51. A seminal study remains that of George Huntston Williams, *The Radical Reformation* (Philadelphia: Westminster, 1962). For an introduction to apocalyptic themes in the Radical Reformers, see Walter Klaassen, *Living at the End of the Ages: Apocalyptic Expectation in the Radical Reformation* (Lanham, MD: Univ. Press of America, 1992), esp. chap. 4, "The Age of Antichrist."

52. Müntzer is a controversial figure. In modern times his reputation has often been split between Marxist historiography that hails him as a great revolutionary and Lutheran treatments anxious to show why Luther was right in attacking him. A sense of the continued debate can be found in the review of six recent studies issued for the four-hundredth anniversary of his birth; see James M. Stayer, "Thomas Müntzer in 1989: A Review Article," *Sixteenth-Century Journal* 21(1990): 655–70. For general accounts, see Williams, *Radical Reformation,* pp. 44–58; and Norman Cohn, *The Pursuit of the Millennium,* 2nd ed. (New York: Oxford, 1970), pp. 234–51.

53. Anabaptism (i.e., second baptism) is really a misnomer, since those who opposed infant baptism held that it was no baptism at all. This position was found among the Swiss Brethren in Zürich c. 1523–24. One of the early leaders there, George Blaurock,

said of infant baptism: "Luther and Zwingli defended with the sword this false teaching, which they really learned from the father and head of Antichrist. . . ." See *Spiritual and Anabaptist Writers: Documents Illustrative of the Radical Reformation,* ed. George H. Williams and Angel M. Mergal (Philadelphia: Westminster, 1957), p. 42.

54. For an example of Müntzer's rhetoric, consider the following passage from his letter of April 1525 to his community at Allstedt: "Forward, forward, strike while the fire is hot! Don't let your swords become cold or blunt! Smite, cling, clang on Nimrod's anvil; cast their towers to the ground! As long as they [the authorities] remain alive you can never rid yourselves of the fear of men." This is the translation of Elizabeth Bender, "The Mystic with the Hammer: Thomas Müntzer's Theological Basis for Revolution," *Mennonite Quarterly Review* 50(1976): 100. The full text can be found in *Thomas Müntzer: Schriften und Briefe, Quellen und Forschungen zur Reformationsgeschichte,* vol. 33, ed. Paul Kirn and Gunther Franz (Gutersloh: Mohn, 1968), pp. 454–56.

55. Thomas Müntzer, "Letter to Nicholas Hausmann" of June 1521, as found in *Müntzer: Schriften und Briefe,* 373.4–6.

56. *Müntzer: Schriften und Briefe,* 373.7–9.

57. On the Peasants' Revolt, see Williams, *Radical Reformation,* chap. 4.

58. On Hoffman's teaching, see Williams, *Radical Reformation,* pp. 259–64, 307–09, 328–32, and 355–60. For his teaching on Antichrist, see Klaassen, *Living at the End,* chap. 4 passim.

59. For a survey of the Radicals' teaching regarding the marks of Antichrist, see Klaassen, *Living at the End,* pp. 62–72.

60. I quote from the translation of Klaassen, p. 66.

61. For the story of the Melchiorites and the events at Münster, see Williams, *Radical Reformation,* chaps. 13 and 14; and the lively, if not always accurate, account of Norman Cohn, *Pursuit of the Millennium,* chap. 13.

62. Bernard Rothmann, *On the Vengeance and Punishment of the Abomination of Babylon,* as translated in Erwin Iserloh, Joseph Glazik, and Hubert Jedin, *History of the Church,* vol. 5, *Reformation and Counter Reformation* (New York: Seabury, 1980), p. 185. Rothmann's works have been edited by Robert Stupperich, *Die Schriften Bernhard Rothmanns* (Münster: Aschendorff, 1970), where this passage is found on p. 297.

63. The signs of Antichrist's church are: (1) an easy, vain, and false doctrine; (2) an unscriptural practice of sacramental signs, such as infant baptism and the impenitent supper; (3) disobedience to the word; (4) contempt for the neighbor; (5) dissimulation and repudiation of the name of God and Christ; and (6) tyranny and spite against the pious. For an account, see John D. Willis, "'Love Your Enemies': Sixteenth-Century Interpretations of the Love Command" (Ph.D. diss., University of Chicago, 1989), pp. 407–9.

64. Sebastian Franck, *A Letter to John Campanus,* in *Spiritual and Anabaptist Writers,* p. 151. On Franck's theology, see Steven E. Ozment, *Mysticism and Dissent: Religious Ideology and Social Protest in the Sixteenth Century* (New Haven: Yale Univ. Press, 1973), pp. 137–67.

65. Franck, *Letter to Campanus,* p. 160.

66. Franck argued his case historically in his major work called *The Chronicle, Book of the Times and Historical Bible* (1531). Despite his overarching collective view, he continued to believe in a final individual Antichrist who would be the devil's incarnation. On his views, see Preuss, *Die Vorstellungen,* pp. 218–19.

67. Seebass, "Antichrist IV," p. 36.

68. For some examples, see Barnes, *Prophecy and Gnosis,* pp. 112–13 and 133.

69. Alsted, *The Beloved City* (London: n.p., 1643), p. 37.

70. There is a considerable literature on English Reformation apocalypticism and Antichrist views down through the Civil War. Besides K. Firth's *The Apocalyptic Tradition,* see Christopher Hill, *Antichrist in Seventeenth-Century England* (London: Oxford Univ. Press, 1971), and the same author's *The World Turned Upside Down: Radical Ideas During the English Revolution* (London: Smith, 1972). See also Paul Christianson, *Reformers and Babylon: English Apocalyptic Visions from the Reformation to the Eve of the Civil War* (Toronto: Univ. of Toronto, 1978); Bryan W. Ball, *A Great Expectation: Eschatological Thought in English Protestantism to 1660* (Leiden: Brill, 1975). On Scotland, see Arthur H. Williamson, "Antichrist's Career in Scotland: The Imagery of Evil and the Search for a Scottish Past" (Ph.D. diss., Washington University, 1973).

71. K. Firth, *Apocalyptic Tradition,* pp. 24–25, 37–38, 53, emphasizes the Wycliffite tone of the generic view of Antichrist evident, for example, in Tyndale's *Parable of the Wicked Mammon*: "Mark this above all things; that Antichrist is not an outward thing: that is to say a man that should suddenly appear with wonders as our fathers talked of him. No verily; for Antichrist is a spiritual thing . . . Antichrist is now and shall (I doubt not) endure to the world's end." See William Tyndale, *Doctrinal Treatises,* ed. Henry Walter (Cambridge: Parker Society, 1848), p. 42.

72. This sermon has not survived. Christianson, *Reformers and Babylon,* pp. 13 and 23, claims that at this stage Cranmer in medieval fashion held that the present pope was the Final Enemy and only later expanded this to include the reformation belief in the institution of the papacy as Antichrist.

73. John Jewel, *Works,* ed. by John Ayre, vol. 2 (Cambridge: Parker Society, 1840–50), p. 902.

74. On Bale, see Firth, *Apocalyptic Tradition,* pp. 38–58, 78–80; and Christianson, *Reformers and Babylon,* pp. 14–22.

75. John Bale, *Select Works* (Cambridge: Parker Society, 1849), p. 251.

76. Ibid., p. 461.

77. On Foxe's view of history and the role of Antichrist, see Firth, *Apocalyptic Tradition,* pp. 82–84, 89–106; and Christianson, *Reformers and Babylon,* pp. 39–46.

78. On the role of the Apocalypse in England, see the papers in *The Apocalypse in English Renaissance Thought and Literature,* ed. C. A. Patrides and Joseph Wittreich (Ithaca, NY: Cornell Univ. Press, 1984), esp. the overview of Bernard Capp, "The Political Dimension of Apocalyptic Thought," pp. 93–124.

79. Edwin Sandys, *Sermons,* as quoted in Christianson, *Reformers and Babylon,* p. 34.

80. Quoted in Hill, *Antichrist,* p. 32.

81. Some Elizabethan Calvinists continued to adhere to the classic view that only the pope was truly Antichrist. See the discussion of William Whitaker's views by Peter Lake, "The Significance of the Elizabethan Identification of the Pope as Antichrist," *Journal of Ecclesiastical History* 31(1980): 161–78.

82. On the Separatists, see Christianson, *Reformers and Babylon,* chap. 2.

83. Ibid., p. 50.

84. Ibid., p. 47.

85. Thomas Brightman, *The Works . . . viz: A Revelation of the Apocalyps, etc.* (London: Samuel Cartwright, 1644). On Brightman's views, see Firth, *Apocalyptic Tradition,* 164–76; Christianson, *Reformers and Babylon,* pp. 101–06; Ball, *Great Expectation,* pp. 82–84, 116–18, 168–69; and Brian G. Cooper, "The Academic Rediscovery of Apocalyptic Ideas in the Seventeenth Century," *Baptist Quarterly* 18(1960): 351–62 and 19(1961): 29–34.

86. Brightman, *A Revelation . . . ,* e.g., pp. 805, 816, 831.

87. Ibid., p. 824. Actually, Brightman believed that the Apocalypse had described two bindings of Satan for a thousand years: The first (c. 300–1300) comprised the absence of open persecution; the second, which was the true millennium of the freedom of reformed teaching for its first 390 years, coexisted with the revived persecution of that Satan who is to be seen in the papal Antichrist.

88. Millenarianism was attacked, for instance, by David Pareus, professor of Scripture at Heidelberg, whose *Commentary on the Apocalypse* was translated into English in 1644.

89. See Michael Murrin, "Revelation and two seventeenth-century commentators," *The Apocalypse in English Renaissance,* pp. 125–46, for a comparison of Pareus and Mede. On Mede also see Ball, *Great Expectation,* pp. 136–38; Firth, *Apocalyptic Tradition,* pp. 213–28; and Christianson, *Reformers and Babylon,* pp. 124–29.

90. On the role of learned millenarianism in the Civil War, see Ball, *Great Expectation,* chap. 5; and Christianson, *Reformers and Babylon,* pp. 128–31.

91. See esp. Hill, *Antichrist,* chap. 3.

92. This point is emphasized by Hill, *Antichrist,* both in his comments on the vagueness of usage (e.g., pp. 44–48, 66, 78, 101, 162) and his discussion of the reasons for the decline of Antichrist after 1660 (pp. 155–74).

93. Quoted in Christianson, *Reformers and Babylon,* pp. 120–21.

94. For a list of some, see Hill, *Antichrist,* pp. 81–88.

95. Milton's treatises of 1641–42, esp. *Of Reformation, Animadversions,* and *The Reasons,* attacked the notion of the "godly prince" and saw prelacy as always allied with Antichrist: "Beleeve it Sir right truly it may be said, that Antichrist is Mammons Son. The soure levin of humane Traditions mixt in one putrif'd Masse with the poisonous dregs of hypocrisie in the hearts of Prelates that lye basking in the Sunny warmth of Wealth, and Promotion, is the Serpents Egge that will hatch an Antichrist wheresoever. . . ." See John Milton, *Complete Prose Works,* vol. 1 (New Haven: Yale Univ. Press, 1953), p. 590.

96. Quoted from Hill, *Antichrist,* pp. 79–80.

97. On the Fifth Monarchists, see P. G. Rogers, *The Fifth Monarchy Men* (London: Oxford Univ. Press, 1966); and B. S. Capp, *The Fifth Monarchy Men: A Study in Seventeenth-Century English Millenarianism* (London: Faber & Faber, 1972).

98. Quoted from Hill, *Antichrist,* p. 109.

99. On Spittlehouse and Rogers, see Rogers, *Fifth Monarchy Men,* pp. 26–27, 30–40.

100. On Cromwell as Antichrist, see the texts in Hill, *Antichrist,* pp. 121–23.

101. Among the Levellers, for example, Henry Denne held that Antichrist, "that mystical body of iniquity," filled "the pulpits of England." The Ranter, William Erberry, came to believe that Antichrist resided in all kingdoms and churches. Gerrard Winstanley, who founded the Diggers in 1649, arrived at a completely immanent view of Christ and Antichrist as powers within every heart: "There is no man or woman needs go to Rome nor to hell below ground, as some talk to find the Pope, Devil, Beast or power of darkness; neither to go up into heaven above the skies to find Christ the word of life. For both these powers are to be felt within a man, fighting against each other." On Winstanley, see Hill, *Antichrist,* pp. 116–19 and 141–46.

102. See Ben Jonson, *The Alchemist* (1610) and *Bartholomew Fair* (1614), as cited in Hill, *Antichrist,* pp. 60–61.

103. Cited in Hill, *Antichrist,* p. 149.

104. Ibid., p. 159.

105. This is not to say that all Catholics abandoned such language, particularly figures on the fringes. For example, the learned, strange, and half-mad Guillaume Postel

(1510–1581), writing to Melanchthon in 1555, asserted that the pontificates of Paul III and Julius III were years of Antichrist.

106. Catholic identification of Luther with Antichrist built upon the traditional association of heresy with the Final Enemy. A few of Luther's original German opponents, such as John Eck and Jerome Emser, vilified him as the *Antichristus mixtus,* that is, the immediate predecessor of the Final Antichrist (see Preuss, *Die Vorstellungen,* pp. 215–16). The same accusation was made in Italy by the prophet Paulus Angelus in his work *For the Ruin of Satan's Tyranny* (Venice: n.p., 1524), fol. 7v. Other works, such as the *Prognosticon on Antichrist's Advent* (1524), without explicitly calling Luther Antichrist, associated his protest with the troubles to come immediately before the end of time.

107. Preuss, *Die Vorstellungen,* p. 247.

108. I have used the edition of Robert Bellarmine's *Disputations on the Controversies . . .* found in his *Opera omnia* (Venice: Malachinus, 1721), in which the section rebutting the view that the pope is Antichrist can be found in vol. 1, pp. 348–91.

109. Little has been written on Bellarmine's Antichrist views. Older surveys, such as Preuss, *Die Vorstellungen,* pp. 248–52, are not very helpful.

110. Bellarmine, *Controversies* III.3, chap. 9 (p. 362).

111. See his *Commentaries and Disputations on the Summa of Thomas Aquinas* found in Francis Suarez, *Opera Omnia,* ed. Charles Bertin (Paris: Vivés, 1860), *In Tertiam Partem,* Disputation 54, on Q. 59, art. 6 (vol. 19, pp. 1025–44).

112. There is no good modern study of these important exegetes. For some introductory notes, see Wilhelm Bousset, *Die Offenbarung Johannis* (Göttingen: Vandenhoeck & Ruprecht, 1906), pp. 91–95.

113. The Portuguese Viegas's *Exegetical Commentaries on the Apocalypse of the Apostle John* was first printed in 1601. In the 1602 Venice edition, the comment on Apoc. 13 includes a summary section on Antichrist (pp. 693–714) disproving the Protestant view. Benedict Pereyra's commentary of 1606 was heavily Joachite (see Reeves, *Prophecy,* pp. 283–85).

114. Bousset, *Die Offenbarung,* p. 91. On Ribera's exegesis, I have profited from the unpublished paper of my colleague Michael Murrin, "Francisco de Ribera: The Apocalypse as Science Fiction."

115. On Alcazar, see Reeves, *Prophecy,* pp. 282–83, where the quotation on Joachim is to be found.

116. Thomas Malvenda, *De Antichristo: Libri Undecim* (Rome: C. Vulliettus, 1604).

117. Malvenda sometimes adds recent information to help defend elements in the legend. For example, in book 2, chap. 8, he supports the tradition that Antichrist will be conceived by demonic incubation making use of human semen by appealing to examples of such demonic mischief in the Americas—"Writers on matters American tell us that the devil in the form of a satyr is accustomed to deal in a very familiar way with American [i.e., Indian] women and to have sex with them from which are born children, some of whom are held to be important when they are known to have such a father" (p. 76).

118. Tommaso Campanella, *De Antichristo,* ed. Romano Amerio (Rome: International Center of Humanistic Studies, 1965).

119. The fourth chapter of *On Antichrist,* taking up just over 40 percent of the whole, is devoted to proving that the pope is neither Antichrist nor a part of Antichristianism.

120. Campanella, *De Antichristo,* pp. 10 and 14. On the signs of the end, which include Columbus's discovery of America in 1492 and Luther's revolt of 1518, see p. 78.

121. Ibid., p. 62.

Chapter Nine

1. I have used a late edition, Dionysius von Lützenberg, *Leben Antichristi* (Vienna: G. Lehmann, 1729). There is little literature on this perhaps justly forgotten work, but see Preuss, *Die Vorstellungen,* pp. 254–56.

2. Typical is that in Lützenberg, *Leben Antichristi,* chap. 31, devoted to Antichrist's miracles where the author suddenly exclaims, "O my God and my heart! What is that? Who has ever heard the like? Who has ever thought the like?" (p. 239).

3. Lützenberg, *Leben Antichristi,* chap. 8, p. 62; cf. p. 88.

4. Preuss, *Die Vorstellungen,* p. 254.

5. See Marina Caffiero, "La fine del mondo. Profezia, apocalisse e millennio nell'Italia rivoluzionaria," *Cristianesimo nella Storia* 10(1989): 389–442, who discusses these two figures on pp. 391–94. I wish to thank Roberto Rusconi for bringing this important article to my attention.

6. For details, see P. Stella, "Per una storia del profetismo apocalittico cattolico ottocentesco," *Rivista di storia e letteratura religiosa* 4(1968): 448–69.

7. See Caffiero, "La fine del mondo," pp. 436–39.

8. For what follows, see esp. Robert O. Crummey, *The Old Believers and the World of Antichrist: The Vyg Community and the Russian State 1694–1855* (Madison: Univ. of Wisconsin Press, 1971); and Michael Cherniavsky, "The Old Believers and the New Religion," *Slavic Review* 25(1966): 1–39.

9. See Crummey, *Old Believers,* p. 7; and Cherniavsky, "Old Believers and New Religion," pp. 16–17.

10. A weak and distant analogy in contemporary America might be the question of proper respect for the American flag.

11. Crummey, *Old Believers,* p. 16.

12. The fact that the date of the synod (1666) contained the number of the Beast was not lost on later Old Believers who frequently worked it into their apocalyptic calculations.

13. Cherniavsky, "Old Believers and New Religion," p. 20.

14. On Peter as Antichrist, see the materials in Cherniavsky, "Old Believers and New Religion," pp. 23–39. In modern times this view has received a fictional presentation in Dmitri Merezhkovski's *The Antichrist: Peter and Alexis* (1905), the final novel in his historical trilogy *Christ and Antichrist* (see chap. 10 below).

15. On these three figures, see Cherniavsky, "Old Believers and New Religion," pp. 23–27. Syseov proved that Peter was the Beast in part because his pigeon toes and loud voice matched the Apocalypse's description of the Beast "with feet like a bear and a mouth like a lion" (Apoc. 13:2).

16. Crummey, *Old Believers,* p. 211.

17. See Preuss, *Die Vorstellungen,* pp. 261–63; and Seebass, "Antichrist IV," pp. 37–38.

18. Bengal's special contribution to this ancient delusion was the distinction between the Greek terms *chronos* and *kairos,* which he calculated respectively at 1111 1/9 and 222 2/9 years.

19. Preuss, *Die Vorstellungen,* pp. 267–74, and Seebass, "Antichrist IV," pp. 39–40, have discussed the various reprises of Pietist and of more traditional Lutheran views of Antichrist in late eighteenth- and nineteenth-century German theology.

20. It is significant that the Savoy Declaration of 1658, which was a modification of the Westminster Confession according to Congregational tenets and was accepted by

the New England churches, was one of the few Christian creeds to include a declaration of millenarianism (Article V).

21. Thomas More Brown, "The Image of the Beast: Anti-Papal Rhetoric in Colonial America," *Conspiracy: The Fear of Subversion in American History,* ed. Richard O. Curry and Thomas M. Brown (New York: Holt, Rinehart, & Winston, 1972), pp. 13–14.

22. Newton's *Observations upon the Prophecies of Daniel and the Apocalypse of St. John* were published posthumously in 1733 (London: Darby and Browne).

23. Newton saw the successful interpretations of the recent investigators as a proof that the millennium was near, but he cautiously refrained from giving a date— "Amongst the Interpreters of the last age there is scarce one of note who hath not made some discovery worth knowing; and thence I seem to gather that God is about opening these mysteries" (*Observations upon Daniel and the Apocalypse,* p. 253).

24. See the comment on Dan. 7 of Newton, *Observations upon Daniel and the Apocalypse* (pp. 74–89); and the comment on Apoc. 3 of Newton, *Observations upon Daniel and the Apocalypse* (pp. 281–84).

25. Eighteenth-century England saw some interesting developments in exegesis of the Apocalypse that had repercussions on speculation on Antichrist. The premillenarian view popular among the Puritans that held that Jesus would physically return to earth to inaugurate the millennium before the end began to cede to postmillenarian positions that expected an amelioration of society after Antichrist's defeat that would prepare the way for Christ's return at the end. Two important spokesmen for this were Daniel Whitby and Moses Lowman. For an account of their views, see James West Davidson, *The Logic of Millennial Thought: Eighteenth-Century New England* (New Haven: Yale Univ. Press, 1977), pp. 141–49. There was also the ongoing activity of apocalyptic and prophetic sects, such as the "French Prophets," Huguenot exiles who came to England as a result of Louis XIV's persecutions and preached the imminent destruction of the papal Antichrist.

26. Newton's pupil, the mathematician William Whiston, was another, and later the Presbyterian turned Unitarian (and famous scientist) Joseph Priestley (1733–1804) also was much concerned with prophetic interpretation.

27. Along with the works cited below, see Stephen J. Stein, "Transatlantic Extensions: Apocalyptic in Early New England," *The Apocalypse in English Renaissance,* pp. 266–98.

28. For comments on these figures, see Stein, "Transatlantic Extensions," pp. 267–70. On Mather and Cotton, see also Robert Middlekauff, *The Mathers: Three Generations of Puritan Intellectuals, 1596–1728* (New York: Oxford Univ. Press, 1971), pp. 20–34.

29. For what follows, see esp. W. Clark Gilpin, *The Millenarian Piety of Roger Williams* (Chicago: Univ. of Chicago Press, 1979).

30. Roger Williams, *Queries of Highest Consideration,* as quoted in Gilpin, *Millenarian Piety,* p. 83.

31. Gilpin, *Millenarian Piety,* pp. 40–45, 51–61, 81–83, 113–14, and 125–26.

32. Brown, "The Image of the Beast," p. 10.

33. On Mather's views, besides Stein's "Transatlantic Extensions," pp. 276–79, see his "Cotton Mather and Jonathan Edwards on the Number of the Beast: Eighteenth-Century Speculation about the Antichrist," *Proceedings of the American Antiquarian Society* 84(1975): 293–315.

34. Stein summarizes in "Cotton Mather and Jonathan Edwards" thus: "The identification of the beast was transmitted uncritically from generation to generation with Potter, Mather, and Edwards forming a continuum in the process of transmission" (p. 314).

35. *An Humble Attempt . . . ,* in *The Works of Jonathan Edwards,* vol. 5, *Apocalyptic Writings,* ed. Stephen J. Stein (New Haven: Yale Univ. Press, 1977), p. 412.

36. See Stein, "Cotton Mather and Jonathan Edwards," pp. 313–15. C. C. Goen, "Jonathan Edwards: A New Departure in Eschatology," *Church History* 28(1959): 25–40, is also useful despite overstressing Edwards's originality.

37. Quoted in Stein, "Transatlantic Extensions," p. 287.

38. The case for a strong influence has been argued by Ruth Bloch in *Visionary Republic: Millennial Themes in American Thought, 1756–1800* (Cambridge: Cambridge Univ. Press, 1985), who contends that the general cultural pattern of millenarianism "was basic to the formation of American revolutionary ideology in the late eighteenth century" (p. xiii). Previous studies, such as Davidson, *The Logic of Millennial Thought,* chap. 6, are more guarded. See also Nathan O. Hatch, *The Sacred Cause of Liberty* (New Haven: Yale Univ. Press, 1977).

39. Quoted from Davidson, *The Logic of Millennial Thought,* p. 238. See Bloch, *Visionary Republic,* pp. 54–60.

40. Quoted in Stein, "Transatlantic Extensions," p. 288. For a more detailed treatment, see Bloch, *Visionary Republic,* chaps. 3–4; and Hatch, *Sacred Cause,* pp. 21–24, 51–52, 86–87, and 151–54.

41. Bloch, *Visionary Republic,* p. 60.

42. This is especially true of England and America, where the the Antichrist element was strong, but apocalyptic interpretations were also found in Catholic Europe. For England and America, see Clarke Garrett, *Respectable Folly: Millenarians and the French Revolution in France and England* (Baltimore: Johns Hopkins Univ. Press, 1975); W. H. Oliver, *Prophets and Millennialists: The Uses of Prophecy in England from the 1790s to the 1840s* (Auckland: Univ. of Auckland and Oxford Univ., 1978), chap. 3; and Ronald R. Nelson, "Apocalyptic Speculation and the French Revolution," *Evangelical Quarterly* 53(1981): 194–206. There is also considerable information in Bloch, *Visionary Republic,* chaps. 7 and 9; and in the uncritical survey of Leroy E. Froom, *The Prophetic Faith of Our Fathers,* vol. 2 (Washington, DC: Review & Herald, 1954).

43. On this probably pseudonymous work, see Bloch, *Visionary Republic,* pp. 24–28, 161–67.

44. Quoted from Nelson, "Apocalyptic Speculation," p. 200. France as the tenth part of the city (Apoc. 11:13) was easily equated with France as the tenth and last horn of the papal Antichrist (Apoc. 13:1).

45. Fleming arrived at the date of 1794 by calculating 1260 years of 360 days from 552 C.E., the year he chose for the beginnings of the papal Antichrist. See the account in Nelson, "Apocalyptic Speculation," pp. 198–200.

46. On this treatise, see Nelson, "Apocalyptic Speculation," p. 202.

47. Bloch, *Visionary Republic,* pp. 130–33 and 144–45, joins others in arguing that it was only toward the end of the eighteenth century that the split between an optimistic postmillennial and a pessimistic premillennial view of the coming of Christ became evident.

48. Among these propagandists, we can note the English preacher Elhanan Winchester and the Baptist tract writer James Bicheno, both active in 1793. Joseph Priestly's 1794 "Fast Sermon" also interpreted the French Revolution in light of Apocalypse 11. In the United States, Samuel Langdon, former president of Harvard, produced his *Observations on the Revelation of Jesus Christ to St. John* in 1791, in which he argued for the imminent end of Antichrist. The message seemed confirmed by the news from France, as a

number of American commentators, such as John Winthrop, Elias Lee, and William Staughton, noted. On these writers, see Bloch, *Visionary Republic,* pp. 151–58.

49. As the effects of the Revolution moved outside France itself, the attention of the apocalypticists shifted to the opposition developing between the revolutionary forces and the papacy. For example, Edward King's *Remarks on the Signs of the Times* (1798) hailed the French expulsion of Pius VI from Rome as the end of the fated 1260 years.

50. On Horseley, see Oliver, *Prophets and Millennialists,* pp. 51–54.

51. On Faber, see Oliver, *Prophets and Millennialists,* pp. 54–64.

52. See Garrett, *Respectable Folly,* p. 211.

53. Bloch, *Visionary Republic,* p. 204. See the discussion in chap. 9. See also Hatch, *Sacred Cause,* pp. 133–35, 168–69, and 173.

54. Besides Oliver's *Prophets and Millennialists,* e.g., see Ernest R. Sandeen, *The Roots of Fundamentalism: British and American Millenarianism 1800–1930* (Chicago: Univ. of Chicago Press, 1970); and J. F. C. Harrison, *The Second Coming: Popular Millenarianism 1780–1850* (London: Routledge & Kegan Paul, 1979).

55. Sandeen, *Roots,* p. 42.

56. Living Antichrist belief played a more restricted role in Catholicism in the nineteenth century, generally being connected with traditionalist Catholic reaction to revolutionary and liberal religious and political movements, as we have seen above. Such traditionalism was often allied with Marian miracles and manifestations. It is noteworthy that the earliest in the modern series of Marian appearances, that of La Salette in 1846, is said to have included references to Antichrist in its secrets about the approaching end. See Sandra L. Zimdars-Swartz, *Encountering Mary: From La Salette to Medjugorje* (Princeton: Princeton Univ. Press, 1991), pp. 177–84.

57. On Irving and Drummond, see Oliver, *Prophets and Millennialists,* chap. 5.

58. G. S. Farber, *The Revival of the French Emperorship* (London: Thomas Bosworth, 1853).

59. Ibid., pp. 45–56.

60. Quoted in Sandeen, *Roots,* pp. 97–98. For American attitudes to Napoleon III, see Sandeen, *Roots,* pp. 94–98.

61. Nathan O. Hatch, "Millennialism and Popular Religion in the Early Republic," in *The Evangelical Tradition in America,* ed. Leonard I. Sweet (Macon, GA: Mercer Univ. Press, 1984), pp. 113–30.

62. Quoted in Hatch, *Sacred Cause,* p. 121.

63. On Darby, see Sandeen, *Roots,* pp. 36–40. For more on his view of Antichrist, see Timothy P. Weber, *Living in the Shadow of the Second Coming,* 2nd ed. (Chicago: Univ. of Chicago Press, 1987), pp. 22–24.

64. Antichrist's decline might well profit from a study parallel to the insightful account of D. P. Walker, *The Decline of Hell: Seventeenth-Century Discussion of Eternal Torment* (Chicago: Univ. of Chicago Press, 1964).

Chapter Ten

1. E.g., G. J. Dyer, "Antichrist," *New Catholic Encyclopedia,* vol. 1 (New York: Macmillan, 1967), p. 618; and Rudolph Pesch, "Antichrist," *Encyclopedia of Theology: The Concise Sacramentum Mundi,* ed. Karl Rahner (New York: Seabury, 1975), p. 15.

2. E.g., H. Tüchle, "Antichrist. III. Kirchengeschichtlich," *Lexikon für Theologie und Kirche* (Freiburg: Herder, 1957), c. 637.

3. Karl Rahner, "Antichrist. II. Dogmatisch," *Lexikon für Theologie und Kirche,* cc. 635–36.

4. On these Marian apparitions, see Sandra L. Zimdars-Swartz, *Encountering Mary.*

5. See Emile Appolis, "En marge du catholicism contemporain: millénarists, cordiphores et naundorffistes autour de 'Secret' de La Salette," *Archives de Sociologie des Religions* 14(1963): 106.

6. Quoted from the article of Alan Riding, "Mexican Wrath Falls on Defiant Sect," *New York Times,* 12 November 1982, p. 4.

7. First published in 1951, the book was republished in 1974. Rev. R. Gerald Culleton, *The Reign of Antichrist* (Rockford, IL: Tan Books, 1974). The work, though totally uncritical, is useful for its collection of obscure nineteenth- and twentieth-century Catholic prophecies of Antichrist (pp. 156–224).

8. See Yves Dupont, *Catholic Prophecy: The Coming Chastisement* (Rockford, IL: Tan Books, 1973). On the Antichrist, see, e.g., pp. 55, 57–58 (Antichrist possibly born in 1962), and 89–91 (a summary of the author's apocalyptic scenario).

9. Vincent P. Miceli, *The Antichrist* (West Hanover, MA: Christopher Publishing House, 1981), esp. chaps. 8–10. On p. 168, the eighty-seven American theologians (including myself) who in 1968 protested Paul VI's Encyclical "Humanae Vitae" are accused of "acting as forerunners of the Antichrist."

10. For a sketch of these differences, see the introduction to Weber, *Living in the Shadow.*

11. See Weber, *Living in the Shadow,* pp. 17–23.

12. However, as Timothy Weber points out (*Living in the Shadow,* pp. 9–12), futurist premillennialism comes in three varieties: *pretribulational,* which believes the church will be raptured before the tribulation; *midtribulational,* which thinks that the rapture will take place during the time of troubles; and *posttribulational,* which holds that their rescue will come after the trial. The great majority of modern premillennial apocalypticism is pretribulational.

13. Ernest R. Sandeen, *The Roots of Fundamentalism,* pp. xiii–xv (quotation from p. xv); cf. pp. 219–20, 246–47.

14. Weber, *Living in the Shadow,* p. 159.

15. The scenario of the tribulation, which is still basic to contemporary premillennialism, includes:

1. the revival of the Roman Empire as a ten-nation confederacy (see Dan. 7);

2. the rise of a ruler of the confederacy (the "little horn" of Dan. 7:8; that is, Antichrist) who will make a treaty with the state of Israel that will allow the Jews to rebuild the temple;

3. Antichrist's declaration of his divinity in the temple after three and a half years and the beginning of a reign of terror orchestrated by his assistant, the False Prophet (2 Thess. 2 and Apoc. 13:11–18);

4. the attack of a northern confederacy led by Russia against Antichrist (Ezek. 38–39) and their defeat (this sometimes involves a southern alliance led by Egypt; see Dan. 11:40–41);

5. the gathering of vast armies from the East against Antichrist at Armageddon (Dan. 11:44; Apoc. 9:13–21 and 16:12–16);

6. the return of Christ with the saints to destroy the armies of the world, cast the Beast and the False Prophet into hell, and set up the millennial kingdom (Apoc. 19:11–21).

16. On World War I and premillennialism, see Weber, *Living in the Shadow,* chap. 5.

17. For an overview, see Weber, *Living in the Shadow,* chap. 6. A more detailed consideration can be found in Yaakov S. Ariel, *On Behalf of Israel: American Fundamentalist Attitudes toward Jews, Judaism, and Zionism, 1865–1945* (Brooklyn: Carlson Publishing, 1991).

18. John F. Walvoord, *Armageddon, Oil and the Middle East Crisis* (Grand Rapids, MI: Zondervan, 1990), p. 218.

19. I. M. Haldeman, *Why I Preach the Second Coming* (New York: Fleming H. Revell, 1919), pp. 121–22. See Weber, *Living in the Shadow,* p. 126.

20. Oswald J. Smith, *Is the Antichrist at Hand?—What of Mussolini?* (Harrisburg and New York: Christian Alliance Publishing Company, 1927), pp. 24–25; cf. pp. 64–67. On the basis of Apoc. 17:8, Smith even claimed that the Antichrist would be a reincarnation of an evil dead person, possibly Antiochus Epiphanes, Judas, or Nero (pp. 36–37).

21. See Weber, *Living in the Shadow,* pp. 178–81.

22. Quoted from Weber, *Living in the Shadow,* p. 183.

23. Ibid., p. 238.

24. For another survey of Lindsey's views, see Weber, *Living in the Shadow,* pp. 211–21.

25. Hal Lindsey, *The Late Great Planet Earth,* 86th printing (Grand Rapids, MI: Zondervan, 1981), p. 43.

26. Lindsey's book proved to be so popular that he could not resist authoring seven clones during the following decade, concluding with *The 1980's: Countdown to Armageddon* (New York: Bantam Books, 1981), which solemnly asserts, *"The decade of the 1980's could very well be the last decade of history as we know it"* (his italics—p. 8). Weber, *Living in the Shadow,* pp. 217–21, notes an important shift in the latter book, not one involving apocalyptic hopes but rather an increasingly right-wing political agenda that seems at odds with premillennial expectations for the rapture that will remove Christians from the scene.

27. The message is repeated several times. See John F. Walvoord, *Armageddon, Oil and the Middle East Crisis* (Grand Rapids, MI: Zondervan, 1990), pp. 24–29, 201–02, 219–25, and the handy charts on pp. 147 and 185.

28. Ibid., chap. 15 (p. 194 for the dangerous hailstones).

29. Among the fuller treatments is that found in H. L. Willmington's *The King Is Coming,* reprint (Wheaton, IL: Tyndale House, 1991), chaps. 7–9 (pp. 76–216), which discuss the three parts of the tribulation. Dr. Willmington is a graduate of the Moody Bible Institute who is vice president of Jerry Falwell's Liberty University in Lynchburg, Virginia.

30. The social psychological power of such beliefs has been investigated by a number of works, such as the classic study of Leon Festinger, Henry W. Rieken, and Stanley Schachter, *When Prophecy Fails: A Social and Psychological Study of a Modern Group that Predicted the Destruction of the World* (Minneapolis: Univ. of Minnesota Press, 1956). For an attempt to delineate both the positive and the negative aspects of the religious values in apocalypticism, see my introduction in McGinn, *Apocalyptic Spirituality,* pp. 7–16.

31. For information concerning some of the more bizarre premillennial views, see William M. Alnor, *Soothsayers of the Second Advent* (Old Tappan, NJ: Fleming H. Revell, 1989).

32. Edgar C. Whisenant, *On Borrowed Time: Biblical Dates of the 70th Week of Daniel, Armageddon and the Millennium* (Nashville: World Bible Society, 1988).

33. Ibid., pp. 12–13.

34. Jeane Dixon, *My Life and Prophecies,* pp. 178–80, as cited in Willmington, *The King Is Coming,* pp. 89–91.

35. Noah Hutchins, "The Vatican Connection," *Gospel Truth* for April 1984, p. 4, as cited in Alnor, *Soothsayers,* pp. 22–23.

36. Robert W. Faid published a book entitled *Gorbachev! Has the Real Antichrist Come?* in which he claimed that fourteen of the sixteen biblical marks of Antichrist were already fulfilled in Gorbachev's career. See the account of Art Levine, "The Devil in Gorbachev," *Washington Post,* 5 June 1988.

37. David Webber and N. W. Hutchings, *Countdown for Antichrist,* rev. ed. (Oklahoma City: Southwest Radio Church, 1984), p. 121, as cited in Alnor, *Soothsayers,* pp. 21–22

38. Alnor, *Soothsayers,* pp. 82–83, claims this rumor was spread after the attempted assassination of Reagan, though he cites no specific publications.

39. See Alnor, *Soothsayers,* pp. 23–25.

40. See Weber, *Living in the Shadow,* pp. 241–42.

41. Ibid., pp. 222–24.

42. Ibid., pp. 224–26. See also Alnor, *Soothsayers,* pp. 24, 83–86.

43. Mary Stewart Relfe, *When Your Money Fails* (Montgomery, AL: Ministries, 1981). An earlier, less developed witness can be found in Chuck Smith, *The Soon to Be Revealed Antichrist* (Costa Mesa, CA: Maranatha Evangelical Association, 1976), pp. 16–20. Smith believes that the coming Antichrist will indeed be *Nero redivivus* in the sense that the same demon who possessed Nero will possess the Final Enemy (see p. 34).

44. Fears of the evil connotations of 666 remain one of the powerful folkloric aspects of Antichrist beliefs. For example, several newspaper accounts of early 1990 noted that British license plates with the prefix 666 had to be canceled because too many people who owned them had reported untoward events befalling them. One report cited the case of the mother of a convicted murderer who claimed that her son had been a good boy until his job required him to drive a van with a 666 license (see *Chicago Tribune,* 4 February 1990, p. 16).

45. Some literary uses of the term Antichrist and associated symbolism in the past century have little to do with the Antichrist legend. Thus, I will not comment on Friedrich Nietzsche's noted *Der Antichrist* (1895), which should be translated as *The Antichristian,* because it deals with the philosopher's reasons for opposing Christianity rather than with the Antichrist legend per se. Nietzsche's view of the post-Christian "superman" did, however, play a role in some conservative Christian views of the modern form of the Antichrist, as we shall see below. Similarly, the occult English writer Aleister Crowley, who publicly identified himself as "666, or the Great Beast," belongs to the history of English Satanism and magic rather than of apocalyptic thought.

46. Frank Kermode, *The Sense of an Ending: Studies in the Theory of Fiction* (London: Oxford Univ. Press, 1967).

47. Among these works, see M. N. Abrams, *Natural Supernaturalism* (New York: Norton, 1971); John R. May, *Toward a New Earth: Apocalypse in the American Novel* (Notre Dame: Univ. of Notre Dame Press, 1972); W. Warren Wagar, *Terminal Visions: The Literature of the Last Things* (Bloomington: Univ. of Indiana Press, 1982); Douglas Robinson, *American Apocalypses: The Image of the End of the World in American Literature* (Baltimore and London: Johns Hopkins Univ. Press, 1985); and esp. David M. Bethea, *The Shape of the Apocalypse in Modern Russian Fiction* (Princeton: Princeton Univ. Press, 1989).

48. David Bethea in his important book, *Shape of Apocalypse,* has argued for the existence of a distinctive form of "apocalyptic fiction" in modern Russian literature. Ac-

cording to his view, an apocalyptic fiction is "a kind of sacred text or version of *the Book* [i.e., the Apocalypse] through which the character and the narrator and, by implication, the reader—all in their separate, self-enclosed realms—are made privy to a 'secret wisdom' from another space-time" (p. 33). For further discussion, see pp. 39–42 and 105.

49. For some examples, see Bethea, *Shape of Apocalypse,* pp. 26–31.

50. One text from the *Diary,* cited in Bethea, *Shape of Apocalypse* (p. 30), proclaims: "The Antichrist is coming to us! He is coming! And the end of the world is near—nearer than they think!"

51. Bethea, *Shape of Apocalypse,* pp. 95–102.

52. On Solovyev, see Bethea, *Shape of Apocalypse,* pp. 110–16; and Czeslaw Milosz, "Science Fiction and the Coming of Antichrist," in *Emperor of the Earth: Modes of Eccentric Vision* (Berkeley: Univ. of California Press, 1977), pp. 15–31. For an introduction to his thought, see Egbert Munzer, *Solovyev: Prophwet of Russian-Western Unity* (New York: Philosophical Library, 1956). Considerable information about Solovyev's life (though to be used with caution) is to be found in Paul M. Allen, *Vladimir Soloviev: Russian Mystic* (Blauvelt, NY: Steinerbooks, 1978).

53. Hans Urs von Balthasar, *The Glory of the Lord: A Theological Aesthetics. III: Studies in Theological Styles: Lay Styles* (San Francisco: Ignatius, 1986), p. 284. Von Balthasar's chapter on Solovyev (pp. 279–352) is an insightful presentation of his thought.

54. Ibid., p. 297, distinguishes three periods in Solovyev's thought: (1) 1873–83, the initial construction of his theosophical system; (2) 1883–90, the period of his ecumenical project for the reconciliation of the churches; and (3) 1890–1900, the time of "outlining the system in its final form, with the accent this time on 'theurgy' and apocalypse."

55. I will use the translation of Alexander Bakshy, *War, Progress, and the End of History, Including a Short Story of the Anti-Christ: Three Conversations by Vladimir Soloviev* (London: Univ. of London Press, 1915); see p. xx for the quote. For details about the composition of the work, see Allen, *Vladimir Soloviev,* chap. 7. See also Munzer, *Solovyev,* chap. 5.

56. Bakshy, *War, Progress,* p. xix.

57. For reflections on Solovyev's view of evil, see von Balthasar, *Glory of the Lord,* pp. 296–97, 318–21, 340–41, and 350–52.

58. Bakshy, *War, Progress,* pp. 123–26.

59. Von Balthasar, *Glory of the Lord,* p. 296.

60. Bakshy, *War, Progress,* p. 129.

61. Ibid., p. 165; cf. the whole discussion on pp. 161–66. On the role of resurrection in his thought, see von Balthasar, *Glory of the Lord,* pp. 340–41.

62. Bakshy, *War, Progress,* p. 173.

63. Milosz, "Science Fiction and the Coming of Antichrist," p. 16.

64. Bakshy, *War, Progress,* pp. 187–90.

65. As von Balthasar points out in *Glory of the Lord,* p. 352: "Soloviev quite unconcernedly surrenders great parts of his philosophy of cosmic process into the hands of Antichrist. As regards the *facts* of the process, he has not abandoned a single detail; the one thing he has given up is the idea that the process comes to perfection within history."

66. Bakshy, *War, Progress,* pp. 190–93. See esp. the culminating point when Satan infuses Antichrist with his own spirit: "'Receive thou my spirit! As before my spirit gave birth to thee in *beauty,* so now it gives birth to thee in *power.*' With these words of the stranger, the mouth of the superman involuntarily opened, two piercing eyes came close up to his face, and he felt an icy breath which pervaded his whole being. At the same time he felt in himself such strength, vigor, lightness, and joy as he had never before experienced."

67. On this, see Milosz, "Science Fiction and the Coming of Antichrist," pp. 28–31.

68. Bakshy, *War, Progress,* p. 227.

69. Vladimir Nabokov ranked it with Joyce's *Ulysses,* Kafka's *Transformation,* and Proust's *In Search of Lost Time.* See "Translators' Introduction," in Andrei Bely, *Petersburg,* trans. Robert A. Maguire and John E. Malmstad (Bloomington: Indiana Univ. Press, 1978), p. viii.

70. Bethea, *Shape of Apocalypse,* p. 114.

71. Ibid., p. 127 n. 33, points out the apocalyptic associations of the name Apollyon, both with Apoc. 9:11, and the magician Apollonius in Solovyev's *Three Conversations.*

72. Alexander Pushkin's famous poem, "The Bronze Horseman," plays a crucial role in Russian apocalyptic fiction, as detailed by Bethea, *Shape of the Apocalypse,* e.g., pp. 44–61.

73. Bely, *Petersburg,* pp. 213–14.

74. Mereshkovsky's belief in a coming "third humanity" at times sounds almost Joachite, but there is no evidence for influence from the Calabrian abbot. See Bernice Gatzer Rosenthal, "Merezhkovski, Dmitrii," in vol. 9, *The Encyclopedia of Religion,* pp. 379–80; and Marjorie Reeves and Warwick Gould, *Joachim of Fiore and the Myth of the Eternal Evangel in the Nineteenth Century* (Oxford: Clarendon Press, 1987), pp. 306–8.

75. The Swedish Nobel Prize winner Selma Lagerlof (1858–1940) used the Antichrist legend in one of her admittedly less successful works, *The Miracles of Antichrist,* which appeared in 1897. Antichrist, for Lagerlof, is not a person but a statue, a false copy of a wonder-working image of the Christ child, and actually a symbol for socialism in the novel.

76. Wagar, *Terminal Visions,* p. 216 n. 16, mentions two works I have not seen: Constancia Serjeant, *When the Saints Are Gone* (1908), and Sydney Watson, *The Mark of the Beast* (1911).

77. Robert Hugh Benson, *Lord of the World,* reprint (Long Prairie, MN: Neumann Press, n.d.). The science fiction aspects of Benson's novel mark him as a younger contemporary of Jules Verne.

78. Ibid., p. 264.

79. Charles Williams, *All Hallows' Eve,* reprint (New York: Farrar, Straus and Giroux, 1979), p. xvi.

80. Ibid. Humphrey Carpenter in his study of Lewis, Williams, J. R. R. Tolkien, and their friends entitled *The Inklings* (New York: Ballantine, 1981), pp. 212–15, notes the role that Lewis and Tolkien had in helping to shape the novel.

81. The relation between the Simon Magus legend and that of Antichrist was probably known to Williams, given his wide reading. Williams's position is not unlike that of Cyril of Jerusalem for whom Antichrist was primarily a wicked magician who lusts for world domination (see chap. 3 above, pp. 70–71).

82. For particular passages that reflect elements of the Antichrist legend, see Williams, *All Hallows' Eve,* e.g., pp. 30–34, 59–65, 118–20, 153, 160–61, 200–01, 216–18, 255, and so on.

83. Williams, *All Hallows' Eve,* pp. 263–66. I have taken the liberty of excerpting from this powerful scene of Simon's end, which needs be read in its entirety.

84. See, e.g., Salem Kirban, *666* (Wheaton, IL: Tyndale House, 1970); Carol Balizet, *The Seven Last Years* (New York: Bantam, 1980); and Dan Betzer, *Beast: A Novel of the Future World Dictator* (Lafayette, LA: Prescott Press, 1985).

85. Neil Gaiman and Terry Pratchett, *Good Omens* (New York: Workman Publishing, 1990).

86. However, a made-for-TV sequel entitled *Damien IV: The Awakening* shows that someone still thought there was money to be made in the Antichrist story.

87. The trilogy also gave birth to a book, though in this case not an actual script, but a Fundamentalist tract claiming to be by the "Biblical technical advisor" to the first two parts. See W. S. McBirnie, *Antichrist* (Dallas, TX: Acclaimed Books, 1978).

88. On these and other Antichrist movies, see Kim Newman, *Nightmare Movies: A Critical Guide to Contemporary Horror Films* (New York: Harmony Books, 1988), esp. pp. 39, 44–47.

89. C. G. Jung, *Aion: Researches into the Phenomenology of the Self,* Bollingen Series XX (Princeton: Princeton Univ. Press, 1978), "Foreword," p. ix. "Enantiodromia" for Jung signified the emergence of an unconscious opposite over the course of time. Jung also comments on Antichrist elsewhere in his voluminous writings, esp. in the 1952 *Answer to Job* as found in C. G. Jung, *Psychology and Religion: West and East,* Bollingen Series XX (Princeton: Princeton Univ. Press, 1969), pp. 355–470 (cf. pp. 412, 432–35, 447, and 458).

90. Jung, *Aion,* p. 47; see pp. 45–55 for his view of evil. Jung admits that *privatio boni* may be a metaphysical truth but denies that it can ever be a psychological one.

91. Ibid., p. 41.

92. Ibid., p. 42.

93. E.g., see Jung, *Aion,* pp. 42–45, 71, 84–85, 94, and 98.

94. C. G. Jung, *Psychological Commentaries on "The Tibetan Book of Great Liberation" and "The Tibetan Book of the Dead"* in *Psychology and Religion: West and East,* p. 488.

95. E.g., John A. Sanford, *Evil: The Shadow Side of Reality* (New York: Crossroad, 1989).

96. Thomas J. J. Altizer, *The New Apocalypse: The Radical Christian Vision of William Blake* (n.p.: Michigan State Univ. Press, 1967), chap. 5, "Christ and Antichrist." The quotations are from pp. 217 and 213.

97. Robert L. Heilbroner, *An Inquiry into the Human Prospect* (New York: Norton, 1974).

98. Rudolf Bultmann, *History and Eschatology: The Presence of Eternity* (New York: Harper Torchbook, 1957).

99. Ernesto Cardenal, *Apocalypse and Other Poems* (New York: New Directions, 1977). For another recent example, see Daniel Berrigan, *The Nightmare of God* (Portland, OR: Sunburst Press, 1983). Neither poet, however, makes use of Antichrist.

100. See McGinn, *Apocalyptic Spirituality,* pp. 7–16.

101. See, for example, Jean-François Revel, *The Flight from Truth: The Reign of Deceit in the Age of Information* (New York: Random House, 1992).

102. Denis the Carthusian, *Dialogue on the Catholic Faith* 6, in *Opera omnia,* vol. 18 (Tournai: n.p., 1899), p. 468.